Thomas Leo McCluskey • Apostolos Kotsialos •
Jörg P. Müller • Franziska Klügl • Omer Rana •
René Schumann
Editors

Autonomic Road Transport Support Systems

Editors

Thomas Leo McCluskey
School of Computing and Engineering
University of Huddersfield
Huddersfield
West Yorkshire, United Kingdom

Apostolos Kotsialos
School of Engineering
and Computing Science
Durham University
Durham, United Kingdom

Jörg P. Müller
Department of Informatics
TU Clausthal
Clausthal-Zellerfeld, Germany

Franziska Klügl
School of Science and Technology
Örebro University
Örebro, Sweden

Omer Rana
School of Computer Science
and Informatics
Cardiff University
Cardiff, United Kingdom

René Schumann
Institute of Information Systems
HES-SO Valais-Wallis
Sierre, Switzerland

2012 ACM Computing Classification System: Artificial Intelligence, Machine Learning, Modelling and Simulation, Software System Structures, Enterprise Computing, Data Management Systems, Information Systems Applications

Autonomic Systems
ISBN 978-3-319-25806-5 ISBN 978-3-319-25808-9 (eBook)
DOI 10.1007/978-3-319-25808-9

Library of Congress Control Number: 2016931280

Cover design: deblik, Berlin

Printed on acid-free paper

This book is published under the trade name Birkhäuser
The registered company is Springer International Publishing AG Switzerland (www.birkhauser-science.com)

Contents

Autonomic Road Transport Support Systems: An Introduction

Thomas Leo McCluskey, Apostolos Kotsialos, Jörg P. Müller, Franziska Klügl, Omer F. Rana, and René Schumann

1 Motivation and Challenges

One of the most persistent problems that plague modern-day road transport facilities is the quality of service provided. Especially during rush hours, this expensive infrastructure does not operate at capacity nor does it provide the level of service required by its users. Congestion has become a problem with severe economic and environmental repercussions. Hence, efficient road traffic management is more important than ever.

T.L. McCluskey
School of Computing and Engineering, University of Huddersfield, Huddersfield, West Yorkshire, UK
e-mail: lee@hud.ac.uk

A. Kotsialos
School of Engineering and Computing Science, Durham University, Durham, UK
e-mail: apostolos.kotsialos@durham.ac.uk

J.P. Müller (✉)
Department of Informatics, TU Clausthal, Clausthal-Zellerfeld, Germany
e-mail: joerg.mueller@tu-clausthal.de

F. Klügl
School of Science and Technology, Örebro University, Örebro, Sweden
e-mail: franziska.klugl@oru.se

O.F. Rana
School of Computer Science and Informatics, Cardiff University, Cardiff, UK
e-mail: ranaof@cardiff.ac.uk

R. Schumann
Institute of Information Systems, HES-SO Valais-Wallis, Sierre, Switzerland
e-mail: rene.schumann@hevs.ch

T.L. McCluskey et al. (eds.), *Autonomic Road Transport Support Systems*, Autonomic Systems, DOI 10.1007/978-3-319-25808-9_1

Despite the fact that a lot of research has been conducted in this field and, more importantly, huge amounts of money have been invested in hardware, communication and software systems, the average traffic conditions are still far from the desired level. In fact, a paradox can be observed: Although very good and well-designed methods are reported in the academic literature, a persistent theory-practice gap appears [1]. Methods that are reported to perform well in simulated environments do not often translate to a realistic deployment, thereby limiting benefits to the potential and not the actual.

There are many reasons for this situation. Administrative inertia and institutional conflicts is one, but as the need for more and more efficient systems increases so does the pressure on network operators to become more efficient.

The theory-practice gap, however, is mainly due to the complex nature of the traffic phenomena and the associated decision-making problems road operators are faced with. The traffic flow complexity can be attributed to the erratic nature of the collective outcome of thousands of individual driving decisions and the random occurrence of capacity-reducing events. For network operators, this is compounded by the rules, regulations and policies they are bounded to and by the complex methods/tools used to support decision-making within a Traffic Control Centre (TCC).

TCC operators receive copious information from a diverse set of resources, and therefore it is not an understatement to claim that they suffer from information overload. The decision-making problems encountered when viewed in their totality are beyond the human capability to solve efficiently. Even if highly efficient (at least in simulation) methods are applied, the operators still face a problem of understanding them. Highly efficient algorithms come at the cost of design and development sophistication, which is beyond the reach of the normal operator. This effect is compounded by the deployment of vehicle automation systems that are becoming available. From various on-board devices to driverless vehicles, a new type of driver-vehicle-infrastructure system emerges.

The background that these developments are based on is the communication network capability of various agents involved in the traffic flow process. As communication technology becomes more advanced and higher channel capacity and bandwidth become available, traffic management system architectures can be realised in an ever-increasing variety of centralised/de-centralised notions. This allows the design and development of systems with a high degree of intelligence embedded within them capable of displaying highly sophisticated behaviour.

Hence, there is a *need* for intelligent, automated assistance to deal with the complexity of traffic management, while at the same time the technical platform *exists* to support such a capability. But what form should this assistance take? This leads us to the notion of autonomic computing as introduced in the following and from there to the field of *Autonomic Road Transport Support* (ARTS) Systems, which are the topic of this volume.

2 Autonomic Computing

A system that carries out a process by itself, without human intervention, can be said to be automatic. Generally humans create the automatic process to achieve certain goals, though the system is not usually explicitly aware of what its goals are. For example, a thermometer informs people of the room temperature automatically (it happily performs this process over time without anyone intervening), but it has no explicit knowledge of what it is doing.

Nowadays, we have systems that can interact with the outside world and carry out a process involving situations where the system makes decisions itself, based on sense data from a dynamic and unpredictable environment. In other words, the system can sense, interpret the sensed data and use that interpretation to control how the system affects the outside world. We call these systems *autonomous*, and current examples in the transport area are driverless cars and so-called "managed motorway" systems. Generally humans create the autonomous process to achieve certain goals, though the system itself need not be aware of what its goals are or what they mean.

For more intelligent management assistance, it would be desirable if the system embodied some understanding of its own functions. Human operators could then communicate service expectations to the system (such as to keep to certain limits of road congestion or emissions of pollutants), and in response the system would assess its performance against expectations, derive outstanding goals to achieve from this self-assessment, and plan how to act in order to achieve its goals while protecting its currently achieved goals. We also require that the system be able to carry out and monitor the execution of those plans and learn and adapt from its experience. We call a system that displays these kinds of self-management properties "autonomic".

Whereas we are concerned with transportation systems that are constituted with hardware and software, autonomicity as a separate and distinctive system feature was originally put forward as an important system design objective in the context of computer software systems. Such desirable system features had been discussed by other researchers, e.g. [2, 3], but in an effort to characterise system automation that goes beyond the traditional notions of automatic control, it was IBM through the Autonomic Systems vision who characterised the properties of such systems in [4] and subsequent initiatives[1] that promoted autonomics and supported their development in the computer systems domain.

In [4] general definitions of "self-$*$" properties that characterise autonomicity were given and a discourse started which, just few years later, had already resulted in a large body of literature. Different self-$*$ properties have been defined for addressing the needs of various functionalities, such as self-healing, self-configuration,

[1]In fact, IBM launched the Tivoli Systems division to specifically implement autonomic properties into their computer systems.

self-optimisation, self-protecting, which may be considered as falling under the general term of self-management for the computer systems domain.

Many self-$*$ properties have been introduced by design at different levels of hierarchy within computer systems (e.g. software application level, hardware management level, etc.) in the literature, resulting to autonomic system behaviour at the component level. Different methodological approaches have been used for enabling systems to possess them, including optimisation, control theory, machine learning and artificial intelligence. The outcome of this design effort are systems with increased resilience in the presence of uncertainty, improved levels of service and learning capabilities.

Furthermore, autonomic systems interact with users at a higher policy and requirements level rather than at a lower operational level. Hiding complexity from a user is important, in order to minimise potential concern about a potentially large number of micro-actions that may need to be orchestrated/executed. Hence, the information overload, e.g. of system administrators, is avoided and interactions with the computing system are performed at a higher policy level.

3 Autonomics Applied to Transport Systems

The vast majority of the published literature on autonomics has been concerned with the design of autonomic computer systems. This is natural since the core design concepts that have been applied in autonomics stem from this domain area. Gradually other domains have found their way towards designing autonomic systems by developing systems with some self-$*$ properties. Examples are financial markets [5], household energy management [6], telecommunication networks [7], spacecraft operations [8] and transportation systems [9].

There are two main views regarding the use of autonomics in the traffic management context. The first one adopts the narrow perspective of the use of autonomic computing and communication systems for supporting centralised or decentralised traffic operations. There is an increased demand for computing power, monitoring and control application information and data exchange in real time for any real-world network. Autonomics can be the computing and communications systems technology leading to the required level of service for components installed inside a TCC, over the road network infrastructure and in the vehicles themselves.

A more general view, which can be adopted beyond the computing and communications technologies, is that of designing systems explicitly having a range of self-$*$ properties. This is a far more complicated task holding a higher promise. It requires a fundamental approach enabling to consider phenomena of bottom-up emergence of component and system behaviour. This exceeds the mere analysis of (completely designed) systems, but instead covers all stages of design, operation and optimisation, e.g. based on appropriate simulation models and tools. It is no coincidence that simulation technologies play an important role in quite a few chapters of this book.

In addition, different technologies and methodologies can be used for system design purposes, such as optimisation, scheduling, feedback and model predictive control, machine learning and automated planning. These methods in conjunction with technological advancements in the form of vehicle automation create a fertile ground for the design of autonomic systems at different operational levels, from the TCC general policy implementation to vehicle-to-vehicle coordination.

4 Overview of This Volume

This volume covers a broad range of views—theory, models, architectures (including platforms and development methods) and applications, showcasing autonomic concepts and features in autonomic road transport support systems. It blends into, extends and generalises the emerging discussion on the use of autonomic concepts in the domain of road traffic flow management.

This discussion is relatively new and has taken place along different dimensions of related research covering the full range of traffic operations, including modelling, control, surveillance, scheduling and routing behaviour. As such, this volume aspires to become one of the first texts in the literature where the notion of systems supporting traffic management operations with self-$*$ properties is discussed. The scope of the individual contributions covers different aspects of traffic management with an explicit effort dedicated to the selection and interpretation of self-$*$ properties.

The volume's chapters focus on methods that are used for designing, developing and implementing systems that demonstrate an autonomic property in their operation. Every chapter explains how autonomic properties can be developed and used in the context of the particular problem considered. The definition of autonomic behaviour is given within the context of the specific problem and target application. A whole range of applications related to the traffic management operations are considered. More specifically, routing control is considered in chapters "A Game Theory Model for Self-adapting Traffic Flows with Autonomous Navigation" and "TIMIPLAN: A Tool for Transportation Tasks"; signalised junction control in chapters "Self-management in Urban Traffic Control: An Automated Planning Perspective", "An Experimental Review of Reinforcement Learning Algorithms for Adaptive Traffic Signal Control", "Learning-Based Control Algorithm for Ramp Metering" and "Traffic Signal Control with Autonomic Features"; simulation verification in chapters "Simulation Testbed for Autonomic Demand-Responsive Mobility Systems" and "Multi-Agent Traffic Simulation for Development and Validation of Autonomic Car-to-Car Systems"; traffic flow model validation in chapters "Autonomic Systems Design for ITS Applications Modelling and Route Guidance" and "Performance Maintenance of ARTS Systems"; integrated control in chapters "A Multiagent Approach to Modeling Autonomic Road Transport Support Systems", "A Self-optimization Traffic Model by Multilevel Formalism", "An Organic Computing Approach to Resilient Traffic Management", "An Autonomic

Methodology for Embedding Self-tuning Competence in Online Traffic Control Systems" and "Applying the PAUSETA Protocol in Traffic Management Plans"; and electric vehicle management in chapter "Electric Vehicles in Road Transport and Electric Power Networks".

In order to design and eventually deploy these systems, we can distinguish two broad approaches that have been followed. Artificial Intelligence (AI) and Multi-Agent Systems (MAS) methods form the core of the first approach, whereas control methods are at the heart of the second. Both computer science and engineering are represented as disciplines. This book presents their confluence on the broader subject of traffic management. In order to facilitate the presentation and coverage of the subject's wide range, the volume is divided into three parts.

4.1 Part I: Models, Concepts, Architecture and Theories of ARTS

The first part of the book contains a collection of state-of-the-art research concerned with models, concepts, architectures and theories that provide a foundation for use in the development of autonomic traffic management systems.

In the first chapter of this part (chapter "A Game Theory Model for Self-adapting Traffic Flows with Autonomous Navigation"), Varga presents an application of game theory for modelling and analysing the self-organisation of routing behaviour. Routing games are used for modelling autonomous self-adaptive navigation providing in this way an interesting theoretical foundation for autonomic routing systems. Game-theoretic modelling of the interaction among self-interested entities enables the study of the resulting collective autonomic phenomena.

The second contribution by Jimoh and McCluskey (chapter "Self-management in Urban Traffic Control: An Automated Planning Perspective") is concerned with urban junction signal control using Automatic Planning (AP) and how to develop a system with self-management properties. It is argued that in order to create such self-awareness functionality the traffic management system (or a suitably defined subsystem) needs to be situation-aware and have knowledge of its components, its environment and the reasoning between them. Hence, autonomic systems must be deliberative with respect to their actions in real time in order to apply control.

Within such a framework the system can respond on its own, without external guidance, during unforeseeable situations. One of the tools that can be used for enabling such capability is AP. In order to use this technology, a specific application domain requires its formal description using a suitable language and the subsequent use of heuristics for dynamically finding plans and schedules that aim to satisfy a set of objectives. The domain in this case is the urban road junction equipped with traffic lights and the vehicle volume that needs to be served. The chapter elaborates on the architecture of a self-managing system based on AP.

A different approach towards control of signalised intersections is discussed in chapter "An Experimental Review of Reinforcement Learning Algorithms for Adaptive Traffic Signal Control" by Mannion, Howley and Duggan. In this contribution, a Traffic Signal Control regime based on Reinforcement Learning (RL-TSC) is presented. A wide overview of RL is provided, and its importance as a method supporting the evolution of learning of a system is highlighted. RL is described as a Markov decision process where the reward function, the set of states, the set of actions and the state transition function are defined for the signalised intersection. It is argued that RL can be used for developing systems with autonomic properties because it enables system adaptability, learning capability and self-optimisation through flexible goal orientation based on online learning.

In chapter "A Multiagent Approach to Modeling Autonomic Road Transport Support Systems", Fiosins, Friedrich, Görmer, Mattfeld, Müller and Tchouankem provide a conceptual agent-based model of a traffic system comprised of drivers and traffic control centres as participants. Drivers are modelled as locally autonomous agents, which act to optimise their operational and tactical decisions, such as their route choice. Traffic management centres act as agents influencing the traffic flow process according to dynamically selected policies.

Two autonomic features emerging from the local decisions and actions of traffic participants are considered: (1) autonomic routing, whereby vehicle agents individually adapt routing decisions based on local learning capabilities and traffic information, and (2) vehicle grouping, i.e. collective decision-making of vehicles, which dynamically form and operate groups to drive in a convoy, thus aiming at higher speed and increased throughput. In this framework, autonomicity is studied as a property emerging from the decentralised agents' interactions.

The final contribution of the first part is chapter "Self-optimization Traffic Model by Multilevel Formalism" by Stoilov and Stoilova. In this work, the authors propose to use a bi-level optimisation formalism for developing an urban junction signal control strategy with a self-optimising behaviour. The self-optimisation aspect of a complex system is implemented by simultaneous solutions of interconnected local optimisation problems which are part of a hierarchical structure. An example of this approach is given for urban junction signal control where the green splits of a cycle are determined in one level and the cycle duration on the other.

4.2 Part II: Platforms and Methods for Engineering ARTS

This part of the volume presents software platforms, methods and other tools that can be used for further studying and developing ways of designing autonomic traffic management applications.

The first contribution of this part, chapter "An Organic Computing Approach to Resilient Traffic Management", by Sommer, Tomforde and Hähner, explores the application of organic computing to the management of decentralised junction signal and vehicle routing control systems. The organic traffic control system described provides a self-organised and self-adaptive solution combining the principles of autonomic and organic computing. A basic requirement behind this approach to system design is for parts of the design-time process tasks to be transferred to the system's responsibility at runtime showing at the same time robustness and flexibility. Based on the discussion of these two properties, the chapter discusses resilience of a traffic management system, i.e. proactive robustness.

In chapter "Autonomic Systems Design for ITS Applications Modelling and Route Guidance", Kotsialos and Poole provide a general methodology for system design based on the autonomic nervous system. Autonomics is put forward as a more general system design approach where self-$*$ properties are considered design requirements, and tools from control theory and optimisation are used for endowing feedback control loops with autonomic properties. A distinction between sympathetic and parasympathetic system functionalities is drawn as two partially competing but mostly complementary components of an autonomic system.

The authors evaluate their approach through an application of macroscopic traffic flow model validation METANET. Optimisation is used for calibrating and verifying the model in such a way that the spatial distribution of fundamental diagram capacities is automatically detected, without the need for expert engineering judgement. At a higher level of policy determination and expression, the requirements for an autonomic route guidance application are discussed.

In the third chapter of this part (chapter "Simulation Testbed for Autonomic Demand-Responsive Mobility Systems"), Čertický, Jakob and Píbil present an open-source simulation testbed for emerging autonomic mobility systems, in which transport vehicles and other resources are automatically managed to serve a dynamically changing transport demand. The contribution acknowledges the need of providing usable frameworks and platforms that enable the controlled experimentation with autonomic systems. This will help accelerate the development of control mechanisms for autonomic mobility systems and to facilitate their mutual comparison using well-defined benchmark scenarios.

In their contribution (chapter "Multi-Agent Traffic Simulation for Development and Validation of Autonomic Car-to-Car Systems"), Vokrinek, Schaefer, Pinotti and Tango propose another simulation testbed. They apply the multi-agent paradigm to the study of decentralised coordination strategies applied in cooperative car-to-car systems, such as an Autonomic Lane Change Assistant. The focus of their work differs from the previous chapter in that it acknowledges and takes into account the role of the human user (in their case the driver) in an autonomic system. Thus, the chapter provides a methodological basis to study a number of interesting phenomena that occur when advanced driver assistance systems meet autonomic features aiming at increasing safety and efficiency.

In chapter "Performance Maintenance of ARTS Systems", Schumann focuses on the problem of analysing the performance of autonomic systems. The chapter points out that the performance of an autonomic, self-managing system not only depends on characteristics of the environment but also on the adaptation history of the system. The chapter further stresses the important role of experimental, empirical validation for these systems. The main contribution of this chapter is that it identifies and exemplifies strategies for increasing the resilience of ARTS systems against undesired adaptations. In doing so, two principles for avoiding undesired adaptations are explored, by design or by self-regulation.

Greguric, Ivanjko and Mandzuka describe in chapter "Learning-Based Control Algorithm for Ramp Metering", how machine learning techniques can be used to automatically adjust ramp metering strategies for highways. Instead of manually fixed strategies for different scenarios, the assignment of strategies to particular traffic situations is made automatically. It is an example of how self-configuration strategies can be implemented in a situation where a number of mutually non-dominant control strategies are available.

The advantage of applying self-configuration based on a traffic simulation of different scenarios enables it to automatically compare different strategies, often developed for different scenarios, and to adjust the strategy selection towards a unified objective function.

4.3 Part III: Emerging and Innovative Applications of ARTS

The final part of this volume is devoted to applications of autonomic road transport support systems. It features five chapters that describe and evaluate innovative demonstrators and prototypes of emerging applications, which showcase interesting future ITS use cases.

The first chapter (chapter "An Autonomic Methodology for Embedding Self-tuning Competence in Online Traffic Control Systems") of this part, authored by Kouvelas, Manolis, Kosmatopoulos, Papamichail and Papageorgiou, presents a methodology for embedding self-tuning competence in online traffic control systems. They aim at the development and validation of algorithms that can embody autonomic properties within the existing strategies for managing and controlling Intelligent Transportation Systems. The contribution described in this book is Adaptive Fine-Tuning (AFT), a novel adaptive optimisation algorithm that combines methodologies from the fields of traffic engineering, automatic control, optimisation and machine learning. The algorithm has been successfully evaluated in simulation experiments, and promising field results reported for the urban network of Chania, Greece, are presented in the chapter.

In their contribution (chapter "Electric Vehicles in Road Transport and Electric Power Networks"), Marmaras, Xydas, Cipcigan, Rana and Klügl investigate the consequences of the upcoming e-mobility on the future grid. It is expected that mainly in urban areas the share of electric vehicles is going to increase in the near future. This will bring additional load to the electric grids in those areas. Both traffic networks and electric grids are currently enriched with techniques from autonomic computing.

In their contribution, the authors demonstrate that these developments cannot be handled independently from each other and that different objectives and constraints are going to be relevant in the near future for decision-making in both fields, increasing the need for further improvement in control strategies that can handle those high-fluctuations and less predictable system behaviour. In particular, this development can and will foster the application of autonomic computing in the electric vehicles, the management of the road network and also in the management of the grids, transforming them to smart grids.

In chapter "Traffic Signal Control with Autonomic Features", Kosonen and Ma outline the application of autonomic architecture and methods for traffic signal control. The authors apply the multi-agent approach both for controlling the signals and for modelling the prevailing traffic situation. The key methods to achieve autonomic management of the system involve a combination of a real-time micro-simulation together with a signal group control and fuzzy logic supported self-calibration and self-optimisation. What makes the work described in this chapter special is that it does not restrict itself to evaluation by simulation but provides a use case for autonomic traffic signal control in the form of an operational control system.

The fourth chapter in this part, chapter "TIMIPLAN: A Tool for Transportation Tasks", addresses the domain of multimodal transportation planning and scheduling. Torralba, Garcia, Borrajo, Lopez and Garcia-Olaya present autonomic aspects of self-management in the design of the TIMIPLAN tool. TIMIPLAN is a software tool developed for solving real-world multimodal transportation problems.

The tool includes a solver that combines Linear Programming with Automated Planning techniques. Features of TIMIPLAN of special relevance for the topics of this book are the underlying mixed-initiative approach (allowing the users to modify the plans provided by the planning module) and the integration of an autonomic execution component monitoring the execution, keeping track of failures and re-planning if necessary.

The final contribution in this volume, chapter "Applying the PAUSETA Protocol in Traffic Management Plans" by Prades-Farron, Garcia and Tomas, introduces a distributed combinatorial auction protocol for replacing manual negotiations during incident response. Response time forms a critical aspect when setting up and activating a traffic management plan. Such a plan organises resource access and utilisation from different agencies and the amount contributed by each of them. The PAUSETA protocol extends previous distributed combinatorial auctions by explicitly dealing with item types exhibiting different self-$*$ properties. The protocol is illustrated using a simulated accident on a highway near Barcelona.

The collection at hand represents the state-of-the-art in Autonomic Road Traffic Support (ARTS) systems. It is the sincere hope (and expectation) of the editors of this book that readers will find the selection of contributions in this volume instructive and enjoyable. We believe that this volume will stimulate further research in ARTS systems, further foster the integration and collaboration between the disciplines of traffic engineering, artificial intelligence and autonomic computing systems, and as such make a valuable contribution to promote this fascinating field of research and application.

The focus and objective of this volume are to provide an overview of the state of the art in the ARTS area. To conclude, let us direct the reader's attention to the forthcoming Roadmap on Autonomic Road Transport Support Systems [10]. The

Roadmap will complement this volume by pointing out *future* research opportunities and challenges in the ARTS research area.

Acknowledgements This book displays results achieved by members of COST Action TU1102 "Towards Autonomic Road Transport Support Systems" (ARTS). COST (European Cooperation in Science and Technology) is a pan-European intergovernmental framework. Its mission is to enable breakthrough scientific and technological developments leading to new concepts and products and thereby contribute to strengthening Europe's research and innovation capacities. It allows researchers, engineers and scholars to jointly develop their own ideas and take new initiatives across all fields of science and technology, while promoting multi- and interdisciplinary approaches. COST aims at fostering a better integration of less research-intensive countries to the knowledge hubs of the European Research Area. The COST Association, an International not-for-profit Association under Belgian Law, integrates all management, governing and administrative functions necessary for the operation of the framework. The COST Association has currently 36 member countries (see www.cost.eu).

We do acknowledge the support of the COST Action TU1102, run from 2011 to 2015, which has contributed immensely in building this research community and facilitating our discussions and collaborations, part of which are reported here.

References

1. Papageorgiou, M., Diakaki, C., Dinopoulou, V., Kotsialos, A., Wang, Y.: Review of road traffic control strategies. Proc. IEEE **91**(12), 2043–2067 (2003)
2. Tincknell, D., Radcliffe, D.: A generic model of manufacturing flexibility based on system control hierarchies. Int. J. Prod. Res. **34**(1), 19–32 (1996)
3. Williams, B.C., Nayak, P.P.: Immobile robots. AI in the new millennium. AI Mag. **17**(3), 16 (1996)
4. Kephart, J., Chess, D.: The vision of autonomic computing. IEEE Comput. **36**(1), 41–50 (2003)
5. Cheliotis, G., Kenyon, C.: Autonomic economics. In: Proceedings of the IEEE International Conference on E-Commerce (2003)
6. Warnier, M., van Sinderen, M., Brazier, M.: Adaptive knowledge representation for a self-managing home energy usage system. In: Proceedings of the Fourth International Workshop on Enterprise Systems and Technology (I-WEST), Athens, 24–25 July 2010, pp. 132–141
7. Agoulmine, N.: Autonomic Network Management Principles: From Concepts to Applications. Academic, Burlington (2010), http://www.sciencedirect.com/science/book/9780123821904
8. Truszkowski, W., Hallock, H., Rouff, C., Karlin, J., Rash, J., Hinchey, M., Sterritt, R.: Autonomous and Autonomic Systems: With Applications to NASA Intelligent Spacecraft Operations and Exploration Systems. Springer, London (2009), http://www.springer.com/gb/book/9781846282324
9. Etemadnia, H., Abdelghany, K., Hariri, S.: Toward an autonomic architecture for real-time traffic network management. J. Intell. Transp. Syst. **16**(2), 45–59 (2012)
10. McCluskey, T.L., et al.: Autonomic road transport support systems: a roadmap. University of Huddersfield and EU COST Action TU 1102. http://www.cost-arts.org (2015)

A Game Theory Model for Self-adapting Traffic Flows with Autonomous Navigation

László Z. Varga

Abstract It is widely believed that road traffic as a whole self-adapts to the current situation to make travel times shorter, if the navigation devices exploit real-time traffic information. A novel theoretical approach to study this belief is the online routing game model. This chapter describes the model of online routing games in order to be able to determine how we can measure and prove the benefits of online real-time data in navigation systems. Three different notions of the benefit of online data and two classes of online routing games are defined. The class of simple naive online routing games represents the current commercial car navigation systems. Simple naive online routing games may have undesirable properties: stability is not guaranteed, single flow intensification may be possible and the worst case benefit of online data may be bigger than one, i.e. it may be a "price". One of the approaches to avoid such problems of car navigation is intention propagation where agents share their intention and can forecast future travel times. The class of simple naive intention propagation online routing games represents the navigation systems that use shortest path planning based on forecast future travel times. In spite of exploiting intention propagation in online routing games, single flow intensification may be possible, the traffic may fluctuate and the worst case benefit may be bigger than one. These theoretical investigations point out issues that need to be solved by future research on decision strategies for self-adapting traffic flows with autonomous navigation.

Keywords Performance • Games • Online routing games • Benefit of online data

1 Introduction

This chapter investigates the properties of autonomous car navigation devices with access to real-time data. If all the information about the road network, the cars on the roads and the destination of the cars could be collected by a centralized system, then

---

L.Z. Varga (✉)
ELTE Regional Knowledge Centre, Irányi Dániel u. 4., Székesfehérvár H-8000, Hungary
e-mail: lzvarga@inf.elte.hu; http://people.inf.elte.hu/lzvarga/

T.L. McCluskey et al. (eds.), *Autonomic Road Transport Support Systems*,
Autonomic Systems, DOI 10.1007/978-3-319-25808-9_2

it would be able to create an optimal plan for the trips of the cars. Optimality may be measured in several ways, but usually we assume that the goal is to optimize some "global" parameter of the traffic, like the sum of the travel times. We also assume that the goal is to assure some kind of fairness for all traffic participants, for example, none of the cars pays with some extra long travel time to achieve the global optimum of the whole traffic. Everyday traffic is not coordinated by a centralized system, and even if the traffic was coordinated by such centralized system, there would be the question whether the individual traffic participants would conform to its instructions. In reality, the traffic participants make their own autonomous decisions based on their intentions and the information available for them locally. This means that instead of centralized decision making, we have a set of autonomous distributed decision makers, i.e. a multi-agent system. In this aspect autonomy refers to the autonomous route planning by the navigation devices in the individual cars instead of following the instructions of some centralized planner.

Another aspect of the autonomous behaviour of navigation systems is related to the ability of the traffic as a whole to self-organize and adapt to the current situation, which is a kind of autonomicity. The major trends that became more and more accomplished in the history of computing are ubiquity, interconnection, intelligence, delegation and human orientation [14]. The current wave of this progress is marked by the widespread availability of online real-time data. The navigation devices in cars can get up-to-date information on the current status of the traffic, like the current travel time on each road, indicating the current situation of the traffic that needs to be adapted to. The routing algorithms implemented in the navigation devices must be able to utilize this real-time data to self-heal the global traffic; for example, if a road becomes congested, then the navigation devices autonomously tell the individual cars how to adapt to the current traffic situation and send the cars to less congested roads. Although current navigation devices are already able to utilize real-time data for route planning, these systems were implemented without clear understanding of the impact of real-time data on traffic as a whole and how real-time data affects the above-mentioned self-adaptation aspects of the traffic flows. Note that in this chapter we focus on online-data-based self-adaptation which is different from self-adaptation based on previous experiences, like in the case of route selection from home to work based on the experience of the previous day.

Two well-known examples of real-time information based navigation systems are Google Maps and Waze. The planning in these systems is done on central server(s) which may play similar role to the virtual environment in the anticipatory vehicle routing of Claes et al. [3]. There are other traffic management systems that combine central planning and local freedom, like the PLANETS system [8] in which global control strategy is provided from a Traffic Management Centre, but traffic participants have a freedom to make decisions autonomously. In our view, self-interested agents will not conform to a central strategy if it is not individually rational, so the global strategy must emerge from the autonomous agents' decision. Therefore, we believe that the basic theoretical model of the online route planning problem should not have an explicit concept of a central planner or a virtual environment even if the agents use the services of these abstractions.

It is widely believed and intuitively we might think that traffic route planning is able to self-adapt to the current situation and plan trips with shorter travel time if we take into account real-time traffic information; however, the classical theoretical models do not have definite answer if online-data-based car navigation is able to self-adapt and produce better traffic or not. There is need for new theoretical studies like the one described in this chapter, because autonomous cars are being designed and the usage of online-data-based navigation systems is spreading and we do not even know how to measure their benefit, not to mention how to optimize their self-healing behaviour.

This chapter has four main sections. In Sect. 2 we shortly describe the classical non-adaptive game theory model for the routing problem, which does not handle real-time information. In Sect. 3 we describe the new online game theory model, which is able to model self-adaptation to real-time information. In Sect. 4 we show the properties of the class of simple naive online routing games, which model the behaviour of traffic using the currently available commercial online-data-based navigation devices. In Sect. 5 we show the properties of the class of simple naive intention propagation (SNIP) online routing games, which model the prediction utilizing anticipatory vehicle routing systems proposed by researchers to improve the currently available commercial online-data-based navigation devices. Finally in Sect. 6 we summarize the main messages of the chapter. The description of these models and the analysis results are based on formal proofs of previous papers [11, 12], but here we present them in an easier understandable way and put them in the context of autonomy and self-adaptation.

2 Classic Non-adaptive Approach

In this section we highlight the main theoretical findings of routing games and online mechanism design, because the model of autonomously self-adapting navigation is based on them and the research in the new field of online routing games[1] has to answer similar questions.

Routing Games Algorithmic game theory studies networks with source routing (Sect. 18 in [9]), in which end users simultaneously choose a full route to their destination and the traffic is routed in a congestion sensitive manner. Two models are used: non-atomic selfish routing and atomic selfish routing. Non-atomic routing is meant to model the case when there are very many actors, each controlling a very small fraction of the overall traffic, so a traffic flow from a source to a destination can be divided among several routes. Atomic routing is meant to model the case when each actor controls a considerable amount of traffic, so a single traffic flow is not divided among several routes. Both models are studied in detail and showed

[1] In the generic form joint resource utilization games [11].

similar properties. The main difference is that the non-atomic model basically has continuous functions having unique extreme values, while the atomic model has discrete functions which can approximate extreme values at several points. The *algorithmic game theory model* of the routing problem is based on the triple (G, r, c), where G is the road network given by a directed graph, r is the total traffic flow given by a vector of r_i traffic flows from source to destination vertices and c is the throughput characteristic of the road network given by a cost function.

A flow distribution is optimal if it minimizes the cost of the total traffic flow over all possible flow distributions. A flow distribution is an *equilibrium flow distribution* if none of the actors can change its traffic flow distribution among its possible paths to decrease its cost. The equilibrium flow distribution is a rational choice for every actor, because deviating from the equilibrium would increase the cost for the actor.

It is proven (Sect. 18 in [9]) that every non-atomic routing problem has at least one equilibrium flow distribution and all equilibrium flow distributions have the same total cost. The *price of anarchy* is the ratio between the cost of an equilibrium flow distribution and the optimal flow distribution. If the cost functions are linear, then the price of anarchy in any non-atomic routing problem is not more than $4 \div 3$. If the cost functions can be non-linear, then one can create cost functions to exceed any given bound on the price of anarchy of non-atomic routing problems.

In atomic routing problems, the existence of equilibrium flow distribution is not always guaranteed. Atomic routing problems have equilibrium flow distribution if every traffic flow r_i has the same value or if the cost functions are linear. If there are more than one equilibrium flow distributions, then their total costs may be different. If the cost functions of an atomic routing problem are linear, then the price of anarchy is at most $(3 + \sqrt{5}) \div 2$. If the cost functions of an atomic routing problem are linear and in addition every traffic flow r_i has the same value, then the price of anarchy is at most $5 \div 2$.

It is known that if the routing problem has an equilibrium and the actors try to minimize their own cost (best-response), then the traffic flow distribution converges to an equilibrium.

The algorithmic game theory investigations of the routing game revealed important properties; however, the algorithmic game theory model contains the following assumptions: (a) The throughput characteristic of the network does not change with time, and the drivers can compute this characteristic or learn it by repeatedly passing the road network. (b) The drivers simultaneously decide their optimal route. (c) The outcome travel time for a given driver depends on the choice of all the drivers and the characteristic of the network, but not on the schedule of the trip of the drivers. These assumptions are not valid for car traffic where the drivers use a navigation device exploiting online data.

The issue of traffic dynamism is studied in the field of dynamic traffic assignment [5], but there they investigate the time-varying properties of traffic flow, whereas here we assume that the traffic flow is basically constant and only the cost functions may change. In our investigations the critical issue is the adaptive sequential decision making of the agents. In the classical game theory approach, the issue of sequential decision making of agents is studied in online mechanism design.

Online Mechanisms Online mechanism design problem is a multi-agent sequential decision-making problem [10]. When agents participate in the mechanism, they report to a central planner for a given period their request for certain resources at given valuations (which may be different from their private values). The central planner decides which resources at which cost are allocated to which agent in each time step. All agents are trying to maximize their utility. The *model of the online mechanism problem* is the five tuple (t, θ, k, c, u), where t is a sequence of time periods, θ is the set of agent types where each agent type is characterized by the arrival/departure time of the agent and its valuation of goods, k is a sequence of decision vectors in each time period by each agent, c is the cost function of the decisions and u is the utility function of the agents.

In this model the θ set of agent types may be model-free when no probabilistic information is known about the agents or may be model based if probabilistic information is known. The agents may report values different from their private agent type, but only for the time period when they are present, at the beginning of the reported time period and without knowing the reports of the other agents (closed direct revelation). Usually the goal is to design online mechanisms where the truthful revelation is the dominant strategy. The *effectiveness of online mechanisms* is measured similarly as that of online algorithms: the performance of the online mechanism is compared with that of an offline mechanism that has the complete information about all future agent types.

The dynamic nature of online mechanisms is a good starting point to model the online-data-based adaptive routing problem; however, the differences are considerable: in contrast with online mechanisms, in the online-data-based adaptive routing problem, there is no central planner (agents make their own plan), the arrival and departure times are not flexible (agents want to start their plan when they arrive) and the actual cost is determined not at the decision time but at utilization time.

3 Game Theory Model for the Online-Data-Based Self-adapting Routing Problem

The online-data-based self-adapting routing problem is a challenging application, because in this problem autonomous agents have access to real-time data, and based on this information, they autonomously try to self-organize themselves by creating adapted plans to achieve their individual goals in an environment where they jointly utilize resources that become more costly as more agents use them. In this problem agents are dynamically arriving and departing after completing their plans. The plans are created by exploiting online data that describe the current status and the current cost of the resources. There is uncertainty about the feasible decision of an agent, because the cost of the resources will change by the time the agent starts to use them: departing agents will release the resources as they complete their plans, agents simultaneously creating their plans will influence each other's costs and agents arriving later may also influence the costs of the resources used by agents already executing their plans. This is somewhat similar to typical game theory problems, where the outcome of the action of the agent depends on its own decision plus the decisions of the other agents; however, in the self-adapting routing problem, the outcome depends on even more circumstances as written above. This type of applications are called *online joint resource utilization games* [11] which is derived from algorithmic game theory [9] and online mechanisms [10]. Note that these games are different from resource allocation or minority games [7] which are simultaneous one shot or repeated simultaneous games where there might be some coordination among some of the agents. In contrast, online joint resource utilization games are continuous and non-cooperative games exploiting real-time data.

Adaptive car navigation using real-time data is a special case of online joint resource utilization games, because the allowed order of the resource utilization in the plan of the agents is restricted by the structure of the road network. From theoretical point of view, online-data-based car navigation applications are called *online routing games* [11]. Note that in this approach each driver makes an individual online-data-based decision at the time of entering the network, whereas in other approaches [2] drivers learn the best route to select, based on past experiences.

3.1 The Model of Online Routing Games

In order to have a generic model, the model of the online joint resource utilization game was defined [11] as an extension of the algorithmic game theory model of the routing problem and the online mechanisms. The model resembles the algorithmic game theory routing game model in the concepts of flow, cost and resource, and it resembles the model of online mechanisms in the sequences of time periods and decisions. Time unit T is introduced in order to be able to compute the rate of resource utilization. The model of online routing games [11] is like the model of online joint resource utilization games but with a restriction on the allowed plans represented by a graph and with somewhat different cost functions. The formal model is described in this subsection, and there are a few examples in Sects. 4 and 5.2.

The *model of the online routing game* is the sextuple (t, T, G, c, r, k), where

- $t = \{1, 2, \ldots\}$ is a sequence of equal time periods.
- T is a natural number with T time periods giving one time unit (e.g. 1 min).
- G is a directed graph $G = (V, E)$ with vertex set V and edge set E where each $e \in E$ is characterized by a cost function c_e which is equal to the utilization time of the edge.
- c is the cost function of G with $c_e : R^+ \rightarrow R^+$ for each edge e of G mapping the incoming flow at each time period to the travel time on that edge, which is

never less than the remaining cost of any other agent currently utilizing that edge increased with the time gap of the flow.[2]

- r is the total flow given by a vector of r_i flows with r_i denoting the flow aiming for a trip P_i from a source vertex s_i of G to a target vertex t_i of G.
- $k = (k^1, k^2, \ldots)$ is a sequence of decision vectors with decision vector $k^t = (k^t_1, k^t_2, \ldots)$ made in time period t and k^t_i the decision made by the agent of the flow r_i in time period t.

In this model, the graph G may contain parallel edges. The cost functions are non-negative, continuous and non-decreasing. The cost functions have a constant part which does not depend on the flow on the edge and a variable part which depends on the flow on the edge. The variable part is not known to any of the actors of the model until an agent exits an edge and reports it. The flow r_i is given by $T \div n_i$ where n_i is a natural number constant, meaning that the following distance of the units of the flow r_i are n_i time periods.[3] The k^t_i decision is how the trip P_i is routed on a single path of the paths leading from s_i to t_i. The actual cost of a path $(e_1, e_2, e_3, ...)$ for a flow starting at time period t is the sum of the cost of the edges, and the actual cost of an edge is determined at the time when the flow enters the edge.

The actual cost of the edges becomes known for the agents only when an agent reports its actual cost. Because agents do not report cost values in each time step, the agents interested in the cost values must decrease the last reported value by taking into account the time elapsed since the last reporting event (it is similar to the pheromone evaporation in [4]).

The online routing game model can accommodate changes of the cost function c over the sequence of time periods t, because the agents can get information about the actual cost only from the cost reported by the agents exiting an edge.

Routing Strategy The critical point in the online routing game is how to determine the best decision vector k. The algorithmic game theory approach assumes that the agents have full information about the cost functions, and the theory tells what the best strategy is in the case of simultaneous decisions but does not tell how the agents can achieve this. In online mechanisms a central planner decides which resources at which cost are allocated to which agent. In online routing games there is no central planner. The agents in online routing games will have to apply algorithms similar to online algorithms [1]. At this time we are not investigating how the agents of online routing games determine their strategy; instead, we are investigating the performance of the strategies of current navigation devices.

Simple Naive Strategy Typical navigation software currently installed in cars use simple shortest path search in the road network, possibly modifying the distances with the online information about the actual traffic delay. We call this decision

---

[2]In this model cars cannot overtake the cars already on the road and there is a time gap, i.e. minimum "following distance".

[3]So if $T = 6$ time steps and $n_i = 2$, then one car enters the network every second time step and the intensity of the flow is 3, because 3 cars enter the network in a time unit.

strategy *simple naive strategy*. This strategy is investigated because of its practical importance. Note that the simple naive strategy is by definition deterministic; thus it is a pure strategy.

3.2 The Benefit of Online Real-Time Data

We would like to be able to tell if the agents are better off by autonomously trying to self-adapt to the observed online real-time data or not. In order to be able to compare the costs of the agents using online data with the costs of the agents not using online data, we have to know what we are going to compare with what.

If we take the approach of online algorithms, then we would compare the results of the online routing game with the results of an oracle that has all the information needed. One might think that in our case the oracle with all information would be the central planner, because the central planner has all the information and can tell each agent which route to take.

The central planning oracle might be good to measure the global effectiveness of the agents in the online routing game model; however, it evaluates not only the benefits of making decisions based on online data, but in addition, it evaluates the different decision-making strategies as well. In the online routing game model there is no coordination among the agents and the agents make decisions using, for example, the simple naive strategy, while in the central planning and the algorithmic game theory approaches, the agents are coordinated and they exploit their knowledge about the cost functions. Therefore, if we want to evaluate only the benefits of autonomous self-adaptation using online real-time data, then we want to compare the results with an "oracle" using the same decision-making strategy.

In the algorithmic game theory model, there is equilibrium and the price of anarchy concept is the ratio between the equilibrium and the optimum. Later in this chapter (in Theorem 1), we will see that there are simple naive strategy online routing games which do not have equilibrium at some flow values. If there is no equilibrium, then we must have different measures for the best, worst, and average cases (which are guaranteed to exist if there is finite sequence of time periods). Depending on the type of application, we are interested in the different types of benefits. The most important is the worst case, because it can be used to provide a guarantee in critical applications. The best case can be used in applications, where we have to make sure that a certain value is achieved at least once. The average case is seldom useful in itself; usually we have to consider statistical distribution parameters as well.

The above discussion is concluded with the definition of the different benefits of online real-time data [11]. If these benefits are below 1, then the agents have a benefit, because their costs (travel times) are reduced. If these benefits are greater than 1, then they are in fact a "price" like the price of anarchy.

Definition 1 The *worst/best/average case benefit* of online real-time data at a given flow is the ratio between the cost of the maximum/minimum/average cost of the flow and the cost of the same flow with an oracle using the same decision-making strategy and only the fixed part of the cost functions.

Classes of Online Routing Games Online routing games using the same type of decision strategies belong to the same class of online routing games. Each class needs to be evaluated how much benefit they make out of online real-time data, in order to be able to determine the type of application where they are suitable. The evaluation should include formal proofs. In this paper we discuss the formal analysis of the class of simple naive strategy online routing games and the class of SNIP online routing games.

Although the simple naive decision strategy is often applied in real world, it is not the best, because it does not alternate the agents of a flow among two or more paths, whereas the optimal central planning and the algorithmic game theory approach use several paths for the same flow. Further research is needed to study different online routing game decision strategies derived from other related games like resource allocation or minority games [7] and the El Farol Bar problem in [6].

4 Simple Naive Strategy Online Routing Games

The simple naive strategy was introduced in Sect. 3.1 and now we discuss properties of simple naive strategy online routing games [11]. The first property states that if the agents of the car navigation system use simple naive strategy to autonomously adapt to the current situation of the traffic, then at some flow values they may make the traffic fluctuate.

Theorem 1 *There are simple naive strategy online routing games which do not have equilibrium at certain flow values.*

Proof The proof [11] is informally illustrated in Fig. 1. The traffic will fluctuate between the roads e_1 and e_2 if at some flow value the non-congested travel time on e_2 is smaller than the non-congested travel time on e_1, which is smaller than the

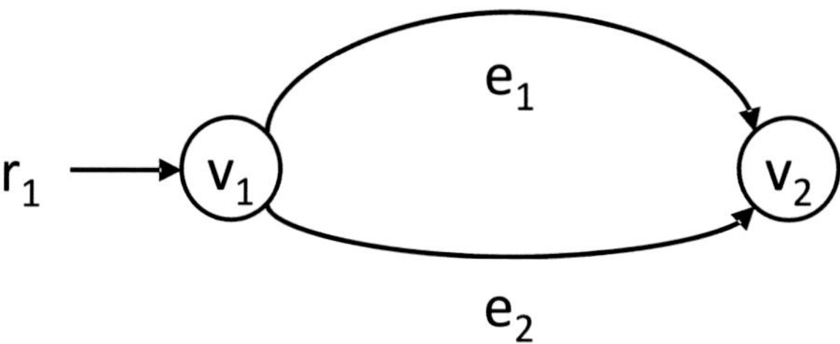

Fig. 1 Simple naive online routing game with fluctuation

congested travel time on e_2, which is smaller than the congested travel time on e_1. In the beginning the traffic starts to flow on e_2, so the travel time on e_2 starts to increase, and when the travel time on e_2 exceeds the non-congested travel time on e_1, then the traffic at vertex v_1 switches to e_1, and then the travel time on e_2 starts to decrease, and when the travel time on e_2 drops below the travel time of e_1, the traffic switches to e_2, so the travel time on e_2 starts to increase and the cycle starts again. □

The second property is the possibility of *single flow intensification*: if the agents of the navigation system use simple naive strategy to autonomously adapt to the current situation of the traffic and only a single flow enters the road network, then at some flow value at some time there may be a road somewhere in the network, where the flow is bigger than the flow that entered the network. The formal statement is the following:

Theorem 2 *There are simple naive strategy online routing games, where the total traffic flow has only one incoming flow, i.e.* $r = (r_1)$*; however, the flow on some of the edges of the road network G sometimes may be more than* r_1.

Proof The proof [11] is informally illustrated here with the network of Fig. 2, where road e_2 is not susceptible to congestion, the non-congested travel time on road e_1 is smaller than the travel time on e_2, which is smaller than the congested travel time on e_1 at some flow value, which is smaller than 1.5 times the travel time on e_2. In addition, the travel time on e_2 is more than 2 time units. In this network it may happen that a platoon of the full incoming flow going on e_1 is caught up by some agents that go on e_2 and arrive at vertex v_2 at the same time, so a bigger flow will go into e_3 than the one that enters the network. □

The third property is that the online information may have a "price": if the agents of the car navigation system use simple naive strategy to autonomously adapt to the current situation of the traffic, then sometimes they may be worse off than without exploiting information about the current situation. The formal statement is the following:

Theorem 3 *There are simple naive strategy online routing games where the worst case benefit of online real-time data is greater than one, i.e. in these games the worst case benefit is a "price".*

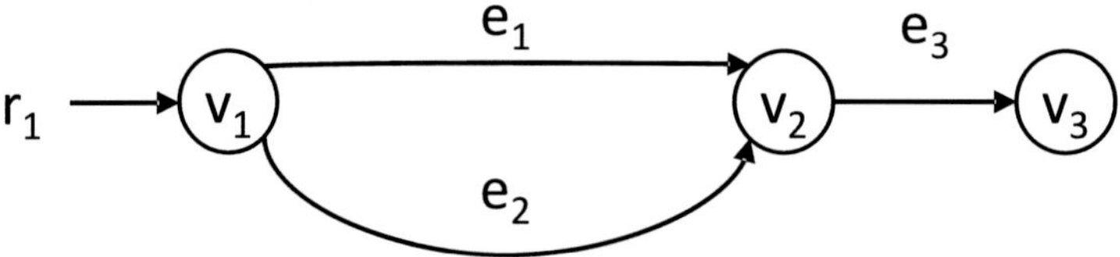

Fig. 2 Simple naive online routing game with "single flow intensification"

Proof The proof [11] is informally illustrated here with the network of Fig. 2 if road e_3 is susceptible to congestion. Without online information all the agents would select the path (e_1, e_3); however, if the agents exploit online information, then in accordance with Theorem 2, at some flow value at some time, the incoming flow of e_3 will be a platoon of the full incoming flow of the network from e_1 plus some other flow from e_2. The result is that the travel time on path (e_1, e_3) in this case will be longer than the travel time without online information. □

5 Simple Naive Intention Propagation Strategy Online Routing Games

As we have seen, if the agents of car navigation systems use the simple naive strategy to autonomously adapt to the current situation of the traffic, then the traffic may have properties that we are not happy with. These findings are in line with the simulation results, like the simple scenario consisting of two parallel routes investigated in [13]. The simulations also showed that online information often leads to oscillations in the number of cars on the routes, the velocity and the travel times, which lead to worse overall performance. In the discussion the authors conclude that one of the reasons for the oscillations is that the real-time travel information reflects the state of the network some time ago. Another reason for the oscillation is that the agents do not coordinate their actions. In order to improve these, the authors advise the usage of anticipatory traffic forecast based on the broadcast route choice of the agents, which basically means that the agents share or propagate their intentions. In order to improve the simple naive strategy, the approach of intention propagation was proposed in the anticipatory vehicle routing system using delegate multi-agent systems [3]. In this section we discuss how the online routing game model [11] is used to investigate some of the properties of the usage of intention-propagation-based prediction in autonomously self-adapting car navigation.

5.1 *Intention Propagation*

The anticipatory vehicle routing proposed in [3] uses the individual planned routes of the agents to forecast future traffic density. Every vehicle is represented by a vehicle agent running on a smart device inside the vehicle. Vehicle agents communicate with the delegate multi-agent system. The delegate multi-agent system represents the traffic environment and is able to make forecast of future traffic density based on the current traffic situation and the planned routes of the vehicles. The delegate multi-agent system provides the traffic forecast back to the vehicle agents which use this information to plan their trip.

The delegate MAS can predict future travel times based on the intention notifications that it has received from all vehicle agents. The delegate MAS has a parametrized model that describes the relationship between the travel time and the intention notifications. The parameters are continuously updated based on both historical and real-time data, so basically the delegate MAS computes the cost functions of the online routing game model with the ability to handle adapting cost functions.

If the predicted future travel times show that a new travel route is preferable, then the vehicle agent is free to change its route plan. If the vehicle agent changes its route plan, then it notifies the delegate MAS of its change of intention. The old intention is then invalidated and the new intention is registered in the delegate MAS.

Although the vehicle agent could use several strategies to revise its intention, we assume that vehicle agents always select the shortest travel time which is called simple naive decision strategy in the online routing game model.

5.2 *Properties of Intention-Propagation-Based Prediction in Online Routing Games*

A slightly modified version of the above anticipatory vehicle routing system is used to define and formally analyse the class of online routing games that use intention-propagation-based prediction in their decision mechanism [12]. This class of online routing games are called SNIP online routing games.

Definition 2 Simple naive intention propagation online routing games (SNIP online routing games) are online routing games where the decision-making agents of the flows r_i are the vehicle agents of the anticipatory vehicle routing system; the vehicle agents use the delegate MAS as described in the previous section to predict the travel time for each path p_j of their trip P_i; and their decision k_i^t is to select the path with the shortest travel time among the predicted travel times on the different paths of their trip P_i. The vehicle agent notifies the delegate MAS of its selected path, and the delegate MAS remembers this selection while the vehicle agent is in the network and invalidates it when the vehicle agent exits the road network.

Note that SNIP online routing games are a little bit different from the anticipatory vehicle routing system of Claes et al. [3], because the SNIP vehicle agents select their route when they enter the road network, and in accordance with the online routing game model, they do not revise it during their trip.

The agents receive a prediction of future traffic in SNIP online routing games, so we would expect that this additional information can be used to improve the properties of simple naive online routing games. Unfortunately intention propagation does not solve the “single flow intensification” problem, as the next Theorem 4 says.

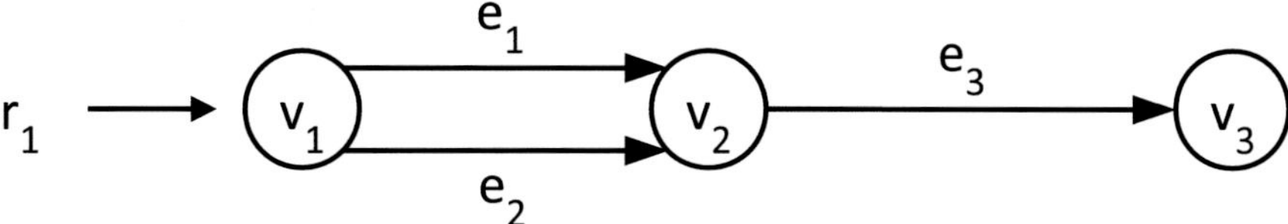

Fig. 3 The network of the SNIP online routing game $SN_{5.1}$

Theorem 4 *There are SNIP online routing games where the total traffic flow has only one incoming flow, i.e.* $r = (r_1)$*; however, the flow on some of the edges of the network G sometimes may be more than* r_1.

Proof In this paper we are informally highlighting the essence of the proof [12] of the theorem with the SNIP online routing game $SN_{5.1}$. The network of $SN_{5.1}$ is shown in Fig. 3. The cost functions are $c_{e1} = 10 + x$, $c_{e2} = 10,5 + x$ and $c_{e3} = 1 + x$, where x is the total incoming flow on the edge. The network has only one incoming flow from v_1 to v_3. Because the flow receives predictions, normally it alternates the flow between the roads e_1 and e_2. Because the cost functions of e_1 and e_2 are different, the flow fluctuates on road e_3. As a result, the flow on e_3 will be bigger, for a short time, than the incoming flow. □

The above Theorem 4 shows that "single flow intensification" may happen in SNIP online routing games, but it does not happen the same way as in simple naive online routing games. The proof of the above theorem cannot be continued to prove that the worst case benefit of online data in SNIP online routing games may be more than one the same way as it was done in [11]. However, there is an additional alternative proof in the next Theorem 5, and this proof points out another reason for possible worst case benefit above one.

Theorem 5 *There are SNIP online routing games where the worst case benefit of online real-time data is greater than one.*

Proof We are informally highlighting the essence of the proof [12] of the theorem with the SNIP online routing game $SN_{5.2}$. The network is shown in Fig. 4. The cost functions are $c_{e1} = 1$, $c_{e2} = 1$, $c_{e3} = 10 + x$ and $c_{e4} = 10.5 + 10 \times x$, where x is the total incoming flow on the edge. The total traffic flow is $r = (r_1, r_2)$ with flow $r_1 = 1$ from the source v_0 to the target v_3 and flow $r_2 = 1$ from v_1 to v_3. Without online data, both flow would select the road e_3, so the cost of both flow would be 13 and the total cost 26. With online data, the flows realize at some time that the cost of e_3 will go above the cost of e_4. This happens at the same time for both flows, and they are not aware that the other flow is going to change to e_4 at the same time, so they do not take into account the additional cost on e_4. This is because the traffic forecaster is only aware of the intention propagations before the current time step, but does not know and cannot forecast the decisions at the current time

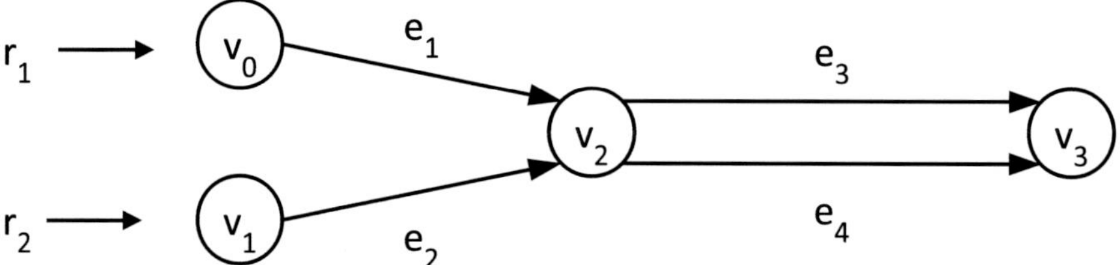

Fig. 4 The network of the SNIP online routing game $SN_{5.2}$

step. Because e_4 is more susceptible to congestion than e_3, the cost on e_4 will be more than on e_3, so the total cost may go above 26. □

The situation is even worse than in the theorem above, because the worst case benefit of online data can be arbitrarily large as the next theorem shows. Note that Theorem 6 is not specific to intention propagation, just this property was not investigated for simple naive online routing games.

Theorem 6 *Given any arbitrarily large number α, there are SNIP online routing games with linear cost functions, where the worst case benefit of online real-time data is bigger than α.*

Proof Basically the proof [12] of this theorem is based on the SNIP online routing game $SN_{5.2}$ of the above Theorem 5. In short and informally, if the cost function of the road e_4 is steep enough, then the flows can incur big enough cost when they change to e_4 at the same time. □

The last question is whether intention propagation can help to avoid fluctuation? Unfortunately the answer is not positive, as the next theorem shows.

Theorem 7 *There are SNIP online routing games which do not have equilibrium at certain flow values.*

Proof In short and informally, the proof [12] of this theorem is the continuation of the scenario of Theorem 5. Once the two flows change to e_4 at the same time, they immediately realize from the prediction that this has high cost, so they revert to e_3, but after a while the cost of e_4 drops below the cost of e_3, so both flows change to e_4 again at the same time. Then this fluctuating cycle continues. □

6 Conclusions

Information and communication technologies allow that modern car navigation devices utilize live online data from road traffic networks to optimize the route of vehicles. The navigation devices in cars are autonomous agents, because they plan their route based on their intentions and local information instead of following the instructions of some centralized planner. The routing algorithms implemented in the navigation devices must be able to utilize real-time data to self-heal the global traffic and autonomously tell the individual cars how to adapt to the current traffic situation. Although current navigation devices are already able to utilize real-time data for route planning, these systems were implemented without clear understanding of how real-time data affects the autonomous and self-adaptation aspects of traffic flows.

In order to be able to measure and prove properties of autonomous traffic routing based on online data, the formal model of online routing games was developed. This model is an extension of the models of routing games of the algorithmic game theory approach and the online mechanisms. Different classes of online routing games are foreseen, and two of them were discussed here. One is the class of simple naive online routing games, which models the currently available commercial real-time-data-based navigation devices. The other is the class of SNIP online routing games, which models the prediction utilizing anticipatory vehicle routing systems proposed by researchers to improve the currently available commercial online-data-based navigation devices.

Several properties of these two classes of online routing games were proved in [11, 12]. Here we informally presented these proofs, discussed them in an easily understandable way and highlighted the critical phenomena that are behind these properties. In the class of simple naive online routing games, stability is not guaranteed, so it makes sense to talk about worst, average and best case benefit of online data. Simple naive online routing games may have the "single flow intensification" property. The result of this is that the worst case benefit of online data may be bigger than 1, which means that sometimes some of the autonomous cars are worse off with utilizing online data for the self-adaptation of traffic flows, than without utilizing online data.

The class of SNIP online routing games may also have the "single flow intensification" property. The worst case benefit of online data may also go above 1 and the traffic may fluctuate. We have pointed out that one of the reasons of this surprising result is the "simultaneous decision" problem: the traffic forecaster predicts future traffic conditions based on the intentions of the vehicles already on the road, but it does not predict the intentions of the vehicles currently making decisions. If many vehicles make decisions at the same time, then they may try to take the same alternative route to avoid the already predicted congestion and cause congestion on the alternative route. Obviously, intention propagation helps the vehicles to detect the possibility of congestion formation before the congestion is actually formed, and thus there is smaller "time window" to make the same "wrong" decision to head towards the newly forming congestion than in the case of the simple naive online routing games. The technique of intention propagation and traffic forecast is therefore an important improvement to the simple naive online strategy.

The issues discussed here point out notions and characteristics that can become the basis to guide future research. These issues also challenge future research to develop online routing game decision strategies that have worst case benefits of online data below 1 or prove that it is not possible to develop such strategy.

If such strategies are possible, then we expect that the application of these new strategies will be individually rational choice, and therefore the decision strategies can be implemented in the navigation devices themselves instead of the centralized planning approaches like those of Google Maps and Waze, because some users are reluctant to provide private data for the centralized approach.

Acknowledgements This research is supported by the European Union and the European Social Fund through project FuturICT.hu (grant no.: TÁMOP-4.2.2.C-11/1/KONV-2012-0013).

References

1. Albers, S.: Online algorithms. In: Goldin, D.Q., Smolka, S.A., Wegner, P. (eds.) Interactive Computation: The New Paradigm, pp. 143–164. Springer, Berlin (2006)
2. Bazzan, A.L.C., Klügl, F.: Case studies on the Braess Paradox: simulating route recommendation and learning in abstract and microscopic models. Transp. Res. Part C Emerg. Technol. **13**(4), 299–319 (2005)
3. Claes, R., Holvoet, T., Weyns, D.: A decentralized approach for anticipatory vehicle routing using delegate multi-agent systems. IEEE Trans. Intell. Transp. Syst. **12**(2), 364–373 (2011)
4. Dallmeyer, J., Schumann, R., Lattner, A.D., Timm, I.J.: Don't go with the ant flow: ant-inspired traffic routing in urban environments. In: 7th International Workshop on Agents in Traffic and Transportation (ATT 2012) held at AAMAS 2012, pp. 59–68 (2012)
5. Dynamic Traffic Assignment: A Primer. Transportation Research Circular Number E-C153, Transportation Research Board, 500 Fifth Street, NW, Washington, DC 20001 (2011)
6. Galafassi, C., Bazzan, A.L.C.: Evolving mechanisms in Boolean games. In: Proceedings of Multiagent System Technologies, 11th German Conference, MATES 2013, Koblenz, pp. 73–86. Springer, Berlin/Heidelberg (2013)
7. Galstyan, A., Kolar, S., Lerman, K.: Resource allocation games with changing resource capacities. In: Proceedings of the International Conference on Autonomous Agents and Multi-Agent Systems (AAMAS-2003), Melbourne, pp. 145–152. ACM, New York (2003)
8. Görmer, J., Ehmke, J.F., Fiosins, M., Schmidt, D., Schumacher, H., Tchouankem, H.: Decision support for dynamic city traffic management using vehicular communication. In: Proceedings of 1st International Conference on Simulation and Modeling Methodologies, Technologies and Applications, pp. 327–332. SciTePress Digital Library (2011)
9. Nisan, N., Roughgarden, T., Tardos, E., Vazirani, V.V.: Algorithmic Game Theory. Cambridge University Press, New York (2007)
10. Parkes, D.C.: Online mechanisms. In: Nisan, N., Roughgarden, T., Tardos, E., Vazirani, V.V. (eds.) Algorithmic Game Theory, pp. 411–439. Cambridge University Press, New York (2007)
11. Varga, L.Z.: Online routing games and the benefit of online data. In: Proceedings of Eighth International Workshop on Agents in Traffic and Transportation, held at the 13th International Conference on Autonomous Agents and Multiagent Systems (AAMAS 2014), Paris, pp. 88–95 (2014). Available at http://www.ia.urjc.es/ATT/documents/ATT2014proceedings.pdf. Cited 15 Jan 2015
12. Varga, L.Z.: On intention-propagation-based prediction in autonomously self-adapting navigation. In: Proceedings of IEEE Eighth International Conference on Self-Adaptive and Self-organizing Systems Workshops, London, pp. 38–44. IEEE, London (2014)
13. Wahle, J., Bazzan, A.L.C., Klügl, F., Schreckenberg, M.: Decision dynamics in a traffic scenario. Phys. A Stat. Mech. Appl. **287**(3–4), 669–681 (2000)
14. Wooldridge, M.: An Introduction to MultiAgent Systems, 2nd edn. Wiley Publishing, Chichester (2009)

Self-management in Urban Traffic Control: An Automated Planning Perspective

Falilat Jimoh and Thomas Leo McCluskey

Abstract Advanced urban traffic control (UTC) systems are often based on feedback algorithms. They use road traffic data which has been gathered from a couple of minutes to several years. For instance, current traffic control systems often operate on the basis of adaptive green phases and flexible coordination in road (sub)networks based on measured traffic conditions. However, these approaches are still not very efficient during unforeseen situations such as road incidents when changes in traffic are requested in a short time interval. For such anomalies, we argue that systems that can sense, interpret and deliberate with their actions and goals to be achieved are needed, taking into consideration continuous changes in state, required service level and environmental constraints. The requirement of such systems is that they can plan and act effectively after such deliberation, so that behaviourally they appear self-aware.

This chapter focuses on the design of a generic architecture for autonomic UTC, to enable the network to manage itself both in normal operation and in unexpected scenarios. The reasoning and self-management aspects are implemented using automated planning techniques inspired by both the symbolic artificial intelligence and traditional control engineering. Preliminary test results of the plan generation phase of the architecture are considered and evaluated.

Keywords Automated planning • Autonomic systems • Urban traffic control

1 Introduction

The need for planning and execution frameworks has increased interest in designing and developing system architectures which use state-of-the-art plan generation techniques, plan execution, monitoring and recovery in order to address complex tasks in real-world environments [1]. An example of such an architecture is teleo-reactive executive (T-Rex): a goal-oriented system architecture with embedded automated

---

F. Jimoh (✉) • T.L. McCluskey (✉)
School of Computing and Engineering, University of Huddersfield, Huddersfield, West Yorkshire, UK
e-mail: Falilat.Jimoh@hud.ac.uk; t.l.mccluskey@hud.ac.uk

T.L. McCluskey et al. (eds.), *Autonomic Road Transport Support Systems*, Autonomic Systems, DOI 10.1007/978-3-319-25808-9_3

planning for on-board planning and execution for autonomous underwater vehicles to enhance ocean science [2, 3]. Another recent planning architecture, planning and execution learning architecture (PELEA), is a flexible modular architecture that incorporates sensing, planning, executing, monitoring, replanning and even learning from past experiences [4].

This means that advanced control systems should be able to reason with their surrounding environment and take decisions with respect to their current situation and their desired service level. This could be achieved by embedding situational awareness into them, giving them the ability to generate necessary plans to solve problems themselves with little or no human intervention. We believe this is the key to embody autonomic properties in systems.

Self-managed (SM) systems are required to have an ability to learn process patterns from the past and adopt, discard or generate new plans to improve control systems. The ability to identify the task is the most important aspect of any SM element; this enables SM to select the appropriate action when healing, optimising, configuring or protecting itself.

Our self-managed system architecture is inspired by the functionality of the human autonomic nervous system (HANS) that handles complexity and uncertainty with the aim to realise computing systems and applications capable of managing themselves with minimum human intervention.

2 Urban Traffic Control

There are several applications of artificial intelligence to urban traffic control (UTC) with the aim of creating intelligent systems that will optimise the flow of traffic in urban centres [5–7]. Yet, the existing UTC approaches are not generally optimal during unforeseen situations such as road incidents, car breakdown or when traffic demand changes rapidly within a short time interval [8, 9]. This increases the need for autonomy in UTC. Such an autonomic system (AS) would need to be able to consider the factors affecting the situation at hand: the road network, the state of traffic flows, the road capacity limit, accessibility or availability of roads within the network, etc. All these factors will be peculiar to the particular set of circumstances causing the problem [10]. Hence, there is a need for a system that can reason with the capabilities of the control assets, and the situation parameters as sensed by road sensors, and generate a set of actions or decisions that can be taken to alleviate the situation. Therefore, we need systems that can plan and act effectively in order to restore an unexpected road traffic situation into a normal order. A significant step towards this is exploiting automated planning techniques which can reason about unforeseen situations in the road network and come up with plans (sequences of actions) achieving a desired traffic situation.

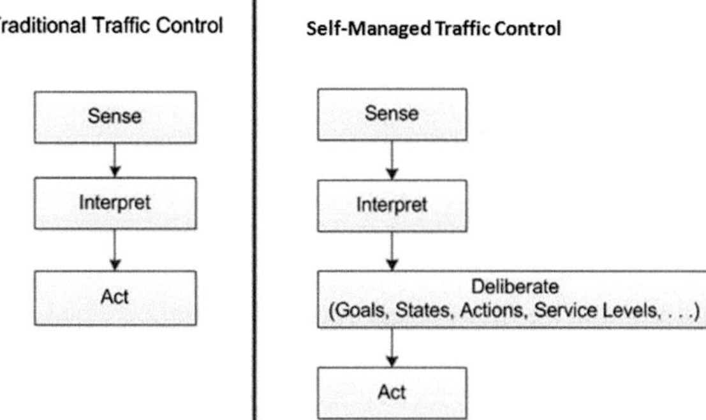

Fig. 1 Comparison of traditional and deliberative controls in urban transport systems

2.1 *Role of AI Planning in UTC*

The field of *Artificial Intelligence Planning*, or AI Planning, has evidenced a significant advancement in planning techniques, which has led to the development of efficient planning systems [11–14] that can input declarative representation of models of applications. The existence of these general planning tools has motivated engineers in designing and developing complex application models which closely approximate real-world problems. Thus, it is now possible to deploy deliberative reasoning to real-time control applications [15, 16]. Consequently, AI Planning now has a growing role in the realisation of autonomy in control systems, and this architecture is a leap towards the realisation of such a goal. The main difference between traditional and our autonomic control architecture is depicted in Fig. 1. Traditionally, a control loop consists of three steps: sense, interpret and act [17]. In other words, data are gathered from the environment with the use of sensors, and the system interprets information from these sensors as the state of the environment. The system acts by taking necessary actions which are fed back into the system in order to keep the environment in a desirable state. Introducing deliberation in the control loop allows the system to reason and generate effective plans in order to achieve desirable goals. Enabling deliberative reasoning in UTC systems is important because of its ability to handle unforeseen situations which has not been previously learnt nor hard-coded into a UTC. Ultimately, this would help to reduce traffic congestion and carbon emissions.

3 Automated Planning

AI Planning deals with the problem of finding a totally or partially ordered sequence of actions whose execution leads from a particular initial state to a state in which a goal condition is satisfied [18]. Actions in plans are ordered in such a way that the executability of every action is guaranteed. Hence, an agent is able to transform the environment from an initial state into a desired goal state [19]. A planning problem thus involves deciding "what" actions to do and "when" to do them [20].

In general, state space of AI Planning tasks can be defined as a state-transition system specified by three-tuple (S, A, γ) where:

- S is a set of states
- A is a set of actions
- $\gamma : S \times A \rightarrow 2^S$ is a transition function

Actions can modify the environment (a state is changed after an action is triggered). Application of an action a in some state s results in a state in $\gamma(s, a)$ ($\gamma(s, a)$ contains a set of states). It refers to nondeterministic effects of actions.

Classical planning is the simplest form of AI Planning in which the transition function γ is deterministic (i.e. $\gamma : S \times A \rightarrow S$). Hence, the environment is assumed to be static and fully observable. Also, in classical planning actions have instantaneous effects.

Temporal planning extends classical planning by considering time. Actions have durative effects which means that executing an action takes some time and effects of the action are not instantaneous. Temporal planning, in fact, combines classical planning and scheduling.

Conformant planning considers partially observable environments and actions with nondeterministic effects. Therefore, the transition function γ is nondeterministic (i.e. $\gamma : S \times A \rightarrow 2^S$).

For describing classical and temporal planning domain and problem models, we can use PDDL [21], a language which is supported by most planning engines. For describing conformant planning domain and problem models, we can use PPDDL [22] (an extension of PDDL) or RDDL [23], languages which are supported by many conformant planning engines. Our architecture can generally support all the above kinds of planning.

4 Autonomic Computing Paradigm

We use the term "autonomic system" (AS) rather than autonomic computing to emphasise the idea that we are dealing with a heterogeneous system containing hardware and software. Sensors and effectors are the main component of this type of autonomic system architecture [24]. AS needs sensors to sense the environment and executes actions through effectors. In most cases, a control loop is created: the system processes information retrieved from the sensors in order to be aware of its effect and its environment; it takes necessary decisions using its existing knowledge from its domain, generates effective plans and executes those plans using effectors. Autonomic systems typically execute a cycle of monitoring, analysing, planning and execution [25].

System architecture elements are self-managed by monitoring and behaviour analysing, and the response is used to plan and execute actions that move or keep the system in a desired state. Overall self-management of a system is about doing self-assessment, protection, healing, optimisation, maintenance and other overlapping terms [24]. It is important to stress that these properties are interwoven. The existence of one might require the existence of others to effectively operate. For instance, a self-optimisation process might not be complete until the system is able to self-configure itself. Likewise, an aspect of a proactive self-healing is an ability of the system to self-protect itself. A system that is meant to satisfy the above objectives will need to have the following attributes:

- Self-awareness of both internal and external features, process resources and constraints
- Self-monitoring of its existing state and processes
- Self-adjustment and control of itself to the desirable/required state
- Heterogeneity across numerous hardware and software architectures

In a quest to embed these autonomic attributes into an UTC system, we explore the feasibility of embedding an automated planning component into an UTC system. The next section gives an overview of the architectural design of our approach.

5 A Self-managing System Architecture Using Automated Planning

We describe the system's modules in the section below, using the diagram in Fig. 2.

Key to the contents of the architecture is a declarative description of the system itself: the individual components that make up such a system, the dynamic environment that can influence the performance of such system and its sensing and controlling capabilities. A novel feature is its ability to reason and deliberate using a combination of model predictive control (MPC) approach [26] and AI Planning paradigm.

5.1 Road Traffic Network

A real traffic network contains information about the state of a road traffic environment at any time of the day.

Where historic data is available, or where behaviour is caused by anticipated circumstances, a road network will continue to flow normally using its programmed or adaptive intelligence. This means that signal heads will be able to control traffic as long as the traffic pattern is closed to the programmed or learnt pattern [27]. Changes to the state of a traffic network are under the influence of various disturbances. For

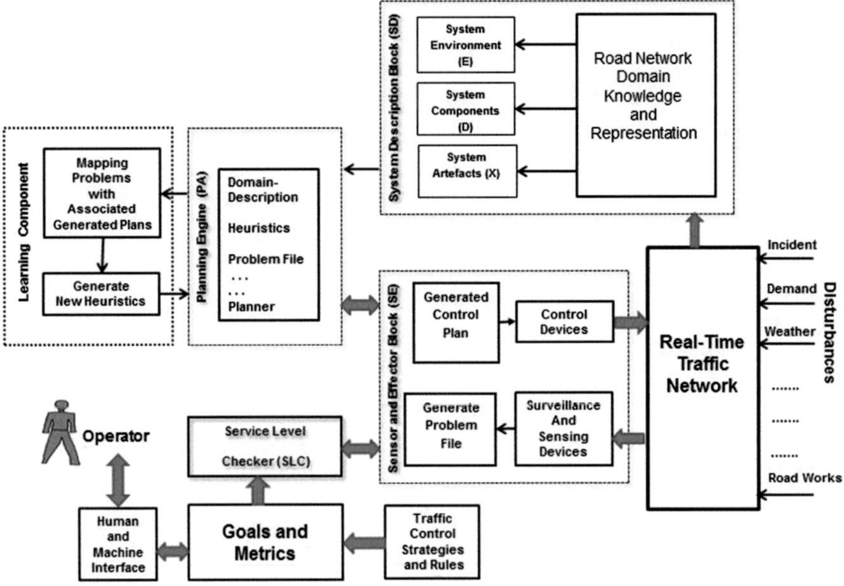

Fig. 2 Diagram of a self-managing system architecture using automated planning

example, a sudden increase in the volume of traffic because of the end of a football game in a nearby arena becomes a disturbance to a road network, if the network has not been previously programmed or adapted to such a traffic change.

Thus, our perception of the traffic situation within a network of roads is that a network of traffic will continue to operate as planned until a disturbance makes it act otherwise. In this work, a network of roads, as shown in Fig. 3, within Huddersfield town centre area of the United Kingdom was considered for our experimental analysis [28, 29].

5.2 *Disturbances*

The factors that affect the normal functioning of a road network are planned and unplanned disturbances. An example of planned disturbance is a set of road works. This disrupts the normal flow of traffic for the entire duration of its construction. During such road works, the adjoining route and intersection signal need to be optimised in order to minimise the effect of road or lane blockage during the period of the maintenance or upgrade. There are several examples of unplanned disturbances. This includes but is not limited to road incident, unexpected change in traffic demand and severe weather conditions. Whenever a road incident occurs, the portion of the road would be blocked to allow comprehensive investigation

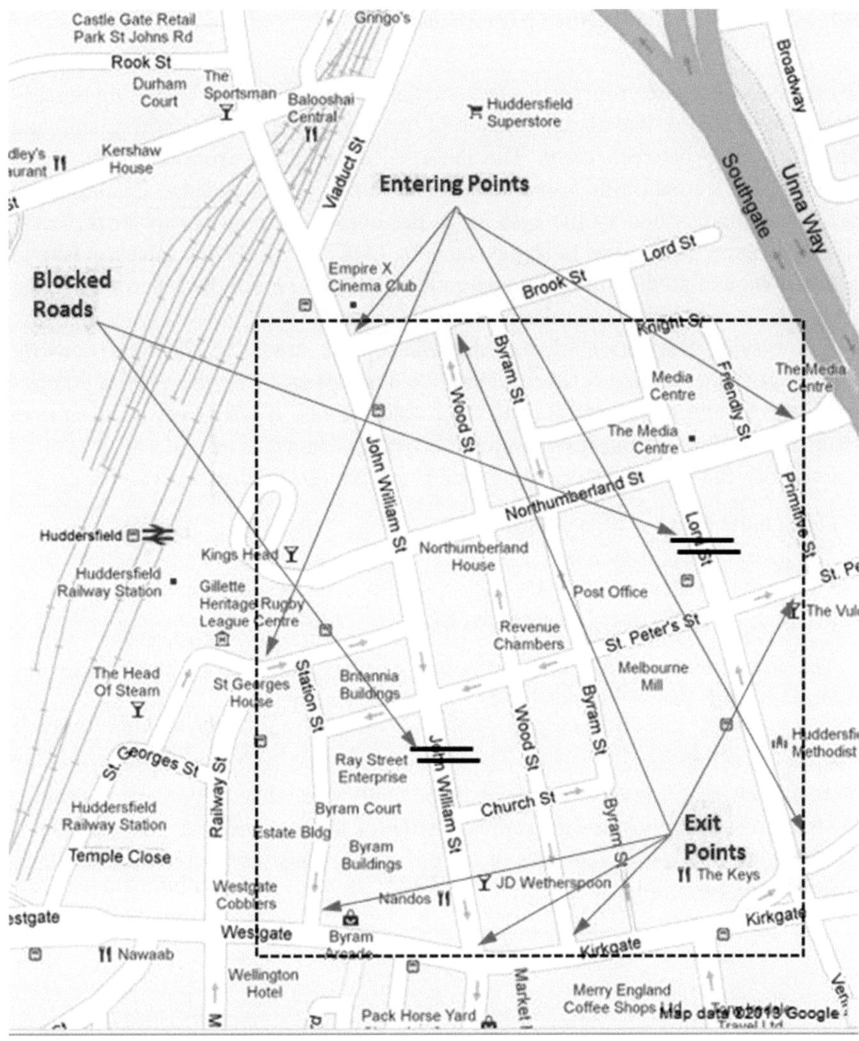

Fig. 3 Map showing the network entry and exit points and the blocked roads in a part of town centre of Huddersfield, West Yorkshire, United Kingdom. It is used for our empirical analysis

for a period of time. During this period, the signal head should be aware of the status of the vehicles on the road through the use of road sensors and existing surveillance. Necessary alerts should be sent to the operator for medical emergency and security staff. Also the signal heads in adjoining routes should also be optimised to allow outflow of vehicles from the incident point to connected roads and the inflow of vehicle to the effected roads. This would be achieved automatically by a self-managed system by the use of message boards and switching all signal heads appropriately.

5.3 System Description (SD) Block

To create a self-aware property in a system, the system needs both to be situationally aware *and* have a knowledge model of its components, its environment and the relationship between them. The latter is achieved by extracting operational knowledge of a road traffic domain and representing that knowledge in a language that can be understood by the system. In the implementation of this work, much of the domain knowledge is represented in PDDL [21]. PDDL gives a formal representation of all the entities and operation policy of a road network in a language that is understood by an automated planning function.

The system description block comprises of the model of the road network domain. It is the storage for the declarative description of all the system components, the system environments and their components. It also gives a declarative description of the relationship between those components.

Formally, the system description block is a triple $\langle D, X, S \rangle$ where:

- D is a finite set of system components
- X is a finite set of artefacts
- S is a set of states, where each state $s_i \in S$ is a set of assignments $f_k(y_l) = v_m$ where $y_l \in D \cup X$ and v_m is a value of y_l

The components are all the objects that can be controlled by the system, for example, traffic control signal heads, variable message signs (VMS) and traffic cameras.

In the UTC domain, for instance, SD consists of a declarative description of the road network of an area that needs to be controlled while optimising the traffic flow patterns. This includes the representation of the road map as, for example, a directed graph. Below is a snippet of the the connections between individual roads in our regional example:

```
. . .
(:objects
    markStr //there exist a road in the network called mark street
....

  ((:init
  (:init
   (conn JWInts north brookStr)//north of Brook street is connected
                                to south of John William's intersection.
   (link lordStr south brookStr) //south of Brook street is
                                   linked with Lord street
. . . .
```

The system components are the available objects in the system that can be manipulated and optimised for smooth traffic flow. This includes the signal heads and message boards. These objects have a set of properties and relations which record information, and changes to the objects are recorded through changes to these properties and relations. For example, an object called road has a name property called "byramStr" and a road capacity limit of 20 cars. Capacity limit is the maximum number of vehicle the road can contain at any given period of time.

```
        ....
(= (capacity brookStr) 11)//the maximum capacity of Brook street
                             is 20 cars
(= (capacity byramStr) 20) //the maximum capacity for Byram
                             Street is 11 cars
        ...
```

This implies that whenever the road sensor shows a total of 20 vehicles on Byram street for a period of time without a dynamic change in the state of the vehicle (i.e. not moving), then such road is blocked and vehicles should be diverted from using it until the number of vehicles in such road is reduced.

5.4 Sensor and Effector (SE) Block

This is the sensory nerves of the system. It serves as the information interchange between the high-level reasoning component of the system and the road network. It has an input mode and an output mode.

The Input Mode Surveillance and sensing devices are embedded into almost every road network. Road traffic monitoring agencies make use of surveillance and sensing devices for retrieving the status of road networks. These devices upload the real-time data in a format that can be retrieved and understood by the system. The raw sensor data is then the start of an information processing pipeline which ends up as values that describe the properties and relationships of objects that are defined in the SD described in the section above.

For example, in the UTC domain, sensing can be done by road sensors and CCTV cameras. After information processing, this would result in a state file for urban traffic, for example:

```
. . .
(operational brookStr)// Brook street is operational with no
                        disruption
(operational byramStr)// Byram Street is operational with no
                        disruption
 . . .
(= (val north brookStr) 3)// number of vehicles on Brook Street
(= (val south byramStr) 12)// number of vehicles on Byram Street
  . . .
```

An excellent example of recovering information from an array of sensors, and extracting PDDL-like states and activities from them via information processing, is given in Laguna's recent thesis [30]. Here the sensors were Radio-frequency identification (RFID) and camera, and the activity being sensed was cooking in a kitchen, but the parallel between this and the UTC domain is clear.

The Output Mode Control devices are called actuators in classical control terminology. They are embedded into systems to change their performance to a desirable state. Control devices play a vital role in UTC environment, from the simple traffic light to the complex controller box for signal heads. They all help to control and maintain smooth traffic operation in road network. SE is responsible for executing control plans (sequences of actions) retrieved from the planning and action block. Generated control plans are received from this block, formatted and passed as system instructions to appropriate control devices for execution. The control devices change the state of the road network to desired state. An excerpt from the generated control file is:

```
. . .
25.010: (enable v2 north brookStr)  [50.000] //release vehicles on
        Mark Street for 50 seconds
26.007: (disAble v1 south JW)  [30.000] //stop vehicles on south of
        John Williams for 30 seconds
27.009: (divert-through-intersection y2 JWInts north brookStr)[60.000]
        //divert vehicles through south of john William's intersection
. . .
```

Executing actions is done by system components via the control devices. Since we have to consider uncertainty, after executing a sequence of actions, the sensors sense the current state, and if the current state is different from the expected one, the information is propagated to the planning and action block which provides a new plan.

5.5 Planning and Action (PA) Block

PA can be understood as a core of deliberative reasoning and decision making in the system. This is "the brain" of our architecture. It has several components:

- an estimated current state
- a description of desired states or service levels [18]
- the model of the domain
- the planning problem file
- the planner program
- heuristics, such as ways of estimating how far a goal is away from a state

The PA block receives an update to the estimated current state of the system from SE and system goals [desired states or service levels input from the service-level checker (SLC), explained below]. It produces a plan which aims to meet the system goals from the current state. The default planning technology to carry out this technique is AI Planning [18]. The plan produced is passed to the SE block for execution. However, it is well known from planning and execution systems [31] that producing a plan given a planning problem does not guarantee its successful execution. The SE block, which is responsible for plan execution, verifies whether executing an action provides the desired outcome. If the outcome is different (for whatever reason), then this outcome and current estimated state are passed back to the PA which is requested to replan.

In the UTC domain, if some road is congested, then the traffic is navigated through alternative routes. Hence, PA is responsible for producing a plan which may consist of showing information about such alternative routes on VMS and optimising signal heads towards such route. There are theoretical limits to the success of automated planning (even simple planning problems are intractable in general), however, and hence PA might not guarantee generating plans in a reasonable time. In a dynamic environment, where a system must be able to react quickly to avoid imminent danger, this may be a significant problem.

Real-time processes require fast response times to deal with exogenous events. In order to cope with this, we need to be able to satisfy two situations where:

- no valid plan can be found to meet the system goals
- the environment has changed prior to the generation and execution of a control plan

These two planning problems can be minimised by utilising an MPC approach [26] to supplement an automated planner.

MPC techniques help to reduce the situation whereby the environment has changed prior to generation and execution of plans. Rather than using only the system model, generating the problem file takes all possible disturbances into consideration. It also sends the planning problem to the planner in a receding horizon approach. This means that the problem represents what is likely to happen in few seconds ahead. This allows the planner to generate plans with consideration for future timing and reduces the possibility of a totally changed environment prior to plan execution.

The MPC approach also helps to reduce the likelihood of situations where no valid plan can be found for given system goals.

This is achieved by breaking search exploration into horizons such that the best node at every horizon is explored further if planner time limit is not exceeded. This is because exploring more search space will delay output time for a real-time system, and the output time might not be predictable since the time taken to generate valid plans depends on the complexity of the task. This complexity varies at different stages of the entire process life span. The planner searches, considering all the possible combinations of the input constraints over a period of time and/or node counts, and returns a sequence of steps that will take the road network from its current state to a partial or goal state. We use the phrase partial or goal state because the planner will return a plan from its current state irrespective of whether the goals are met or not. This will make sure a plan is available to follow at every instance of time. Thus, allowing the planner to search for a limited resource count and returning the partial or complete goal plan at every time stamp ensures that the planner will always generate a plan that will take the system closer to the goal trajectory provided that the fixed searching time and the node count are well guided.

Specifically, after searching for a fixed time and/or node count, the planner communicates the partial or completely generated control plan to the network control devices through the sensor and effector block, aiming to effect a change in state from an initial state to a fully or partially desirable state. The SE takes new samples from the reaction of the network to the effect of these sequences of control action. The network's new state with the corresponding dynamic input parameters from the environment is fed back into the planner to generate another sequence of steps that will take the network traffic from its current state to another partial/goal state for another sampling time and so on.

This generates a control loop, which, when continued over a period of time, will generate a continuous curve like that of an MPC as shown in Fig. 4. This process takes the road network from its initial state to a goal state and maintains that goal state as long as the process is still active. The ability of the system to take the current state of the dynamic changing input parameters into consideration during planning process increases the robustness to unexpected events in the environments or system itself. This feedback loop also compensates for the few deviations in the production of suboptimal plans. In fact, the smooth series of state changes can only be achieved if the heuristics for the planner are sound. This means that the planner must always produce a correct (but not necessarily optimal) partial plan in the time allotted for plan generation.

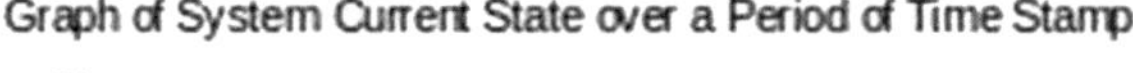

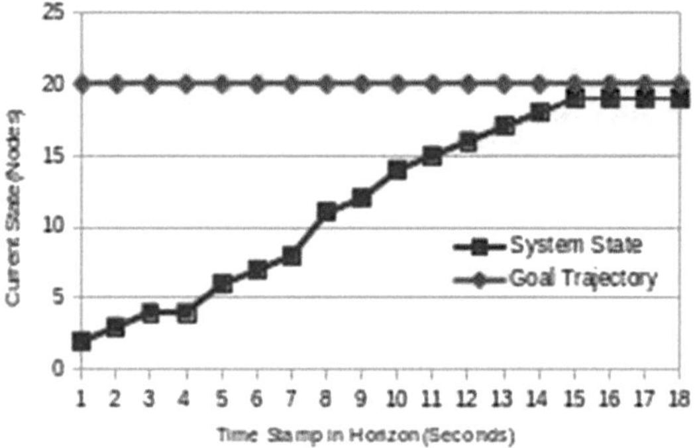

Fig. 4 Illustration of a well-guided real-time process curve

5.6 *Learning Block*

The inputs to the learning component are the generated plans and the associated problem files within the domain.

Generated plans and associated problems are mapped and stored for adaptation purposes.

A common learning technique in UTC research systems is reinforcement learning: this learns appropriate actions for traffic patterns over a period of time, utilising the idea of assigning blame or positive feedback over repeated trials [27, 32]. Learning has also been implemented in several planning applications. One such method is to use a decision tree classifier to combine the generated plans with problem instances and learn a policy for the Markov decision process (MDP) from which the problems were drawn [33]. Thus, our emphasis in this part of the architecture is not on learning the pattern alone but on generating new heuristics from the learning component to improve the performance of the planning engine. These heuristics include macro actions for specific goals, the best horizon limit set for similar problems and the goal distance heuristics common to that environment at certain period of time. One clear advantage of the use of AI Planning in UTC is that the actions, goals and states are all defined in a declarative fashion. This means that why plans achieve a certain set of goals can be explained logically, using the operational semantics of the actions. Through this explanation, we can derive the *weakest precondition* of a plan, in other words the smallest set of features on a state such that if those features are seen again, the same plan can be reused to achieve the same goals.

5.7 *Service-Level Checker*

The SLC, as the name implies, repeatedly checks the service level of the entire system to see if the system is in a "good condition". It gets the current state of the system from SE and compares it with the "ideal" service level. If the current state is far from being "ideal", then the system should act in order to recover its state to a "good condition".

Formally, we can define an error function $\epsilon : S \rightarrow \mathbb{R}_0^+$ which determines how far the current state of the system is from being "ideal". $\epsilon(s) = 0$ means that s is an "ideal" state. If a value of the error function in the current state is greater than a given threshold, then SLC generates goals (desired states of a given components and/or artefacts) and passes them to the problem file to generate new goals and metrics.

An example of this in UTC domain can be seen in an accident scene at a junction. The "ideal" service level for such a junction is to maximise traffic flow from the junction to neighbouring routes. The present state of the system shows that the traffic at that junction is now static with road sensors indicating static vehicles (i.e. vehicles are no longer moving). Such a situation is not "ideal", and the error function in such a state is high; hence, new goals are generated by SLC to re-route incoming traffic flowing towards such junction as well as divert existing traffic in such locations to a different route through connected roads.

It is also possible to alter the error function by an external system controller. For instance, a self-managed UTC system can also accept inputs from the traffic controller (motoring agencies). This means that the system behaviour can be altered by the user if needed.

6 Preliminary Evaluation

We have created a prototype architecture along the lines described in the sections above, integrating a UTC scenario, environmental knowledge, etc., with AI Planning engines, but in a simulated rather than real environment. The experimental setting consists of several "specific" problems which are defined on the top of the road network as depicted in Fig. 3.

Uncertainty is not considered in this experiment, due to the limitation of AI Planning approaches to reason with uncertainty in a complex domain. Problem 1 addresses the problem of navigating five cars from Lord Street (bottom right corner of the map) to Wood Street (upper part of the map). Problem 2 addresses the problem navigating cars (two at each entry point) through the network such that they are evenly distributed at south, north and east exit points (individual vehicles are not distinguished). Problem 3 has the same settings but has five cars at each entry point. Problems 1–3 are considered in two different variants, that is, without blockages and with blockages. Experiments were run on Intel Core i7 2.9 GHz, 5 GB RAM, Ubuntu 12.04.1 LTS.

For evaluation purposes, we selected known planning engines, Crikey [12], Optic [34] and LPG-td [11], which are capable of handling PDDL 2.1 features (including timed initial literals). LPG-td, however, is not very useful for our problem for two reasons. Firstly, it does not successfully complete preprocessing when the problem has more than a few objects (e.g. roads). Secondly, it cannot handle well concurrency from actions sharing some fluent(s), that is, actions having the same fluent in their descriptions are never considered as concurrent.

Table 1 shows the results of our preliminary experimental settings using the Crikey and Optic planners. We can see that Optic clearly outperforms Crikey in both criteria—makespan (a time needed for executing the plan) and runtime (a time needed by a planner to provide a plan). Moreover, Optic is an incremental planner, that is, after finding a plan, it searches for a better one (with lower makespan) until a given time limit is reached.

The results of Optic are very promising given the fact that plans have been retrieved in a very reasonable time (at worst slightly above 1 s) and their quality (makespan) is satisfactory. Cars can be therefore navigated reasonably through the road network even in case of some unexpected event which could lead to road

Table 1 Our experimental results showing planners' performance in given settings

		Crikey		Optic	
Prob. no.	Blockages	Runtime	Makespan	Runtime	Makespan
1	No	0.16	156	0.19	53
1	Yes	0.14	156	0.16	64
2	No	1.22	122	0.35	43
2	Yes	1.28	170	0.40	52
3	No	36.84	299	1.79	57
3	Yes	51.52	446	1.54	70

Runtime (in seconds) stands for a time needed by a planner to produce a plan. Makespan stands for a duration in which the plan can be executed

blockage. Also, given the fact that in the real-world environment, cars are entering the road network continuously, good quality plans (in terms of makespan) can somehow ensure that the traffic flow remains continuous and roads will not become congested.

A sample plan shows a solution of Problem 1 (no blockage) given by the Optic planner and some interesting aspects. Firstly, despite going from the same entry point to the same exit point, cars are split along the way such that some cars are navigated through Northumberland Street (e1) and some cars are navigated through St. Peter Street (v2). This might be useful when some unexpected event occurs (e.g. an accident on St. Peter Street) and there is no time to redirect traffic. Secondly, the Optic planner is not very able to consider more than one car in a single action (nn1) even though it is possible. This is a shortcoming because it does not lead to optimal (or very nearly optimal) solutions. Basically, if such a plan when executed allows one car to go through the junction, then the other cars have to wait until that car drives through the following road. This is quite counter-intuitive and consequently these plans are not optimal.

In summary, embedding planning components into the UTC might be beneficial since it enables (centralised) reasoning in the given area which, for instance, can more easily overcome non-standard situations (e.g. road blockage after an accident). Our results showed that the makespan of the plans (given by the Optic planner) did not increase much even though some roads were blocked. Minimising makespan, which is a goal of any UTC system, will help to reduce road congestion and pollution in the environment. However, as we demonstrated, using state-of-the-art domain-independent planning engines does not lead to optimal solutions even in quite simple cases. Also, it is questionable whether a planner's performance will not significantly decrease on larger road networks. On the other hand, developing a domain-dependent planner specifically tailored to road transport domains (RTDM) might overcome (some of) these issues.

7 Challenges

This architecture is presently implementable in systems that have time delay. It cannot be implemented with real-time processes that require continuous changes in nanoseconds/microseconds. This is due to the fact that prediction can be computationally demanding, so posing a challenge to implement it in real time. However with technology advancement on CPU processing speed and the introduction of high-performance computing (HPC), future implementations are possible. It is also important to know that the controller might anticipate set-point changes which may not be desirable. This could be a result of a grossly inaccurate model which will yield poor control decisions, although the method is surprisingly robust. To achieve a highly tuned controller, a very accurate model is needed, because one can only control as precisely as one can model. The sampling of the environment at every period of time (state selection) for control plan generation should also encompass all significant dynamics and disturbances; otherwise performance may be poor and important events may be unobserved.

The most important lesson learnt through our experiments with this deliberative architecture is that the heuristics that the planners use must be well guided. This is directing our research into developing specialised planners which are tuned for UTC use. This will allow us to take advantage of the peculiarities of the application area and result in operationally successful planners.

8 Conclusion

This chapter describes our vision of self-management at the architectural level within a UTC management system, where autonomy is the ability of the system components to configure their interaction in order for the entire system to achieve a set service level. We created an autonomic architecture made of several blocks which are discussed in the context of the UTC domain. We described the functionality of each block, highlighting their relationship with one another. We also highlighted the role of AI Planning in enabling a self-management property in an autonomic system architecture. We believe that creating a generic architecture that enables control systems to automatically reason with knowledge of their environment and their controls, in order to generate plans and schedules to manage themselves, would be a significant step forward in the field of autonomic systems.

In a real-world scenario where data such as road queues are uploaded in real-time from road sensors with traffic signals connected to a planner, we believe that our approach can optimise and restore road traffic disruption with little or no human intervention. To that end, the development of specialised, deliberative AI planners, tuned to UTC applications, is necessary.

References

1. Myers, K.L.: Towards a framework for continuous planning and execution. In: Proceedings of the AAAI Fall Symposium on Distributed Continual Planning, AAAI Press (1998)
2. McGann, C., Py, F., Rajan, K., Thomas, H., Henthorn, R., McEwen, R.: A deliberative architecture for AUV control. In: International Conference on Robotics and Automation (ICRA), Pasadena (2008)
3. Pinto, J., Sousa, J., Py, F., Rajan, K.: Experiments with deliberative planning on autonomous underwater vehicles. In: IROS Workshop on Robotics for Environmental Modeling, Algarve (2012)
4. Jiménez, S., Fernández, F., Borrajo, D.: Integrating planning, execution, and learning to improve plan execution. Comput. Intell. **29**(1), 1–36 (2013)
5. Smith, S., Barlow, G., Xie, X.F., Rubinstein, Z.: Surtrac: scalable urban traffic control. In: Transportation Research Board 92nd Annual Meeting Compendium of Papers, Transportation Research Board (2013)
6. Tettamanti, T., Luspay, T., Kulcsar, B., Peni, T., Varga, I.: Robust control for urban road traffic networks. IEEE Trans. Intell. Transp. Syst. **15**(1), 385–398 (2014)
7. Mitsakis, E., Salanova, J.M., Giannopoulos, G.: Combined dynamic traffic assignment and urban traffic control models. Proc. Soc. Behav. Sci. **20**, 427–436 (2011)
8. Roozemond, D.A.: Using intelligent agents for pro-active, real-time urban intersection control. Eur. J. Oper. Res. **131**(2), 293–301 (2001)
9. Oliveira, D.D., Bazzan, A.L.: Multiagent learning on traffic lights control: effects of using shared information. In: Bazzan, A., Klügl, F. (eds.) Multi-Agent Systems for Traffic and Transportation Engineering, pp. 307–321. Information Science Reference, Hershey (2009). doi:10.4018/978-1-60566-226-8.ch015
10. Jimoh, F., Chrpa, L., Gregory, P., McCluskey, T.: Enabling autonomic properties in road transport system. In: The 30th Workshop of the UK Planning and Scheduling Special Interest Group, PlanSIG 2012 (2012)
11. Gerevini, A., Saetti, A., Serina, I.: An approach to temporal planning and scheduling in domains with predictable exogenous events. J. Artif. Intell. Res. **25**, 187–231 (2006)
12. Coles, A.I., Fox, M., Long, D., Smith, A.J.: Planning with problems requiring temporal coordination. In: Proceedings of 23rd AAAI Conference on Artificial Intelligence (2008)
13. Penna, G.D., Intrigila, B., Magazzeni, D., Mercorio, F.: Upmurphi: a tool for universal planning on pddl+ problems. In: Proceedings of 19th International Conference on Automated Planning and Scheduling (ICAPS), pp. 19–23 (2009)
14. Eyerich, P., Mattmüller, R., Röger, G.: Using the context-enhanced additive heuristic for temporal and numeric planning. In: Proceedings of 19th International Conference on Automated Planning and Scheduling (ICAPS) (2009)
15. Lhr, J., Eyerich, P., Keller, T., Nebel, B.: A planning based framework for controlling hybrid systems. In: International Conference on Automated Planning and Scheduling (2012)
16. Ferber, D.F.: On modeling the tactical planning of oil pipeline networks. In: Proceedings of 18th International Conference on Automated Planning and Scheduling (ICAPS), AAAI (2012)
17. Gopal, M.: Control Systems: Principles and Design. McGraw-Hill, London (2008)
18. Nau, D., Ghallab, M., Traverso, P.: Automated Planning: Theory & Practice. Morgan Kaufmann Publishers Inc., San Francisco (2004)
19. Garrido, A., Onaindia, E., Barber, F.: A temporal planning system for time-optimal planning. In: Progress in AI. Lecture Notes in Computer Science, vol. 2258 (2001)
20. Hoffmann, J., Nebel, B.: The FF planning system: fast plan generation through heuristic search. J. Artif. Intell. Res. **14**, 253–302 (2001)
21. McDermott, D., et al.: PDDL-the planning domain definition language. Technical report. Available at: www.cs.yale.edu/homes/dvm (1998)
22. Younes, H.L.S., Littman, M.L., Weissman, D., Asmuth, J.: The first probabilistic track of the international planning competition. J. Artif. Intell. Res. **24**, 851–887 (2005)

23. Sanner, S.: Relational dynamic influence diagram language (RDDL): language description. http://users.cecs.anu.edu.au/~ssanner/IPPC_2011/RDDL.pdf (2010)
24. Ganek, A., Corbi, T.: The dawning of the autonomic computing era. IBM Syst. J. **42**(1), 5–5 00188670 (2003). Copyright International Business Machines Corporation 2003
25. Lightstone, S.: Seven software engineering principles for autonomic computing development. Innov. Syst. Softw. Eng. **3**(1), 71–74 (2007)
26. Camacho, E., Bordons, C.: Model Predictive Control. Springer, London (1999)
27. Bazzan, A.L.: A distributed approach for coordination of traffic signal agents. Auton. Agent. Multi-Agent Syst. **10**(1), 131–164 (2005)
28. Shah, M.M.S., Chrpa, L., Kitchin, D.E., McCluskey, T., Vallati, M.: Exploring knowledge engineering strategies in designing and modelling a road traffic accident management domain. In: 23rd International Joint Conference on Artificial Intelligence (IJCAI 2013), AAAI (2013)
29. Jimoh, F., Chrpa, L., McCluskey, T.L., Shah, S.: Towards application of automated planning in urban traffic control. In: 2013 16th International IEEE Conference on Intelligent Transportation Systems-(ITSC), pp. 985–990, IEEE (2013)
30. Laguna, J.O., Olaya, A.G., Millan, D.B.: Building planning action models using activity recognition. Ph.D. thesis, Universidad Carlos III de Madrid (2014)
31. Fox, M., Long, D., Magazzeni, D.: Plan-based policy-learning for autonomous feature tracking. In: International Conference on Automated Planning and Scheduling (2012)
32. Dusparic, I., Cahill, V.: Autonomic multi-policy optimization in pervasive systems: overview and evaluation. ACM Trans. Auton. Adapt. Syst. **7**(1), Article 11, 1–25 (2012). doi:http://dx.doi.org/10.1145/2168260.2168271
33. Fox, M., Long, D., Magazzeni, D.: Plan-based policies for efficient multiple battery load management. Comput. Res. Rep. abs/1401.5859 (2014)
34. Benton, J., Coles, A.J., Coles, A.: Temporal planning with preferences and time-dependent continuous costs. In: International Conference on Automated Planning and Scheduling (2012)

An Experimental Review of Reinforcement Learning Algorithms for Adaptive Traffic Signal Control

Patrick Mannion, Jim Duggan, and Enda Howley

Abstract Urban traffic congestion has become a serious issue, and improving the flow of traffic through cities is critical for environmental, social and economic reasons. Improvements in Adaptive Traffic Signal Control (ATSC) have a pivotal role to play in the future development of Smart Cities and in the alleviation of traffic congestion. Here we describe an autonomic method for ATSC, namely, reinforcement learning (RL). This chapter presents a comprehensive review of the applications of RL to the traffic control problem to date, along with a case study that showcases our developing multi-agent traffic control architecture. Three different RL algorithms are presented and evaluated experimentally. We also look towards the future and discuss some important challenges that still need to be addressed in this field.

Keywords Reinforcement Learning • Adaptive Traffic Signal Control • Intelligent Transport Systems • Multi-Agent Systems • Smart Cities

1 Introduction

Traffic congestion has become a major issue that is familiar to the majority of road users, and the environmental, social and economic consequences are well documented. Ever-increasing vehicle usage rates, coupled with the lack of space and public funds available to construct new transport infrastructure, serve to further complicate the issue. Against this backdrop, it is necessary to develop intelligent and economical solutions to improve the quality of service for road users. A relatively inexpensive way to alleviate the problem is to ensure optimal use of the existing road network, e.g. by using Adaptive Traffic Signal Control (ATSC). Improvements in ATSC have a pivotal role to play in the future development of Smart Cities, especially considering the current EU-wide emphasis on the theme of Smart, Green

---

P. Mannion (✉) • J. Duggan • E. Howley
National University of Ireland Galway, Ireland
e-mail: p.mannion3@nuigalway.ie; jim.duggan@nuigalway.ie; enda.howley@nuigalway.ie

T.L. McCluskey et al. (eds.), *Autonomic Road Transport Support Systems*,
Autonomic Systems, DOI 10.1007/978-3-319-25808-9_4

and Integrated Transport in Horizon 2020 [1]. Setting optimal traffic light timings is a complex problem, not easily solved by humans.

Autonomic systems exhibit several key properties such as adaptability, self-management and self-optimisation. Efforts are now underway to incorporate these highly desirable properties into future transportation networks, leading to the creation of Autonomic Road Transport Support Systems (ARTS). True ATSC capabilities are an important component of this vision. In recent years, applications of machine learning methods such as fuzzy logic, neural networks and evolutionary algorithms have become increasingly common in ATSC research.

The approach that will be examined in this chapter is reinforcement learning (RL), a field that has many potential applications in the intelligent transportation systems (ITS) area. Reinforcement learning for traffic signal control (RL-TSC) has many benefits; RL agents can learn online to continuously improve their performance, as well as adapting readily to changes in traffic demand. RL-TSC systems may be classified as autonomic control systems since they exhibit many autonomic and intelligent characteristics. Flexible goal orientation via customised reward functions allows us to choose which system parameters we wish to optimise. RL-TSC agents are capable of learning ATSC strategies autonomously with no prior knowledge. Online learning once the system is deployed allows real-time refinement of the control policy and continuous self-management and self-optimisation.

Traffic control problems have been shown to be a very attractive test bed for emerging RL approaches [11] and present non-trivial challenges such as developing strategies for coordination and information sharing between individual agents. While we deal here only with the use of RL-TSC, there are other reviews of the applications of machine learning and agent-based technologies in the broader ITS field that may be of interest to the reader [5, 11, 12, 15, 29].

The remainder of this chapter is structured as follows: the second section discusses the concept of RL, while the third section describes specific applications that we have investigated for this study. The following section details the design of our experimental set up, after which we present our experimental results. Finally, we conclude by discussing our findings, our plans for future work and a number of challenges that still need to be addressed in the RL-TSC domain.

2 Reinforcement Learning Algorithms

The term reinforcement learning describes a class of algorithms that have the capability to learn through experience. An RL agent is deployed into an environment, usually without any prior knowledge of how to behave. The agent interacts with its environment and receives a scalar reward signal r based on the outcomes of previously selected actions. This reward can be either negative or positive, and this feedback allows the agent to iteratively learn the optimal control policy. The agent must strike a balance between exploiting known good actions and exploring the consequences of new actions in order to maximise the reward received during its lifetime. Q values represent the expected reward for each state action pair, which aid the agent in deciding which action is most desirable to select when in a certain state. The Q values are typically stored in a matrix, which represents the knowledge learned by an RL agent. For further detail on RL beyond the summary presented in this chapter, we refer the reader to [14, 42, 49].

2.1 Markov Decision Processes, Policies and Optimality

An RL problem is generally modelled as a Markov decision process (MDP), which is considered the de facto standard when formalising problems involving learning sequential decision making [49]. An MDP may be represented using a reward function R, set of states S, set of actions A and a transition function T [36], i.e. a tuple $\langle S, A, T, R\rangle$. When in any state $s \in S$, selecting an action $a \in A$ will result in the environment entering a new state $s' \in S$ with probability $T(s, a, s') \in (0,1)$ and give a reward $r = R(s, a, s')$.

A policy π determines the agent's behaviour in its environment. Policies provide a mapping from states to actions that guide the agent when choosing the most appropriate action for a given state. The goal of any MDP is to find the best policy (one which gives the highest overall reward) [49]. The optimal policy for an MDP is denoted $\pi*$.

2.2 Model-Based Reinforcement Learning

RL can be classified into two categories: model-free (e.g. Q-learning, State-Action-Reward-State-Action (SARSA)) and model based (e.g. Dyna, Prioritised Sweeping). To implement model-based approaches successfully, it is necessary to know the transition function T [49], which may be difficult or even impossible to determine even in relatively simple domains. By contrast, in the model-free approach, this is not a requirement. Exploration is required for model-free approaches, which sample the underlying MDP in order to gain knowledge about the unknown model. The use of a model-based approach in a highly stochastic problem domain like traffic control also adds unnecessary extra complexity when compared with a model-free approach [21]. Our analysis in this chapter will focus in the main on model-free approaches to this problem domain for the reasons outlined above.

One of the most popular RL approaches in use today is Q-learning [44]. It is an off-policy, model-free learning algorithm that is commonly used in RL-TSC literature, e.g. [6, 7, 10, 19–21, 30, 38, 39, 52]. It has been shown that Q-learning converges to the optimum action values with probability 1 so long as all actions are repeatedly sampled in all states and the action values are represented discretely [45]. In Q-learning, the Q values are updated according to the equation below:

$$Q_{t+1}(s_t, a_t) = Q_t(s_t, a_t) + \alpha(r_t + \gamma Q_{\max_a}(s_{t+1}, a) - Q_t(s_t, a_t)) \qquad (1)$$

SARSA [37] (meaning State-Action-Reward-State-Action) is another common model-free RL approach. This algorithm has also been proven to converge to the optimal value function so long as all state action pairs are visited infinitely often, and the learning policy becomes greedy in the limit [40]. SARSA is very useful in nonstationary environments, where an optimal policy may never be reached, and also in situations where the use of function approximation (FA) is desired [49]. Use of SARSA is also quite common in RL-TSC literature, e.g. [13, 33, 43, 47]. When using SARSA, the Q values are updated as follows:

$$Q_{t+1}(s_t, a_t) = Q_t(s_t, a_t) + \alpha(r_t + \gamma Q_t(s_{t+1}, a_{t+1}) - Q_t(s_t, a_t)) \tag{2}$$

The learning rate $\alpha \in [0, 1]$ is an input parameter required for many RL algorithms and determines by how much Q values are updated at each time step t. The learning rate is typically initialised as a low value (e.g. 0.05) and may be a constant, or may be decreased over time. Setting $\alpha = 0$ would halt the learning process altogether, which may be desirable once a satisfactory solution is reached. Selecting a value of α that is too large may result in instability and make convergence to a solution more difficult.

The discount factor $\gamma \in [0, 1]$ controls how the agent regards future rewards and is typically initialised as a high value (e.g. 0.9). Setting $\gamma = 0$ would result in a myopic agent, i.e. an agent concerned only about immediate rewards, whereas a higher value of γ results in an agent that is more forward-looking.

2.3 *Exploration vs. Exploitation*

When using RL, balancing the exploration–exploitation trade-off is crucial. Exploration is necessary for a model-free learning agent to learn the consequences of selecting different actions [49] and thus determine the potential benefit of selecting those actions in the future. Exploitation of known good actions is necessary for the agent to accumulate the maximum possible reward. As we have seen above, two of the most common model-free RL algorithms have been proven to converge to an optimum solution when all states are visited infinitely often (thus exploring all possible states is a condition for convergence to the optimum policy). While this is not practical in real-world transportation problems, it is logical that the RL agent will make better informed decisions, and thus perform better, when an efficient exploration strategy is in place that allows for sufficient exploration. Conversely, selecting an inappropriate exploration strategy may result in the agent getting stuck in a local optimum and not converging to the best possible solution. Excessive exploration limits the agent's capacity to accumulate rewards over its lifetime and may reduce performance. Two algorithms that are commonly used to manage the exploration–exploitation trade-off are ϵ-greedy and softmax (Boltzmann) [49].

3 Reinforcement Learning for Traffic Signal Control

In this section, we discuss the development of RL-TSC approaches by various researchers and the challenges associated with implementation, as well as the current state of the art. The use of RL as a method of traffic control has been investigated since the mid-1990s, but the number of published research articles has increased greatly in the last decade, coinciding with a growing interest in the broader ITS field among the research community. The potential for performance improvements in traffic signal control offered by RL when compared to conventional approaches is vast, and there are many published articles reporting promising results, e.g. [4, 6, 13, 21, 25, 28, 48]. Thorpe describes some of the earliest work in this area, and even at this initial stage in the development of RL-TSC, it offered significant improvements over fixed signal plans [43].

3.1 Problem Formulation

The traffic control problem may be considered as a multi-agent system (MAS), where each agent is autonomous and responsible for controlling the traffic light sequences of a single junction. In the context of RL-TSC, this scenario is described by the term Multi-agent Reinforcement Learning (MARL), which consists of multiple RL agents like those detailed in Sect. 2, learning and acting together in the same environment. The scenario is a partially observable Markov decision process, as it is impossible for agents to know every detail about the environment in large-scale transportation networks in the real world.

The MAS paradigm is inherently very suitable for the management of transportation systems [12] and also for transport simulations. Modern transportation networks may contain thousands or millions of autonomous entities, each of which must be represented in simulations. Vehicles, drivers, pedestrians and traffic signal controllers can all be modelled as agents. Use of MAS allows large-scale representation of these agents, while also allowing fine-grained detail for each individual agent if desired. Additionally, MAS is innately robust and highly scalable [14]; there is no single point of failure and new agents can easily be inserted into the system. Wooldridge [51] gives a good overview of the main concepts in multi-agent systems (MAS), which may be of interest to the reader.

A naïve way of using RL to control traffic signals is to train a single RL agent to control all junctions in the system. However, this approach is not feasible when considering large networks, due to a lack of scalability and the huge number of potential actions that may be selected [9]. Thus, MARL is the standard approach in RL-TSC research, as it scales much better than a single agent controlling an entire network.

3.2 Challenges of Applying RL to Traffic Signal Control

A significant challenge in RL-TSC is implementing coordination and information sharing between agents [11, 21, 28]. The effect of any single agent's actions on the environment is also influenced by the actions of other agents [14]. Single agents are self-interested and will seek only to maximise their personal rewards. For example, a control policy selected by an agent may result in a local optimum in terms of traffic movements, but may have a detrimental effect on traffic flows in the network as a whole, limiting the effectiveness of the other agents. Thus, having multiple agents that are primarily greedy or self-interested is not necessarily the best option, and some sort of coordination or information sharing mechanism is necessary to implement systems relevant to the real world.

One of the main difficulties associated with determining optimal traffic control policies is the sheer scale of the problem. With respect to RL, the term "curse of dimensionality" is frequently used to describe the difficulty of dealing with the plethora of information that must be handled [21, 34, 42, 49]. As each individual intersection has its own controller agent, the problem complexity increases vastly in larger road networks. When implementing coordination between agents, this increase in dimensionality is even more pronounced. In many commonly used MARL coordination methods, each agent has to keep a set of tables whose size is exponential in the number of agents [21]. Later, we will examine some of the approaches used by researchers to tackle these formidable problems. Model-free RL methods become even more attractive as network size increases, as the absence of a model reduces the computational complexity when compared with model-based methods. The continual increase in available computational power is another factor that will make this challenge easier to deal with in the future.

3.3 State Definitions

One of the most important issues to be considered when designing an RL-TSC system is that of determining how the state of the environment will be represented to the agent. Various different approaches to defining the environment state in RL-TSC problems have been proposed in the literature, with each having its own relative merits. Queue length is one of the most common state definitions used in RL-TSC [6] and has been used as a means of state representation in many RL-TSC research papers, e.g. [3, 4, 6, 16, 19–21]. Wiering [48] proposed a vehicle-based state definition, based on the expected total waiting time for a vehicle to reach its destination. Delay-based approaches are also considered in e.g. [7–9, 23, 28, 41, 50]. In [10] the traffic state is estimated by considering both queue length and traffic flow rate, while [13] presents an approach based on queue length and elapsed time since the previous signal change.

3.4 Reward Function Definitions

Choosing an appropriate reward function is equally important as the choice of state representation when designing an RL-TSC agent. These issues are somewhat interrelated, in that the reward received by an agent is often related to the difference in utility between the current and previous states, i.e. the agent is rewarded for actions that improve the state of the environment. Equivalently, we can think of optimising some parameter as the agent's objective, and this objective is specified in the reward function.

Many different objectives have been considered by authors when defining the reward function used by RL-TSC agents. These include average trip waiting time (ATWT)/trip delay, average trip time (ATT), average junction waiting time (AJWT), junction throughput/flow rate (FR), achieving green waves (GW), accidents avoidance (AA), speed restriction, fuel conservation and average number of trip stops (ANTS). Brys et al. [13] have proposed delay squared as a possible alternative reward signal, the idea being that large delays will be punished more severely than small delays. Their results suggest that the use of delay squared as a reward signal may result in faster learning rates than simple delay.

It should be noted that many of the proposed reward definitions above rely on information that is easy to obtain in a simulation, but quite difficult or impractical to obtain in a real-world setting using current technologies. Data about ATWT, ATT, ANTS, fuel usage or emissions could not be collected reliably without some form of Vehicle to Junction (V2J) communication, whereby a vehicle could report these parameters to a controller agent via wireless communications. This research area is still under development and is not yet mature enough for widespread deployment. Also, all or nearly all vehicles using the network would have to have V2J capabilities for the statistics to be useful in assigning the agent a reward.

Dresner and Stone [18] have suggested using RL in their Autonomous Intersection Management architecture with V2J communications. This approach treats the intersection as a marketplace where vehicles pay for passage or pay a premium for priority, and the controller agent's goal is to maximise the revenue collected. In future, revenue collected could be used in reward functions for RL-TSC.

3.5 Performance Metrics

Evaluating the merits of any traffic control system requires suitable performance metrics. In RL-TSC these parameters are doubly important, as an agent must receive an assessment of its own performance in order to learn. In some cases, these can be the same or similar parameters used in the environment state definitions or the reward functions of the individual agents, but aggregated on a network-wide level to give an assessment of an RL-TSC system. Some performance metrics used in transportation and RL-TSC literature include reduction in emissions or fuel consumption, number of stops in a trip, percentage of stopped vehicles, delay time/ATWT, vehicle density in various parts of the network, junction queue lengths, mean vehicle speed and junction throughput.

3.6 Single Agent Reinforcement Learning Approaches

The most basic applications of RL to traffic control in the literature consider only a single junction controlled by a single agent, in what is called Single Agent Reinforcement Learning (SARL). While this approach may be appropriate for signalised intersections that are isolated and not part of a larger control network (e.g. junctions in small towns), it is not suitable for deployment in large urban networks. As SARL approaches do not exploit the full potential of RL-TSC, they will not be discussed in great detail, although they still prove its potential to outperform conventional approaches. There are a number of published works describing RL controlled isolated signalised junctions [6, 16, 19, 30, 47].

One such approach is that of Abdulhai et al. [6], where the authors present a case study of the application of Q-learning to control an isolated two-phase signalised junction. The Q-learning agent was found to perform on a par with pre-timed signals on constant or constant-ratio flows and to significantly outperform pre-timed signals under more variable flows. The authors attributed the latter result to the ability of the agent to adapt to changing traffic conditions.

In [19], the authors present a study based on a single junction in the Downtown Toronto area. The designs of three Q-learning agents with different state representations are outlined, and the performance of these agents is compared to a reference Webster-based [46] fixed time signal plan. The state definitions considered were based on (1) arrival of vehicles to the current green direction and queue length at red directions, (2) queue length and (3) vehicle cumulative delay. The authors reported that Q-learning outperformed the reference fixed signal plan, regardless of the state representation used or traffic conditions. The Q-learning agent using vehicle cumulative delay for state representation was found to produce the best results in heavy traffic conditions.

3.7 Multi-Agent Reinforcement Learning Approaches

Most authors have focused on developing approaches based on MARL, i.e. networks consisting of multiple signalised intersections, each controlled by an independent RL agent. These cases are much more relevant to real-world traffic signal control problems than the SARL cases described above. One of the most significant early works in Multi-agent RL-TSC is that of Wiering [48]. Several authors have since extended Wiering's approach or used his algorithms as a benchmark for their own approaches, e.g. [8, 9, 23, 28, 41, 50]. Wiering developed a model-based approach to

RL-TSC and presents three such algorithms: TC-1, TC-2 and TC-3. He found that the RL systems clearly outperformed fixed time controllers at high levels of network saturation, when testing on a simple 3×2 grid network. Another interesting aspect of this research is that a type of co-learning is implemented; value functions are learned by signal controllers and driver agents, and the drivers also learn to compute policies that allow them to select optimal routes through the network.

Steingröver et al. [41] extend the work of Wiering, by introducing a basic form of information sharing between agents. Three new traffic controllers are described by the authors: TC-SBC (Traffic Controller-State Bit for Congestion), TC-GAC (Traffic Controller-Gain Adapted by Congestion) and TC-SBC+GAC which combines the latter approaches. In TC-SBC, a congestion bit is added to the state tuple which represents the amount of traffic congestion at neighbouring intersections. One major disadvantage of TC-SBC is that it increases the size of the state space, which makes the problem more difficult to compute. TC-GAC uses congestion information from neighbouring junctions when estimating the optimal action selection. An advantage of this method is that it does not increase the size of the state space, but it never learns anything permanent about congestion in the network. The algorithms are tested on a simple grid network, under both fixed and variable flows. All three methods proposed were found to outperform Wiering's TC-1, and TC-GAC was found to provide the best performance under variable traffic flows. A further extension of this work is presented by Isa et al. in [23]. Two new algorithms called TC-SBA (Traffic Controller-State Bit for Accidents) and TC-SBAC (Traffic Controller-State Bit for Accidents and Congestion) are presented, both based on TC-1. In TC-SBA, similar to TC-SBC, an extra bit is added to the state tuple, this time representing whether the lane ahead is obstructed by an accident. TC-SBAC adds both the state and accident bits to TC-1. Both of these approaches suffer from the same problem as TC-SBC, namely, a substantial increase in the state space. In the case of TC-SBAC, the state space is four times larger than that of the original TC-1 algorithm.

In [3], Abdoos et al. present a Multi-agent RL-TSC implementation, tested on a relatively large abstract network consisting of 50 junctions. The authors based their algorithm on Q-learning, which was tested against reference fixed time signal plans. At each junction, average queue length (AQL) over all approaching links is used for state representation, and action selection is by means of selecting the green time ratio between different links. The proposed algorithm is found to offer a substantial performance improvement over fixed time control, greatly reducing delay times in the network.

Salkham and Cahill [38] developed a Multi-agent RL-TSC system, Soilse. This approach utilises a pattern change detection (PCD) mechanism that causes an agent to relearn based on the degree of change detected in traffic flows. A collaborative version SoilseC is also described, which adds a collaborative reward model to the Soilse architecture to incorporate reward information exchanged between agents. The authors test their system on a simulated network based on Dublin City centre consisting of 62 signalised junctions, using assumed traffic flow data. Two baseline fixed time control schemes were also tested. Soilse and SoilseC were shown to outperform both baselines in terms of vehicle AWT and average number of stops. This work is significant in that a large-scale test of RL-TSC on a real urban traffic network is presented.

3.8 Coordinated MARL Approaches

A natural extension to the approaches described above is to use MARL to achieve decentralised and coordinated traffic signal control. Use of RL and game theoretic approaches to achieve coordination in traffic control agents is certainly plausible [11], and this is an active research theme in RL-TSC.

Kuyer et al. [28] extend the work of Wiering [48] to develop a coordinated model-based RL-TSC system using the Max-Plus algorithm as a coordination strategy. Max-Plus is used to compute the optimal joint action by means of message passing between connected agents. However, this approach is very computationally demanding, as agents must negotiate when coordinating their actions. The authors report improved performance when comparing their approach to that of Wiering [48] and Bakker et al. [8].

El-Tantawy and Abdulhai [20] and El-Tantway et al. [21] present a coordinated Multi-agent RL-TSC architecture called MARLIN-ATSC. This is a model-free architecture based on Q-learning, where the state definition is based on queue length and the reward definition is based on total cumulative delay. The authors deal with the dimensionality problem by utilising the principle of locality of interaction among agents [31] and the modular Q-learning technique [32]. The former principle means that each agent communicates only with its immediate neighbours, while the latter allows partitioning of the state space into partial state spaces consisting of only two agents. This approach significantly reduces the complexity of the problem while still producing promising results.

In [20], the architecture is tested on a five-intersection network against a Webster-based fixed time plan, as well as uncoordinated Q-learning controllers. MARLIN-ATSC was reported to outperform both the fixed timing and uncoordinated RL approaches, resulting in a reduction in average delay. The proposed architecture was also found to offer improved convergence times when compared to a network of independent learning agents.

The authors extend their approach in [21], where the system is tested on a simulated network of 59 intersections in Downtown Toronto, using input data provided by the City of Toronto, including traffic counts and existing signal timings. In this instance, MARLIN-ATSC outperformed the currently implemented real-world control scheme as well as the uncoordinated RL approach, resulting in a reduction in average delay, average stop time, average travel time, maximum queue lengths and emissions. The results presented in [21] are very encouraging, and this work is one of the largest and most realistic simulation tests of an RL-TSC approach to date, due to the use of a real urban network, along with real-world traffic data and signal timings.

3.9 Multi-Objectivity

Multi-objectivity is an emerging research theme in RL-TSC that has received some attention in recent years [13, 22, 24–26]. In RL-TSC, this approach seeks to optimise a number of parameters in the network at once, the idea being that considering multiple parameters may lead to better solutions and convergence times, as well as allowing consistent performance even under varying demand levels. This is typically achieved by expanding the agent's reward function definition to include multiple parameters.

The majority of traditional traffic control methods are single objective [26], seeking optimal solutions based on a single parameter only. As we have seen in Sect. 3.5, some reward function definitions are more suited to certain traffic patterns, so combining several definitions may be beneficial where the demand is highly variable. Multi-objective RL is comparable to single-objective RL in terms of time complexity [25]; this is because the only extra operation required to extend a single-objective approach is scalar addition to determine the combined reward signal. This means that the potential performance improvements can be gained quite cheaply in terms of computational complexity.

Houli et al. [22] present a multi-objective RL-TSC algorithm, which is tuned for three different scenarios: light, medium and heavy traffic. Each level of traffic has a corresponding Q function. However, adaption occurs offline, as one Q function is activated at a time based on the number of vehicles entering the network in a given timeframe.

Brys et al. [13] observed in their experiments that the objectives throughput and delay are correlated. They implemented a multi-objective RL-TSC algorithm by replacing the single-objective reward signal with a scalarised signal, which was a weighted sum of the reward due to both objectives. The onus is on the user, however, to select weightings that will give good results. They report that the proposed multi-objective approach exhibits a reduced convergence time, as well as decreasing the average delay in the network when compared to a single-objective approach. While performance gains can be seen from this multi-objective approach, selecting appropriate values for the weightings of rewards was reported to be a very time-consuming task.

A more advanced approach is presented by Khamis and Gomaa [24, 25] and Khamis et al. [24]. In [24, 26] the authors develop multi-objective RL-TSC systems with weighted sum reward functions. Multiple reward criteria are considered in the combined reward function (FR, ATWT, ATT, AJWT, safety/speed control). The systems were tested on simple grid-type networks with varying demand levels. The authors report that their approach outperforms Wiering's TC-1 [48] algorithm, resulting in a reduction in the average number of stops and waiting time in each trip [24], as well as increasing the average speed for each trip [26]. In [25] the authors extend their work further, considering a total of seven different parameters in the reward function proposed. This extended approach is tested against TC-1, Self-Organising Traffic Lights (SOTL) [17] and a genetic algorithm proposed by

Wiering [50]. The proposed multi-objective approach outperforms the other three control schemes, again showing a significant reduction in ATWT and number of stops, as well as an increase in the average speed of vehicles in the network.

3.10 Function Approximation

In complex environments, it is not possible for the RL agent to visit each state action pair infinitely often to ensure convergence. RL literature describes a technique called function approximation (FA), whereby explicit tabular representations of rewards due to each state action pair are not required; instead, it is possible to generalise across different states and/or actions. By approximating state action pairs, the agent can learn reasonable behaviour more quickly than a tabular implementation [42]. In general, the values of the approximate function are defined using a set of tuneable parameters [49].

Prashanth and Bhatnagar [34, 35] present the first published application of FA to RL-TSC. Two RL algorithms based on Q-learning are presented: one with full state representation (FSR) and one using FA. The latter algorithm uses features in place of FSR, namely, traffic demand and wait. Demand level is classified based on queue lengths (low, medium or high) and wait is classified based on time that a red signal has been displayed to the lane. This approach does not require precise queue length information, and it does not require a precise value of elapsed time, as time is defined as being above or below a threshold. The goal is to minimise queue lengths while ensuring fairness so that no lane has an overly long red time. In [34], the algorithms are benchmarked against reference fixed timings and SOTL [17] in four test networks. The proposed Q-learning with FA approach consistently outperformed the other approaches tested, while also being more efficient in terms of memory usage and computation time compared to RL with FSR.

Abdoos et al. [4] also applied FA to RL-TSC, using tile coding. In tile coding, the receptive fields of the features are grouped into partitions called tilings in which each element is called a tile, and the overall number of features that are present at one time is strictly controlled and independent of the input state [42]. Each intersection is controlled by a Q-learning agent, and these agents are grouped together to be controlled by superior agents. These superior agents use tile coding as a method of linear function approximation because of the large state space involved. This hierarchical control algorithm was tested on a 3×3 junction grid and was found to outperform a standard Q-learning approach, resulting in reduced delay times in the network.

Pham et al. [33] present an RL-TSC system based on SARSA that also uses tile coding as a method of function approximation. In contrast to the approach above, this system does not include any form of coordination between agents. Instead, each SARSA agent is completely independent, and tile coding is used only as a method of approximating the value function for the agent's local states.

Arel et al. [7] propose a Q-learning algorithm with function approximation for traffic signal control. The authors implement a feedforward neural network trained using back-propagation to provide an approximation to the state action value function. Testing was conducted on a five-intersection grid, using the proposed algorithm, along with a longest queue first approach. The authors report that their Q-learning with function approximation algorithm outperformed the longest queue first approach at high demand levels.

4 Experimental Design

We now present a case study, which is based on the RL-TSC test bed that we are currently developing. The microscopic traffic simulation package SUMO (Simulation of Urban MObility) [27] is the basis for our experimental setup. Agent logic is defined in our external MARL framework, which is implemented in Java. Each RL agent is responsible for controlling the light sequences of a single junction. The TraaS library [2] is used to feed simulation data to the agents and also to send commands from the agents back to SUMO.

For each agent, state is defined as a vector of dimension $2 + P$, where the first two components are the index of the current phase and the elapsed time in the current phase. The remaining P components are the maximum queue lengths for each phase. This is a similar state definition to that of El-Tantawy and Abdulhai [20]. We used a mixed radix conversion to represent this state vector as a single number, which is used when setting and retrieving values in the Q values matrix. For all junctions in our simulations, the number of phases is two. We limit the maximum number of queueing vehicles considered by an agent to 20, and the maximum phase elapsed time considered is limited to 30 s. By imposing these limits, we reduce the possible number of states considered by an agent. Even so, there are over 27,000 possible states that arise from the ranges used.

The actions available to the agents at each time step are to keep the currently displayed green and red signals and to set a green light for a different phase. Phases are subject to a minimum length of 10 s, to eliminate unreasonably low phase lengths from consideration. There is no fixed cycle length, and agents are free to extend the current phase or switch to the next phase as they see fit. When changing phases, an amber signal is displayed for 3 s, followed by an all red period of 2 s and then by a green signal to the next phase. Actions are selected using the ϵ-greedy algorithm, which chooses either a random action or the action with the best expected reward, where ϵ is the probability of choosing a random action. All agents begin with ϵ set to 0.9 at the beginning of the experiments, and initialising ϵ with a high value encourages early exploration of different states and actions, as well as improving convergence times. The value of ϵ is decreased linearly over time, to a final value of 0.1 after 10 h of simulated time. This final value promotes exploitation of the knowledge the agent has gained, but still allows for some exploration.

We tested our agents on a 3 × 3 grid network, with a total of nine signalised junctions. We have chosen a grid-type network for a number of reasons: this is the most common type of network used in the RL-TSC literature (e.g. [4, 7, 9, 25, 33–35, 41, 50]), which makes it easy for researchers to replicate experimental conditions and compare results. Also, many cities are based on a grid-type layout (e.g. New York, Washington DC, Miami), and therefore the results presented are relevant to real urban traffic networks and give an indication of the potential performance improvements. All lanes in our network have a maximum speed of 50 km/h. Two distinct traffic demand definitions are used during each 72 h experiment run. The first 36 h is used as a training period for the agents, which allows them to gain the required experience. Simple horizontal and vertical routes are defined for this period, with 200 vehicles per hour travelling on each of the routes AD, BE and CF and 300 vehicles per hour travelling on each of the routes GJ, HK and IL. These routes are shown in Fig. 1.

In the second 36 h period, a random traffic pattern is used to simulate a more unpredictable user demand. A set of random trips were defined and processed using the SUMO DUAROUTER tool, with a frequency of 1800 vehicles per hour and a minimum trip distance of 450 m. The results presented for each RL algorithm are derived by taking an average of ten simulation runs, to give results that are representative of the algorithm's performance.

We evaluate three different RL-TSC algorithms, RLTSC-1, RLTSC-2 and RLTSC-3, all of which are based on Q-learning. In RL-TSC-1, we define the reward as the difference between the previous and current average queue length (AQL) at the junction ($R(s, a, s') = \text{AQL}_{s'} - \text{AQL}_{s}$), and we have defined a queueing vehicle as one travelling below 10 km/h. The reward function for RL-TSC-2 is based on waiting times at the junction. The average waiting times (AWT) for each junction approach are added, and the reward the agent receives

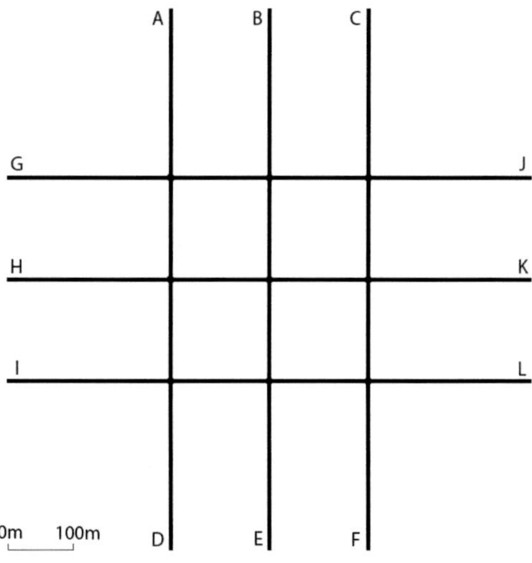

Fig. 1 The nine-junction test network

is the difference between the sums of the current and previous waiting times ($R(s, a, s') = \Sigma \text{AWT}_{s'} - \Sigma \text{AWT}_s$). RL-TSC-3 has a multi-objective reward function, which is the unweighted sum of the reward functions used in RL-TSC-1 and RL-TSC-2 ($R(s, a, s') = \text{AQL}_{s'} - \text{AQL}_s + \Sigma \text{AWT}_{s'} - \Sigma \text{AWT}_s$). The learning rate α for all agents is set to 0.08, while the value used for the discount factor γ is 0.8. A fourth agent type which implements fixed signal timing is also tested as a reference. The fixed timing agent has a cycle length of 60 s and divides the available green time in the ratio of the fixed flows defined in the first simulation period (40 % green time to the north to south phase and 60 % green time to east to west phase). The fixed timing agent maintains the same control scheme throughout the entire 72 h test period.

5 Experimental Results and Discussion

Results are reported for each of the four algorithms described in the previous section. The performance metrics we have chosen for the evaluation of our simulation results are junction queue length, waiting times and vehicle speeds. The values reported are averages of the results in the entire test network. In Table 1, a summary of the results for each control method under random flows is shown. Figures 2 and 3 show queue lengths and waiting times, respectively, which are plotted for the full 72 h test period. During the first 36 h of each experiment, we see a gradual improvement in both waiting times and queue lengths for each of the three RL-TSC approaches, as the agents learn more about the effects of their actions on the traffic conditions. Of the three RL agent types, RL-TSC-2 offers the best performance under steady flows, with slightly lower waiting times than the fixed time agent by the end of the 36 h learning period.

These graphs show a marked difference between the fixed time and RL-TSC control schemes under random traffic flows during the second 36 h phase of the experiments. We see that the fixed time agents clearly cannot cope with the random traffic patterns in the network; this is expected as these agents are optimised for fixed ratio flows. However, all three RL-TSC-based algorithms can adapt to this random traffic load, albeit with fluctuations in the queues and waiting times due to the unpredictability of the demand. From the summary of experimental results presented in Table 1, it is clear that RL-TSC-1 performs the best under these

Table 1 Summary of performance under random traffic flows (average values)

Algorithm	Queue length	Vehicle speed (km/h)	Waiting time (s)
Fixed timing	8.55	7.98	346.49
RL-TSC-1	2.93	12.91	39.26
RL-TSC-2	3.68	12.29	57.42
RL-TSC-3	3.37	12.58	48.32

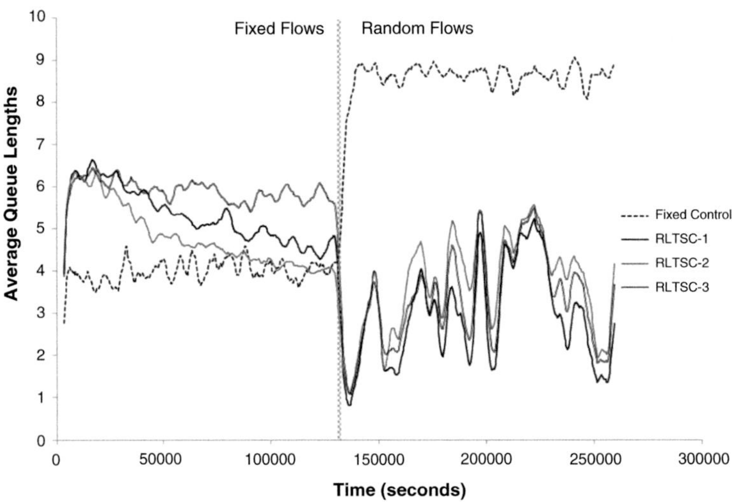

Fig. 2 Average junction queue length

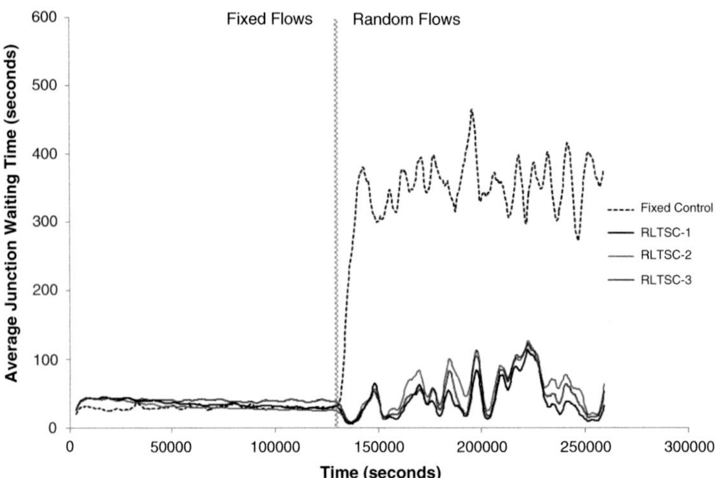

Fig. 3 Average junction waiting times

unpredictable traffic conditions, with the highest vehicle speeds and the lowest queue lengths and waiting times. RL-TSC-2 performs slightly worse here, with lower vehicle speeds and increased waiting times and queues compared to RL-TSC-1. RL-TSC-3 performs somewhere between the latter two algorithms; this is reasonable as it is effectively a hybrid of these approaches.

By taking an average of ten simulation runs for each agent type, we have demonstrated that RL-based approaches offer consistently better performance under variable traffic flows than fixed time traffic signal plans. Each RL algorithm is also competitive with fixed traffic signals under more predictable flows, with RL-TSC-2 offering the best performance under this type of flow regime. Further work is required on RL-TSC-1 and RL-TSC-3 in order for them to achieve the same performance under predictable flows as a fixed time controller. In general, our findings concur with those of Abdulhai et al. in [6], who showed that a Q-learning agent can perform on a par with pre-timed signals under fixed flows and outperform pre-timed signals under more variable flows. Further work is also required on our multi-objective algorithm RL-TSC-3, in order to improve its performance. These refinements may include considering different reward definitions, along with determining the optimal weighting for each of the parameters considered. Determining the optimal parameter weightings in multi-objective reward functions is a time-consuming endeavour, so we may consider implementing a learning-based approach to determine these weightings automatically.

In summary, we recommend the use of RL-TSC-2 for conditions where there are fixed flows or fixed ratio flows. RL-TSC-1 is recommended for highly variable traffic conditions, while the multi-objective RL-TSC-3 algorithm performs somewhere between the two and offers good all-round performance.

6 Conclusions and Future Work

As we have outlined in this chapter, the field of RL-TSC is a very promising one. We have provided the reader with a general introduction to the concept of RL, as well as discussing the factors that need to be taken into consideration when designing MARL architectures capable of controlling traffic signals and how various authors have addressed these challenges in their own research. In our experiments, we have demonstrated the suitability of RL-TSC to deal with time-varying flows and random traffic patterns when compared to a fixed time control scheme. RL-TSC has matured significantly in the last decade, and while much has been accomplished, it has yet to advance beyond theory and simulations. There have been no reported field deployments at the time of writing, but this is the ultimate goal of RL-TSC research.

Real-world deployment would of course necessitate a blend between both offline and online learning to be successful. Ideally, agents would first be trained offline in a simulator, using real-world network geometry and traffic demand data. Incorporating some online learning would allow the agents to adapt to changing traffic patterns, if this behaviour is desired. Finding the right balance between online and offline learning will be important when deploying RL-TSC systems in the field and remains unaddressed in the literature. Further studies using real road networks and corresponding traffic demand data should be conducted to further this aim, preferably using the existing signal plans as a benchmark.

Questions concerning the robustness and reliability of controllers and the effect of a failure on traffic dynamics also remain unanswered at the time of writing. One must also consider how RL-TSC will interface with other promising approaches in ITS in the future, e.g. Autonomous Intersection Management [18]. Many approaches in the literature use parameters for state and reward definitions that are not easily obtained in real traffic networks, e.g. ATWT. To apply these approaches, we will need to develop and include the required data gathering capabilities in our traffic networks, e.g. vehicle detecting cameras, vehicle to junction communications or even floating car data.

Some of the recently emerging themes in RL-TSC, e.g. function approximation, multi-objectivity and coordination, also deserve further attention. There is certainly great potential in these areas, and only a handful of papers in the literature have investigated these themes. There may also be scope for further theories from mainstream RL literature to be applied to the RL-TSC domain in the future.

References

1. Horizon 2020: http://ec.europa.eu/programmes/horizon2020/en (2014)
2. Traas: Traci as a service. http://traas.sourceforge.net/cms/ (2014)
3. Abdoos, M., Mozayani, N., Bazzan, A.: Traffic light control in non-stationary environments based on multi agent q-learning. In: 14th International IEEE Conference on Intelligent Transportation Systems (ITSC), 2011, pp. 1580–1585 (2011). doi:10.1109/ITSC.2011.6083114
4. Abdoos, M., Mozayani, N., Bazzan, A.: Hierarchical control of traffic signals using q-learning with tile coding. Appl. Intell. **40**(2), 201–213 (2014). doi:10.1007/s10489-013-0455-3
5. Abdulhai, B., Kattan, L.: Reinforcement learning: introduction to theory and potential for transport applications. Can. J. Civ. Eng. **30**(6), 981–991 (2003). doi:10.1139/l03-014
6. Abdulhai, B., Pringle, R., Karakoulas, G.: Reinforcement learning for true adaptive traffic signal control. J. Transp. Eng. **129**(3), 278–285 (2003). doi:10.1061/(ASCE)0733-947X(2003)129:3(278)
7. Arel, I., Liu, C., Urbanik, T., Kohls, A.: Reinforcement learning-based multi-agent system for network traffic signal control. IET Intell. Transp. Syst. **4**(2), 128–135 (2010). doi:10.1049/iet-its.2009.0070
8. Bakker, B.: Cooperative multi-agent reinforcement learning of traffic lights. In: ACM Transactions on Multimedia Computing, Communications, and Applications (2005)
9. Bakker, B., Whiteson, S., Kester, L., Groen, F.: Traffic light control by multiagent reinforcement learning systems. In: Babuška, R., Groen, F. (eds.) Interactive Collaborative Information Systems. Studies in Computational Intelligence, vol. 281, pp. 475–510. Springer, Berlin/Heidelberg (2010). doi:10.1007/978-3-642-11688-9_18
10. Balaji, P., German, X., Srinivasan, D.: Urban traffic signal control using reinforcement learning agents. IET Intell. Transp. Syst. **4**(3), 177–188 (2010). doi:10.1049/iet-its.2009.0096
11. Bazzan, A.L.C.: Opportunities for multiagent systems and multiagent reinforcement learning in traffic control. Auton. Agent. Multi Agent Syst. **18**(3), 342–375 (2009). doi:10.1007/s10458-008-9062-9
12. Bazzan, A.L.C., Klügl, F.: A review on agent-based technology for traffic and transportation. Knowl. Eng. Rev. **29**, 375–403 (2014). doi:10.1017/S0269888913000118
13. Brys, T., Pham, T.T., Taylor, M.E.: Distributed learning and multi-objectivity in traffic light control. Connect. Sci. **26**(1), 65–83 (2014). doi:10.1080/09540091.2014.885282
14. Busoniu, L., Babuška, R., Schutter, B.: Multi-agent reinforcement learning: an overview. In: Srinivasan, D., Jain, L. (eds.) Innovations in Multi-agent Systems and Applications - 1. Studies in Computational Intelligence, vol. 310, pp. 183–221. Springer, Berlin/Heidelberg (2010). doi:10.1007/978-3-642-14435-6_7
15. Chen, B., Cheng, H.: A review of the applications of agent technology in traffic and transportation systems. IEEE Trans. Intell. Transp. Syst. **11**(2), 485–497 (2010). doi:10.1109/TITS.2010.2048313

16. Chin, Y.K., Bolong, N., Yang, S.S., Teo, K.: Exploring q-learning optimization in traffic signal timing plan management. In: 2011 Third International Conference on Computational Intelligence, Communication Systems and Networks (CICSyN), pp. 269–274 (2011). doi:10.1109/CICSyN.2011.64
17. Cools, S.B., Gershenson, C., D'Hooghe, B.: Self-organizing traffic lights: a realistic simulation. In: Prokopenko, M. (ed.) Advances in Applied Self-organizing Systems, Advanced Information and Knowledge Processing, pp. 41–50. Springer, London (2008). doi:10.1007/978-1-84628-982-8_3
18. Dresner, K., Stone, P.: Multiagent traffic management: opportunities for multiagent learning. In: Tuyls, K., Hoen, P., Verbeeck, K., Sen, S. (eds.) Learning and Adaption in Multi-agent Systems. Lecture Notes in Computer Science, vol. 3898, pp. 129–138. Springer, Berlin/Heidelberg (2006). doi:10.1007/11691839_7
19. El-Tantawy, S., Abdulhai, B.: An agent-based learning towards decentralized and coordinated traffic signal control. In: 13th International IEEE Conference on Intelligent Transportation Systems (ITSC), 2010, pp. 665–670 (2010). doi:10.1109/ITSC.2010.5625066
20. El-Tantawy, S., Abdulhai, B.: Multi-agent reinforcement learning for integrated network of adaptive traffic signal controllers (marlin-atsc). In: 15th International IEEE Conference on Intelligent Transportation Systems (ITSC), 2012, pp. 319–326 (2012). doi:10.1109/ITSC.2012.6338707
21. El-Tantawy, S., Abdulhai, B., Abdelgawad, H.: Multiagent reinforcement learning for integrated network of adaptive traffic signal controllers (marlin-atsc): methodology and large-scale application on downtown Toronto. IEEE Trans. Intell. Transp. Syst. **14**(3), 1140–1150 (2013). doi:10.1109/TITS.2013.2255286
22. Houli, D., Zhiheng, L., Yi, Z.: Multiobjective reinforcement learning for traffic signal control using vehicular ad hoc network. EURASIP J. Adv. Signal Process. **2010**, 7:1–7:7 (2010). doi:10.1155/2010/724035
23. Isa, J., Kooij, J., Koppejan, R., Kuijer, L.: Reinforcement learning of traffic light controllers adapting to accidents. In: Design and Organisation of Autonomous Systems (2006)
24. Khamis, M., Gomaa, W.: Enhanced multiagent multi-objective reinforcement learning for urban traffic light control. In: 11th International Conference on Machine Learning and Applications (ICMLA), 2012, vol. 1, pp. 586–591 (2012). doi:10.1109/ICMLA.2012.108
25. Khamis, M.A., Gomaa, W.: Adaptive multi-objective reinforcement learning with hybrid exploration for traffic signal control based on cooperative multi-agent framework. Eng. Appl. Artif. Intell. **29**, 134–151 (2014). doi:10.1016/j.engappai.2014.01.007
26. Khamis, M., Gomaa, W., El-Shishiny, H.: Multi-objective traffic light control system based on Bayesian probability interpretation. In: 15th International IEEE Conference on Intelligent Transportation Systems (ITSC), 2012, pp. 995–1000 (2012). doi:10.1109/ITSC.2012.6338853
27. Krajzewicz, D., Erdmann, J., Behrisch, M., Bieker, L.: Recent development and applications of SUMO - Simulation of Urban MObility. Int. J. Adv. Syst. Meas. **5**(3&4), 128–138 (2012)
28. Kuyer, L., Whiteson, S., Bakker, B., Vlassis, N.: Multiagent reinforcement learning for urban traffic control using coordination graphs. In: Daelemans, W., Goethals, B., Morik, K. (eds.) Machine Learning and Knowledge Discovery in Databases. Lecture Notes in Computer Science, vol. 5211, pp. 656–671. Springer, Berlin/Heidelberg (2008). doi:10.1007/978-3-540-87479-9_61
29. Liu, Z.: A survey of intelligence methods in urban traffic signal control. Int. J. Comput. Sci. Netw. Secur. **7**(7), 105–112 (2007)
30. Lu, S., Liu, X., Dai, S.: Incremental multistep q-learning for adaptive traffic signal control based on delay minimization strategy. In: 7th World Congress on Intelligent Control and Automation, 2008. WCICA 2008, pp. 2854–2858 (2008). doi:10.1109/WCICA.2008.4593378
31. Nair, R., Varakantham, P., Tambe, M., Yokoo, M.: Networked distributed POMDPs: a synthesis of distributed constraint optimization and POMDPs. In: Proceedings of the 20th National Conference on Artificial Intelligence, AAAI'05, vol. 1, pp. 133–139. AAAI Press, Pittsburgh (2005)

32. Ono, N., Fukumoto, K.: A modular approach to multi-agent reinforcement learning. In: Weiß, G. (ed.) Distributed Artificial Intelligence Meets Machine Learning in Multi-Agent Environments. Lecture Notes in Computer Science, vol. 1221, pp. 25–39. Springer, Berlin/Heidelberg (1997). doi:10.1007/3-540-62934-3_39
33. Pham, T., Brys, T., Taylor, M.E.: Learning coordinated traffic light control. In: Proceedings of the Adaptive and Learning Agents workshop (at AAMAS-13) (2013)
34. Prashanth, L., Bhatnagar, S.: Reinforcement learning with average cost for adaptive control of traffic lights at intersections. In: 14th International IEEE Conference on Intelligent Transportation Systems (ITSC), 2011, pp. 1640–1645 (2011). doi:10.1109/ITSC.2011.6082823
35. Prashanth, L., Bhatnagar, S.: Reinforcement learning with function approximation for traffic signal control. IEEE Trans. Intell. Transp. Syst. **12**(2), 412–421 (2011). doi:10.1109/TITS.2010.2091408
36. Puterman, M.L.: Markov Decision Processes: Discrete Stochastic Dynamic Programming, 1st edn. Wiley, New York (1994)
37. Rummery, G.A., Niranjan, M.: On-line Q-learning using connectionist systems. Tech. Rep. 166, Cambridge University Engineering Department (1994)
38. Salkham, A., Cahill, V.: Soilse: a decentralized approach to optimization of fluctuating urban traffic using reinforcement learning. In: 13th International IEEE Conference on Intelligent Transportation Systems (ITSC), 2010, pp. 531–538 (2010). doi:10.1109/ITSC.2010.5625145
39. Salkham, A., Cunningham, R., Garg, A., Cahill, V.: A collaborative reinforcement learning approach to urban traffic control optimization. In: IEEE/WIC/ACM International Conference on Web Intelligence and Intelligent Agent Technology, 2008. WI-IAT '08, vol. 2, pp. 560–566 (2008). doi:10.1109/WIIAT.2008.88
40. Singh, S., Jaakkola, T., Littman, M., Szepesvári, C.: Convergence results for single-step on-policy reinforcement-learning algorithms. Mach. Learn. **38**(3), 287–308 (2000). doi:10.1023/A:1007678930559
41. Steingröver, M., Schouten, R., Peelen, S., Nijhuis, E., Bakker, B.: Reinforcement learning of traffic light controllers adapting to traffic congestion. In: Proceedings of the Belgium-Netherlands Artificial Intelligence Conference, BNAIC '05 (2005)
42. Sutton, R.S., Barto, A.G.: Introduction to Reinforcement Learning, 1st edn. MIT Press, Cambridge (1998)
43. Thorpe, T.L., Anderson, C.W.: Traffic light control using sarsa with three state representations. Tech. rep., IBM Corporation (1996)
44. Watkins, C.J.C.H.: Learning from delayed rewards. Ph.D. thesis, King's College (1989)
45. Watkins, C., Dayan, P.: Technical note: Q-learning. Mach. Learn. **8**(3–4), 279–292 (1992). doi:10.1023/A:1022676722315
46. Webster, F.V.: Traffic signal settings. Road Research Technical Paper No. 39, Road Research Laboratory, London, published by HMSO (1958)
47. Wen, K., Qu, S., Zhang, Y.: A stochastic adaptive control model for isolated intersections. In: IEEE International Conference on Robotics and Biomimetics, 2007. ROBIO 2007, pp. 2256–2260 (2007). doi:10.1109/ROBIO.2007.4522521
48. Wiering, M.: Multi-agent reinforcement learning for traffic light control. In: Proceedings of the Seventeenth International Conference on Machine Learning, ICML '00, pp. 1151–1158. Morgan Kaufmann, San Francisco (2000)
49. Wiering, M., van Otterlo, M. (eds.): Reinforcement Learning: State-of-the-Art. Springer, Heidelberg (2012)
50. Wiering, M., Vreeken, J., van Veenen, J., Koopman, A.: Simulation and optimization of traffic in a city. In: IEEE Intelligent Vehicles Symposium, pp. 453–458 (2004). doi:10.1109/IVS.2004.1336426
51. Woolridge, M.: Introduction to Multiagent Systems. Wiley, New York (2001)
52. Xu, L.H., Xia, X.H., Luo, Q.: The study of reinforcement learning for traffic self-adaptive control under multiagent markov game environment. Math. Probl. Eng. **2013** (2013)

A Multiagent Approach to Modeling Autonomic Road Transport Support Systems

Maksims Fiosins, Bernhard Friedrich, Jana Görmer, Dirk Mattfeld, Jörg P. Müller, and Hugues Tchouankem

Abstract In this chapter, we investigate a multiagent based approach to modeling autonomic features in urban traffic management. We provide a conceptual model of a traffic system comprising traffic participants modeled as locally autonomous agents, which act to optimize their operational and tactical decisions (e.g., route choice), and traffic management center(s) (TMC) which influence the traffic system according to dynamically selected policies. In this chapter, we focus on two autonomic features which emerge from the local decisions and actions of traffic participants and their interaction with the TMC and other vehicles: (1) *Autonomic routing*, in which we study how vehicle agents can individually adapt routing decisions based on local learning capabilities and traffic information communicated truthfully by a traffic management center; and (2) *Autonomic grouping*, i.e., collective decision-making of vehicles, which exchange route information and dynamically form and operate groups to drive in a convoy, thus aiming at higher speed and increased throughput. Communication is based on a (simulated) vehicle-to-infrastructure (V2I) and vehicle-to-vehicle (V2V) protocols. Initial experiments are reported using a real-world traffic scenario modeled in the Aimsun software, which is extended by the decision logic of TMC and vehicles. The experiments indicate that autonomic routing and grouping can improve the performance of a traffic management network, even though negative effects such as unstable behavior can be observed in some cases.

M. Fiosins (✉) • J. Görmer • J.P. Müller
Department of Informatics, TU Clausthal, Clausthal-Zellerfeld, Germany
e-mail: maksims.fiosins@gmail.com; jana.gormer@tu-clausthal.de; joerg.mueller@tu-clausthal.de

B. Friedrich
Institute of Transportation and Urban Engineering, Technische Universität Braunschweig, Braunschweig, Germany
e-mail: friedrich@tu-braunschweig.de

D. Mattfeld
Decision Support Group, Technische Universität Braunschweig, Braunschweig, Germany
e-mail: d.mattfeld@tu-bs.de

H. Tchouankem
Institute of Communications Technology, Leibniz Universität Hannover, Hannover, Germany
e-mail: hugues.tchouankem@ikt.uni-hannover.de

T.L. McCluskey et al. (eds.), *Autonomic Road Transport Support Systems*,
Autonomic Systems, DOI 10.1007/978-3-319-25808-9_5

Keywords Autonomic grouping • Autonomic rountig • Communication • Distributed systems • Intelligent transport systems • Multi-agent systems • Traffic modelling

1 Introduction

The need for individual mobility creates ecological and traffic problems in metropolitan areas, which constitute major limiting factors for urban development. The complexity of managing traffic is steadily increasing. At the same time, new technological trends are about to heavily affect traffic management systems and create new challenges and opportunities: Vehicle-to-infrastructure (V2I) and vehicle-to-vehicle (V2V) communication (collectively referred as V2X) enable real-time data exchange and coordination among vehicles and traffic infrastructure. Vehicles themselves become more and more autonomous through advanced assistance functions such as dynamic navigation and adaptive cruise control over speed, distance, and intersection assistants [4] as well as autonomous driving support [19]. Also, the interplay of advanced sensor systems, ubiquitous mobile networks, and large-scale intelligent data processing [12, 15] is about to transport the vision of the Internet of Things to the traffic management domain.

Traditional traffic management systems have largely attempted to reconcile system optimality with user-optimality conditions in a Wardropian sense [10], i.e., under the restricting behavioral assumption that users make decisions (e.g., choose routes) that minimize time and cost; thus, traditional traffic management policies are largely focusing on the part of user optimality that is not in potential conflict to societal traffic management goals; for instance, proposing a shorter or faster route to a driver will mostly be compliant with his preferences, so the driver is likely to follow such proposal. Also, in the past, users often have not been able to assess how traffic control actions affect their own goals, due to the absence of up-to-date information. With this being subject to change, individual traffic participants may be more likely to take decisions that are not the ones intended or predicted by traffic management. Before this background, sustainable cooperative traffic management systems (TMS) will require new models that enable them to interconnect enforcing system-optimal behavior in terms of safety and efficiency while taking the preferences and goals of the users into account, acknowledging that not all aspects of compliance can be enforced and giving users as much as possible degrees of freedom in acting according to their preferences.

In particular, these new dynamic models need to be able to explain and predict interdependencies between top-down control and bottom-up local strategy. In this context, theories and models of autonomic computing [20] come into play.[1]

[1]We refer to the introductory chapter of this book for a discussion of the core terminology and concepts of autonomics and autonomic traffic management.

Autonomic multiagent systems (MAS) [27] extend the notion of autonomicity to loosely coupled, decentralized systems and—as we argue in Sect. 2.1—are a promising modeling approach for autonomic traffic management systems (TMS).

In this chapter, we report on work studying autonomic features of traffic systems by using a multiagent-based model. The conceptual model and a corresponding technical architecture are described in Sect. 2. In Sect. 3, we study how vehicle agents can individually adapt their routing decisions based on local learning capabilities and traffic information communicated truthfully by a traffic management center (TMC).[2] We found that the local ability to adaptively optimize route choice can lead to reduced travel times, thus increasing both societal and local welfare. We call this feature *autonomic routing*, because the routes of vehicles are not centrally or statically determined, but rather the overall behavior of the traffic system emerges as a reaction of the experiences of the vehicles and the current situation without a central control.

In Sect. 4, we report on initial work considering a type of collective decision-making of autonomous vehicles and its influence on traffic performance. Vehicles exchange route information and vehicles with similar routes dynamically form and operate groups which drive in a convoy, thus aiming at higher speed and increased throughput due to reduced safety distances required. We call this feature *autonomic grouping* because vehicle groups are formed locally without a centralized control, leading to dynamic self-configuration of the traffic system without a central locus of control. In particular, we study the question what market penetration rate of autonomic grouping is required to actually lead to emergent (and desirable) autonomic behavior, measuring, e.g., overall travel times and number of stops in our example scenario for different penetration rates.

Before we start with defining the underlying conceptual and technical model of our approach in Sect. 2, we relate this chapter to the topic of autonomics: While we model our traffic system based on *autonomous* agents, the overall *autonomic* behavior of the system emerges from the interaction of these autonomous agents. Putting it differently, it is not the vehicle or the intersection control which are autonomic, but the system as a whole reveals autonomic behavior.

In our view, truly autonomic traffic systems that fully comply with the definition in the introduction of this book still do not exist. In the context of autonomicity, our work is an initial attempt to study how a multiagent-based approach can support adaptive and collective self-organization, self-configuration, and self-optimization, considering two specific features, i.e., routing and grouping. Based on these results, we hope to be able to tackle some of the challenging issues that are required to be solved to support truly autonomic traffic management systems.

[2]By this we mean that the TMC does not communicate information strategically, but to the best of its knowledge.

2 Conceptual Model and Technical Architecture

In this section, we define the basic concepts underlying our approach and discuss our research methodology (Sect. 2.1); in Sect. 2.2, we sketch the corresponding technical architectures based on which the autonomic features described in this chapter were implemented and validated.

2.1 Conceptual System Model

Our conceptual view (and related modeling approach) of next-generation traffic systems is illustrated in Fig. 1. It shows three basic sets of entities: The traffic management (TM), a smart traffic infrastructure, and the traffic participants (in this work we focus on vehicles). *Vehicles* are represented as general self-interested and autonomous software agents [21], whose internal architecture is based on a sense-update-decide-act model and whose informational state, motivations, and capabilities are modeled by a Belief, Desire Intention (BDI) architecture [22]. While the agents aim to meet their goals (or to maximize their utility according to a local utility function, involving, e.g., individual travel times, energy consumption, and speed or route preferences), we assume for the scope of this chapter that vehicles will comply with basic traffic laws and also will not voluntarily violate these types of rules, but act towards their local ends within the boundaries of these rules. We also do not consider changes in traffic management policies and concentrate on the behavior of (autonomous) vehicles given some fixed traffic management regime.

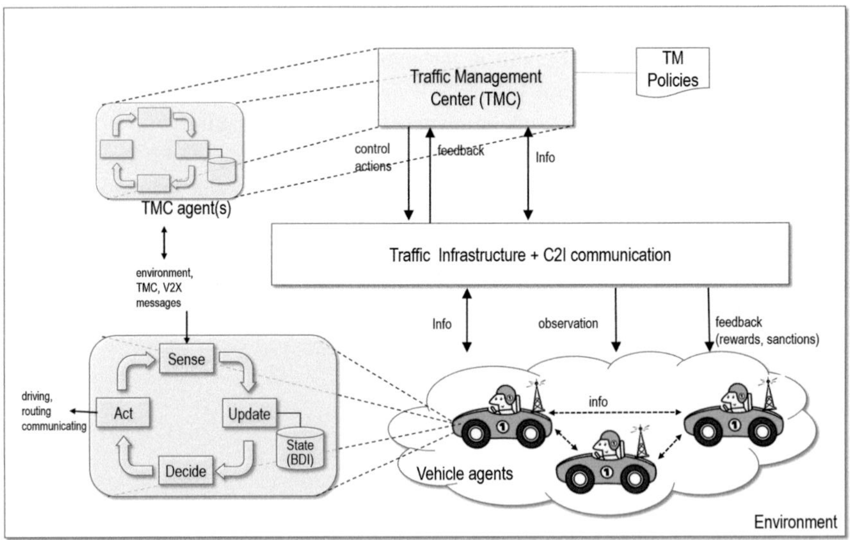

Fig. 1 Conceptual system model

The objective of *traffic management* is to optimize the overall traffic performance, which can be measured by criteria such as overall travel times or distance travelled, fuel consumption, and emissions, but possibly also criteria such as driver satisfaction. Thus, the objectives of traffic management and individual drivers may be partly conflicting. TM can influence the behavior of traffic participants mostly through exerting control (guided by some TM policies) on the traffic infrastructure, even though also direct communication between TM and traffic participants may be possible in some cases. The intelligent *traffic infrastructure* is the third major entity of our overall system. This infrastructure comprises intelligent sensing, light signaling, traffic signs, road side units, V2X communication infrastructure, and other components. It observes the traffic situation and communicates with vehicles and TM.

Another general conceptual approach, labeled *micro-meso-macro approach* (abbreviated M3 in the following), for analyzing and describing complex self-organizing systems has been proposed by Sanderson et al. in [24]. This approach, depicted in Fig. 2, is complementary to our conceptual system model of Fig. 1 in that it refines the architecture by identifying three interacting levels relevant for system modeling and analysis: the micro level, the meso level, and the macro level. At the micro level, we model and analyze individual agent behavior, in our case a vehicle; the meso level describes clusters or groups of micro-level individuals and their local interactions; in our case, meso-level interactions could be cooperative driving maneuvers such as platooning, but also, e.g., interactions between vehicles and light signals for cooperative intersection management [28]. Finally, the macro level represents infrastructure and system-wide, societal goals such as the reduction of overall congestion, the increase of throughput, or the minimization of travel times.

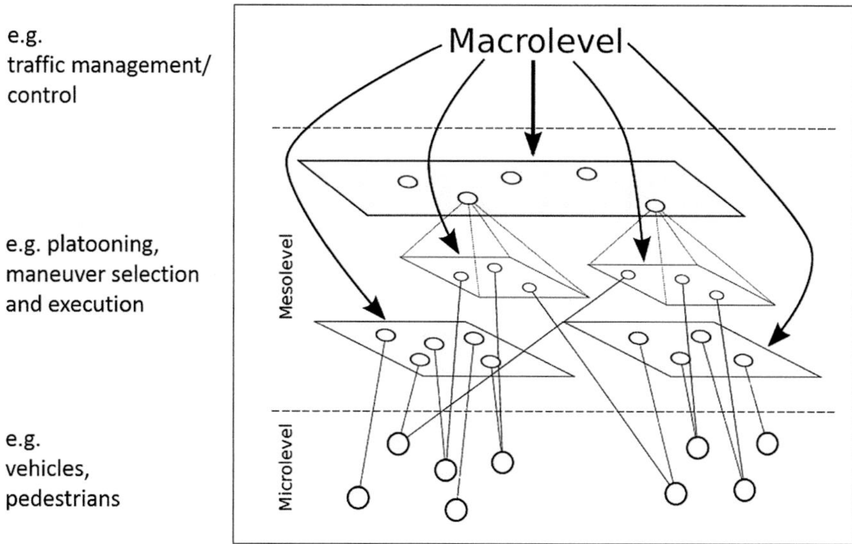

Fig. 2 Sanderson's micro-meso-macro approach [24]

The M3 model also provides a valuable framework for modeling interactions between the processes and systems at and across the three layers. For example, in Sect. 3 we study effects of autonomic behavior at micro and macro level, whereas in Sect. 4, we investigate how autonomic meso-level phenomena impacts the micro and macro level. While M3 is not restricted to multiagent models, the three-level model is well suited as a methodology for describing and analyzing multiagent systems, which can be very naturally described using these levels and their interactions.

Before we outline our conception of and assumptions on these components, we note that the study of self-adaptation and resilience of this overall system, according to the definition of autonomicity underlying this book, can be approached in three differing ways: *A first line of research*, starting from classical traffic control and engineering, would study how TM and infrastructure can cooperate and self-adapt using autonomic features based on static or probabilistic models of traffic participant behavior. *A second line of research* would assume that TM remains static (or predictable using some probabilistic models), while infrastructure and traffic participants reveal collective autonomic behavior; it is this line of research we start from in this chapter.

A third, most challenging line of research, towards which our long-term research is aiming at, will study the complex interactions of autonomic behavior both at TM and traffic participants side, possibly leading to effects such as oscillations or the type of game-theoretic phenomena such as the tragedy of the commons. Following the third line, a major objective (and success criteria) for autonomic behavior is the degree to which it can reliably prevent or dampen these negative effects, degrade gracefully and recover quickly when faced with disturbances (e.g., road blockings), and maximize overall (societal) utility, possibly measured by aggregated individual satisfaction of traffic participants. In such a setting, traffic management (TM) will have direct and indirect instruments at its disposal to influence the behavior of traffic participants. Direct instruments include dynamic signal plans, speed limits, or modifying the direction of lanes. Indirect instruments include incentivizing mechanisms such as (real or virtual) payments made for behavior of traffic participants that complies with the goals of traffic managements (such as certain routes being taken or avoided) and sanctions enforced on traffic participants whose behavior does not comply with traffic management goals; the latter can be implemented, e.g., by dynamic pricing schemes for the usage of traffic infrastructure (such as roads or parking space).

We found the paradigm of autonomous agents and multiagent systems (see [5] for an up-to-date review of agent-based models, methods, and applications in traffic and transport) to be an appropriate conceptual model for studying autonomic traffic management systems, because it supports (1) the notion of autonomy including restricted local states, local preferences, motivations, and capabilities; (2) the notion of communication and coordination; (3) a unified view of human and automated agents (e.g., vehicles operated by human drivers and autonomous vehicles); and (4) models and mechanisms that allow an integrated study of the relationship between individual and collective reasoning and decision-making, including multiagent planning, game-theoretic models (see [30]), auctions and market mechanisms (see, e.g., [16, 31]), and models of computational social choice (see, e.g., [7]).

2.2 The PLANETS Technical Architecture

In this section we describe a technical architecture in which the conceptual model described above has been prototypically implemented. The PLANETS simulation architecture used for the work described in this chapter is based on the Aimsun traffic simulator (see Fig. 3). Aimsun is used as the traffic environment to create realistic traffic demand and vehicle behavior; the vehicles [assumed to be equipped with an on-board unit (OBU)] are modeled as agents using the Jade framework; also the TM is modeled as a separate component which interacts with Aimsun, e.g., by modifying signal plans. Finally, OMNET++ is used as a platform for realistic simulation of wireless V2X communication.

The TM component represents the top-down control of the system. It collects information from vehicles in the form of Floating Car Data (short messages with locations and speeds of the vehicles) as well as from detectors in order to estimate actual vehicle flows in the streets of the network and convert them to the Level of Service (LoS), denoting different degrees of road congestion [23]. Based on the LoS, one of a number of predefined strategies for traffic light control is selected and corresponding information is sent to vehicles. We refer to [18] for a description of the TMC component.

The vehicle with OBU component implements the basic agent cycle illustrated in Fig. 1 above. Next to basic operational decisions (speed and lane choice), a vehicle agent can make tactical decisions relating to route choice (detailed in Sect. 3) and vehicle group formation (see Sect. 4). Routing decisions are based on the vehicle

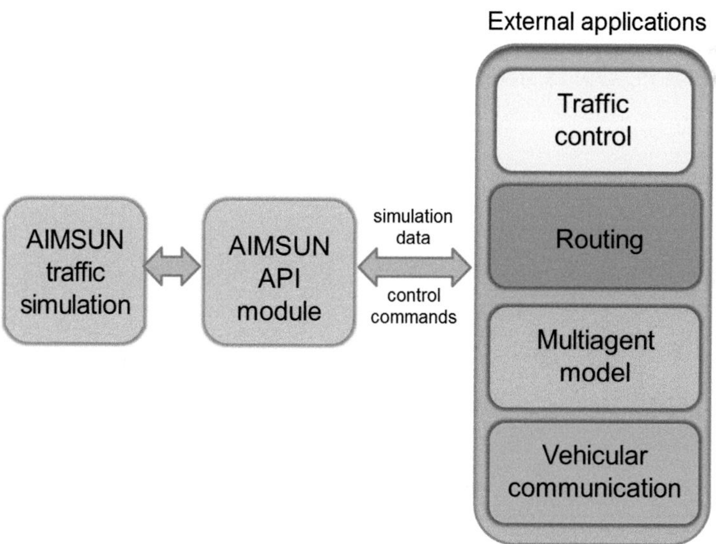

Fig. 3 Technical architecture overview

preferences and information from TMC; grouping decisions are based on V2V information exchange and speed coordination.

The technical architecture of the OBU is modular and extensible and (in the version underlying the work described in this chapter) comprised of the following components (called Apps for easier understandability by non-computer scientists):

- Learning App—updates a model of travel times for different routes based on local history and information provided by the TMC
- Routing App—provides access to external (or vehicle-internal) routing services
- Grouping App—implements group formation protocols and corresponding decisions
- CommBox—provides access to basic V2X (V2I and V2V) communication
- setRoute App—translates the vehicle's tactical plans (route) to corresponding operational actions (e.g., lane choices, turns)

The V2X communication module implements realistic V2X communication, taking influence of buildings into account. It implements V2I communication between OBU and Road Side Units, assumed to be installed in the streets (intersections) as well as V2V communication in the form of broadcast messages sent by OBU and received by other OBUs.

As a main simulation environment for our experiments, we use a road network that models a part of Hanover (Germany) with two parallel and five perpendicular streets (see Fig. 4, left part) and a real exemplary traffic demand profile for a 1 h morning rush hour period. Figure 4 (right part) illustrates the road network model as defined in Aimsun.

In the following two sections, we describe the autonomic features enabling self-organized routing and group formation, which have been realized and evaluated based on the PLANETS architecture.

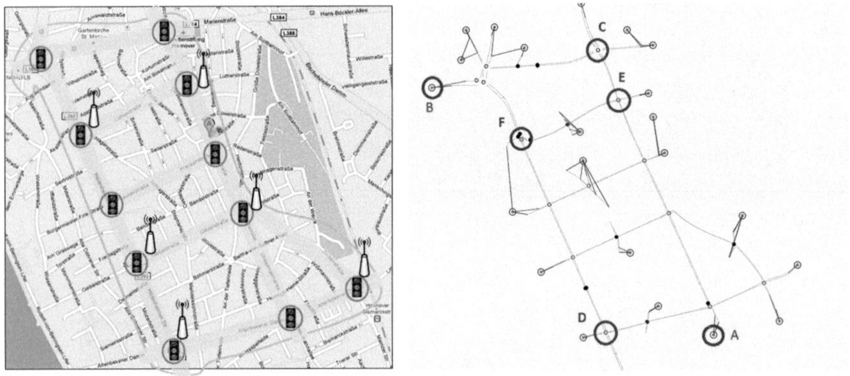

Fig. 4 Simulated traffic network (*left*); representation in Aimsun (*right*)

3 Autonomic Routing

In this section, we study how vehicle agents can individually adapt their routing decisions based on micro-level learning capabilities and traffic information communicated truthfully by a traffic management center (TMC) via some (possibly decentralized) infrastructure (meso level). We call this feature *autonomic routing*, because the routes of vehicles are not centrally or statically determined, but rather the overall behavior of the traffic system emerges as a reaction of the experiences of the vehicles and the current situation without a central control. In Sect. 3.1, we describe the underlying models and methods; Sect. 3.2 describes experimental results carried out to validate the autonomic routing feature.

3.1 Models and Methods

The process of route choice (in the following called *routing*) is performed by the OBU component of the PLANETS architecture; its result can be displayed as a route recommendation to the vehicle driver (or, depending on the scenario, be used to control an autonomous vehicle). As we have seen in Sect. 2.2, each OBU is controlled by an intelligent agent. In this section, we use the term *agents* to denote the intelligent in-vehicle units.

Routing decisions of the agents are based on their individual preferences, derived from their past experience, as well as on current information from the TMC. Individual preferences are modeled through utility functions [11]. We model agent preferences on the level of road segments: each agent has its own opinion about each road segment, based on its previous experience (e.g., related to congestion level or travel time). Road segment preferences may be easily converted to route preferences, used in the routing process. We suppose that agents make routing decisions that maximize their utility values.

The TMC periodically sends updated information about road segments to the agents. Receiving this information, each agent decides to what extent it trusts this information and correspondingly incorporates it into its preferences. Some agents may simply ignore received information and rely on their own experience, while others may fully accept the received information and use it for making their decisions. So we can model different types of external information acceptance by the agents. These concepts are presented in detail in [13, 14, 18].

Now let us describe the routing process formally. The agent environment is represented as a search graph $G = (V, E)$ (cf. [6, 18]). The vertices V of this graph correspond to road segments; the edges E correspond to turns, which connect these segments. The search graph contains information about allowed turns (not only about roads and intersections). Numerical values (weights) are used to denote the preference values which an agent attributes to a road segment (see Fig. 5).

The planning process of the agent j is based on the individual weights $c_j^{\text{ind}}(t) = \langle c_j^{v,\text{ind}}(t), c_j^{e,\text{ind}}(t) \rangle$, where the weights of the road segments $c_j^{v,\text{ind}}(t) =$

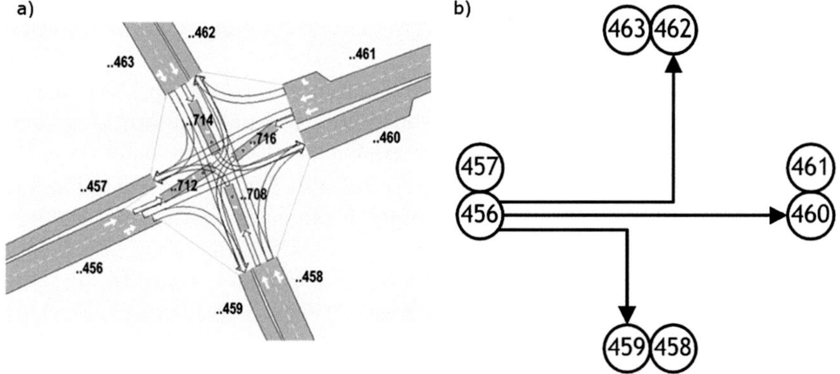

Fig. 5 (**a**) Intersection in Aimsun; (**b**) corresponding search graph

$\{c_{j,1}^{v,\text{ind}}(t), c_{j,2}^{v,\text{ind}}(t), \ldots, c_{j,n_v}^{v,\text{ind}}(t)\}$ correspond to the nodes of the graph and the weights of the turns $c_j^{e,\text{ind}}(t) = \{c_{j,1}^{e,\text{ind}}(t), c_{j,2}^{e,\text{ind}}(t), \ldots, c_{j,n_e}^{e,\text{ind}}(t)\}$ correspond to the edges of the graph at time t.

In order to initialize the weights of an agent, we suppose that there are k initial classes of the agent preferences, each of them representing particular route preferences (this can correspond to inhabitants of the city, guests of the city, transit vehicles, taxis, etc.). For each class i there is a predefined set of the individual weights $\tilde{c}_i^{\text{ind}}$. For each agent entering the network, we assign some class i and initialize its individual weights as $c_j^{\text{ind}}(0) = \tilde{c}_i^{\text{ind}}$.

At time t, each agent receives new information from the TMC in the form of the weights of vertices and edges of the search graph $c^{\text{tmc}}(t)$. As we already mentioned, the agents integrate this new information to their individual weights in different ways. In general, new individual weights depend on old individual weights and new information according to an arbitrary update function U_j, which in general can be different for each vehicle j:

$$c_j^{\text{ind}}(t+1) = U_j(c_j^{\text{ind}}(t), c^{\text{tmc}}(t)). \tag{1}$$

There are different forms of the function U_j in (1). One of the options, used in our simulations, is just a linear combination of individual and received weights:

$$c_{j,i}^{x,\text{ind}}(t+1) = \alpha_j c_{j,i}^{x,\text{ind}}(t) + (1-\alpha_j)c_i^{x,\text{tmc}}(t),$$

where $0 \leq \alpha_j \leq 1$ represents how much the agent j trusts its own weights, but not received information, $x = \{e, v\}$.

According to the individual weights, the shortest path in the search graph is constructed for the individual agent. As all weights are supposed to be non-negative, we can use Dijkstra's algorithm [9] for construction of the shortest path in the graph. The complexity of the planning algorithm is $O(|V|^2)$.

3.2 Results and Benefits

We perform our experiments using the PLANETS simulator using the Hannover data set (see Sect. 2.2). We track a traffic flow from A to B (cf. Fig. 4, right part). We use three initial classes ($k = 3$) of agents: The agents of the first class initially prefer the right vertical street and so will initially prefer a route A-C-B; the agents of the second class have a preference on the left vertical street and so initially will prefer a route A-D-B. The agents of the third class do not have a special preference on the road segments; they will also initially prefer a route A-D-B because it is of shortest distance. The first two classes do not easily change their routes because they have clearly defined preferences ($\alpha_j = 0.8$); the vehicles of the third class easily change their routing on the base of the information from the TMC ($\alpha_j = 0.1$).

When simulating this setting, the road segments from C to B quickly become overloaded. Intersection C is overloaded as well, because many vehicles need to turn left there (see Fig. 6, left part). Assume now that as a reaction to the overload of the street C-B and of intersection C, the TMC decides to close the road segment E-C in the direction C. It informs the vehicles by using variable traffic signs as well as by corresponding V2X messages. In this case, our observed flow will prefer a route A-E-F-B. The intersection D will become heavily loaded as well (Fig. 6, right).

The vehicles of the second class will mostly continue to use this intersection. The vehicles of the third class will mostly switch to the route A-E-F-B. As a result, about 70 % of the vehicles of this flow will follow the route A-E-F-B, about 20 % the route A-D-F-B, and other vehicles follow other routes.

Approximately the same changes are made in other flows. The resulting average time required for one vehicle to cross the street network is shown in Fig. 7. The upper line corresponds to the case where the considered routing scheme is not used. In this case the standard routing scheme of Aimsun is used, which selects the shortest route for each vehicle. The lower line corresponds to the case where 100 % of the vehicles use the proposed routing procedure. We notice a macro-level decrease of travel times by about 10 % by applying the autonomic routing scheme.

To conclude, our initial experiments indicate that the local ability to adaptively optimize route choice can lead to reduced travel times, thus increasing both societal and local welfare. Thus, our *autonomous* vehicles/drivers achieve *autonomic* properties. However, we also found in some cases that the local *autonomous* decisions may lead to oscillating behavior in the traffic network, thus not leading to the

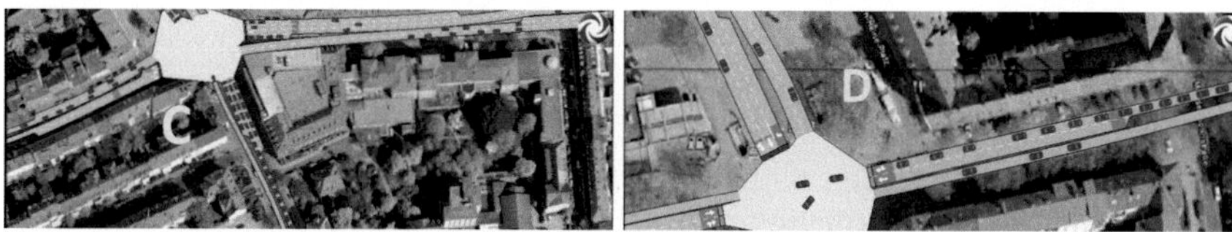

Fig. 6 Screenshots of Aimsun simulation: overload at intersections C (*left*) and D (*right*)

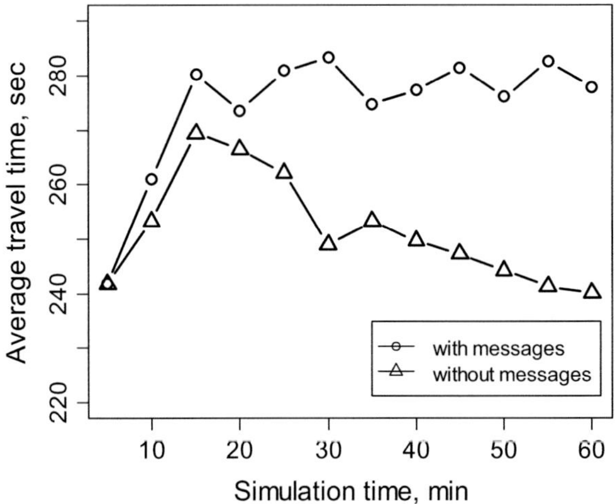

Fig. 7 Travel time without (*above*) and with (*below*) application of the considered routing

desired overall autonomic behavior. So there is a need to more closely study the interaction between TMC policies and local strategies in the future, e.g., by using game-theoretic models [5].

4 Vehicle Group Formation Based on V2V Communication

The autonomic routing showcase discussed in Sect. 3 has shown how autonomic behavior of a traffic system can emerge through local adaptive probabilistic reasoning in combination with information exchange in a multiagent system. In this section we sketch an example of how autonomic behavior can emerge through collective decision-making and acting of autonomous vehicles: In *autonomic grouping*, close-by vehicles exchange route information, and those vehicles with similar routes and preferences dynamically form and operate groups which drive in a platoon [29], thus aiming at higher speed and increased throughput due to smaller safety distances. Group formation is realized by using a multidimensional distance metrics. We call this feature autonomic grouping because vehicle groups are formed locally (at the meso level) without centralized control, leading to dynamic self-configuration of the traffic system on the base of sensing the environment, and TMC/V2X messages individually. The main difference of this work to related research on platooning in automated highway systems [2, 3] is that we consider grouping to occur in the context of urban traffic, which means that vehicles drive with lower speed but dynamics of group formation is much higher with shorter planning horizons. The idea of grouping vehicles also occurs in mesoscopic simulation [8] where a number of vehicles have some common characteristic to save simulation time. In our work, we additionally study how the penetration rate of V2X communication capability influences the macro-level benefit of grouping, measuring, e.g., overall travel times and number of stops in our example scenario (see Fig. 4) for different penetration rates. These results are obtained by using the PLANETS simulator based on Aimsun (see Sect. 2.2). In Sect. 4.1, we describe the underlying models and methods; Sect. 4.2 describes a number of experiments carried out to validate the autonomic vehicle group formation feature.

4.1 Models and Methods

Vehicle group formation is a capability orthogonal to the functionality of routing; it enables a traffic system to adapt speed and lane change decisions in a coordinated fashion aiming to improve traffic flow by minimizing the number of stops and by driving safely with higher speed and less distance in a convoy [17]. Depending on location, destination, routes, and possibly other constraints or preferences, vehicles will consider to form a vehicle group. When driving in a group, speeds and distances can be uniformly agreed and performed; thus several intersections can be crossed by using the green wave, thus avoiding stop times. In our approach, the additional necessary information about the signal plans of the traffic lights will be sent to the members of a group by the Road Side Units (RSU). In these experiments described here, we assume perfect communication between the vehicles. In other work [18], we did investigate group formation with realistic (simulated) communication channels. To avoid the overload of the communication channel, messages are only sent periodically with configurable periods. The data format for the communication is a simplified version of ETSI cooperative awareness messages (CAMs).

Let us consider the example of grouping over a sequence of regulated intersections. Vehicles intend to pass as many successive intersections as possible without stopping, minimizing their individual travel times, whereas an optimal throughput in the network is desired by the centralized traffic management and traffic lights can be regulated accordingly. The idea is to create a motivation for vehicles (at micro level) to join groups (meso level) and act in a coordinated fashion, resulting in reduced overall travel time. In this way, an interaction between macro-level policy and meso-level decentralized grouping is created, which in this example is synergetic, i.e., beneficial for both.

To restrict problems of dynamics and provide enough time for the necessary communication, here we assume that groups in our simulation are (re-)formed at red traffic lights; they then cross the following intersections as a platoon. The first vehicle arriving at the intersection acts as a group leader (first vehicle in the left lane) as illustrated in Fig. 8. It performs a prediction of the traffic state and of the signal plans of subsequent intersections. Depending on the outcome, the leader creates and broadcasts the group plan containing maximal group size, time constraints, and group rules. Each vehicle conducts a relevance check of the received messages; if the goal or partial route fits, it joins the group (dark area in Fig. 8). In detail, vehicles

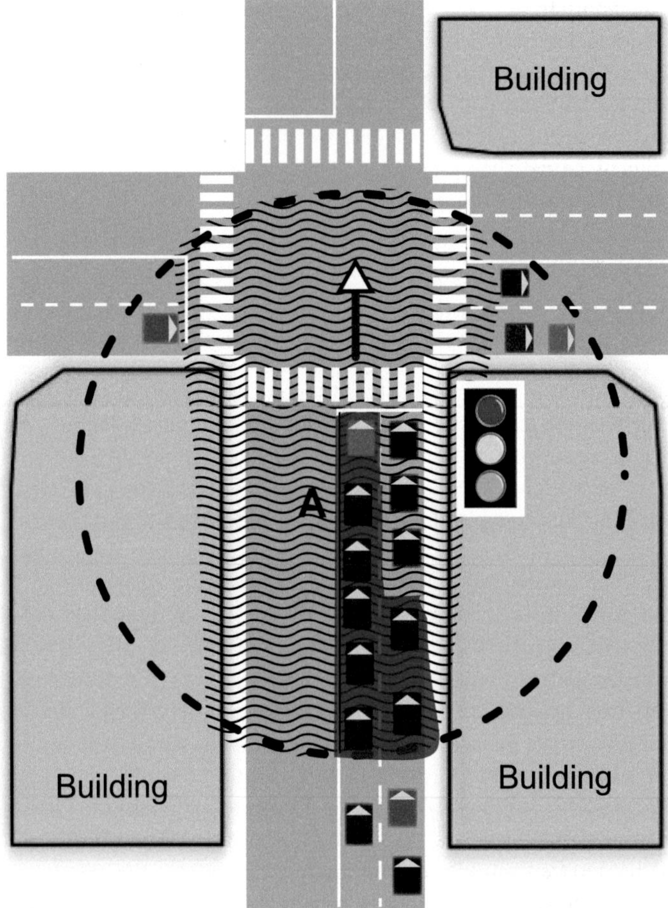

Fig. 8 Communication range of vehicle A computed without (*dashed circular range*) and with consideration of buildings (*shaded area*). Group formation (*dark area*) by a leader (*first vehicle in the left lane*) to pass a green phase

may speed up, slow down, and communicate with other vehicles in order to avoid conflicting situations of slow or blocked vehicles in front; also vehicles may join for coordinated actions. To improve the traffic flow, they can choose lanes and speeds and act dynamically. One benefit of this variant of group formation is simplified control: The group leader makes decisions; other group members contribute to group goals, sharing information and performing local optimization.

The real-time, reliable exchange of information between traffic participants plays an important role to enable autonomic grouping. Moreover, as indicated in Sect. 2.2, a communication model, which includes a complete communication protocol stack, as well as the modeling of the radio propagation channel are essential for application designers—not only for the specification and dimensioning of V2I networks but also for a credible simulation-based investigation of MAS.

Radio propagation models, such as the *Log-Distance Model* or *Two-Ray Ground Reflection Model* are often used for modeling the range of communication in vehicular networks in urban scenarios. In our work [26], we combine a computationally inexpensive radio shadowing model proposed by Sommer et al. [25] with a propagation model which consider the statistic nature of the channel gain amplitude, since the received signal is subject to significant signal fading due to the multipath propagation of radio waves in urban environment. As an illustrative example of the impact of a radio shadowing model on the communication area, Fig. 8 depicts the communication range of vehicle A, which is partially blocked by surrounding buildings (shaded area) and its communication range without consideration of buildings (dashed circle).

4.2 Results and Benefits

To investigate the influence of communication parameters on the effectiveness of the group formation, three input parameters are varied within the simulation setups: transmission power, CAM generation rate, and the ratio of equipped vehicles to the total number of vehicles, i.e., the penetration rate. In order to ensure statistical validity of the results, for all figures in this section, each data point represents the average of ten simulation runs with different random seeds and 1 h simulated time per run. In order to be able to assess the impact of the communication performance related to the traffic efficiency, we focus on the mean travel time (Fig. 9a) as well as the number of stops per vehicle (Fig. 9b) alongside the main road. Figure 9 presents the aforementioned traffic efficiency metrics as a function of the simulation time for different penetration rates. Our measurements indicate no significant improvement

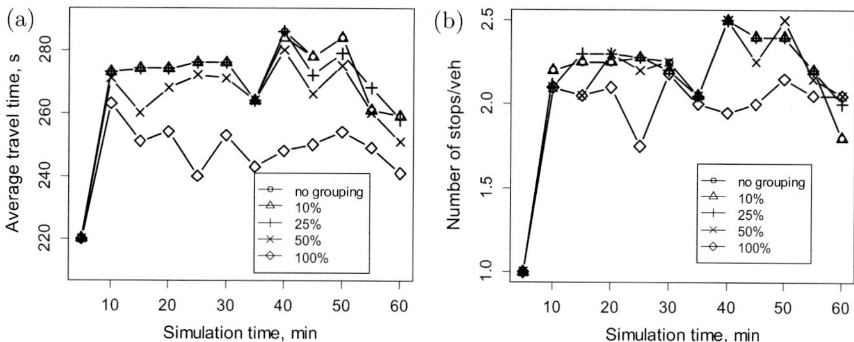

Fig. 9 Mean travel time and mean number of stops per vehicle versus simulation time for different penetration rates. (**a**) Mean travel time. (**b**) Number of stops per vehicle

for penetration rates smaller than 50 %; however, with a 100 % penetration rate, the mean travel time is reduced by up to 14 % and the number of stops per vehicle by up to 20 %.

To summarize, our initial experiments show that in the considered scenario, group formation and coordinated operation of vehicle groups have a positive impact on travel efficiency; it also shows that this overall benefit of self-organized, autonomic grouping behavior strongly depends on the ratio of vehicles that are equipped with the capability of V2X communication and group formation. Also, other experiments (reported in [18]) indicate that the benefit of autonomic grouping depends on the overall traffic density (LoS): Best results can be achieved for dense (but not congested) traffic. In situations of free traffic, too few vehicles are available to form groups, while in a traffic jam, the vehicles are already (involuntarily) grouped, so in these situations grouping does not improve the traffic situation.

5 Conclusion

Cooperative traffic management offers new perspectives to improve traffic safety and traffic flow by means of communication and local optimization. In this context, various new driver assistance systems are under development and partly in an early demonstration stage. However, most of the new cooperative features are designed as individual optimization for the equipped road users and do not necessarily fit a common traffic management plan. In order to overcome this deficiency, this chapter proposes a general conceptual architecture (and an exemplary technical architecture to support it), which allows us to study how aspects of local (autonomous) decision-making can interact with traffic management policies to reveal overall autonomic behavior of a traffic system. In our architecture, strategies are defined as a frame, which provides a flexibility to optimize the individual objectives of the single traffic participants. In this way, traffic planners are allowed to formulate strategies according to the needs of the city's development plan, and cooperative drivers are enabled to optimize their routes and their particular trajectories. Both the general public and the individual driver benefit in this way through the (de-)centralized cooperative traffic management. An analytical description is provided to show how strategies can be formed.

For evaluation purposes, a simulation of the system dynamics, which is able to model the interaction between equipped vehicles and the traffic management system, is necessary. Therefore, as an essential basis for the investigation of various research questions (e.g., concerning the penetration rate of equipped vehicles), the PLANETS simulator was developed. This simulator is based on the commercial traffic simulation software Aimsun and extends Aimsun's capabilities by four external applications, i.e., an external traffic control method, a routing module, a multiagent model, and a communication model (V2X).

Two major shortcomings of the current technical architecture are its limited scalability (due to the choice of Jade, where each agent is represented as a thread) and the fact that Aimsun is a commercial platform with limited access. For this reason, we are currently working on a new architectural approach, using the SUMO simulation platform in order to model the traffic environment, a more lightweight agent model (we are working on a lightweight implementation of the AgentSpeak language), and a more scalable integration approach, which allows for easy parallelization. An initial description of this approach is provided in [1].

Since the real-time exchange of information plays a critical role in MAS, a communication model was developed, which takes into account the frequency-selective and time-variant character of the radio-channel caused by shadowing, reflections, and scattering particularly in urban environments. Simulation shows that communication bottlenecks limit vehicle cooperation possibilities (e.g., multiple group information, cooperative routing, etc.), and broadcast should be used instead of two-sided communication. Cooperative traffic needs more data available for negotiation, and the communication limitations should be taken into account.

In the considered scenario, the routing process is considered to be individual—vehicles do not cooperate in their routing decisions. In our future research we are going to demonstrate how the routing process can be improved by direct exchange of routing preferences between vehicles, which will allow to avoid situations where all the vehicles select an optimal route, making it not optimal. In future, we are going to demonstrate how the groups of heterogeneous vehicles can be formed as well as make group formation and management more decentralized—at the present scenario the group leader was necessary.

Finally, it must be noted that the two autonomic techniques (routing and grouping) described in this chapter have so far been investigated in isolation; they are presented as two possible features of an autonomic traffic system, which have been devised by using the multiagent systems paradigm. Studying how they could be systematically integrated and combined and how this may impact traffic performance is a subject of future research.

Acknowledgements We thank Jan F. Ehmke, Markus Fidler, Daniel Schmidt, and Henrik Schumacher who were also members of the PLANETS project and contributed to the mentioned results as well as Jelena Fiosina for useful discussions.

References

1. Ahlbrecht, T., Dix, J., Köster, M., Kraus, P., Müller, J.P.: A scalable runtime platform for multiagent-based simulation. In: Dalpiaz, F., van Riemsdijk, M.B., Dix, J. (eds.) Engineering Multiagent Systems II. Lecture Notes in Artificial Intelligence, vol. 8758, pp. 81–102. Springer, Cham (2014)
2. Alvarez, L., Horowitz, R.: Safe platooning in automated highway systems, part i: safety regions design. Veh. Syst. Dyn. **32**, 23–55 (1999)
3. Alvarez, L., Horowitz, R.: Safe platooning in automated highway systems, part ii: velocity tracking controller. Veh. Syst. Dyn. **32**, 57–84 (1999)
4. Baskar, L., De Schutter, B., Hellendoorn, J., Papp, Z.: Traffic control and intelligent vehicle highway systems: a survey. IET Intell. Transp. Syst. **5**(1), 38–52 (2011)

5. Bazzan, A., Klügl, F.: A review on agent-based technology for traffic and transportation. Knowl. Eng. Rev. **29**, 375–403 (2014)
6. Bergenthal, T., Frommer, A., Paulerberg, D.: Wege auf Graphen. Mathe Prisma: Fachbereich C/Mathematik der Bergischen Universität Wuppertal (2004)
7. Brandt, F., Conitzer, V., Endriss, U.: Computational social choice. In: Weiss, G. (ed.) Multiagent Systems, 2nd edn., pp. 213–283. MIT Press, Cambridge (2013)
8. Burghout, W., Koutsopoulos, H.N., Andreasson, I.: A discrete-event mesoscopic traffic simulation model for hybrid traffic simulation. In: Proceedings of Intelligent Transportation Systems Conference (ITSC 2006), pp. 1102–1107. IEEE, Toronto (2006)
9. Cormen, T.H., Leiserson, C.E., Rivest, R.L., Stein, C.: Introduction to Algorithms. MIT Press, New York (2001)
10. Correa, J.R., Stier-Moses, N.E.: Wardrop equilibria. In: Cochran, J.J., Cox, L.A., Keskinocak, P., Kharoufeh, J.P., Smith, J.C. (eds.) Encyclopedia of Operations Research and Management Science. Wiley, New York (2011)
11. Desai, P., Loke, S., Desai, A., Singh, J.: Caravan: congestion avoidance and route allocation using virtual agent negotiation. Intell. Transp. Syst. **14**(3), 1197–1207 (2013)
12. Fiosina, J., Fiosins, M., Müller, J.P.: Decentralised Cooperative Agent-Based Clustering in Intelligent Traffic Clouds. Lecture Notes in Computer Science, vol. 8076, pp. 59–72. Springer, Berlin (2013)
13. Fiosins, M., Fiosina, J., Müller, J., Görmer, J.: Agent-based integrated decision making for autonomous vehicles in urban traffic. Adv. Intell. Soft Comput. **88**, 173–178 (2011)
14. Fiosins, M., Fiosina, J., Müller, J.P., Görmer, J.: Reconciling strategic and tactical decision making in agent-oriented simulation of vehicles in urban traffic. In: 4th Int. ICST Conf. on Simulation Tools and Techniques (SimuTools'2011) (2011)
15. Fiosins, M., Fiosina, J., Müller, J.P.: Change point analysis for intelligent agents in city traffic. In: Agents and Data Mining Interaction. Lecture Notes in Computer Science, vol. 7103. Springer, Berlin/Heidelberg (2012)
16. Fischer, K., Kuhn, N., Müller, J.P.: Distributed, knowledge-based, reactive scheduling in the transportation domain. In: Proceedings of the Tenth IEEE Conference on Artificial Intelligence for Applications, pp. 47–53. IEEE, San Antonio (1994)
17. Görmer, J., Müller, J.P.: Multiagent system architecture and method for group-oriented traffic coordination. In: 6th IEEE International Conference on Digital Ecosystem Technologies - Complex Environment Engineering (DEST-CEE), pp. 1–6. IEEE, Campione d'Italia (2012)
18. Görmer, J., Ehmke, J.F., Fiosins, M., Schmidt, D., Schumacher, H., Tchouankem, H.: Decision support for dynamic city traffic management using vehicular communication. In: 1st International Conference on Simulation and Modeling Methodologies, Technologies and Applications (SIMULTECH), pp. 327–332. SciTePress, Noordwijkerhout (2011)
19. Kang, J., Kim, W., Lee, J., Yi, K.: Design, implementation, and test of skid steering-based autonomous driving controller for a robotic vehicle with articulated suspension. J. Mech. Sci. Technol. **24**(3), 793–800 (2010)
20. Kephart, J., Chess, D.: The vision of autonomic computing. Computer **36**(1), 41–50 (2003)
21. Müller, J.P.: The Design of Intelligent Agents. Lecture Notes in Artificial Intelligence, vol. 1177. Springer, Heidelberg (1996)
22. Padgham, L., Nagel, K., Singh, D., Chen, Q.: Integrating BDI agents into a MATSim simulation. In: European Conference on Artificial Intelligence (ECAI 2014), pp. 681–686. IOS Press, Prague (2014)
23. Papacostas, C.S., Prevedouros, P.D.: Transportation Engineering and Planning. Pearson Education, Upper Saddle River (2001)
24. Sanderson, D., Busquets, D., Pitt, J.: A micro-meso-macro approach to intelligent transportation systems. In: IEEE Sixth International Conference on Self-adaptive and Self-organizing Systems Workshops (SASOW), pp. 71–76. IEEE, Lyon (2012)
25. Sommer, C., Eckhoff, D., German, R., Dressler, F.: A computationally inexpensive empirical model of ieee 802.11p radio shadowing in urban environments. Technical Report CS-2010-06. Universitat Erlangen-Nurnberg, Erlangen (2010)

26. Tchouankem, H., Schmidt, D., Schumacher, H.: Impact of vehicular communication performance on travel time estimation in urban areas. In: 6th International Symposium "Networks for Mobility 2012", Stuttgart (2012)
27. Tesauro, G., Chess, D.M., Walsh, W.E., Das, R., Segal, A., Whalley, I., Kephart, J.O., White, S.R.: A multi-agent systems approach to autonomic computing. In: Proceedings of the Third International Joint Conference on Autonomous Agents and Multiagent Systems - Volume 1, AAMAS '04, pp. 464–471. IEEE Computer Society, Washington (2004)
28. VanMiddlesworth, M., Dresner, K., Stone, P.: Replacing the stop sign: unmanaged intersection control for autonomous vehicles. In: AAMAS Workshop on Agents in Traffic and Transportation, pp. 94–101, Estoril. http://www.cs.utexas.edu/users/ai-lab/?ATT08-vanmiddlesworth (2008)
29. Varaiya, P.: Smart cars on smart roads: problems of control. IEEE Trans. Autom. Control **38**, 195–207 (1993)
30. Varga, L.Z.: Game theory model for autonomously self-adapting navigation. In: Kotsialos, A., Müller, J.P., Schumann, R., McCluskey, L., Rana, O., Klül, F. (eds.) Autonomic Road Transport Support Systems. Springer, Heidelberg (2015)
31. Vasirani, M.: A computational market for distributed control of urban road traffic systems. IEEE Trans. Intell. Transp. Syst. **12**, 313–321 (2011)

A Self-Optimization Traffic Model by Multilevel Formalism

Todor Stoilov and Krasimira Stoilova

Abstract This chapter illustrates the ideas of multilevel system theory in the design of a traffic control system that embodies self-optimization properties. These ideas are described in terms of multilevel optimization problems. A simulation example is provided, explaining the methodology of multilevel optimization. The example shows the optimal control evaluation of both traffic arguments: the split of the green light and the duration of the traffic light cycle by two optimization problems. The self-optimization properties are achieved by the extension of the control variables space by an increase of goal functions and a set of requirements towards the control process. The extension is achieved by the integration of optimization problems, which are interconnected by their parameters and arguments. The multilevel theory is proposed as a primary candidate to integrate different self-optimization functionalities. The application of this formalism in transportation systems will give the ground for quantitative formalization of control processes in autonomic traffic control systems.

Keywords Autonomic traffic management • Control theory • Multilevel system theory • Optimization

1 Introduction

In 2001, Paul Horn—senior vice president of IBM research—raised the idea of "autonomic computing". This idea was suggested as a potential solution of the problem of "complexity" of computer and information systems. These systems have become increasingly difficult to manage and ultimately to use [12]. The problem of complexity is met not only in computer systems but in rather wide technological domains. A particular case of a complex system is that of transportation, and problems about traffic control, transport flows and transport services are widely attacked by researches and technological developments for finding better solutions,

T. Stoilov • K. Stoilova (✉)
Institute of Information and Communication Technologies, Bulgarian Academy of Sciences, Acad. G. Bonchev str. bl.2, Sofia 1113, Bulgaria
e-mail: todor@hsi.iccs.bas.bg; k.stoilova@hsi.iccs.bas.bg

T.L. McCluskey et al. (eds.), *Autonomic Road Transport Support Systems*, Autonomic Systems, DOI 10.1007/978-3-319-25808-9_6

in order to improve the exploitation of the existing infrastructure and to provide better qualities of transport services. The idea of "autonomic" operation of the computing systems, translated to the new domain as transport systems, looks beneficial and promises potential improvements in controlling transport systems. This chapter makes an attempt to translate a particular functionality of "self-optimization", coming from the autonomic paradigm to the domain of control in a transportation system. The requirement for self-optimization is realized by the interconnection of several optimization problems. These problems are not related in a sequential order for their solution, but they influence each other by feedbacks through their local optimal solutions. Thus, the global solution of such interconnected problems gives an optimal solution, which concerns more characteristics of the transport system, which is beneficial for its operation and exploitation.

The chapter particularly addresses the term "self-optimization" and the ways for its implementation. But for the sake of completeness, here the meaning of the term "autonomic" and the content of "self-*" functionalities being considered are briefly discussed.

The paradigm for "autonomic computing" has been raised to find new solutions for automating the management of such complex systems like the computational ones. Before finding automatic solutions, the complexity of the systems has been managed mainly by improving the qualification of the humans. However, the technological development in the computing domain crosses the frontier, where only human beings must manage such systems and the necessity for automatic or "autonomic" operation of the complex systems is needed. This chapter discusses the application of the autonomic concept towards the management of an urban transport system. Particularly, how to integrate in a common optimization problem the evaluation of the splits (green lights) and the cycles of the traffic lights for an urban area will be considered. Usually these characteristics are evaluated with the help of independent optimization procedures [6]. The integration of these characteristics in a common optimization problem will increase the control space of the optimization problem, which results in better performance of the transport system in its exploitation.

To motivate our solution and for the right understanding of the particular problem about self-optimization, the inner characteristics of the term "autonomic" are briefly discussed below. Thus, a correct translation of the autonomic concept is searched for another kind of complex systems, such as the transportation ones.

In [12], the automation in the exploitation of computer and communication resources is expected to deal with the problem of complexity. The efforts have to be directed to the development of computer systems, which are "self-controlled" in the same manner as the human nervous system—it regulates a lot of independent subsystems, which control different processes in our body. Thus, the autonomic management can be implemented by developing solutions for self-control of a complex system.

The self-controlling systems will adapt themselves to existing and changeable conditions and can allocate computer resources per arriving requests for servicing. In this manner higher productivity will be realized and at the same time the complexity of the system management for the customer will be less. Thus, the autonomic properties can be achieved by developing "self-controlling" systems. Under the last term, Horn has identified eight general characteristics [12]:

1. The autonomic computing systems have to know themselves. Detailed knowledge of the state of all their components, their capacity, final states and relations to other systems is necessary in order to be controlled. The system has to know the available resources.
2. The autonomic computing systems must change their structure under certain conditions and self-configure. This prestructuring has to be automatically done by dynamical adaptation to the changing environment.
3. The autonomic computing systems have to optimize their work. They have to observe their consisting elements and the tuning working flow in order to reach the preliminary defined goals.
4. The autonomic computing systems have to be able to self-heal themselves from events which can damage some systems' elements. They have to find the problems or potential problems and to discover alternative ways for using resources or to reconstruct the system in order to keep their normal functioning.
5. The autonomic computing systems have to be able to protect themselves. They have to find and protect from different kinds of attacks, to maintain the safety and entity of the system.
6. The autonomic computing systems have to know their environment and act according to it. They have to find and generate rules on how to interact with the neighbour systems. They have to use the most appropriate resources, and, if they are not available, to negotiate with other systems in order to take them from these systems.
7. The autonomic computing systems have to act in various environments and to apply open standards. In this manner, the autonomic computing systems have to continuously make decisions.
8. The autonomic computing system has to predict the necessary optimal resources for accomplishing the current tasks. The system has to satisfy the service quality.

Later on [14, 16] simplified the autonomic functionality and decomposed it into four general aspects: self-configuration, self-optimization, self-healing and self-protection, presented in Table 1. The autonomic properties in regard to the implementation of self-control features have to start with automatic acquiring and aggregating of the information needed for decision making by computer administrators. Because the technologies for automation are improved, it is expected the autonomic computing systems make local decisions at a lower control level. This concept of control, concerning independent local decisions of subsystems, which control parts of the complex system, leads to the formal implementation of multilevel control strategies. Thus, the system administrator, as a high-level control subsystem, will rarely make decisions at low-level control and his/her functions will be allocated at a high decision-making level. The number of control levels can increase for the case of integrating many aspects and targets, which are required by the management of the complex system.

Table 1 Four general aspects of the autonomic systems [14]

Concept	Current computing	Autonomic computing
Self-configuration	Corporate data centres have multiple vendors and platforms. Installing, configuring and integrating systems are time consuming and error prone	Automated configuration of components and systems follows high-level policies. The rest of the system adjusts automatically and seamlessly
Self-optimization	Systems have hundreds of manually set, non-linear tuning parameters, and their number increases with each release	Components and systems continually seek opportunities to improve their own performance and efficiency
Self-healing	Problem determination in large, complex systems can take weeks for a team of programmers	The system automatically detects, diagnoses and repairs localized software and hardware problems
Self-protection	Detection of and recovery from attacks and cascading failures are manual	The system automatically defends against malicious attacks or cascading failures. It uses early warning to anticipate and prevent system-wide failures

Based on the above characteristics of the autonomic management, the chapter targets the development of a formal model for self-optimization, applying the hierarchical approach in the control system.

2 Implementation of Self-Optimization by Hierarchical System Management

From a formal point of view, an optimal solution x^{opt} of an optimization problem

$$\begin{aligned} &\min_x f\,(x, a) \\ &g\,(x, a) \leq 0 \end{aligned} \tag{1}$$

is defined as this value of the vector argument x^{opt}, which satisfies the conditions for the minimization of the goal function f (.) keeping feasibility of the constraints g (.)

$$\begin{aligned} &f\,(x^{opt}, a) \leq f\,(x, a)\,, \qquad \forall x \in g\,(x, a) \leq 0 \\ &g\,(x^{opt}, a) \leq 0, \end{aligned}$$

where $\boldsymbol{x}$ is a vector of n components, $x^{\mathrm{T}} = (x_1, x_2, \ldots, x_n)$; f is the goal function, which has to be minimized; and $\boldsymbol{g}$ is a set of m inequalities, which the optimal solution has to satisfy, $\mathbf{g}^{\mathbf{T}} = (g_1, g_2, \ldots, g_m)$.

In problem (1), the vector of parameters $\boldsymbol{a}$ is denoted. These parameters are assumed to be known for the definition and solution of the optimization problem

(1). This set of parameters $\boldsymbol{a}$ is not a part of the optimal solution x^{opt}. They are defined in advance and their values are not optimal for the management of the transportation system. The optimal solutions x^{opt} are optimal only in the sense of the local problem (1), which means that the values of the set of parameters $\boldsymbol{a}$ have been chosen based on other considerations and they do not have optimal values in the sense of problem (1).

The autonomic aspect for self-optimization gives opportunities to improve the system performance and efficiency (see Table 1). In a formal way, this means to incorporate additional goal functions and constraints into a new optimization problem of the form (1), to increase the space of the system characteristics $\boldsymbol{x}$, which will be evaluated in an optimal way. As a consequence, fewer system characteristics will be defined as parameters (not optimal), and more of them will be evaluated as optimal solutions for the system management. For the local problem (1), this aspect of the self-optimization recommends the subset of the parameters $\boldsymbol{a}$ to be derived also as solutions of the same optimization problem. Hence, self-optimization will reduce the amount of the parameters $\boldsymbol{a}$, which are assumed to be preliminary given as known parameters, and the argument $\boldsymbol{x}$ will increase its dimension.

Thus, for the implementation of the self-optimization aspect for the autonomic management of a complex system, a new optimization problem has to be defined, having an extended space of the problem arguments, such as $(\boldsymbol{x}^{opt}, \boldsymbol{a}^{opt})$. The extension of the problem arguments is desirable; however, methodological difficulties do not allow the definition of such a complex optimization problem. In the real control case, the optimization problems concern a part of the system characteristics, which means that $\boldsymbol{x}$ is an optimal solution only for a part of the system (the notation local optimization problem has been used for this case). The additional system characteristics, which participate in the control problem, are applied as predefined parameters, which are identified by preliminary estimation procedures. For the local problem (1), the set of these predefined parameters are denoted by $\boldsymbol{a}$ (e.g., the parameters of the fundamental diagram are not a part of the optimization solution $\boldsymbol{x}$, but they are a priori estimated, before the application of the optimization and control rules).

Returning back to the aspect of self-optimization, the autonomic management of a complex system comprises the solution of a new optimization problem, which has an extended space of problem solutions as arguments of the optimization problem. In this research, this methodological challenge is solved by the integration of existing optimization local problems. But their integration is achieved by considering the interconnections between these problems. The interconnections take part when a solution of an optimization problem plays the role of a parameter for another problem and vice versa. The formal description of such interconnections is given by the relations presented below.

Optimization problem A	Optimization problem B
$\min_x f_A(x, a)$	$\min_y f_B(y, b)$
$g_A(x, a) \leq 0$	$g_B(y, b) \leq 0$

The arguments x of problem $A\rightarrow$ define the parameters in problem B, $b = x$. The parameters in problem A, $y = a\leftarrow$, are defined as arguments y of problem B.

For the case of self-optimization, it is a benefit to integrate both optimization problems A and B. The integration will result in achieving both problem goals, formalized by the minimization of f_A and f_B, satisfying both sets of constraints g_A and g_B, and the increase of the space of optimal solutions (x^{opt}, y^{opt}). The self-optimization aspect is implemented by the extension of the area of local problem (1) in the aspect that more system characteristics are evaluated as optimal solutions and less of them are assumed as predefined parameters. The system is optimized for more goals and criteria satisfying the extended space of requirements towards the systems.

The methodological problem now is how to integrate such interconnected optimization problems and to solve this new optimization problem. For this purpose the research presented will apply an approach, described in the aspect of the hierarchical system theory. Particularly, hierarchical system management with the application of the prediction coordination principle will be used. It allows the defining and solving of hierarchically interconnected optimization problems. The formal background of the prediction coordination is illustrated for a multilevel system control, given in Fig. 1.

The low-level optimization problem optimizes the value of x, assuming y and z as constant parameters. But x influences the upper-level problem, where x is used as a predefined parameter. The value of y is optimized by the upper optimization problem, assuming x and z as constant parameters. In the same interconnected way, the high-level problem optimizes the argument z, assuming x, y as given parameters.

The overall hierarchical optimization problem gives the three arguments x, y, z as optimal solutions. It optimizes the system management to the three goal functions f_x, f_y, f_z. It satisfies the integrated requirements g_x, g_y, g_z.

Thus, applying the hierarchical system methodology, the self-optimization aspect can be implemented by the integration of several independent optimization problems, which have interconnected components.

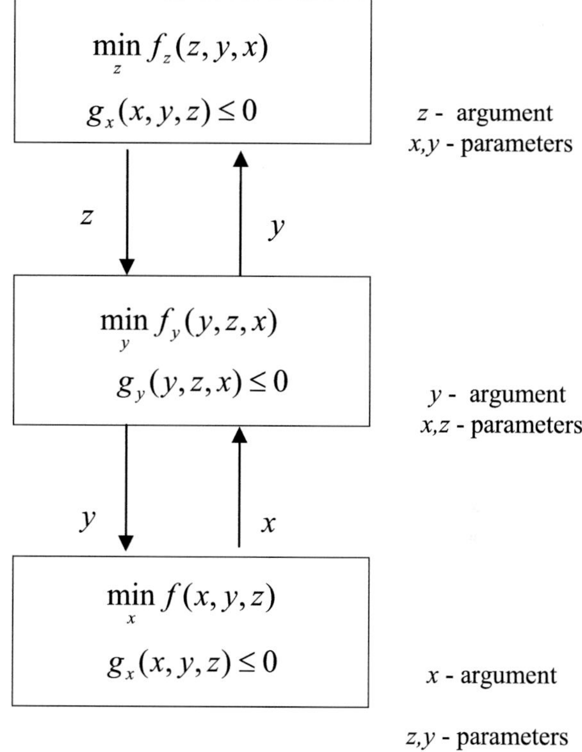

Fig. 1 Hierarchical integration

3 Autonomic Behaviour of the Transportation Systems

The self-optimization behaviour of complex systems can be translated for the case of transportation systems. This research addresses the optimization of traffic flows in urban areas. The autonomic behaviour for the control of the traffic flows is inspired mainly by the complex nature of the traffic phenomena and the necessity to solve the associated decision-making problems by road operators.

The complexity of the traffic management comes from the requirements to solve a set of management traffic tasks and to implement control solutions by technical devices and systems. The basic structure of a road control system is equipped with sets of sensors of different types, which have to make the measurements, needed for the traffic management. Additionally, the traffic processes are subjected to a number of noisy inputs, like weather conditions, subjective driver decisions and incidents which cannot be neither predicted nor controlled in the traffic management system. The traffic management is strongly influenced by the human traffic manager, who decides how to manage the traffic according to his/her competence about the traffic needs. These traffic characteristics have to be estimated and included in the optimization problems, which formalize the management process.

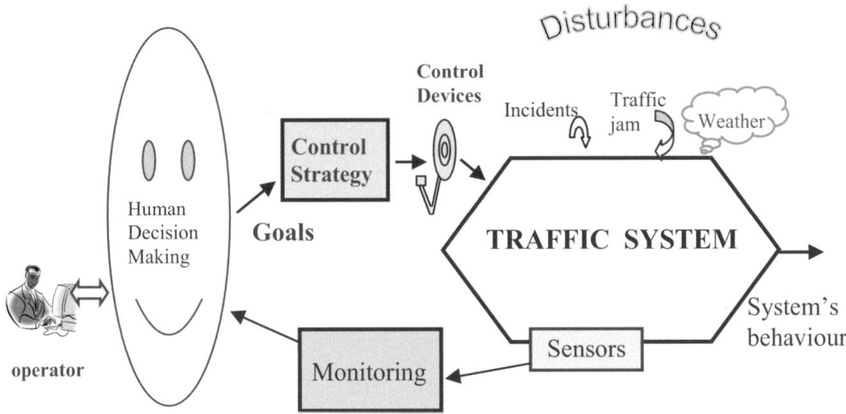

Fig. 2 Traffic control loop

To reduce the information burden towards the traffic operators and to decrease the complexity in managing the transportation system, the principle of closed loop control has to be applied (see Fig. 2). Such a system will implement automatic features for the traffic control, reduce the pressure on the traffic operators in decision making and integrate the different subsystems, solving local control tasks.

A prospective way to tackle the complexity of the problem for traffic management is to apply the concept of self-optimization behaviour of several local control subsystems and to coordinate their functionalities in a multilevel control system. Since the traffic management system is a distributed system with local subsystems, each operating with its own goal and functionality, the challenge is to provide self-optimization properties to each subsystem and to create a cohesive management policy that will integrate the subsystem optimization capabilities, taking into account the subsystem interactions. This will allow the optimal control policies and the optimal local control influences to adapt the overall traffic control accordingly. This interconnected control approach will increase the set of system characteristics to be found as solutions of several optimization problems and will decrease the set of parameters, which are used as predefined parameters.

4 Traffic Control System and Opportunities for Self-Optimization

The traffic control systems mainly address two types of infrastructures: an urban network and freeway traffic. This research addresses only the case of urban traffic. In this case, the traffic processes are generally formalized by a store and forward model of traffic flows. This model of urban network processes is accepted as a simple formal one, and it is widely used for the development of control strategies in urban traffic networks. The model is introduced by [9] and it is actively exploited in previous and recent researches [1, 5, 23, 24]. The engineering meaning of this model concerns the continuity of a flow, which allows estimating the dynamics of vehicles in the links of the urban networks. The number of the vehicles is known as queues, which the control strategies try to reduce and minimize. The model results in a set of linear dynamical discrete-type relations. This model leads to control policy which contains steps for the definition and solution of an appropriate optimization problem. The implementation of these optimal solutions is the content of the traffic management strategy. Following the algorithms for solving the traffic optimization problems, efforts have been done for simplifying the computational workload by means of performing online calculations and online control evaluations in closed and open loop control structures [3, 6, 8]. The developments try to decrease the traffic congestions, which can be additionally assessed by a performance function, addressing the level of emissions, noise, travel time, fuel economy and others. An important overview for the different classes of optimization problems is provided in [18]. The control policies are classified as fixed time control [19] and traffic response control [13]. These models lead to linear time invariant state space problems, which do not present non-linear events as congestion dynamics like spills back in the traffic network. Examples for the inclusion of additional non-linear constraints and deriving a non-linear state space problem to cope more precisely with non-linear events to the traffic model are given by [18]. Particularly, these additional constraints have the form of inequalities, where the control or the state space variables have to take extreme values between predefined limits. In general, the state variables x are assumed to be outflows of the vehicles or the queue lengths, and the control variables are the split g_i of the green light durations and/or the total sum of the green $G = \sum g_i$ for different stages of the traffic lights. The time cycle c_i for the traffic lights is assumed as a given parameter (not as a problem argument) of the optimization problem. Thus, the available control policies evaluate only the green light duration as a problem argument. Attempts to extend the control space are made in [7]. But the split and the cycle are implemented as independent control problems. The self-optimization functionality of an autonomic system will benefit by extending the control space with both these controls as solutions in a common optimization problem.

The research idea of this work is to integrate several optimization problems in a common optimization problem. Thus, the self-optimization aspect of the complex system will be implemented by simultaneous solutions of interconnected local optimization problems. The integration of the local optimization problems will give more traffic characteristics as problem arguments, instead of predefined problem parameters, which is the current case in the traffic control. Thus, the integration of the local control solutions will achieve self-optimization functionalities for the control process by extending the set of problem arguments. For the particular case of traffic light control, self-optimization functionalities can be implemented by solving a global optimization problem, giving as control solutions both the split of the green lights and the duration of the total cycle of the traffic lights. Thus, the control space for the traffic system increases from a split to a composition of splits and cycles. This will benefit the traffic behaviour in the urban network by minimizing the queues and increasing the flows in the network.

Here in the optimization problems, integration is illustrated for the case of an arterial corridor in an urban network. A global multilevel optimization problem is defined, which contains hierarchically connected two optimization local problems. The global control problem is formalized as a bi-level optimization. Its solution (problem arguments) contains two types of control variables: the split of green lights and the cycle time of the traffic lights.

In general, the traffic control system within an arterial corridor targets the maximization of the traffic flow, passing through the corridor. According to [11], the arterial control has also strong impact on the adjacent road traffic. For the sake of simplicity, the store-and-forward traffic model is used. It suits well to the dynamical changes of queues in the arterial corridor even for cases of under congested and saturated traffic conditions.

5 Bi-level and Multilevel Modelling

The multilevel theory develops decomposition approaches applied for solving both mathematical programming and dynamical variation problems. Such decomposition technique allows the original complex optimization problem to be reduced to a set of low-order optimization subproblems. Then the solution of the complex problem is found as a vector of the subproblem solutions. The local subproblems are influenced (coordinated) by the coordination problem to generate the components of the global solution of the original problem. Many practical problems are formulated in terms of multilevel optimization models [21]:

$$\begin{aligned} &\min_{x_k} f_k\left(x_1, \ldots, x_k\right) \\ &g_k\left(x_1, \ldots, x_k\right) \leq 0, \end{aligned} \tag{2a}$$

where x_{k-1} is the solution of

$$\begin{aligned} &\min_{x_{k-1}} f_{k-1}\left(x_1, \ldots, x_k\right) \\ &g_{k-1}\left(x_1, \ldots, x_k\right) \leq 0, \end{aligned} \tag{2b}$$

x_1 is the solution of problem

$$\begin{aligned} &\min_{x_1} f_1\left(x_1, \ldots, x_k\right) \\ &g_1\left(x_1, \ldots, x_k\right) \leq 0. \end{aligned} \tag{2c}$$

Problem (2a) is solved at the upper level, where the coordinator controls the variables of the solutions x_k for minimizing f_k function. Similarly, problem (2c) is solved at the first level and corresponds to the lower hierarchical level. The multilevel optimization problem (2) is hard to be solved [2, 4]. Even in the simplest version of two-level optimization, it becomes non-convex and/or non-smooth and belongs to the class of global optimization [4]. The evaluation of the global optimum for non-smooth optimization problems can be found by applying penalty functions; by satisfying the Karush–Kuhn–Tucker-type conditions, which transforms the optimization problem to a set of non-linear inequalities; and by applying pure non-differentiable optimization technique (bundle optimization algorithm). The computational workload, used for the solution of optimization problems, is also a part of the complexity of the system. But this type of complexity is not under consideration in this work.

For the traffic control, regarded as a complex system, the complexity is related not only to the system dimension (large-scale system) but also to the interconnections between the different characteristics of the system. In general, the traffic control system has to tackle problems with non-linear dynamics of the control processes, but the key issue is the control of interconnected system characteristics. The classical case of a traffic control applies the centralized manner of system management. The data acquisition has to be centralized, which is not suitable for distributed systems like the transportation ones.

To tackle the difficulties in centralized control, a multilevel hierarchical approach is under consideration for traffic management. The multilevel approach implements decomposition and coordination between the different control subsystems [15, 17, 20]. It allows each local control subsystem to operate independently, but at a higher level, a coordination unit integrates the local control influences. The formalism, applied for such a multilevel paradigm, is more general than mathematical programming. It contains hierarchically interconnected subproblems, and their coordination is done by an appropriate high-level coordination problem. Multilevel optimization allows achieving the functionalities of the control process not only as pure control but also optimization, adaptation and self-organization, as shown in Fig. 3. Thus, by hierarchically connected optimization problems, the control system can achieve functionalities belonging to the category of self-* operations. The hierarchical approach can be extended, including not only optimization problems but non-numerical procedures for solving aspects of the self-* operations. This work is

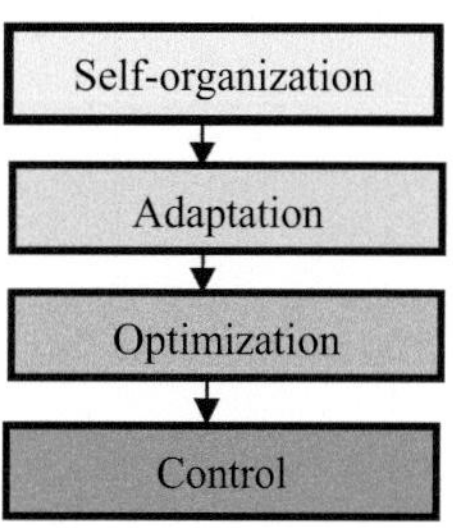

Fig. 3 Multilayer hierarchy of control

narrowed only for the case of optimization problems, which are hierarchically interconnected. Thus, the operation rules in the control system are formalized as a sequence of solutions of hierarchically ordered and interconnected optimization problems [22].

The multilevel hierarchical approach is an opportunity to cope with the different aspects of the traffic modelling, control and optimization. It is regarded as a tool for the integration of different traffic and control characteristics as a complex argument in a set of optimization problems. Such integration allows the traffic control to demonstrate autonomic properties and the control influences to be evaluated automatically, which will reduce the subjective influences of human operators.

6 Bi-level Modelling of an Arterial Road Network

The bi-level model is applied for the case of an arterial traffic infrastructure. This particular case refers to the downtown of Sofia. This traffic network frequently endures congestions not only during the rush hours of the day. Our practical interest is to find alternative solutions for the traffic control which can elaborate the current traffic behaviour.

The bi-level formulation concerns the definition of two interconnected optimization problems. The low-level optimization problem applies a simple store and forward model for the urban network, presented in Fig. 4. The goal of this problem is to minimize the queues of cars $\mathbf{x}(k)$ on each sections, and k is the discrete time step. This problem assumes that the time cycle $\boldsymbol{c}$ of the traffic lights is a predefined and fixed problem parameter. The optimization concerns the evaluation of the relative duration of the green light $\boldsymbol{u}(k)$ for the defined time cycle $\boldsymbol{c}$; $\boldsymbol{x}$, $\boldsymbol{u}$, $\boldsymbol{c}$ are vectors with corresponding dimensions.

For the case given in Fig. 4, the optimization low-level problem has an analytical description as follows:

– *First crossroad section*:

$$x_1(k+1) = x_1(k) + q_{1in}(k) - s_1 u_1(k) c_1,$$

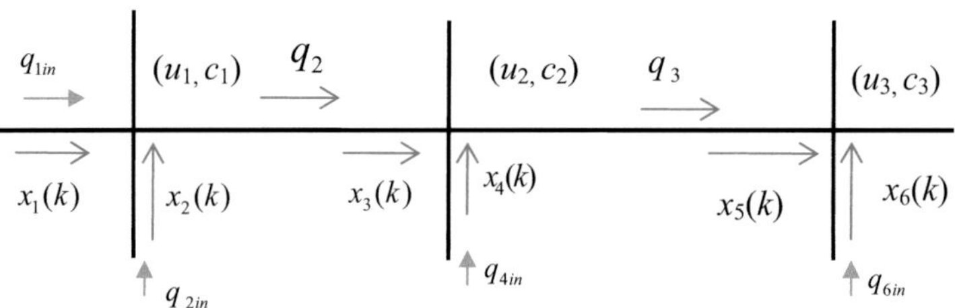

Fig. 4 Road network

where

k is the discrete time moment of the control strategy

x_1 is the queue length on the main stream [veh]

q_{1in} is the incoming flow of cars for the period of k, [veh]

c_1 is the duration of the traffic light cycle [s]

$u_1(k)$ is the split, the control influence of which has to be evaluated as a problem solution [in % or as a relative value]

s_1 is the saturation flow of the crossroad for the period k, [veh/s]

– *Vertical direction of the first crossroad section*

$$x_2\,(k+1) = x_2(k) + q_{2in}(k) - (l_1c_1 - u_1(k)c_1)\,s_1,$$

where l_1 is the relative duration of the amber light. For simplicity of the design, it is assumed that l_1 is a constant value. It is possible to assume that the duration of the amber light is not influenced by the time cycle or the component l_1c_1 is a constant value. Such an assumption will not influence the formal description of the control problem as two interconnected optimization problems.

Following the store and forward modelling, the next constraints of the optimization problem regarding the next sections are:

$$x_3\,(k+1) = x_3(k) + s_1u_1c_1 - s_2u_2c_2$$

$$x_4\,(k+1) = x_4(k) + q_{4in}(k) - (l_2c_2 - u_2c_2)\,s_2$$

$$x_5\,(k+1) = x_5(k) + s_2u_2c_2 - s_3u_3c_3$$

$$x_6\,(k+1) = x_6(k) + q_{6in}(k) - (l_3c_3 - u_3c_3)\,s_3.$$

The goal of this problem is to minimize the values of $x_i\ (k)$, $i = 1, \ldots, 6$ by changing the control influence $u_j\ (k)$, $j = 1, \ldots, 3$. In this low-level problem, the durations of the traffic light cycles $\boldsymbol{c}$ are assumed as given values.

The goal function for the minimization of the queue lengths is defined in a quadratic form

$$\min_{u_1,u_2,u_3} \left\{ f\,(x_1, ..x_6) = x^TQ_1x + u^TQ_2u \right\},$$

where $\boldsymbol{Q}_1$, $\boldsymbol{Q}_2$ are weighting matrices.

For the increase of the control space by additional arguments $\boldsymbol{c}$, a second optimization problem is defined. Its solutions are the time cycles $\boldsymbol{c}$, applying the splits $\boldsymbol{u}$ as known parameters. The second problem targets the maximization of

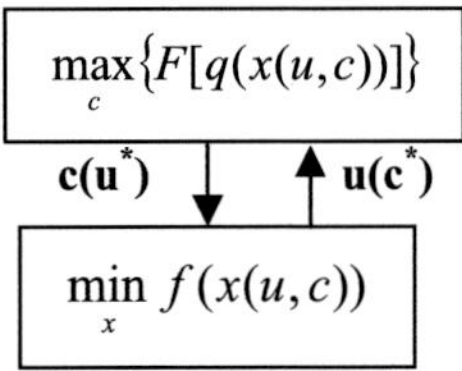

Fig. 5 Bi-level optimization problem

the traffic flow, which passes through the main arterial direction. Following the notations of Fig. 4, the problem is defined as follows:

$$\max_{c} \{q_2 (x (u, c)) + q_3 (x (u, c))\} .$$

The notation $\boldsymbol{q}(\boldsymbol{x}(\boldsymbol{u}, \boldsymbol{c}))$ means that the traffic flows are functions both of the traffic light cycles $\boldsymbol{c}$ and of the splits of the green lights $\boldsymbol{u}$. The upper optimization problem assumes that $\boldsymbol{u}$ have fixed values (not problem arguments), evaluated by the low-level optimization problem. The arguments of the upper-level optimization problem are the time cycles $\boldsymbol{c}$. Thus, the global bi-level optimization problem is defined as interconnected low-level and upper-level optimization problems (Fig. 5). The notations F and f correspond to the goal functions of the optimization problems. The solution $\boldsymbol{c}(\boldsymbol{u}^*)$ of the upper-level problem is found for given $\boldsymbol{u}^*$, and $\boldsymbol{u}(\boldsymbol{c}^*)$ is the solution of the lower problem for given $\boldsymbol{c}^*$.

The bi-level formulation can be described as a general optimization problem, where new optimization is applied in the feasible area:

$$\max_{c} \{F [q (x (u, c))]\} ,$$

where

$$u = \arg \left\{\min_{x} f (x (u, c))\right\}$$

$$x \in g(x).$$

Such form of the general optimization problem contains non-analytically described constraints. As a consequence from the non-analytical relations, it is not possible to apply methods from non-linear programming for solving this problem. That is why the current technique for solving a bi-level problem is a repetitive sequence of solving the lower- and upper-level problems by changing the corresponding values of $\boldsymbol{u}$ and $\boldsymbol{c}$.

To simplify the computations, this work applies a time step for the control $k = 1$, which means that the control variables $\boldsymbol{u}$ and $\boldsymbol{c}$ are evaluated for each control cycle. Thus, the discrete-type dynamical problems are reduced to mathematical programming ones, which simplifies the computational burden.

6.1 Upper-Level Optimization Problem

The goal function of the optimization targets the maximization of the traffic flow for the arterial direction. Following Fig. 4, this is formalized as

$$\max_{c} \{q_2 (x (u, c)) + q_3 (x (u, c))\},$$

where the durations of the cycles $\boldsymbol{c}$ are problem arguments.

In order to derive the relations between $\boldsymbol{q}$ and $\boldsymbol{c}$, the integral relation between the traffic flow and traffic density is used:

$$q = v * \rho,$$

where v is the average speed of the traffic flow and ρ is the density of the flow.

Because v depends also on ρ, $v = v(\rho)$, following a simple approximation of the fundamental diagram, presented in Fig. 6 [10], a linear relation is assumed:

$$v = v_{free} (1 - \rho/\rho_{\max}),$$

where the parameter v_{free} is the value of the freeway traffic on the left side of the fundamental diagram and $\rho_{\max}$ is the traffic density, which results in a zero speed, $v = 0$, on the right side of the fundamental diagram (Fig. 6).

Following these integral dependences, the relation between the traffic flows and the average speed takes a quadratic form:

$$q = v * \rho = v_{free} (1 - \rho/\rho_{\max}) \rho = v_{free}\rho - \rho^2 v_{free}/\rho_{\max}.$$

To introduce the number of vehicles $\boldsymbol{x}$ in $\boldsymbol{q}$, it is assumed that the density is proportional to the cars on a section with length L, or

$$\rho(x) = x/L.$$

Finally, the relation $\boldsymbol{q}(\boldsymbol{x})$ is expressed analytically in a quadratic form:

$$q(x) = \frac{v_{free}}{L} x - \frac{v_{free}}{\rho_{\max} L^2} x^2.$$

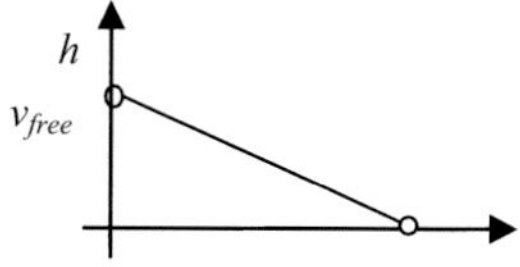

Fig. 6 Linear approximation

Returning back to the upper-level optimization problem, the last takes the analytical definition:

$$\max_{c_1,c_2,c_3} \{q_2(x_3) + q_3(x_5)\}, \tag{3}$$

where

$$q_2(x_3) = \frac{v_{free}}{L_2}x_3 - \frac{v_{free}}{\rho_{\max}L_2^2}x_3^2$$

$$q_3(x_3) = \frac{v_{free}}{L_3}x_5 - \frac{v_{free}}{\rho_{\max}L_3^2}x_5^2.$$

Using the relations of $x_3(k)$ and $x_5(k)$ from the low-level problem, the upper-level optimization problem becomes well defined analytically by the relations $q(x(u^*,c))$ where u^* are assumed as parameters.

The analytical definition of the low-level optimization problem is given below, assuming that the values of $\boldsymbol{c}$ are given parameters:

$$\min_{u_1,u_2,u_3} \{x_1^2 + x_2^2 + x_3^2 + x_4^2 + x_5^2 + x_6^2 + 10u_1^2 + 10u_2^2 + 10u_3^2\}, \tag{4}$$

where

$$x_1 + u_1s_1c_1 = x_{10} + q_{1in}$$

$$x_2 - u_1s_1c_1 = x_{20} + q_{2in} - 0.9s_1c_1$$

$$x_3 - u_1s_1c_1 + u_2s_2c_2 = x_{30}$$

$$x_4 - u_2s_2c_2 = x_{40} + q_{4in} - 0.9s_2c_2$$

$$x_4 = x_{40} + q_{4in} - s_2(0.9c_2 + u_2c_2)$$

$$x_5 - u_2s_2c_2 + u_3s_3c_3 = x_{50}$$

$$x_6 - u_3s_3c_3 = x_{60} + q_{6in} - 0.9s_3c_3.$$

The upper-level optimization problem obtains its analytical form as follows:

$$\max_{c_1,c_2,c_3} \{q_2^2 + q_3^2\} \tag{5}$$

$$q_2 = \frac{v_{free}}{L_2}(x_{30} + u_1 s_1 c_1 - u_2 s_2 c_2) + \frac{v_{free}}{\rho_{\max} L_2^2}(x_{30} + u_1 s_1 c_1 - u_2 s_2 c_2)^2$$

$$q_3 = \frac{v_{free}}{L_3}(x_{50} + u_2 s_2 c_2 - u_3 s_3 c_3) + \frac{v_{free}}{\rho_{\max} L_3^2}(x_{50} + u_2 s_2 c_2 - u_3 s_3 c_3)^2,$$

where $\boldsymbol{u}$ are given parameters.

The arguments of the bi-level optimization problem contain both the splits and the cycles ($\boldsymbol{u}$, $\boldsymbol{c}$) which increase the space of the optimal control influences of the traffic control system. This increase benefits the control process and satisfies additional requirements needed for self-optimization of the transport system.

6.2 Solution of the Bi-level Optimization Problem

In the general form, both lower- and upper-level problems are discrete ones. Assuming $k = 1$, the problem is simplified to a mathematical programming one, which benefits real-time calculation. The control process repetitively calculates the values of $\boldsymbol{u}$ and $\boldsymbol{c}$ for each control cycle. The resulting values of $\boldsymbol{x}$ are applied as initial data for the next control cycle.

Analytical Formulation of the Low-Level Problem

The low-level problem becomes a linear–quadratic optimization one in the form

$$\min_{x,u_3}\left\{[x,u]\,Q\begin{bmatrix}x\\u\end{bmatrix} + R^T\begin{bmatrix}x\\u\end{bmatrix}\right\}$$

$$A\begin{bmatrix}x\\u\end{bmatrix} = B,$$

where

$$x = \{x_i\}, \quad i = 1, 6$$

$$u = \{u_i\}, \quad i = 1, 3 \quad R = \{0\}$$

$$Q = \begin{bmatrix} 1\,0\,0\,0\,0\,0 & 0 & 0 & 0 \\ 0\,1\,0\,0\,0\,0 & 0 & 0 & 0 \\ 0\,0\,1\,0\,0\,0 & 0 & 0 & 0 \\ 0\,0\,0\,1\,0\,0 & 0 & 0 & 0 \\ 0\,0\,0\,0\,1\,0 & 0 & 0 & 0 \\ 0\,0\,0\,0\,0\,1 & 0 & 0 & 0 \\ 0\,0\,0\,0\,0\,0 & 10 & 0 & 0 \\ 0\,0\,0\,0\,0\,0 & 0 & 10 & 0 \\ 0\,0\,0\,0\,0\,0 & 0 & 0 & 10 \end{bmatrix},$$

$$A = \begin{bmatrix} 1\,0\,0\,0\,0\,0 & s_1c_1 & 0 & 0 \\ 0\,1\,0\,0\,0\,0 & -s_1c_1 & 0 & 0 \\ 0\,0\,1\,0\,0\,0 & -s_1c_1 & s_2c_2 & 0 \\ 0\,0\,0\,1\,0\,0 & 0 & -s_2c_2 & 0 \\ 0\,0\,0\,0\,1\,0 & 0 & -s_2c_2 & s_3c_3 \\ 0\,0\,0\,0\,0\,1 & 0 & 0 & -s_3c_3 \end{bmatrix},$$

$$B = \begin{bmatrix} x_{10} + q_{1in} \\ x_{20} + q_{2in} - 0.9s_1c_1 \\ x_{30} \\ x_{40} + q_{4in} - 0.9s_2c_2 \\ x_{50} \\ x_{60} + q_{6in} - 0.9s_3c_3 \end{bmatrix}.$$

The solutions $\boldsymbol{x}^*(\boldsymbol{c})$, $\boldsymbol{u}^*(\boldsymbol{c})$ depend on the values of the traffic cycles $\boldsymbol{c}$, which are assumed to be constant parameters for the low-level problem. Thus, the solutions $\boldsymbol{x}^*(\boldsymbol{c})$, $\boldsymbol{u}^*(\boldsymbol{c})$ are inexplicit functions of the traffic cycles $\boldsymbol{c}$.

Solution of the Upper-Level Problem

This problem is referred to the maximization of the traffic flow on the arterial direction and analytically it is formulated as

$$\max_{c_1,c_2,c_3} \{q_2\,(x_3\,(c_1, c_2)) + q_3\,(x_5\,(c_2, c_3))\},$$

where $q_2(x_3)$, $q_3(x_5)$ are according to (3).

The values of x_3 and x_5 are taken as solutions from the low-level optimization problem. Following problem (4), it holds

$$x_3 = x_{30} + u_1s_1c_1 - u_2s_2c_2$$

$$x_5 = x_{50} + u_2s_2c_2 - u_3s_3c_3.$$

Using these relations, the upper-level problem becomes analytically well defined in the form

$$\max_{c}\left\{\tfrac{1}{2}c^{T}q_{c}c + r_{c}^{T}c\right\}$$
$$c_{low} \le c \le c_{upper}, \tag{6}$$

where c_{low}, c_{upper} are low and upper bounded constraints for the time cycles, given by reasonable reasons.

The analytical forms of the matrices q_c and r_c for the particular case of (6) are

$$q_c = \begin{bmatrix} \frac{-v_{free}}{\rho_{\max}L_2^2} + u_1^2 s_1^2 & \frac{0.5v_{free}}{\rho_{\max}L_2^2}s_1c_1 + u_2s_2 & 0 \\ \frac{0.5v_{free}}{\rho_{\max}L_2^2}s_1c_1 + u_2s_2 & \frac{-v_{free}}{\rho_{\max}L_2^2}u_2^2s_2^2 - \frac{-v_{free}}{\rho_{\max}L_3^2}u_3^2s_3^2 & \frac{0.5v_{free}}{\rho_{\max}L_3^2}u_2s_2.u_3s_3 \\ 0 & \frac{0.5v_{free}}{\rho_{\max}L_3^2}u_2s_2.u_3s_3 & \frac{-v_{free}}{\rho_{\max}L_3^2}u_3^2s_3^2 \end{bmatrix}$$

$$r_c = \begin{bmatrix} \frac{v_{free}}{L_2}u_1s_1 - \frac{v_{free}}{\rho_{\max}L_2^2}2x_{30}.u_1s_1c_1 \\ \frac{-v_{free}}{L_2}u_2s_2 - \frac{v_{free}}{\rho_{\max}L_2^2}2x_{30}.u_2s_2 + \frac{v_{free}}{L_3}u_2s_2 - \frac{v_{free}}{\rho_{\max}L_3^2}2x_{50}.u_2s_2 \\ \frac{-v_{free}}{L_3}u_3s_3 + \frac{v_{free}}{\rho_{\max}L_3^2}2x_{50}.u_3s_3 \end{bmatrix}.$$

6.3 Simulation Results

The initial values used for the traffic network were applied after an estimation procedure for several working days of the week. For easier assessment of the bi-level control policy, it has been compared with a currently used traffic plan, which applies fixed values of the time cycles $\boldsymbol{c}$. The initial values, used for the simulation, are

$$\begin{array}{lll} x_{10} = 60\ veh; & x_{40} = 10 & s_1 = 0.44\ vehicles/s \\ x_{20} = 10 & x_{50} = 10 & s_2 = 0.28\ vehicles/s \\ x_{30} = 10 & x_{60} = 10 & s_3 = 0.28\ vehicles/s \end{array}$$

$$L_2 = L_3 = 0.8\ km;\quad v_{free} = 60\ km/h \quad \rho_{\max} = 120\ \ vehicles/km$$

$$q_{1\text{in}} = 15\ veh/min;\qquad q_{2\text{in}} = 10;\quad q_{4\text{in}} = 10;\quad q_{6\text{in}} = 10.$$

The lower and upper optimization problems have additions for non-negativity and bounded constraints for the problem arguments: $\boldsymbol{u}, \boldsymbol{c}, \boldsymbol{x}$. The numerical simulations were performed in a sequence, assuming a time step $k = 1$. The calculations were repeatedly performed, assuming constant inflows $\boldsymbol{q_{in}}$. This results in sequential

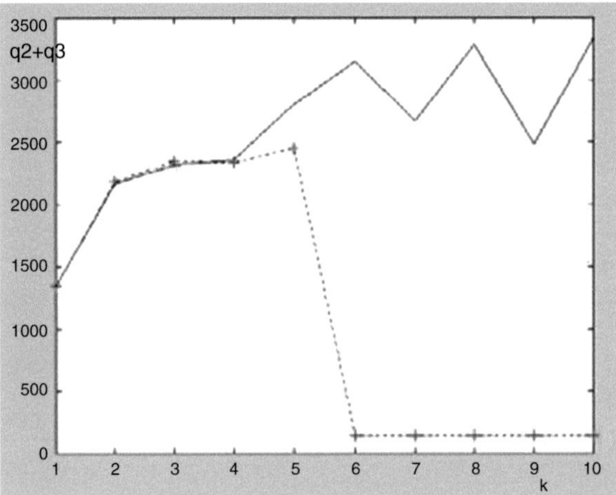

Fig. 7 Total traffic flow—upper-level control

solving of the upper- and lower-level optimization problems. A comparison has been done between the two control policies:

– The traffic light cycles $\boldsymbol{c}$ and the green durations $\boldsymbol{u}$ are evaluated by the bi-level problem.
– The traffic light cycles $\boldsymbol{c}$ are used as constants and only the relative green durations $\boldsymbol{u}$ are optimized.

The numerical evaluation of the efficiency of these two control cases was done by the value of the total traffic flow $q_2 + q_3$, which passes on the arterial direction. It was proved that the bi-level optimization leads to a bigger traffic flow in comparison with the constant values of the traffic light cycles, as seen from Fig. 7. The figures given below also prove the efficiency of inclusion of the upper-level control.

The benefit of the lower-level control is assessed by the evaluation of the total queue, integrated for the sequence of the numerical simulation steps. Figure 8 proves that the low-level control (the thick blue line) provides better control strategy in comparison with the current case (the red dashed line).

Additional illustrations are given in Figs. 9, 10, 11 and 12 for the dynamics of the relations of $x(k)$ $u(k)$ of the main stream of the traffic flow network. The benefit of the bi-level control can be seen, the thick graphics presenting the bi-level control and the dashed lines the constant time cycles $c(k)$.

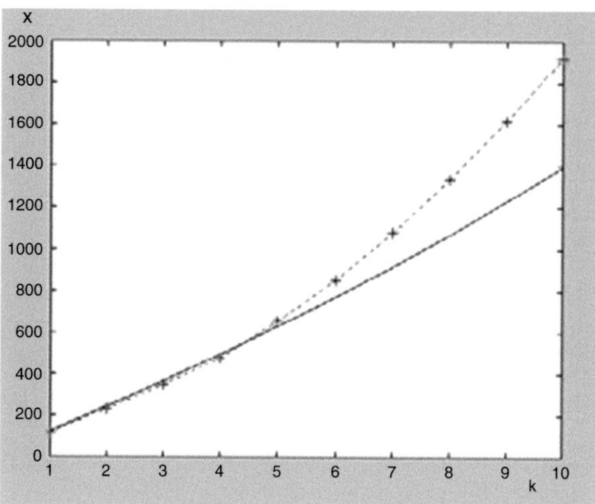

Fig. 8 Total queue lengths—low-level control

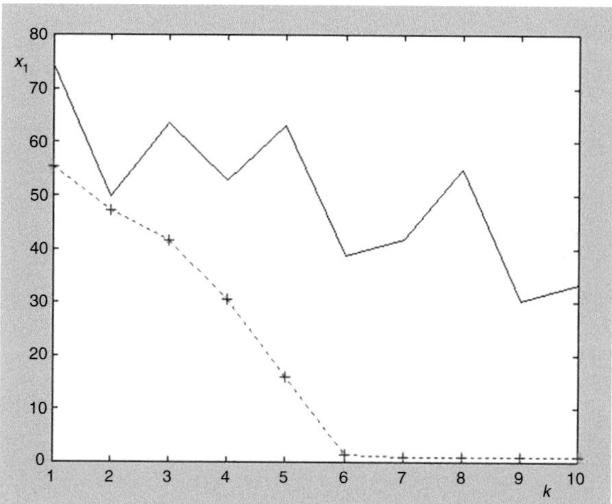

Fig. 9 Values of x_1 towards k

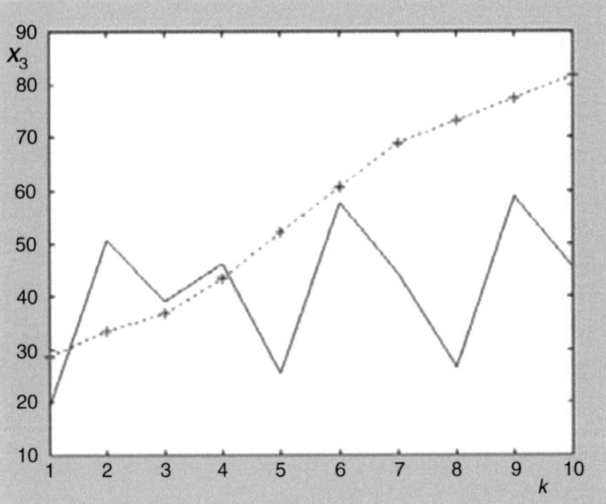

Fig. 10 Values of x_3 towards k

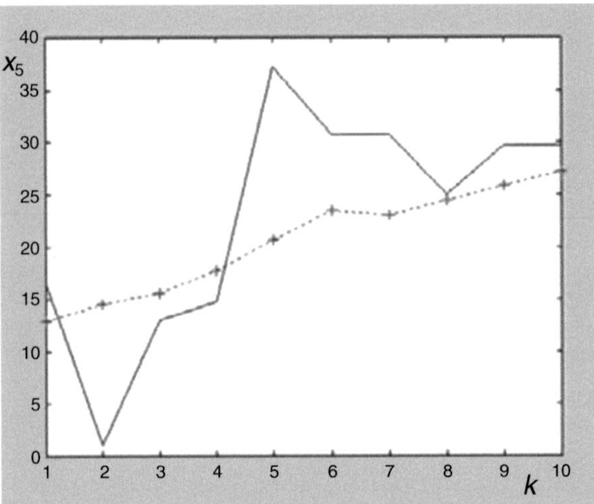

Fig. 11 Values of x_5 towards k

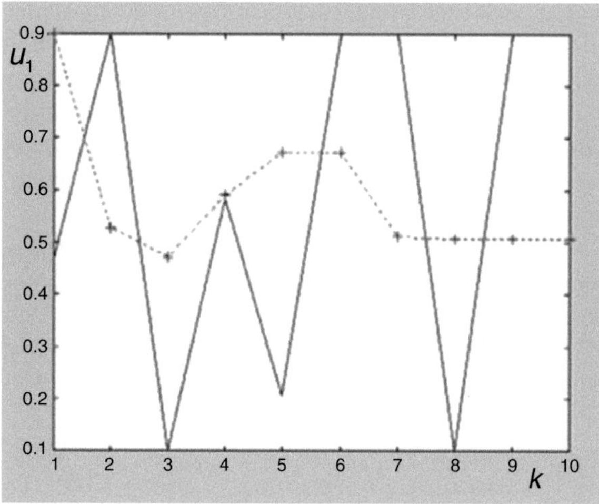

Fig. 12 u_1 changes towards k

7 Conclusions

The bi-level control provides extension of the control space by the inclusion of new system characteristics as control variables. These characteristics allow the increase of the number of optimal arguments, which the control system can implement. The increased number of optimal arguments results in the evaluation of more system parameters in an optimal way, considering more criteria for the optimization procedure and taking into consideration more sets of constraints. This extended content of the optimization components (goals, arguments, constraints) is a prerequisite to implement the self-optimization functionalities of the control system.

This work is an illustration of the way to achieve self-optimization properties. They are achieved by the increase of the space of problem solutions, which can be implemented for complex system management. The increase of the control variables space is suggested by hierarchically ordered optimization problems. The latter are interconnected, but as a result the control process satisfies more sets of constraints and more goal functions and evaluates more system characteristics as optimal solutions.

For an illustration, two control problems have been used in this work. Each problem has a limited area of optimization. But in bi-level formulation, the optimal characteristics are integrated in wider meaning, comprising the optimization features of both problems. For the current case, such integration of the optimization features is achieved by the hierarchical approach. The bi-level formalism results in an increase of the problem arguments: the splits $\boldsymbol{u}$ and the cycles $\boldsymbol{c}$. The potential drawback in this hierarchical approach could be the need for additional computational power of the local traffic light controllers. Since optimization problems have to be solved at each time cycle, such tasks are time consuming and this can delay the implementation of the control influences. Hence, the implementation of autonomic functionalities in the control of a transportation system needs not only additional computational power but fast algorithms for the solution of multilevel hierarchically connected optimization problems. The computational complexity of the multilevel optimization needs additional exploration by tools to find the real-time considerations for the traffic control.

Potential increase in the self-optimization aspect can be searched for by the inclusion into the hierarchical structure not only optimization problems but non-analytical procedures, which perform tasks of parameter identification, diagnosis and high-level decision making. Then multiplication of the self-optimization properties by the self-management properties of a complex control system can be expected.

Acknowledgement This research is partly supported by projects COST, TU1102 "Towards Autonomic Road Transport Support System" and "AComIn: Advanced Computing for Innovation" grant 316087 funded by the European Commission in FP7 Capacity (2012–2016).

References

1. Aboudolas, K., Papageorgiou, M., Kosmatopoulas, E.: Store and forward base methods for the signal control problem in large-scale congested urban road networks. Transp. Res. C Emerg. Technol. **17**, 163–174 (2009)
2. Bard, J., Plummer, J., Sourie, J.: Determining tax credits for converting non-food crops to biofuels: an application of bi-level programming. In: Multilevel Optimization: Algorithms and Applications, pp. 23–50 (1998)
3. Barisone, A., Giglio, D., Minciardi, R., Poggi, R.: A macroscopic traffic model for real time optimization of signalized urban areas. In: Proceedings of the 41st IEEE Conference on Decision and Control (Las Vegas, 2002), pp. 900–903
4. Dempe, S.: Annotated bibliography on bi-level programming and mathematical programs with equilibrium constraints. J. Optim **52**(3), 333–359 (2003)
5. De Oliveira, L., Camponogara, E.: Multiagent model predictive control of signaling split in urban traffic networks. Transp. Res. C Emerg. Technol. **18**(1), 120–139 (2010)
6. Diakaki, C., Papageorgiou, M., Aboudolas, K.: A multivariable regulator approach to traffic-responsive network – wide signal control. Control. Eng. Pract. **10**(2), 183–195 (2002)
7. Diakaki, C., Dinopoulou, V., Aboudolas, K., Papageorgiou, M., Ben-Shabat, E., Seider, E., Leibov, A.: Extensions and new applications of the traffic-responsive urban control strategy: coordinated signal control for urban networks. Transp. Res. Rec. **1856**, 202–211 (2003)
8. Dotoli, M., Fanti, M., Meloni, C.: A signal timing plan formulation for urban traffic control. Control. Eng. Pract. **14**(11), 1297–1311 (2006)
9. Gazis, D., Potts, R.: The oversaturated intersection. In: Proceedings of the Second International Symposium on Traffic Theory (London, 1963), pp. 221–237
10. Greenshields, B.D.: A study of traffic capacity. Highway Research Board Proceedings, vol. 14 (1935), pp. 448–477
11. Haj-Salem, H., Papageorgiou, M.: Ramp metering impact on urban corridor traffic: field results. Transp. Res. A **29A**(4), 303–319 (1995)
12. Horn, P. Autonomic Computing: IBM's Perspective on the State of Information Technology (2001), http://people.scs.carleton.ca/~soma/biosec/readings/autonomic_computing.pdf

13. Hunt, P., Robertson, D., Bretherton, R.: The SCOOT on-line traffic optimization technique. Traffic Eng. Control **23**(1), 190–192 (1982)
14. Kephart, J., Chess, D.: The vision of autonomic computing. IEEE Comput. **36**, 41–50 (2003)
15. Mesarovich, M., Macko, D., Takahara, Y.: Theory of Hierarchical Multilevel Systems. Academic, New York (1970)
16. Murch, R.: Autonomic Computing. IBM Press, Englewood Cliffs (2004). ISBN 0-13-144025-X
17. Nachane, D.: Optimization methods in multilevel systems: a methodology survey. Eur. J. Oper. Res. **21**, 25–38 (1984)
18. Papageorgiou, M., Diakaki, C., Dinopulou, V., Kotsialos, A., Wang, Y.: Review of road traffic optimal control strategies. Proc. IEEE **91**, 2043–2067 (2003)
19. Robertson, D.: TRANSYT method for area traffic control. Traffic Eng. Control **10**(2), 276–281 (1969)
20. Roberts, P.D., Wan, B., Lin, J.: Steady state hierarchical control of large-scale industrial processes: a survey, Preprints of IFAC/IFORS/IMACS Symposium on Large Scale Systems: Theory and Applications, vol. 1(1992), pp. 1–10
21. Stackelberg, H.: The Theory of the Market Economy. Oxford University Press, Oxford (1952)
22. Stoilov, T., Stoilova, K.: Noniterative Coordination in Multilevel Systems. Kluwer Academic Publisher, Dordrecht/Boston/London (1999). 268 p.. ISBN 0-7923-5879-1
23. Tamura, H.: Decentralized optimization for distributed lag models of discrete systems. Automatica **11**, 593–602 (1975)
24. Tettamanti, T., Varga, I., Kulcsar, B., Bokor, J.: Model predictive control in urban traffic network management. In CD ISBN: 978-1-4244-2505-1 (Ajaccio, Corsica, France, 2008), pp. 1538–1543

An Organic Computing Approach to Resilient Traffic Management

Matthias Sommer, Sven Tomforde, and Jörg Hähner

Abstract Growing cities and the increasing number of vehicles per inhabitant lead to a higher volume of traffic in urban road networks. As space is limited and the extension of existing road infrastructure is expensive, the construction of new roads is not always an option. Therefore, it is necessary to optimise the urban road network to reduce the negative effects of traffic, for example, pollution emission and fuel consumption. Urban road networks are characterised by their large number of signalised intersections. Until now, the optimisation of these signalisations is mostly done manually through traffic engineers. As urban traffic demands tend to change constantly, it is almost impossible to foresee all runtime situations at design time. Hence, an approach is needed that is able to react adaptively at runtime to optimise signalisations of intersections according to the monitored situation. The resilient traffic management system offers a decentralised approach with communicating intersections, which are able to adapt their signalisation dynamically at runtime and establish progressive signal systems (PSS) to optimise traffic flows and the number of stops per vehicle.

Keywords Traffic Managament • Resilience • Organic Computing • Forecasting

1 Introduction

Increasing mobility and rising traffic demands cause serious problems in urban road networks. As traffic is constantly changing, the approach of optimising signalisations at design time is no longer suitable. Therefore, solutions that are able to adapt the signalisation of traffic lights at runtime based on the current situation have to be considered. Approaches to reduce the negative impacts of traffic include an improved control of traffic lights and the introduction of dynamic

M. Sommer (✉) • S. Tomforde • J. Hähner
Organic Computing Group, University of Augsburg, Eichleitnerstr. 30, 86159 Augsburg, Germany
e-mail: matthias.sommer@informatik.uni-augsburg.de;
sven.tomforde@informatik.uni-augsburg.de; joerg.haehner@informatik.uni-augsburg.de
http://www.informatik.uni-augsburg.de/lehrstuehle/oc/

T.L. McCluskey et al. (eds.), *Autonomic Road Transport Support Systems*, Autonomic Systems, DOI 10.1007/978-3-319-25808-9_7

traffic guidance systems that take current conditions into account. One integrated solution is organic traffic control (OTC) [20] which provides a self-organised and self-adaptive system founding on the principles of autonomic computing (AC) [14] and organic computing (OC) [16].

Both initiatives state that the increasing complexity of technical systems is hardly manageable with traditional methods. Therefore, decentralised, self-organised and self-optimising solutions are needed in which parts of the design-time process are transferred to the system's responsibility at runtime. The resulting OC systems offer robust, adaptive and flexible solutions. In traffic control, *decentralised* means that each intersection has an additional control component that focuses on the local intersection only. Thereby, a self-configuration of the intersection's control strategy is performed by adapting the control strategy to observed changes in the traffic conditions—which results in a robust behaviour with respect to disturbances in the traffic state. In order to self-optimise this adaptation process, OTC is equipped with safety-oriented learning mechanisms. Furthermore, collaboration among neighbouring intersection controllers is needed to perform higher-level tasks like coordination (e.g. to form progressive signal systems) and route guidance.

Based on the existing OTC system, current research activities focus on turning AC and OC systems from robust into resilient systems. In particular, this means (a) to proactively change the control and routing strategies to predicted future states and (b) to become aware of the impact of the decisions taken by the intersection controllers. This chapter describes the current status of the OTC system and gives an overview of current and future work in the context of traffic-based research on OC techniques. The remainder of this chapter is organised as follows. Section 2 describes the OTC approach with its three research areas and the corresponding state of the art. Afterwards, the current research activities are outlined that focus on turning the OTC system into a resilient traffic management system, followed by an evaluation of the OTC system and a short section about resilience in OTC. The chapter concludes with a summary and an outlook.

2 Organic Traffic Control

Urban road networks are characterised by their large number of signalised intersections located close to each other. Considering the dynamic nature of urban traffic, the rising number of traffic participants and their autonomous behaviour, the traffic domain offers several characteristics that make it a suitable and interesting application domain for OC techniques. Earlier work applied the observer/controller architecture [22] to traffic signal control resulting in the OTC system. This traffic management system is able to optimise an intersection's signalisation based on the monitored flows. Furthermore, OTC-controlled intersections can communicate with neighbouring intersections and thereby establish progressive signal systems, so-called green waves. An additional route guidance system offers drivers recommendations for their route choices to prominent places in the network through variable message signs (VMSs). It was shown that OTC is able to minimise the network-wide number of stops as well as the average travel times of drivers and in consequence the fuel consumption and pollution emission [20].

2.1 Traffic-Adaptive Signalisation

As shown in Fig. 1, the OTC architecture extends existing intersection controllers, the so-called System under Observation and Control (SuOC). Here, a three-layered observer/controller architecture is used. Layer 0 passes observed raw data from detectors in the street surface or other sensors to Layer 1. This Layer 1 contains a modified learning classifier system (based on Wilson's XCS [38]), where parameter sets for the signalisation are chosen according to the observed traffic flow data. The observer collects and preprocesses the local traffic data and passes this on to the controller where the classifier system is situated. If the observed traffic pattern is unknown to the classifier system (no parameter set is known), the offline learning component on Layer 2 is activated. Based on an optimisation heuristic, Layer 2, here represented by an evolutionary algorithm [37], evolves new classifiers and analyses them in a simulation tool. Simulation-based optimisation is time-consuming and prevents reaction in real time if not coupled with the Layer 1 online component. Figure 2 depicts the structure of a classifier. The condition is defined by the situation

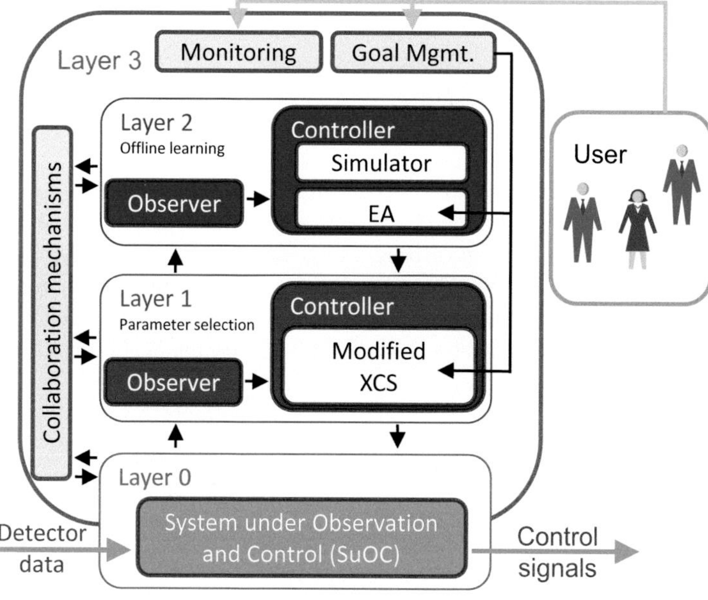

Fig. 1 A three-layered architecture for organic traffic control

ID	Situation	TLC	P	ε	F
1	[{75,90},{130,150},...]	TLC_1	43	.01	99
2	[{90,110},{25,55},...]	TLC_2	40	.03	86
	⋮				

Fig. 2 Schematic view of a classifier set

of the corresponding intersection, containing the flow of every turning of this intersection. The action part represents a parameter set for the traffic light controller (i.e. phase durations). The prediction p is an estimation of the average future payoff of the executed action. The prediction error ϵ estimates the mean absolute deviation of a classifier's prediction in comparison to the actual payoff. A classifier's fitness F is based on the inverse function of its prediction error (higher values are better). The best parameter set is then passed back to Layer 1. This distinction between Layer 2 and the underlying layers bears the advantage that new classifiers are not directly executed on the live system, which could cause the system to perform badly or even malfunction. The classifier system is now able to apply this new classifier to the underlying intersection controller. As the offline learning process is time and resource intensive, Layer 1 reacts with the execution of the best fitting parameter set, while Layer 2 searches for a new solution to the unknown situation.

2.2 *Self-organised Coordination*

Every intersection controller is able to communicate with its neighbouring intersection controllers (directly connected by a section). Thereby, they have the ability to collaborate in the establishment of progressive signal systems to allow unaffected passing of vehicles. A distributed approach for dynamic traffic light coordination allows intersection controllers to establish *distributed progressive signal systems* (DPSS) based on locally available traffic data and communication among neighbouring intersections. The DPSS is generated in a three-step process:

In the **first step**, controllers determine possible partners for forming a PSS. Therefore, each intersection determines its turnings with the strongest flows and communicates this to the respective upstream intersection to initiate a partnership (out of the set of directly connected intersection controllers). Collaborations are acknowledged according to a local matching process.

Once the partnerships are established (**second step**), the collaborating nodes negotiate a common cycle time (the time for an iteration through the signal plan). Every intersection keeps track of its own desired cycle time (DCT) and the agreed cycle time (ACT). The DCT (as a result of Layer 1's selection mechanism) represents the cycle time this node would prefer if it was not part of a DPSS, whereas ACT is the cycle time all nodes in the DPSS agreed on. The DCT is determined by the local learning classifier system which focuses on short average delays at this intersection. The first intersection in a PSS sends its DCT (here equal to ACT) to the next intersection, and this one sets the maximum of its own DCT and the received ACT as new ACT. This is repeated until the last intersection in a PSS is reached and the ACT is communicated backwards to all participants of the PSS.

In a **third step**, the intersection controllers participating in a PSS select signal plans for the signalisation with respect to the common cycle times and offsets and finally established the coordination. The DPSS approach allows for a decentralised coordination of organic intersections at runtime in response to changing traffic demands. In most cases, DPSS comes up with the best solution for the creation of a PSS, but there can be situations where the establishment of a PSS for the strongest traffic stream might not be the optimal solution. One reason can be that it can impede the coordination of several other streams which serve in some more vehicles. Therefore, the DPSS mechanism was extended by an additional hierarchical component, called regional manager (RM) [32]. The RM combines traffic flows of several intersections and uses the resulting regional model to choose the best combinations of partners for the establishment of a PSS. Therefore, it substitutes the first step of the DPSS mechanism.

2.3 Decentralised Route Recommendations

The OTC framework is equipped with techniques for dynamic route guidance (DRG) based on ideas of the distance vector routing protocol [29] (Fig. 3). This self-organising DRG mechanism actively guides vehicles to their destination. Similar

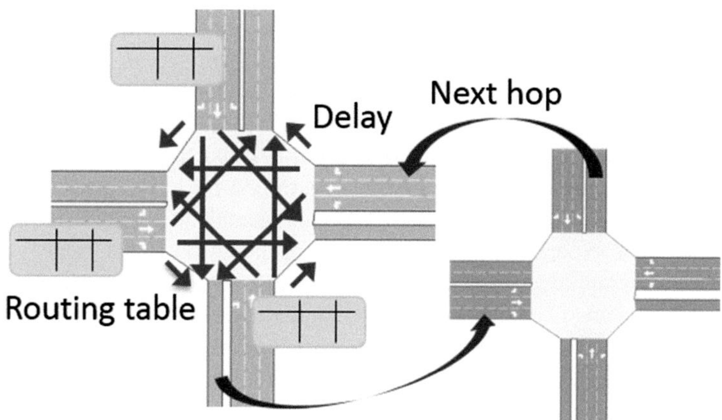

Fig. 3 Dynamic route guidance in OTC

to the establishment of PSS, the communication between intersection controllers allows for the self-organised coordination of intersections. Every intersection controller measures its turning delays (derived on the basis of flows and green times with the help of Webster's formula [33]) and estimates travel times for alternative routes under the current traffic situation to prominent goals in the network. These turning costs are distributed between intersection controllers with the help of the communication infrastructure. The implementation of the DRG functionality is done by a routing component (RC) extending each observer/controller of an intersection controller. Each RC determines the best routes (with lowest estimated travel times) to prominent destinations in the network (e.g. the main station or the city hall). These routes are updated based on the current traffic demands and signalisations. Drivers are routed on a next hop basis from intersection to intersection. The recommended next turns to prominent destinations are visualised through VMSs installed at the intersections. Simulations showed that DRG is especially helpful during disturbed traffic conditions [21]. Thereby, DRG improves the robustness of a road network (with respect to incidents) and lowers the network-wide travel times and number of stops [31].

2.4 State of the Art

The OTC system covers aspects that are also in the focus of approaches from the literature. In the following, we discuss concepts related to traffic signalisation, traffic prediction and route guidance.

Traffic signalisation has been focused by researchers due to the large environmental and economical impact of traffic. Therefore, several commercial traffic control systems have been developed, among them the widely used systems *SCOOT* (Split Cycle and Offset Optimisation Technique, [23]) and *SCATS* (Sydney Coordinated Adaptive Traffic System, [26]). These systems are powerful but also complex and hard to configure. Therefore, offline optimisation techniques such as evolutionary algorithms (EAs) have been successfully applied for the optimisation of control parameters for traffic systems: Recent examples include the work of Sun et al. who rely on multi-objective EAs for this task [28]. Their work uses NSGA-II—a multi-objective EA—to minimise delay times and the resulting number of stops for a two-phase isolated intersection controlled by a fixed-time controller. Approximation formulas by Webster [33] and Akçelik [1] served as objective functions in their experiments. A similar approach can be found in [24], where EAs are used to optimise the traffic lights of an arterial road consisting of 12 intersections in Park City, USA. The OTC system combines EAs and learning classifier systems [40]—which are evolutionary rule-based learning systems—to create an online system with optimisation capabilities resulting in faster and more appropriate responses.

Prediction of traffic conditions can follow different strategies, ranging from statistical analysis to averaged daily load curves to machine learning and to nature-inspired approaches. Statistical analysis tries to detect trends and extrapolates them, while daily load curves assume standard behaviour for classes of days (Monday to Thursday, Friday, Saturday and Sunday/bank holidays). Alternatively, the usage of online simulations for traffic prediction has been investigated [8, 9]. Based on a cellular automaton simulation model that provides "faster than real-time" simulations, the future traffic flows and travel times for the freeway network of North Rhine-Westphalia are predicted here with the simulator configured using local detector counts. The website of North Rhine-Westphalia relies on this approach to provide traffic predictions to travellers [15]. OTC also utilises the idea of using local traffic counts as input for traffic simulations that provide network-wide information. However, the focus is on (decentralised) approaches for urban areas where traffic data can be obtained from (traffic-responsive) traffic lights.

A different approach is a pheromone model for traffic congestion prediction that has been investigated in [2]. The usage of pheromones is inspired by social insects like ants that use trail pheromones as markers to detect shortest paths to food sources. Here, vehicles are regarded as social insects that deposit electronic pheromones on the road network, and the amount of pheromones released by a vehicle on a link depends on the vehicle's speed. Adjacent links propagate their pheromones to neighbours. The accumulated pheromones are used for short-term predictions of travel times.

In [10], a constant and a linear model for short-term traffic prediction is presented. In the constant model, the prediction is derived by using a rolling average over the last measured values, while in the linear model a linear curve fitting of these values is used. Based on traffic data collected by inductive loops in the inner city of Duisburg, Germany, the authors evaluate both prediction models using the mean absolute deviation and the mean relative deviation to the measured value as metrics. They conclude that the models are suitable for a short-term prediction of up to approximately 15 min and propose to combine the models with records of historic traffic data to improve predictions for a longer time horizon.

Alternatively, concepts from machine learning can be found. In [12], genetic programming is used for predicting the journey times on motorways. Several authors investigate the use of neural networks for traffic prediction: For instance, Yasdi [39] applies recurrent Jordan networks, and Ishak and Alecsandru [13] investigate an approach to optimise the performance of neural networks for short-term traffic prediction.

In conclusion, all of these approaches focus on the prediction component in detail, while the usage within a certain system is not evaluated according to a realistic setup, yet.

Route recommendations and driver guidance are used to enable traffic management capabilities and therefore turn the reactive traffic control system into a proactive one. In today's road networks, GPS-based navigation systems [42] installed in many vehicles guide drivers to their destinations. The systems rely on an internal map of the network, which is used on a variant of Dijkstra's algorithm [11] to compute the preferred route (e.g. shortest or fastest route). The route calculation is either based purely on data stored in the map, or it can incorporate up-to-date information from other sources that is transmitted via the radio's *Traffic Message Channel* (TMC) or a mobile Internet connection. TMC provides digitally coded traffic and travel information via public radio, but covers highways and major roads, only. Furthermore, the number of messages is limited to about 300 [6] (internally, a maximum of 300 messages is stored). Data provided via an Internet connection includes urban areas, but its topicality and quality depend largely on the manufacturer-specific penetration rate of a system, since the provided data is based on travel times experienced by other drivers.

In standard traffic signalisation and coordination systems as described before, the route choice of the drivers is not influenced actively by traffic authorities. Current systems rely mostly on VMSs installed at the road network. VMSs are signs next to the road that inform drivers about traffic-related events; examples include road closures, traffic jams or route recommendations. Here, the number of different messages is limited by the size of the sign. Alternatively, *floating car data* can be used to distribute traffic state information. In [35], the Internet routing protocol *BeeHive* [34] has been adapted to be suitable for road traffic. In the resulting *BeeJamA* protocol, vehicles are routed from intersection to intersection on a next hop basis. The routing is performed by regionally responsible navigation servers that store routing tables for their area and routes to other areas. The routing tables are updated based on information provided by vehicles that are assumed to continuously transmit their position, speed and destination to the responsible navigation server. Like *BeeJamA*, the DRG mechanism of OTC relies on routing protocols originally developed for the Internet. However, the difference is in the acquisition of data on the current network state. While *BeeJamA* is based on car-to-infrastructure communication, the flow and signalisation data available at the network's signalised intersections are used in OTC. A related concept without centralised components is the *autonomous* system [36].

Further research investigated possibilities to include route guidance mechanisms into urban traffic control systems. One major example is the European COSMOS project [5], which developed incident management and rerouting strategies for various adaptive network control systems (e.g. MOTION [7]). The approach relies on a centralised simulation-based optimisation for the complete network based on traffic data available in the control system.

3 Resilient Traffic Management

The main purpose of adding adaptation and self-optimisation capabilities to OC systems in general and traffic control in particular is to allow for robust and flexible solutions. In this context, *robust* means that the system is able to deal with a certain set of disturbances by keeping the system performance within a predefined corridor or at least guaranteeing to guide it back within a certain period of time [25]. In contrast, *flexible* means that the system automatically adapts to changing goals provided by the users at runtime [4]. We define the term *resilient* as "proactive robustness" [41], which means that the control mechanism encapsulating the organic and autonomic capabilities of the system does not only react to detected disturbances and dissatisfying system performance but tries to foresee upcoming problems (e.g. automatic incident forecasting, oversaturated situations and shortages). In this case, the control mechanism will guide the system's behaviour in such a way that these disturbances and shortages will be avoided.

Achieving resilience in traffic control means that the intersection controllers have to increase their decision focus towards a longer time horizon and become aware of their decisions' impact. For the pure control tasks, this means to make predictions of the observed traffic flow values per turning that serve as input for the self-adaptation mechanism defined by the organic architecture (cf. Fig. 1). These local predictions can be improved by collaboration between neighbouring intersection controllers since neighbours will observe possible changes earlier in most cases. In order to further transform the reactive traffic *control* system (reactive in terms of responses to observed changes in the traffic situations) into a proactive traffic *management* system, further steps are necessary. Active management of traffic refers to the possibility of influencing traffic streams (or the individual drivers) in order to achieve a certain behaviour of traffic. The most promising example is infrastructure-based traffic guidance, either following a VMS or a TMC approach. Here, traffic streams can be rerouted to avoid jammed regions or parts of the networks with capacity shortages. Additionally, such a route guidance mechanism can act in advance to incidents (i.e. before the impact in terms of backlogs and increased waiting times becomes visible), if these incidents can be detected automatically. The following part of this section describes our current and future research activities in this direction:

1. **Prediction of traffic states:** The first step towards a resilient and anticipatory traffic management system is the self-organised generation of predictions for local traffic states at intersections. Here, historical and current traffic flows of turning movements are used to estimate the most probable traffic state at a certain future point in time. In our scenario, we are interested in the next traffic state that will be observed when performing Layer 1 adaptation loop again. In terms of OTC, Layer 1 operates with respect to the actual cycle time[1] defined by the currently active traffic light controller. Hence, this *next* point in time is typically three times the duration of the current cycle time (typically about $3 \times 90\,\mathrm{s} = 270\,\mathrm{s}$ on average). Using this 270 s interval is a trade-off: A longer cycle time leads to a slower learning process, whereas a too low cycle time prevents learning. Figure 4 describes the embedding of the prediction component into the architectural design of Layer 1's observer component. The generated prediction values can be used to proactively adapt the signalisation and to generate necessary knowledge in advance (rule generation by Layer 2).

[1]For instance, the cycle time is 2 min maximum in England; see http://www.bbc.com/news/magazine-23869955.

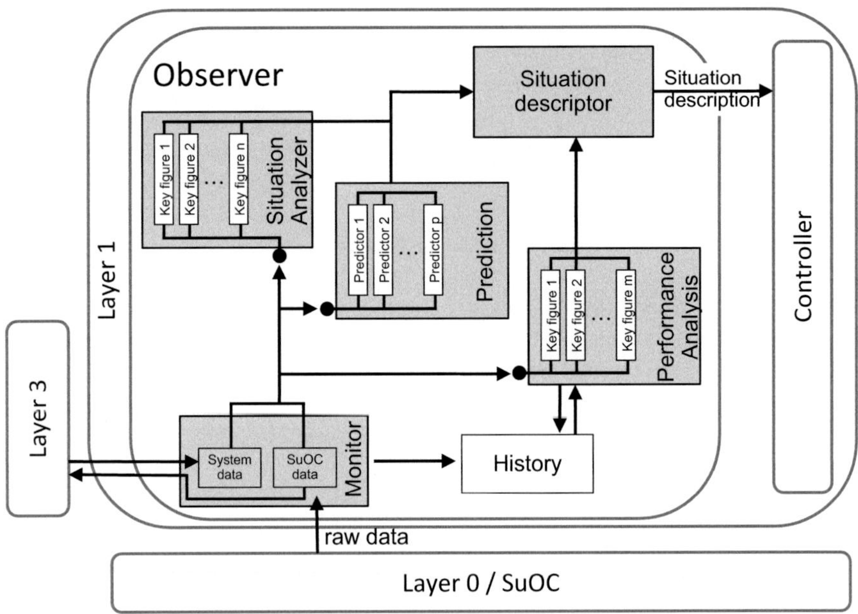

Fig. 4 Detailed view of the observer

In previous work, we investigated which existing prediction techniques show the best performance in realistic traffic networks based on real traffic data [27].[2] In order to be able to deal with reoccurring unanticipated events, we are currently investigating possibilities to combine domain knowledge in terms of regular, static daily load curves and automated learning algorithms. First, an unanticipated event is recognised and a new pattern describing the event is learned. The second time the same or a similar event occurs, it can be recognised and predicted by the system. The goal is to learn the set of possible curves and derive predictions by choosing the best-fitting curve.

2. **Reliable collaboration to improve the prediction horizon:** The OC and AC initiatives postulate to mitigate the complexity of the control problem by distributing it among a set of collaborative nodes. Similarly, we investigate possibilities to take collaborations into account when determining the particular prediction values. With a high probability, neighbouring intersection controllers will observe changes in traffic conditions earlier since the particular vehicles have to travel the connecting road segment until changing the situation at the considered intersection.

[2]We used, for example, traffic data from a census in 2009 provided by local authorities in Hamburg, Germany.

3. **Scalable and resilient route guidance:** Current route guidance mechanisms in OTC work on the principle of proposing route choices to drivers by dynamic message signs in front of intersections. This can result in frequently changing routes, which might affect the acceptability of drivers. In addition, rerouting takes only the current traffic state into account; hence, the impact of providing route recommendations to drivers is not considered. Therefore, we want to generate route recommendations on the basis of predicted values and to introduce regional components responsible for urban districts that aggregate the local decisions. Based on this aggregation, an analysis of the decisions' impact becomes possible by, for example, using flow models. Thereby, we can automatically detect possible capacity shortages in advance and influence the individual intersection controllers to modify their behaviour towards a system-wide optimum, while still operating in a decentralised and scalable manner.
4. **Automated incident detection:** Fully resilient traffic management must also cover the possibility to react on further disturbances besides the "normal" capacity-related problems. Therefore, anomalies in terms of incidents have to be considered. This consists of two basic parts: (a) the knowledge about occurred incidents into the traffic management system's decision process and (b) detecting these incidents automatically. In literature, incidents are defined as "events which cause a need for assistance of involved drivers and/or warning of oncoming traffic in order to maintain safe driving conditions" [30], meaning it is not only restricted to car accidents. In contrast, road blockades, unscheduled maintenance and construction activities or breakdowns and spilled loads are also considered [17]. Current concepts from the literature try to detect such events with different traffic-pattern-based algorithms but focus on highways only (e.g. the *California algorithm* [18, 19]). The challenge is to transfer these highway-based concepts to urban areas where, for example, traffic patterns caused by red traffic lights are similar to those caused by incidents.
5. **Generalisation of investigated OC techniques:** We assume that the concepts and mechanisms developed for the traffic control problem can be transferred to other domains. In previous work, we generalised the architectural framework of the OTC system; applied it to problems in data communication, production and mainframe systems; and investigated for which class of OC systems the approach is applicable (see [31]). We aim at developing a similar general approach for this class of systems with a standardised way to collaboratively and reliably predict future states of observed system variables.

4 Evaluation

In a simulation study, the potential benefits of the OTC system compared to real-world data were evaluated. The simulation was done with the "AIMSUN NG 6.1 Professional" traffic simulation toolkit [3]. AIMSUN is widely used in the field of professional traffic engineering. It was used for the simulation of the daily traffic

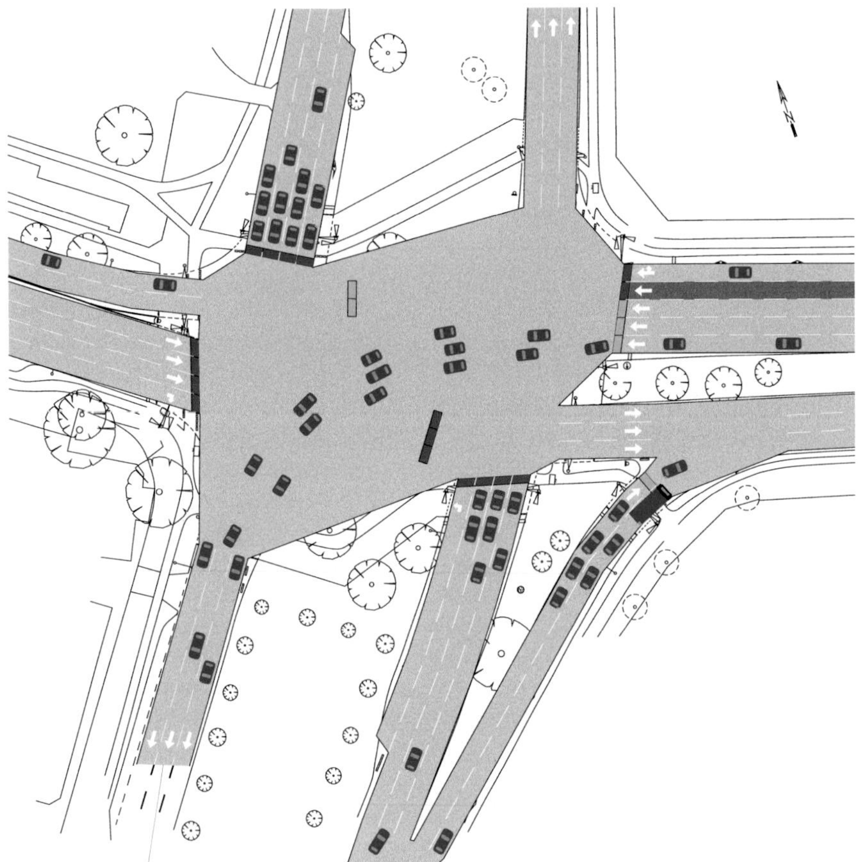

Fig. 5 AIMSUN model of an intersection at Hamburg, Germany

patterns as well as the optimisation runs of Layer 2. The evaluation results depict the average of several simulation runs. In previous work, simulation models for the stadium area in Hannover, Germany (with 13 intersections, Fig. 6), and an intersection in Hamburg, Germany (Fig. 5), as part of a broader network with 11 intersections were developed. Figure 6 depicts an abstracted view of the model of the stadium area in Hannover. The modelled intersections are marked with circles and the modelled roads connecting them with lines. Both models reflect the real topology and are configured based on census data and the actual traffic signalisation (in cooperation with the local authorities). Therefore, it is possible to compare the performance of the OTC system directly to the real-world system.

Additionally, some artificial networks for arterial roads, Manhattan-type networks and regional variants (from 5 to 30 intersections) were developed. These models can be used to evaluate the benefits of the different features of the OTC system in comparison to the expert-designed traffic signalisations with fixed-time

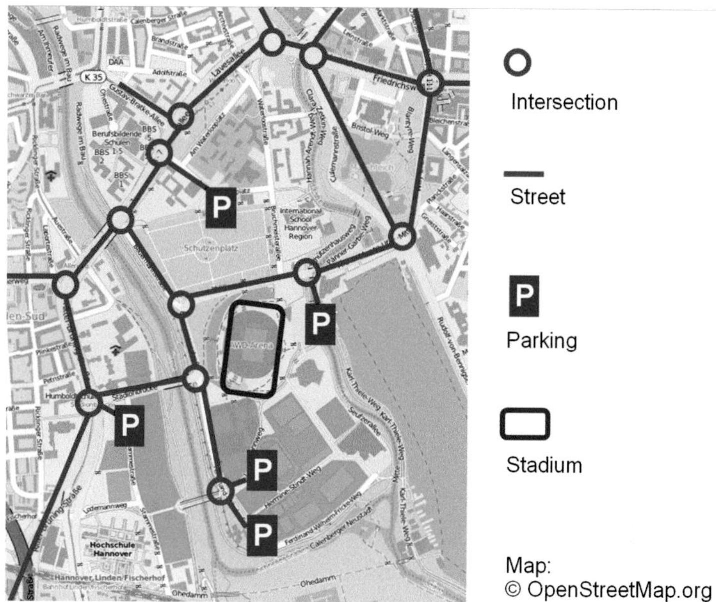

Fig. 6 Map of the stadium area at Hannover, Germany

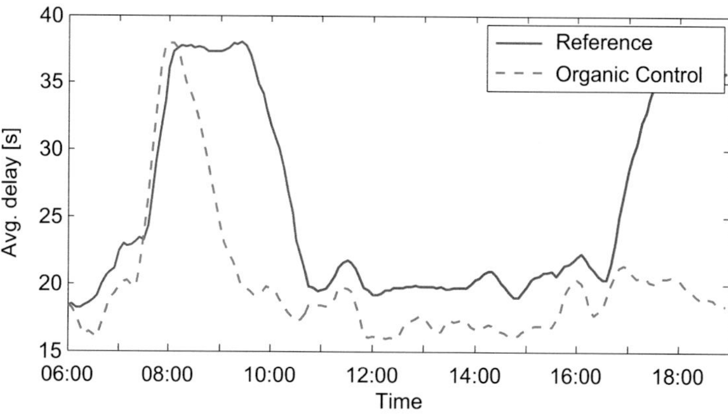

Fig. 7 Vehicular delays

intersection controllers. To indicate the performance of the OTC system, some experimental results from [20] are presented. Figure 7 depicts the average vehicular delays for the time-dependent and the OTC approach for the modelled intersection at Hamburg (cf. the model of the intersection in Fig. 5). Exemplary evaluation results show that the OTC approach leads to a reduction in the average delay compared to the time-dependent switching of signal plans used in the field (labelled *reference*). The depicted delays are averaged over five repeated simulation runs. The obtained

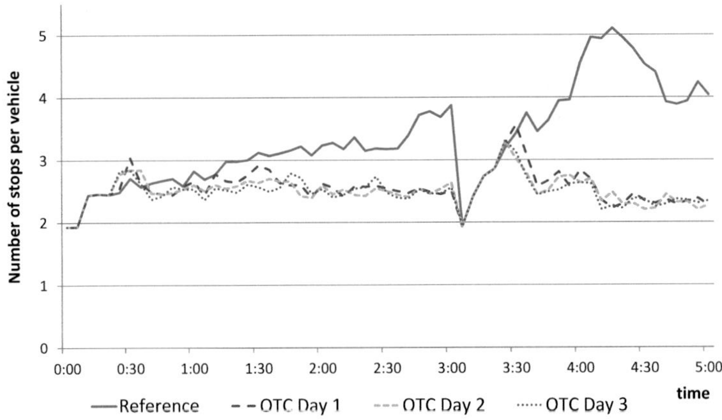

Fig. 8 Averaged number of stops per vehicle in the simulation of the stadium area located at Hannover, Germany

results indicate that an online optimisation (i.e. performing the OTC control loop) outperforms the time-dependent schedule for most of the simulation period. The vehicular delays are reduced by 22.5 % compared to the reference solution used in the field.

Besides the optimisation for 1 day, the OTC system has the ability to improve its performance during runtime. Figure 8 depicts the corresponding results considering the network-wide scenario in Hannover (cf. map in Fig. 6). The drop in the graph is a result of the soccer match which lasted for ca. 90 min. The simulation of the reference solution results in 3.33 stops per vehicle on average, which is reduced by 23.3 % at day 1, to 2.56 stops due to the OTC control. The results are even better for day 2 (reduction of 24.5 % to 2.51 stops) and day 3 (reduction of 25.0 % to 2.49 stops).

Closely connected to delays and stops is the average fuel consumption. Figure 9 depicts the achieved results. A significant reduction can be observed compared to the reference solution (21.4 $\frac{l}{100\,\text{km}}$). During day 1, the OTC system reduced the fuel consumption by 14 % to 18.4$\frac{l}{100\,\text{km}}$, while days 2 (19.6 % to 17.2$\frac{l}{100\,\text{km}}$) and 3 (19.9 % to 17.1$\frac{l}{100\,\text{km}}$) resulted in an even better performance.

Figure 10 compares the network-wide number of stops obtained for coordinated (DPSS) and uncoordinated (reference, without DPSS) intersections at Hannover. The results are averaged over five simulation runs and indicate the benefit of the decentralised coordination as stops are reduced throughout the whole simulation period. The reduction is about 8 % compared to an uncoordinated signalisation.

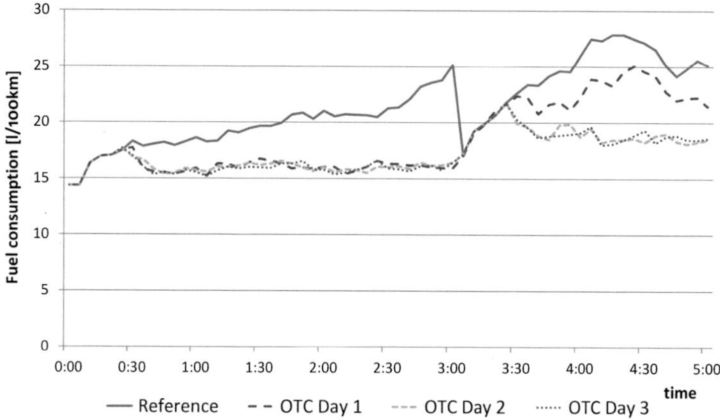

Fig. 9 Averaged fuel consumption per 100 km in the simulation of the stadium area located at Hannover, Germany (lower values are better)

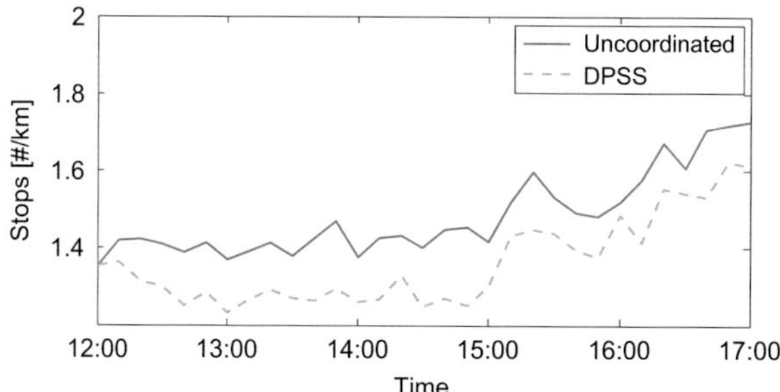

Fig. 10 Network-wide stops

5 OTC and Resilience

OTC works on the basis of self-organisation, adapting route recommendations and traffic light signalisations according to the current traffic conditions within the road network. The performance of traffic-responsive control strategies depends on the early detection of changes in the traffic patterns. Therefore, OTC was extended by a prediction component which is able to forecast traffic data for the (near) future. These forecasts are determined by several prediction techniques (e.g. daily load curves, smoothing algorithms and neural networks) and are then weighted according to the learned accuracy of the respective prediction technique and accumulated into one comprehensive forecast. Based on these predictions, the adaptation of signalisations, the routing decisions and the coordination patterns such as the progressive signal systems can be adapted in advance. Current work showed that the

Table 1 Comparison of OTC with and without forecasts (lower is better)

Parameter	Without forecast	With forecast	Units
Delay time	159.28	157.72	s/km
Density	21.53	21.14	veh/km
Mean queue	47.12	45.58	veh
Speed	24.01	23.81	km/h

performance of OTC can benefit from the use of forecasts (see Table 1).[3] Further integration of these aspects in OTC is subject to current work.

6 Conclusion

This chapter described the current status of the OTC system. Furthermore, it outlined current research activities to turn the existing traffic-adaptive control system into a resilient traffic management system. OTC-based intersection controllers are able to optimise their signal plans on a decentralised basis. By communicating with their neighbours, intersection controllers have the ability to establish progressive signal systems and give route recommendations to drivers through VMSs. Experimental results showed that the online optimisation done by the OTC system is able to decrease the network-wide number of stops (up to 25 %) as well as the vehicular delays (up to 22.5 %). Current and future work focus on the integration of predictive capabilities to enhance existing features of the OTC system towards a proactive traffic management system. Furthermore, comparisons to other self-adapting traffic management systems like SCOOT and SCATS are planned.

References

1. Akçelik, R.: Traffic signals: capacity and timing analysis. Technical Report 123, Australian Road Research Board (1981)
2. Ando, Y., et al.: Pheromone model: application to traffic congestion prediction. In: Engineering Self-Organising Systems – Third International Workshop (ESOA 2005). Lecture Notes in Artificial Intelligence, vol. 3910, pp. 182–196. Springer, Berlin (2006)
3. Barceló, J.: GETRAM/AIMSUN: a software environment for microscopic traffic analysis. In: Proceedings of the Workshop on Next Generation Models for Traffic Analysis, Monitoring and Management, held in Tucson (USA) in Sept 2001 (2001)
4. Becker, C., Hähner, J., Tomforde, S.: Flexibility in organic systems - remarks on mechanisms for adapting system goals at runtime. In: Proceedings of ICINCO 2012, pp. 287–292 (2012)

[3] The results are based on simulations of an intersection as part of a broader network from Hamburg, Germany (Fig. 5) which reflects the real topology and is configured based on census data and the actual traffic signalisation.

5. Bielefeldt, C., Condie, H.: COSMOS – Congestion Management Strategies and Methods in Urban Sites. Final report, The MVA Consultancy (1999)
6. Burton, P., Eveleigh, H., Faber, O.: The UK demonstration of TMC – the final results and update on progress. In: Proceedings of 11th Conference on Road Transport Information and Control, pp. 9–14. IEEE, New York (2002)
7. Busch, F., Kruse, G.: MOTION for SITRAFFIC – a modern approach to urban traffic control. In: Proceedings of IEEE Conference on Intelligent Transportation Systems, pp. 61–64. IEEE, New York (2001)
8. Chrobok, R., Wahle, J., Schreckenberg, M.: Traffic forecast using simulations of large scale networks. In: Proceedings of IEEE Intelligent Transportation Systems Conference, pp. 434–439. IEEE, New York (2001)
9. Chrobok, R., Pottmeier, A., Marinosson, S., Schreckenberg, M.: On-line simulation and traffic forecast: applications and results. In: Internet and Multimedia Systems and Applications (IMSA 2002), pp. 113–118 (2002)
10. Chrobok, R., Kaumann, O., Wahle, J., Schreckenberg, M.: Different methods of traffic forecast based on real data. Eur. J. Oper. Res. **155**(3), 558–568 (2004)
11. Dijkstra, E.W.: Cooperating sequential processes. Technical Report EWD-123, Technische Universiteit Eindhoven (1965)
12. Howard, D., Roberts, S.C.: The prediction of journey times on motorways using genetic programming. In: Applications of Evolutionary Computing – EvoWorkshops 2002. Lecture Notes in Computer Science, vol. 2279, pp. 141–153. Springer, Berlin (2002)
13. Ishak, S., Alecsandru, C.: Optimizing traffic prediction performance of neural networks under various topological, input, and traffic condition settings. J. Transp. Eng. **130**(4), 452–465 (2004)
14. Kephart, J.O., Chess, D.M.: The vision of autonomic computing. IEEE Comput. **36**(1), 41–50 (2003)
15. Mazur, F., Chrobok, R., Hafstein, S.F., Pottmeier, A., Schreckenberg, M.: Future of traffic information – online-simulation of a large scale freeway network. In: Proceedings of IADIS, pp. 665–672 (2004)
16. Müller-Schloer, C.: Organic Computing: on the feasibility of controlled emergence. In: CODES and ISSS 2004 Proceedings, 8–10 Sept 2004, pp. 2–5. ACM Press, New York (2004)
17. Parkanyi, E., Xie, C.: A complete review of incident detection algorithms and their deployment: what works and what doesn't. Technical Report NETCR 37, New England Transp. Consortium, Storrs (2005)
18. Payne, H.J., Knobel, H.C.: Development and testing of incident detection algorithm. FHWA Report FHWA RD 76 21, vol. 3, Federal Highway Administration, US Department of Transportation, Washington DC (1976)
19. Payne, H.J., Tignor, S.C.: Freeway incident-detection algorithms based on decision trees with states. TRB Research Record 682, Transportation Research Board, Washington DC (1978)
20. Prothmann, H., Tomforde, S., Branke, J., Hähner, J., Müller-Schloer, C., Schmeck, H.: Organic traffic control. In: Organic Computing – A Paradigm Shift for Complex Systems, chapter 5.1, pp. 431–446. Birkhäuser, Basel (2011)
21. Prothmann, H., Schmeck, H., Tomforde, S., Lyda, J., Hähner, J., Müller-Schloer, C., Branke, J.: Decentralised route guidance in organic traffic control. In: Proceedings of SASO'11, pp. 219–220. IEEE, New York (2011)
22. Richter, U., Mnif, M., Branke, J., Müller-Schloer, C., Schmeck, H.: Towards a generic observer/controller architecture for organic computing. In: Beiträge zur Jahrestagung der Gesellschaft für Informatik 2006, pp. 112–119 (2006)
23. Robertson, D.I., Bretherton, R.D.: Optimizing networks of traffic signals in real time – the SCOOT method. IEEE Trans. Veh. Technol. **40**(1), 11–15 (1991)
24. Schmeck, H., Müller-Schloer, C.: A characterization of key properties of environment-mediated multiagent systems. In: Proceedings of EEMMAS 2007, pp. 17–38. Springer, Berlin/Heidelberg (2007)

25. Schmeck, H., Müller-Schloer, C., Çakar, E., Mnif, M., Richter, U.: Adaptivity and self-organization in organic computing systems. ACM Trans. Auton. Adapt. Syst. **5**(3), 1–32 (2010)
26. Sims, A.G., Dobinson, K.W.: The Sydney coordinated adaptive traffic (SCAT) system – philosophy and benefits. IEEE Trans. Veh. Technol. **29**(2), 130–137 (1980)
27. Sommer, M., Tomforde, S., Hähner, J.: Using a neural network for forecasting in an organic traffic control management system. In: Proceedings of ICAC '13, International Workshop on Embedded Self-Organizing Systems (2013)
28. Sun, D., Benekohal, R.F., Waller, S.T.: Multiobjective traffic signal timing optimization using non-dominated sorting genetic algorithm. In: Proceedings of the IEEE Intelligent Vehicles Symposium, pp. 198–203 (2003)
29. Tanenbaum, A.: Computer Networks. Prentice Hall Professional Technical Reference, 4th edn. Prentice Hall, Upper Saddle River (2002)
30. Thancanamootoo, B., Bell, M.G.H.: Automatic detection of traffic incidents on a signal-controlled road network. Technical Report H7UNDT RR076, University of Newcastle upon Tyne, Department of Civil Engineering (1988)
31. Tomforde, S.: Runtime Adaptation of Technical Systems. Südwestdeutscher Verlag für Hochschulschriften (2012)
32. Tomforde, S., Prothmann, H., Branke, J., Hähner, J., Müller-Schloer, C., Schmeck, H.: Possibilities and limitations of decentralised traffic control systems. In: International Joint Conference on Neural Networks (IJCNN), pp. 1–9 (2010)
33. Webster, F.V.: Traffic signal settings. Road Research Technical Paper No. 39, Road Research Laboratory, published by HMSO (1958)
34. Wedde, H., Farooq, M.: Beehive: routing algorithms inspired by honey bee behavior. Künstl. Intell. **19**(4), 18–24 (2005)
35. Wedde, H., et al.: Highly dynamic and adaptive traffic congestion avoidance in real-time inspired by honey bee behavior. In: Mobilität und Echtzeit – Fachtagung der GI-Fachgruppe Echtzeitsysteme, pp. 21–31. Springer, Berlin (2007)
36. Wegener, A., Hellbrück, H., Fischer, S., Hendriks, B., Schmidt, C., Fekete, S.: Designing a decentralized traffic information system – autonomos. In: Kommunikation in Verteilten Systemen (KiVS), Informatik aktuell, pp. 309–315. Springer, Berlin/Heidelberg (2009)
37. Wilson, S.W.: The genetic algorithm and simulated evolution. In: ALIFE, pp. 157–166 (1987)
38. Wilson, S.W.: Classifier fitness based on accuracy. Evol. Comput. **3**(2), 149–175 (1995)
39. Yasdi, R.: Prediction of road traffic using a neural network approach. Neural Comput. Appl. **8**(2), 135–142 (1999)
40. Lanzi, P.L.: Learning Classifier Systems, From Foundations to Applications. Lecture Notes in Computer Science, vol. 1813. Springer, Berlin (2000)
41. Hollnagel, E., Woods, D.D., Leveson, N.: Resilience Engineering: Concepts and Precepts. Ashgate Pub Co., Aldershot (2006)
42. Kaplan, E.: Understanding GPS: Principles and Applications. Artech House Inc., Norwood (2006)

Autonomic Systems Design for ITS Applications: Modelling and Route Guidance

Apostolos Kotsialos and Adam Poole

Abstract This chapter discusses a systems design approach inspired from the autonomic nervous system for intelligent transportation system (ITS) applications. This is done not with reference to the employed computing system but with reference to the requirements of traffic engineering applications. It is argued that the design and development of autonomic traffic management systems must identify the control loop that needs to be endowed with autonomic properties and subsequently use this framework for defining a desired set of self-$*$ properties. A macroscopic network modelling application is considered for showing how autonomic system design can be used for defining and obtaining self-$*$ properties, with particular emphasis given on self-optimisation. The interpretation of policies followed by network operators regarding route guidance is also discussed from the perspective of autonomic ITS.

Keywords Autonomic traffic systems • Macroscopic traffic flow model validatin • Route guidance

1 Introduction

The autonomic computing manifesto [1] outlined a vision for the development of highly complex computational systems that are able to hide the complexity of managing them from the system administrator, allowing for high-level policy to change and modify the whole system automatically. This is achieved by designing and embedding a number of self-$*$ properties to the system, such as self-configuration, self-healing, self-protection, self-optimisation and self-management.

Autonomic computing's biological inspiration comes from the nervous system and more specifically from the autonomic nervous system (ANS), a subsystem of the peripheral nervous system. The ANS acts below the level of consciousness controlling visceral functions. These systems operate within a wide range of

A. Kotsialos (✉) • A. Poole
School of Engineering and Computing Science, Durham University, Durham, UK
e-mail: apostolos.kotsialos@durham.ac.uk; a.j.poole@durham.ac.uk

T.L. McCluskey et al. (eds.), *Autonomic Road Transport Support Systems*, Autonomic Systems, DOI 10.1007/978-3-319-25808-9_8

environmental conditions as well as *own* states without the organism conducting a conscious effort to perform them; *this is the important property*. The coordination effort and marshalling of resources allow the conscious part to focus on more important, high-level issues.

The design requirements self-$*$ behaviour imposes necessitate the definition of a set of properties guaranteeing the "unconscious" and efficient operation of the low-level subsystems. *The meaning assigned to these properties is domain and application specific*. Hence, autonomicity should be viewed as a system design approach, rather than just the application of technological solutions. A phenomenological description of a specific self-managed system needs to be given first in order for the corresponding domain-specific design requirements to be specified.

A number of application domains have used the notion of autonomics for system design purposes, including energy management systems [2], communication networks [3], financial markets [4] and spacecraft operations [5]. This chapter takes a look towards defining autonomic systems for intelligent transportation systems (ITS). Similar lines of research have been proposed by the organic computing initiative [6]. An architecture for real-time traffic management using notions from autonomic systems is proposed in [7]. An approach towards optimisation of decentralised autonomic systems for traffic control is reported in [8]. These publications form an initial contribution combining autonomics with traffic management.

2 The Autonomic Control Loop

The first step when trying to design systems with autonomic properties is to identify the level at which to display self-$*$ behaviour. The successful development of systems with "visceral" functions requires the *identification of the control loops* that should possess self-$*$ features. *The criterion, however, for describing a system as autonomic remains that of the unconscious and sustained operation over the full range of environmental and own state conditions*. It is the feedback control loop of the unconscious part that should possess self-$*$ properties.

The general autonomic control loop can be seen in Fig. 1. In order for the whole system to exhibit self-$*$ behaviour, the autonomic manager goes through the monitor-analyse-plan-execute (MAPE) process with knowledge management at the background [1]. The manager uses sensors to collect information about the resource and interacts with it through effectors. This architecture is common in one form or another in control engineering, where sensors attached to the process under control are used to observe the system's state and a controller drives the system to a desired state. Automatic control theory provides good, relevant and sound tools for each of the blocks in the autonomic manager's structure (see also [9]).

The self-$*$ requirement dictates the shape and form of methods to be used. It is the whole system that needs to be autonomic and be at liberty of organising its response for every conceivable combination of environmental conditions and be aware of the

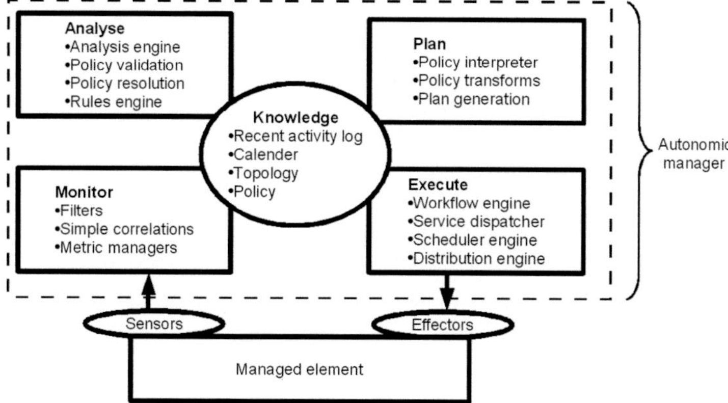

Fig. 1 The autonomic element control loop adopted from [1]

tools (controllers, optimisers, filters, estimators, predictors, etc.) at its disposal. This is one of the points of convergence between control theory and artificial intelligence, necessary for designing autonomic systems [9].

3 Autonomic ITS Applications

The autonomic manager is a system that resides in the virtual computing world, whilst the managed resource can be a computing resource, for example, a processor in a parallel computing system, or an application domain-specific physical resource, for example, the capacity of a controlled on-ramp. In this sense, autonomics can be applied for the computing systems *supporting* ITS applications or as a *design approach* of the ITS applications themselves. The emphasis here is on ITS viewed as operating systems with some self-$*$ properties, rather than on the supporting computational resources. This requires the specific definitions of self-$*$ properties obtaining their meaning with reference to a particular control loop.

The structure of an organism's ANS is used for system design. The ANS consists of two partially competing but mostly complementary components, the *sympathetic* and the *parasympathetic* systems. The sympathetic system is responsible for actions requiring fast responses ("fight or flight"), whilst the parasympathetic for actions not requiring immediate reaction ("test and digest"). This kind of dichotomy and division of labour can be replicated clearly identifying low-level ITS applications acting as visceral functions.

In a living organism, the sympathetic and parasympathetic systems are used by the ANS to achieve *homeostasis*. Homeostasis is a living systems' property whereby the internal state tends to be maintained at a stable band in view of changing environmental conditions. This is achieved by multiple dynamic equilibrium adjustments and using a variety of regulation mechanisms. Hence, an autonomic system must maintain a model of itself *and* a model of its environment, and using both, it should coordinate its resources and regulation mechanisms to achieve a homeostatic condition. This can be a low- or a high-level spatial and/or temporal condition desired and customised by the operator and other users or applications. An interesting discussion on the role of homeostasis for self-healing software may be found in [10].

For ITS applications, such conditions can be expressed as statements made by the network operator, for example, `maintain capacity flow at link` x `and 80% flow at link` y or `maintain mean travel time equal to` x `minutes for route` R `from` A `to` B. The next sections are describing a limited interpretation of a modelling and a route guidance application in those terms.

4 Autonomic Road Network Modelling Application

4.1 The Autonomic Element

The managed resource is the application `network_model`, which in our case is the second-order macroscopic traffic flow model METANET [11]. This modelling approach describes a road network as a directed graph of links and nodes. *Motorway links* are used for representing uniform motorway sections with the same number of lanes and no changes in geometry. The demand originating from the surrounding environment is channelled into the network through flow-receiving boundaries, for example, on-ramps. The flow is sent outside the network via *destination links* used for modelling off-ramps and exit-flow boundaries.

The traffic conditions in a motorway link are described macroscopically by the traffic volume, the vehicular density and the space mean speed at discrete road segments. The traffic conditions in an origin link are described by the queue length of vehicles waiting to enter the network. Traffic conditions in a destination link are modelled through the exit flows from that link. The drivers' routing behaviour is modelled based on turning rates (see [11]). In effect, the model is a dynamic system in the form

$$\mathbf{x}(k+1) = \mathbf{f}\left[\mathbf{x}(k), \mathbf{d}(k); \mathbf{p}\right], \mathbf{x}(0) = \mathbf{x}_0 \tag{1}$$

where k is the index over the model's discrete time steps of duration T; $\mathbf{x}$ is the state vector consisting of the density $\rho_{m,i}$ and space mean speed $v_{m,i}$ of every segment i of motorway link m and the queue length w_j of every origin j; $\mathbf{x}_0$ is the network's initial state at time $k = 0$; $\mathbf{d}(k)$ is the vector of system disturbances consisting of the demand at origins in and the turning rates; $\mathbf{p}$ is a vector of model parameters modelling particular features of the specific network, including the fundamental diagram model parameters, the anticipation and reaction model parameters, weaving and merging modelling parameters, minimum speed and maximum density; and model parameters $\mathbf{p}$ is the outcome of a model validation effort, examined closely later.

The application's functionality is to receive as input the initial state $\mathbf{x}_0$ and measured disturbance trajectories $\mathbf{d}(k)$, $k = 0, 1, \ldots, K - 1$ and deliver the density, speed and queue length profiles, organised in vector $\mathbf{x}(k)$, over K time periods in the future.

4.2 *Definition of Self-∗ Properties*

Several self-∗ properties related to the `network_model` application can be defined with emphasis on the traffic engineering context.

Self-healing: A network model application displays a self-healing property if it is able to heal the input data required for delivering its output. The autonomic manager's MAPE process monitors the disturbance and state trajectories for their integrity and plans a response in case of inconsistencies or missing data.

Self-configuring: It is concerned with the simulation setup, for example, normal conditions or incident simulation, the network configuration and the capability of updating its topology and geometric characteristics, for example, by being capable to import and translate data from geographic information systems (GIS).

Self-optimising: The meaning of this property is defined by considering the model's accuracy, which depends on the input data ($\mathbf{x}_0$ and $\mathbf{d}(k)$) and the *validity* of the model parameters $\mathbf{p}$. The autonomic manager should be able to deliver good sets of parameters for different simulation setups. Hence, the model must be aware of its own accuracy and automatically calibrate itself selecting the best parameter vector $\mathbf{p}^*$ based on real data.

Following the structure of the ANS, the sympathetic and parasympathetic subsystems division is adopted for embedding self-optimisation into `network_model`.

4.3 *Parasympathetic System Functions for Self-optimising*

The interpretation of a self-optimising macroscopic traffic flow modelling application takes the form of a system that can learn over time the most suitable plans and responses to requests for `network_model`. The manager needs to be aware of the model's accuracy for different network configurations over time. The application should have the capability of periodically running *self-assessment tests* using recently archived data for a range of network configurations and decide whether a more detailed validation effort needs to take place.

Another important functionality of the parasympathetic subsystem is the evaluation and configuration of the optimisation method (or solver) used for identifying

$\mathbf{p}^*$. A number of tuning parameters influence a solver's performance. The optimal values can emerge from the continuous assessment of the results obtained. Hence, there is a MAPE loop related to the solver's performance in the autonomic manager setting up the solvers. There is medium- to long-term time scale in this operation as it requires the collection, aggregation and abstraction of knowledge based on repeated experiments. Automatic planning platforms [12] are particularly suitable for developing this kind of systems.

4.4 Sympathetic System Functions for Self-optimising

The sympathetic system function aims at delivering the optimal model parameter vector $\mathbf{p}^*$. A rigorous validation effort is organised automatically by the autonomic manager along the following lines: (a) data collection for performing model calibration; the road data used must cover the entire spectrum of traffic conditions (free, critical and congested); (b) setting up the optimisation problem formulation based on data with different time stamps; (c) selection of data sets that are going to be used for calibration and different data sets to be used for verification only; (d) for every set of data used for calibration, be aware of the journalistic information associated with the network at the particular time (e.g. road works or use of speed limits); (e) run verification tests for a candidate $\mathbf{p}^*$ using data that were not used for obtaining it; (f) set up the requirements for $\mathbf{p}$'s components; default values may be used for some members of $\mathbf{p}$ and only a selected few may be allowed to change.

Even with these requirements, though, in a model validation process, there is still a need for expert opinion on several issues. A self-optimising model application must be able to dispense with expert opinion and replace it explicitly. This requirement gives rise to important modifications to the formulation of the model validation problem.

Expert opinion is required when deciding the spatial extension of the validity of the same fundamental diagram. The fundamental diagram is one of the most important relationships in the whole model (1), determining the equilibrium relationship between density and speed. In METANET it takes the form

$$V[\rho_{m,i}(k)] = v_{f,m} \cdot \exp\left[-\frac{1}{\alpha_m}\left(\frac{\rho_{m,i}(k)}{\rho_{\mathrm{cr},m}}\right)^{\alpha_m}\right] \tag{2}$$

where for a particular motorway link m, $v_{f,m}$ is its free speed, $\rho_{\mathrm{cr},m}$ is its critical density and α_m is a parameter. Assigning a different fundamental diagram to each discrete segment or even to each link would be a mistake, since it leads to over-parametrisation. To avoid this, the engineer setting up the validation process splits the network into parts where a single fundamental diagram applies [11]. The spatial extension of each of the fundamental diagrams used, however, is defined by the expert.

The MAPE process that is able to address this issue for a motorway network leads to a problem formulation and solution algorithms that lift the need for human intervention. This is done by using a black box approach with a population-based optimisation algorithm.

Let us assume that there are M loop detectors available at point j on the motorway providing flow, $y_{j,k,q}$, and speed, $y_{j,k,v}$, measurements for segment i of link m with sample time $T_s = 60\,\text{s}$; k is a time index with reference to the model time discretisation. The model validation problem consists of minimising the total flow and mean speed square error between measurements and model output. This is done by selecting an optimal set of the parameters $\mathbf{p}$ included in Eq. (1).

The contribution to the objective function of the flow square error for a point j is given by

$$J(\mathbf{p})_{j,q} = \sum_{k=1}^{K} \left(y_{j,k,q} - f_{j,k,q}\right)^2 \tag{3}$$

and the same is applied for the mean speed, that is,

$$J(\mathbf{p})_{j,v} = \sum_{k=1}^{K} \left(y_{j,k,v} - f_{j,k,v}\right)^2 \tag{4}$$

where $f_{j,k,q}$ and $f_{j,k,v}$ are the flow and mean speed, respectively, calculated by the model at time interval k for point j. The total square error $J_e\,(\mathbf{p})$ is

$$J_e(\mathbf{p}) = \sum_{j=1}^{M} \left[A_q J(\mathbf{p})_{j,q} + A_v J(\mathbf{p})_{j,v}\right] \tag{5}$$

where A_q and A_v are weights accounting for the variation of the two penalty terms.

In order to achieve the automatic assignment of fundamental diagrams in an intelligent way, penalty terms are included yielding the total objective function in the form

$$J_p(\mathbf{p}) = \sum_{r} \sum_{s} \left[w_v (v_f^r - v_f^s)^2 + w_\rho (\rho_{\text{cr}}^r - \rho_{\text{cr}}^s)^2 + w_\alpha (\alpha^r - \alpha^s)^2\right] \tag{6}$$

where r and s are indices of the different fundamental diagrams and w_v, w_ρ, w_α are weightings [13]. The objective function $J\,(\mathbf{p})$ takes the form

$$J\,(\mathbf{p}) = J_e\,(\mathbf{p}) + J_p\,(\mathbf{p}) \tag{7}$$

The solution of this optimisation problem removes the need for bottleneck identification as used in [14, 15] or choosing an arbitrary point for a change in parameter set [11]. The modelling application is self-optimising itself by auto-

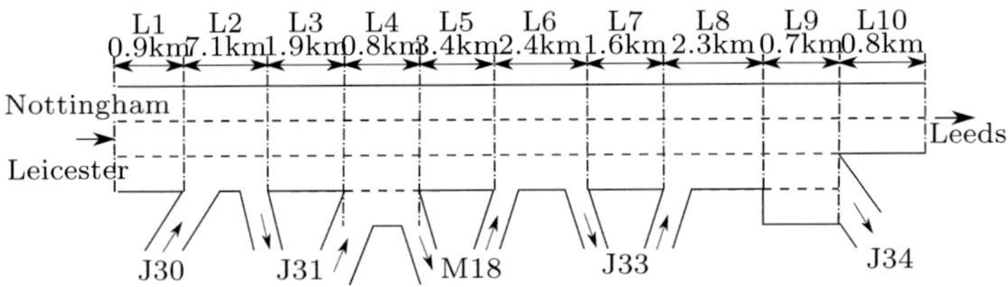

Fig. 2 Schematic of Sheffield site

Table 1 Sheffield optimal solutions for FD parameters

		ρ_{cr}	v_f	α	Start link	End link
1st						
	FD 1	27.23	122.36	2.6760	1	7
	FD 2	30.19	105.35	2.3494	8	9
	FD 3	26.68	109.75	1.1386	10	10
8th						
	FD 1	31.53	122.22	2.5587	1	3
	FD 2	28.50	113.77	1.8865	4	9
	FD 3	38.02	104.72	1.0724	10	10
15th						
	FD 1	28.43	115.96	2.1077	1	7
	FD 2	31.88	103.43	2.0904	8	9
	FD 3	35.17	104.73	1.1459	10	10

matically selecting and making minimal use of fundamental diagrams avoiding over-parametrisation at the same time.

As an example, let us consider the medium-sized motorway network in Sheffield (Northbound M1), which is 21.9 km long (Fig. 2). The recurrent congestion is typically a short wave originating in the centre and difficult to capture. Data was used from the 1st, 8th and 15th of June 2009 to validate the traffic flow model developed in METANET.

The self-optimising property is demonstrated from the results shown in Table 1, where the parameters *and* the extension of each fundamental diagram used are reported for the 3 days of data. The decisions regarding the number of fundamental diagrams that should be used, their extension and their parameters are taken by the system based on the available data without any interference from the operator.

A number of solvers are available for the solution of the resulting optimisation problem. There is a simple genetic algorithm (GA) [16], a number of particle swarm optimisation (PSO) variants (Global PSO (GPSO) [17]; Local PSO (LPSO) [18]; Adaptive PSO 09, 12, 14 (APSO-09, APSO-12, APSO-14; the number indicates year of publication) [19–21]; High Exploration PSO (HEPSO) [21], Chaos Enhanced PSO (CEPSO) [22]), and a classical version of Cuckoo Search (CS) [23] and a Modified CS (MCS) [24]. The performance of these solvers when used for

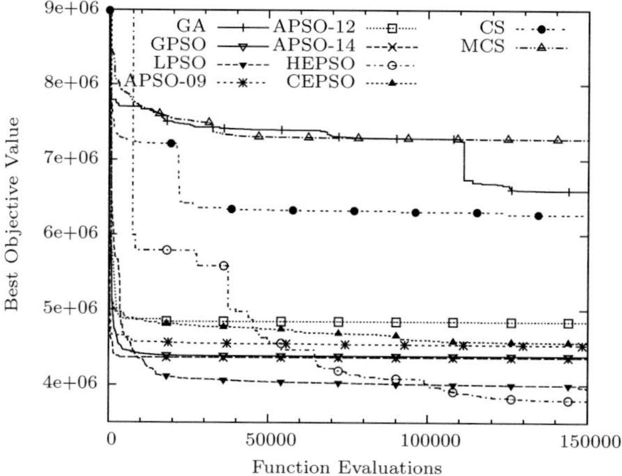

Fig. 3 Convergence profiles for the calibration of Sheffield model using data from the 1st

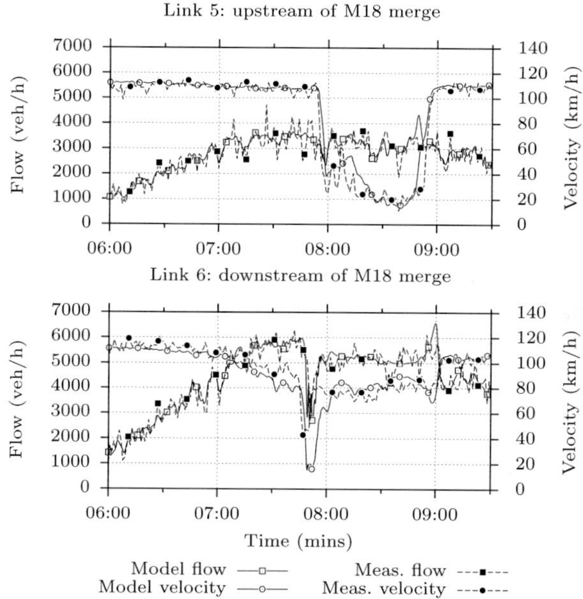

Fig. 4 Sample of time profiles for the calibrated Sheffield model using data of the 1st

calibration of METANET using the data of the 1st is shown in Fig. 3. Figure 4 displays a sample of the model output as compared to real measurements.

The whole effort regarding the selection of the optimisation algorithms, their tuning and the analysis of the obtained results can be automated. In this way it is possible to introduce a sympathetic system component, further supporting the application's self-optimising behaviour.

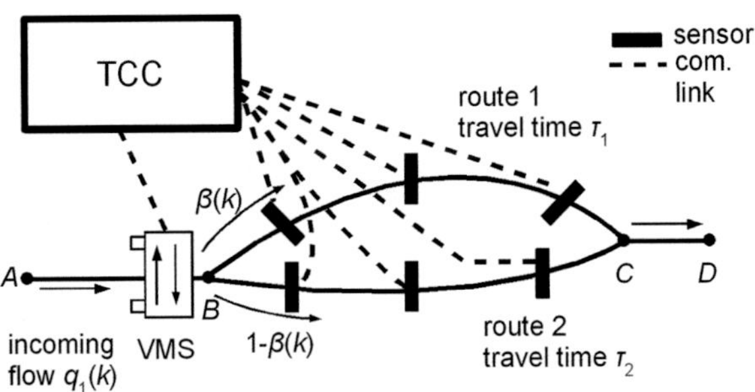

Fig. 5 Simple route guidance example site

5 Autonomic Route Guidance Systems: Policy Interpretation

In this section the behaviour of an autonomic route guidance system is outlined with emphasis on policy statement interpretation as opposed to the more detailed discussion of an autonomic traffic flow modelling application. A detailed discussion on the sympathetic and parasympathetic subsystems of a route guidance application is left for a future paper.

Let us consider the problem of controlling the traffic entering into a simple road system shown in Fig. 5. Traffic flow $q_1(t)$ enters the system at time t at point A. There are no other entry points. All vehicles will exit the system from the single exit point destination D. Vehicles that entered from A proceed to point B, where they need to make a decision about which route they should take to reach point C, after which the two subflows merge and proceed to exit D. Vehicles can either take route 1 or, alternatively, route 2. In the absence of any control measures, a natural split over the considered time horizon H is going to take place, which in most cases is a function of the demand level $q_1(t)$, time of day, congestion in either route, occurrence of a capacity reducing event and weather conditions. This natural split does not necessarily provide the best or more efficient spatio-temporal flow pattern in the network.

A variable message sign (VMS) is used as control device to influence traffic. A gantry over the road with a panel on it showing messages for drivers to go left ("←") or right ("→") is assumed to exist. Drivers approaching C having visual contact with the panel follow its recommendation, assuming a compliance rate $\varepsilon \in [0, 1]$. The task of the traffic control centre (TCC) is to control the VMS in such a way so as to influence traffic. The TCC has under its supervision and control a number of sensors installed over the network in order to monitor the traffic process. The traffic control system for this simple network at the level where the control strategy interacts with the human operator can be considered as an autonomic system if it possesses the properties outlined in Sect. 3.

The important system design property at this stage is to allow for the operator to state the desired objective. This calls for a "language" that is capable of capturing in concise and simple terms the operator's intention without any ambiguities. A simple and intuitive traffic management statement is to "`operate the VMS aiming at equalising the travel time of the two alternative routes`", that is, achieve user optimum conditions. Based on this statement, the first step should be related with the automatic selection of the control strategy that should be followed to support the objective.

Since the objective is to equalise travel times, a feedback regulator can be used [25]. The splitting rate $\beta(k) \in [0, 1]$ is used as control parameter and is defined as the percentage of the flow arriving at B using route 1 to reach point C, where k is an index of the control time step, that is, $t = kT_c$ with T_c the control time step. During this period the left/right signs are shown in such a way so as the average splitting rate over T_c is equal to $\beta(k)$. For known values of $\beta(k)$, the binary left/right operation can be determined, for example, by using a pulse width modulation method [26].

The feedback controllers use estimates of the routes' instant travel times $\tau_1(k)$ and $\tau_2(k)$ and their difference $\Delta\tau(k) = \tau_1(k) - \tau_2(k)$ as follows:

$$\beta(k) = \beta^N(k) - K_P \Delta\tau(k) \text{ (P-regulator)} \tag{8}$$

$$\beta(k) = \beta(k-1) - K_P [\Delta\tau(k) - \Delta\tau(k-1)] - K_I \Delta\tau(k) \text{ (PI-regulator)} \tag{9}$$

where β^N is the nominal split when no control measures are applied and K_P and K_I are regulator parameters. Both aim at sending the value of $\Delta\tau(k)$ to zero. Which of the two will be chosen can be decided based on past experience from the results obtained when either was followed in the field; this is a task for the "test and digest" function of the application's parasympathetic system.

The important issue to note is *the relationship between the policy statement and the control strategy to be followed*. Once the traffic management objective is determined in no uncertain terms, the network operator is out of the operations loop. Hiding the complexity of the related operations is a condition for an autonomic system along with adaptation. The feedback regulators (8) and (9) adapt to the prevailing traffic conditions by receiving updates of the travel times. The autonomic control system should invoke the services of a surveillance application (another service provided by the TCC information infrastructure) for obtaining estimates of $\tau_1(k)$ and $\tau_2(k)$.

The policy statement to equalise the travel times between the two alternative routes, though intuitively simple, can result in inefficient use of the network infrastructure, especially with increasing demand surpassing the capacity supply. The previous requirement may need to be changed when the operator is concerned more with the infrastructure performance and efficiency. If efficiency is understood in terms of congestion severity, extension and duration, then an appropriate and relevant performance index is the total time spent (TTS) by vehicles in the network during the considered time horizon (measured in $veh. * hours$).

Thus, an alternative traffic management policy statement is to "`minimise the TTS when there are no incidents in the system`". This change of requirement calls for a change in the control strategy as well. The VMS panel operation for the resulting flow pattern requires a different methodological approach for calculating the splitting rate $\beta(k)$.

A discrete time traffic model in the form of (1) can be used as shown in [27]. The TTS in terms of the model variables is $T_{\text{TTS}} = T \sum_k \sum_i \rho_{m,i}(k) L_m \Lambda_m$, where Λ_m is the number of lanes in link i, L_m is the segment length of link m (km) and T (h) is the model's time step. The objective function in this case has the following form:

$$\min_{\beta(k)\in[0,1],k=0,\ldots,K-1} J = T_{\text{TTS}} + \sum_{k=0}^{K-1} w\,[\beta(k) - \beta(k-1)]^2 \tag{10}$$

where K is the time horizon number of steps of length T and w a weight penalising strong oscillations of the splitting rate.

A number of other services are necessary for the control strategy to function properly, including a state estimation application for obtaining the system's initial state, a parameter estimation application for updating the traffic model parameters, a demand forecasting system for predicting the incoming flow at A and a real-time compliance rate estimation system for tracking ε. For the purpose of our discussion here, the important element is that of the relationship between the *operator requirement* and the resulting *problem formulation*. The statement that defines the objective is enough for an autonomic traffic control system to take the initiative and conduct all the necessary actions to support this policy.

One step further towards a more challenging situation is for the control system to be aware of the network's anticipated conditions and implement changes in policy, for example, travel time equalisation for light to near capacity demand and TTS minimisation for high demand levels. In other words, it would be left to the autonomic control system to decide which policy should be followed and when it should be changed.

The research challenge for this top-down policy-oriented approach rises from the problem formulation requirements imposed by more complex policies applied to more complex situations. For example, the inclusion of ramp metering control measures at on-ramps on either of the two routes would give rise to more complex management statements, such as "`minimise the TTS by coordinated VMS and ramp meters operation but do not allow the on-ramp queues to spill back to the surface network`". This kind of statement dictates the inclusion of queuing and ramp metering modelling and the solution of a more complex problem. Autonomics are about enabling and supporting the successful operations necessary to make the whole system work.

The guiding force behind this effort should be the needs and requirements from the operator's and drivers' side. It is those needs that should dictate the methods used and not the other way around. *Developing and using policy statement languages capturing user requirements that allow the automatic propagation of actions at the lower system levels is an important step in autonomic ITS deployment.*

6 Conclusions

This chapter described a system design approach inspired from the functioning of the ANS for ITS applications. The autonomic approach towards system design was discussed not with reference to the employed computing system but with reference to the requirements of traffic engineering applications.

It is argued that the design and development of autonomic traffic management systems must identify the control loop that needs to be endowed with autonomic properties and subsequently use this framework for defining a desired set of self-$*$ properties. Once these definitions are in place, the resulting design objectives need to be articulated.

Following the division of the autonomic nervous system into the sympathetic and parasympathetic subsystems is a useful design tactic. The use of control, optimisation and learning tools results to the development of such parasympathetic and sympathetic subsystems for ITS applications. It is the fusion of these approaches within MAPE processes in an autonomic manager that can deliver autonomic elements.

The chapter also presented an interpretation of a macroscopic modelling and a route guidance application within the context of autonomics. For the modelling application, particular attention has been given to the self-optimising property, which is based on an automatic calibration system. It is argued that the ensuing analysis can be automated, removing this way the need for repeated human expert interventions in the use of such applications.

The discussion of the modelling application also reveals the scope and challenge of autonomic traffic management systems. It goes beyond the simple application of a stand-alone application based on a single methodological approach. Instead, it encompasses computer science and traffic engineering knowledge to deliver solutions that perform sophisticated, complicated and challenging activities without the final user being conscious of them.

The discussion on the route guidance application revolved around the problem of designing policy-centric systems. The issue highlighted was that of the language used to describe and set policy goals. Such a language should be able to capture the user requirements in a simple and intuitive way. At the same time, it should be sufficient for formulating actions supporting this policy at lower system levels, hiding the complexity of the required responses from the user. A simplified example was used to highlight the relationship between a general policy statement and the resulting optimisation problem to be solved.

Future work on this area should be focused on the fusion of learning and automated planning algorithms with traffic control methods and on understanding the way high-level user requirements disaggregate and translate into the unconscious low-level autonomic system behaviour requirements.

References

1. Kephart, J., Chess, D.: The vision of autonomic computing. IEEE Comput. **36**(1), 41–50 (2003)
2. Warnier, M., van Sinderen, M., Brazier, M.: Adaptive knowledge representation for a self-managing home energy usage system. In: Proceedings of the Fourth International Workshop on Enterprise Systems and Technology (I-WEST), Athens, pp. 132–141 (2010)
3. Sterritt, R.: Autonomic networks: engineering the self-healing property. Eng. Appl. Artif. Intell. **17**, 727–739 (2004)
4. Cheliotis, G., Kenyon, C.: Autonomic economics. In: Proceedings of the IEEE International Conference on E-Commerce (2003)
5. Truszkowski, W., Hallock, H., Rouff, C., Karlin, J., Rash, J., Sterritt, R.: Autonomous and Autonomic Systems: With Applications to NASA Intelligent Spacecraft Operations and Exploration Systems. NASA Monographs in Systems and Software Engineering. Springer, New York (2009)
6. Richter, U., Mnif, M., Branke, J., Müller-Schloer, C., Schmeck, H.: Towards a generic observer/controller architecture for organic computing. In: GI Jahrestagung (1)'06, pp. 112–119 (2006)
7. Etemadnia, H., Abdelghany, K., Hariri, S.: Toward an autonomic architecture for real-time traffic network management. J. Intell. Transp. Syst. Technol. Plan. Oper. **16**, 45–59 (2012)
8. Dusparic, I., Cahill, V.: Multi-policy optimization in decentralized autonomic systems. In: Proceedings of 8th International Conference on Autonomous Agents and Multiagent Systems (2009)
9. Diao, Y., Hellerstein, J., Parekh, S., Griffith, R., Kaiser, G., Phung, D.: A control theory foundation for self-managing computing systems. IEEE J. Sel. Areas Commun. **23**(12), 2213–2222 (2005)
10. Shaw, M.: "Self-Healing": softening precision to avoid brittleness. In: Proceedings of ACM SIGSOFT WOSS '02, pp. 111–114 (2002)
11. Kotsialos, A., Papageorgiou, M., Diakaki, C., Pavlis, Y., Middelham, F.: Traffic flow modeling of large-scale motorway networks using the macroscopic modelling tool METANET. IEEE Trans. Intell. Transp. Syst. **3**, 282–292 (2002)
12. Guzman, C., Alcazar, V., Prior, D., Onaindia, E., Borrajo, D., Fdez-Olivarez, J., Quintero, E.: PELEA: a domain independent architecture for planning, execution and learning. In: Proceedings of ICAPS'12, pp. 38–45 (2012)
13. Poole, A., Kotsialos, A.: METANET model validation using a genetic algorithm. In: 13th IFAC Symposium on Control in Transportation Systems, pp. 7–12 (2012)
14. Munoz, L., Sun, X., Sun, D., Gomes, G., Horowitz, R.: Methodological calibration of the cell transmission model. In: Proceeding of the 2004 American Control Conference, Boston, pp. 798–803 (2004)
15. Munoz, L., Sun, X., Horowitz, R., Alvarez, L.: A piecewise-linearized cell transmission model and parameter calibration methodology. In: Proceeding of the 85th Transportation Research Board (TRB) Annual Meeting, Washington, DC, pp. 183–191 (2006)
16. Michalewicz, Z.: Genetic Algorithms + Data Structures = Evolution Programs. Springer, Berlin (1996)
17. Shi, Y., Eberhart, R.: A modified particle swarm optimizer. In: The 1998 IEEE International Conference on Evolutionary Computation Proceedings, 1998. IEEE World Congress on Computational Intelligence, IEEE, pp. 69–73 (1998)
18. Kennedy, J., Mendes, R.: Population structure and particle swarm performance. In: Proceedings of the World on Congress on Computational Intelligence, vol. 2, pp. 1671–1676. IEEE, New York (2002)
19. Zhan, Z., Zhang, J., Li, Y., Chung, H.: Adaptive particle swarm optimization. IEEE Trans Syst. Man Cybern. B Cybern. **39**(6), 1362–1381 (2009)

20. Wang, Y., Zhou, J., Zhou, C., Wang, Y., Qin, H., Lu, Y.: An improved self-adaptive PSO technique for short-term hydrothermal scheduling. Expert Syst. Appl. **39**(3), 2288–2295 (2012)
21. Zhang, Z., Jiang, Y., Zhang, S., Geng, S., Wang, H., Sang, G.: An adaptive particle swarm optimization algorithm for reservoir operation optimization. Appl. Soft Comput. **18**, 167–177 (2014)
22. Gandomi, A.H., Yun, G.J., Yang, X.S., Talatahari, S.: Chaos-enhanced accelerated particle swarm optimization. Commun. Nonlinear Sci. Numer. Simul. **18**(2), 327–340 (2013)
23. Yang, X.S., Deb, S.: Cuckoo search via Lévy flights. In: World Congress on Nature & Biologically Inspired Computing, NaBIC 2009, pp. 210–214. IEEE, New York (2009)
24. Walton, S., Hassan, O., Morgan, K., Brown, M.: Modified cuckoo search: a new gradient free optimisation algorithm. Chaos Solitons Fractals **44**(9), 710–718 (2011)
25. Pavlis, Y., Papageorgiou, M.: Simple decentralized feedback strategies for route guidance in traffic networks. Transp. Sci. **33**, 264–278 (1999)
26. Messmer, A., Papageorgiou, M.: Route diversion control in motorway networks via nonlinear optimization. IEEE Trans. Control Syst. Technol. **3**, 144–154 (1995)
27. Kotsialos, A., Papageorgiou, M., Mangeas, M., Haj-Salem, H.: Coordinated and integrated control of motorway networks via non-linear optimal control. Transp. Res. C **10**, 65–84 (2002)

Simulation Testbed for Autonomic Demand-Responsive Mobility Systems

Michal Čertický, Michal Jakob, and Radek Píbil

Abstract In this chapter, we describe an open-source simulation testbed for emerging autonomic mobility systems, in which transport vehicles and other resources are automatically managed to serve a dynamically changing transport demand. The testbed is designed for testing and evaluation of various planning, coordination and resource allocation mechanisms for the control and management of autonomic mobility systems. It supports all stages of the experimentation process, from the implementation of tested control mechanisms and the definition of experiment scenarios through simulation execution up to the analysis and interpretation of the results. The testbed aims to accelerate the development of control mechanisms for autonomic mobility systems and to facilitate their mutual comparison using well-defined benchmark scenarios. We also demonstrate how it can be used to select the most suitable control mechanism for a specific use case and to approximate operational costs and initial investments needed to deploy a specific autonomic mobility system.

Keywords Algorithms • Demand-responsive transport • On-demand transport • Simulation • Testbed

1 Introduction

The increasing deployment of ubiquitous location-aware and Internet-connected devices in transport systems enables the realization of autonomic mobility systems, based on continuous, automated management of transport vehicles to serve a dynamically changing passenger transport demand. Several types of such systems appeared in recent years, including real-time *on-demand transport*, real-time *ridesharing* or *dynamically priced taxis* [12]. More highly innovative services are

M. Čertický (✉) • M. Jakob • R. Píbil
Agent Technology Center, Faculty of Electrical Engineering, Czech Technical University, Prague, Czech Republic
e-mail: certicky@agents.fel.cvut.cz; jakob@agents.fel.cvut.cz; pibil@agents.fel.cvut.cz

T.L. McCluskey et al. (eds.), *Autonomic Road Transport Support Systems*, Autonomic Systems, DOI 10.1007/978-3-319-25808-9_9

likely to emerge with the wider adoption of electromobility and, most importantly, with the advent of autonomous, self-driving cars.

Due to their inherent complexity, such novel mobility systems need to adopt the autonomic systems' principles in order to work reliably, safely and efficiently. They need to be *automatic*, *adaptive* and *aware* [23, 32] in order to deal with the situation at hand quickly and efficiently and to maintain long-term efficiency under ever-changing conditions. Implementing these principles requires the development of planning, coordination and resource allocation algorithms that would orchestrate the operation of all entities of the transport system in a desirable way. The development of such control mechanisms is a challenging task due to many internal and external interdependencies that affect the overall system's behaviour.

To deal with the complexity of mobility systems, various modelling paradigms have been employed. *Analytical modelling*, *simulation modelling* and *agent-based simulations* in particular [35], as well-established approaches for analysing the behaviour of complex sociotechnical systems, have already been applied in this field (see Sect. 2). The agent-based simulation testbed described in this chapter was designed to meet the research community's demand for an experimentation tool tailored specifically for mobility systems, but at the same time universal enough to analyse and compare their numerous variants.

The presented software is called *Flexible Mobility Services Testbed*[1] and was built on top of a transport simulation framework *AgentPolis*.[2] Even though the testbed is not autonomic itself, it allows and encourages experimenting with a wide variety of mechanisms and algorithms necessary for autonomic mobility systems and lets users assess their performance in different scenarios and configurations. Unlike other simulation platforms, the testbed is fully agent based, allowing every agent to perceive the environment, adapt and react to it at any point in time. This gives users the freedom to implement a control logic for individual agents in a way that would lead to self-configuration, self-healing, self-optimization or self-protection properties of the whole system. The testbed supports all stages of the experimentation process, from the implementation of tested control algorithms and the definition of experiment scenarios through simulation execution and visualization up to the analysis and interpretation of simulation results.

To facilitate its use, the testbed provides an easy-to-use application programming interface (API) and allows users to easily plug in their custom control mechanisms by implementing a few predefined abstract Java classes. Furthermore, by providing a standardized way to import and capture key aspects of autonomic transport system deployment scenarios, including road network maps, vehicle properties or transport demand, the testbed also makes it easy to create benchmark scenarios for mutual comparison of different control mechanisms.

This chapter is divided into six sections: After the overview of related work leading up to a brief introduction to agent-based simulation in Sect. 2, we describe the testbed's architecture and underlying modelling ontology in Sect. 3. Sections 4

---

[1] http://github.com/agents4its/mobilitytestbed/.

[2] http://agentpolis.org.

and 5 explain the experimentation process and provide a demonstrative example. The last section merely recapitulates the key ideas and concludes the chapter.

2 Related Work

Since the 1970s, we have seen numerous attempts to study mobility and transport systems in general by analytical modelling. An extensive overview of analytical modelling methodology, along with mathematical background, can be found in a monograph by Ortuzar and Willumsen [8]. Early models of mobility systems were largely based on mathematical programming and continuous approximations. The former technique relied on detailed data and numerical methods, whereas the latter relied on concise summaries of data and analytical models. Geoffrion [15] advocated the use of simplified analytical models to gain insights into numerical mathematical programming models. In a similar spirit, Hall [17] illustrates applications of discrete and continuous approximations and notes that continuous approximations are useful to develop models that are easy for humans to interpret and comprehend. Overview and classification of continuous approximation models can be found in [25].

In some of the more recent work, the attention was focused on demand-responsive mobility systems, which were formalized as mathematical abstractions, such as dial-a-ride problem (DARP) [34] or multiple depot vehicle scheduling (MDVS) problem [5] to allow further formal analysis. For example, Hauptmeier et al. [18] and Lipmann et al. [27] studied formal properties of certain algorithms solving DARP and its variant with restricted information. Haghani and Banihashemi [16] addressed the influence of town size on the performance of algorithms for MDVS and its variant with route time constraints.

However, analytical models and theoretical algorithm analyses were often too abstract for expressing relevant aspects in the structure and dynamics of some transport systems. To deal with this shortcoming, the paradigm of simulation modelling was adopted by the transport research community and has been employed in parallel with the analytical approaches. In 1969, Wilson [36] conducted a pioneer simulation-based study of the influence of the service area, demand density and number of vehicles on the behaviour of transport system. Simulations have since then been extensively utilized in the research of transport and mobility, as a powerful tool for analysing system's behaviour. To mention a few more examples, Regan et al. [31] studied the performance of freight mobility system using different lead acceptance and assignment strategies, Fu [14] developed a simulation model of an urban paratransit system, and Deflorio et al. [9] evaluated demand-responsive transport system under the influence of real-life aspects, such as customer delays and travel time variability.

Simulation modelling also allowed researchers to study DARP or MDVS control mechanisms empirically (in addition to formal algorithmic analysis). Bailey and Clark [3] investigated the performance of one of them in relation to varying vehicle fleet sizes. Jlassi et al. [21] simulated an ambulance service implemented as dial-a-ride system, and Shinoda et al. [33] compared such systems to fixed-route systems under varying circumstances. Diana [10] assessed the effectiveness of scheduling algorithms under different percentages of real-time requests and intervals between call-in time and requested pick-up time, and Quadrifoglio and Dessouky [29] studied the insertion heuristic scheduling algorithm for mobility allowance shuttle transit systems, a hybrid transit solution that merges the flexibility of dial-a-ride systems and the low-cost operability of fixed-route bus services. More recently, d'Orey et al. [11] used simulations to explore the trade-offs between the satisfaction of drivers and passengers.

In these simulations, the system's behaviour could only be centralized—governed in a top-down manner by a single entity or mechanism. Also, any self-initiated interactions, communication or negotiation among individual actors (e.g. passengers) was impossible, severely limiting their level of autonomy. To overcome these limitations, a new paradigm called *agent-based simulation* was introduced. Agent-based simulation has proven to be a highly valuable tool, especially when studying complex self-organizing systems in many domains [24]. Mobility systems modelled under this paradigm are implemented as multi-agent systems—that is, composed of autonomous entities termed *agents* situated in a shared environment which they perceive and act upon, in order to achieve their own goals. In the context of mobility, we usually distinguish between three relevant types of agents: *passengers* (announcing transport requests), *drivers* (serving passenger's requests) and *dispatchers* (optional kind of agents who can negotiate with passengers and coordinate the drivers).

Agent-based simulations have been used to study various aspects of mobility, as well as a number of different control mechanisms. Horn [19] employed a simulation, developed completely from scratch, to study operational characteristics of a multimodal transport system integrating conventional timetabled services (buses, trains, etc.) and flexible demand-responsive mobility services (single- and multiple-hire taxis). A combination of traditional and demand-responsive transit was also simulated by Edwards [13]. The impact of zoning vs. non-zoning strategies on demand-responsive mobility was studied by Quadrifoglio and Dessouky in [30]. Real-time taxi-sharing schemes and ridesharing have been evaluated by Kamar and Horvitz [22], Lioris et al. [26] and Agatz et al. [1], while the efficiency of traditional taxi services has been studied by Cheng and Nguyen [7].

Control mechanisms that govern the behaviour of mobility systems are usually classified by the concentration of decision making into:

- *Centralized* (all the agents controlled by a central entity, e.g. dispatcher)
- *Distributed* (agents act based on their mutual, unorganized interactions)
- *Hybrid* (combination of those two)

Alternatively, control mechanisms may also be divided based on the structure of transport demand they are dealing with into *static* (all transport requests are known in advance) or *dynamic* (future requests are unknown).

Since these control mechanisms represent a cornerstone of mobility system's behaviour and success, significant amount of research has been invested in them and more is still needed. It therefore makes sense to develop software tools that would assist in this research. The general idea of employing simulation testbeds to accelerate the development of multi-agent control mechanisms was put forward, for example, by Pěchouček et al. [28]. A common attribute of simulations used in the works above is that they were developed from scratch using general-purpose programming languages (most often C++ or Java), in order to demonstrate only a single specific mechanism. This is because none of the existing general-purpose (such as AnyLogic[3]) as well as transport-specific simulation tools (such as MATSIM[4] or SUMO[5]) has proven suitable for simulation-based assessment of a wider variety of control mechanisms. The agent-based simulation testbed described in this chapter was created to fill this gap and provide the researchers with a tool necessary to analyse and compare the control mechanisms of various classes without developing their own simulations.

3 Flexible Mobility Services Testbed

An agent-based simulation testbed should not only simulate a mobility system governed by a certain control mechanism—it should be able to support multiple different mechanisms and to compare them under identical benchmark conditions, so that the researchers or public authorities can discover relative strengths and weaknesses of their algorithms and businesses or municipalities can select the most appropriate mechanisms for specific real-world conditions. To satisfy these requirements, a simulation tool should have the following assets:

- Support for *centralized*, *distributed* and *hybrid* control mechanisms
- Functions or protocols for *direct communication* between agents
- Means of importing the transport demand for both *static* and *dynamic* cases
- Agents capable of imposing *custom constraints* on the system (e.g. demand for wheel chair support in a taxi)
- Simple way of *incorporating* various user-provided algorithms

Unlike any of the simulations mentioned in Sect. 2, the open-source *Flexible Mobility Services Testbed* described in this chapter has all of these properties.

3.1 Modelling Ontology of AgentPolis Framework

Transport simulation framework AgentPolis, which serves as the basis for the testbed, provides abstractions, code libraries and software tools for building and

[3]http://www.anylogic.com.

[4]http://www.matsim.org.

[5]http://www.sumo-sim.org.

experimenting with fully agent-based models of interaction-rich mobility systems. The modelling elements provided by AgentPolis are organized in a modelling ontology and can be grouped into three high-level categories:

- *Agent modelling elements:* The concept of the *agent* in AgentPolis is defined rather loosely in order to support modelling of a wide variety of agents (e.g. `DriverAgent`). The behaviour of agents is defined in terms of *activities*—reactive control structures implementing the logic determining which actions or nested activities the agent executes at a certain point in time or in response to sensor information or messages received from other agents (e.g. `DriveVehicle` activity). As part of their behaviour, agents may need to make decisions that require executing complex algorithms, including the ones that comprise the control mechanisms we want to evaluate. In order to promote reusability, such algorithms are encapsulated into so-called reasoning modules. In practice, the reasoning modules are Java classes (e.g. `DriverLogic`) that can be easily rewritten to implement a wide variety of algorithms, or even call external tools or solvers.
- *Environment modelling elements:* The environment models the physical context in which the agents are situated and act. It is represented by a collection of *environment objects*, each representing a fragment of the modelled physical reality (e.g. `Vehicle`), and *queries* that allow agents to be informed about the state of the environment and about the events happening during simulation execution (e.g. `PositionQuery`).
- *Interaction modelling elements:* Modelling complex interactions among the agents or between the agents and the environment is crucial for the analysis of dynamic transport systems. In AgentPolis, agent-environment interactions are realized by *sensors*, which process the percepts from the environment and atomic *actions* that provide a low-level abstraction for modelling how agents actually manipulate the environment (e.g. `MoveVehicle`). Inter-agent interactions are realized by a collection of *communication protocols*. Currently, the testbed provides `1-to-1 messaging`, `1-to-many messaging` and `auction` protocols.

Detailed description of modelling abstractions and corresponding model elements can be found in [20].

3.2 Architecture of the Testbed

Although all the power and flexibility of the AgentPolis framework are accessible to the users of the testbed, it is hidden and only the relevant parts of it are exposed through an API designed specifically for the simulation modelling of demand-responsive mobility systems. The components of the testbed can be broadly divided into three layers (see Fig. 1):

- *AgentPolis transport simulation model:* composed of the core simulation engine and the basic transport domain model. This model implements key elements

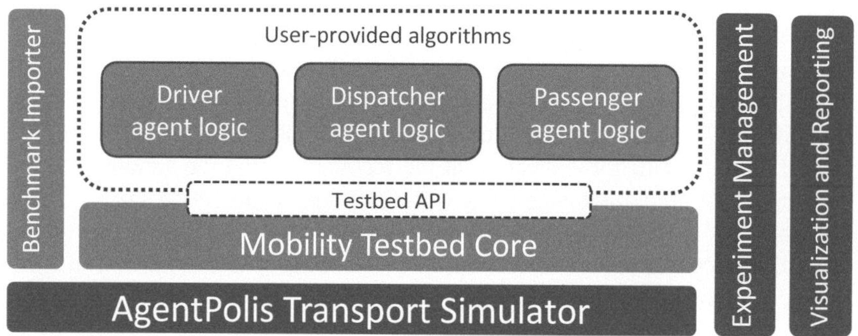

Fig. 1 Testbed's architecture overview

comprising a mobility system, such as road network and vehicles, and basic behavioural logic associated with them. It also provides routing algorithms and communication interfaces designed to simplify the implementation of higher-level simulation logic.

- *Testbed core:* specializes the general AgentPolis simulator for the specific purpose of modelling demand-responsive transport systems. It implements the model of three types of agents (*passengers*, *drivers* and *dispatchers*) and provides extensible abstractions for defining their behaviour.
- *Control mechanism:* a user-supplied implementation of a specific control mechanism that is to be experimentally evaluated.

In addition to these three layers, the testbed provides a suite of tools that facilitate creation, execution and evaluation of simulation experiments:

- *Benchmark importer* loads all the required input data (discussed in detail in Sect. 4), constructs the graph representation of a road network and creates the environment objects and agents accordingly. All the imported data is automatically checked for consistency in order to prevent hard-to-trace errors. Resulting internal representations are simplified by selectively removing redundant information in order to accelerate the reasoning without losing accuracy.
- *Experiment management* is supported by a benchmark generator and tools for the design of experiments. The *generator* allows users to build their own scenarios covering real-world or fictional locations with custom numbers and types of agents. Agents can be generated either based on real-world data or randomly, using various temporal and spatial distributions.

  Since a robust evaluation of the control mechanism under a sufficiently wide range of circumstances may require many simulation runs, the testbed provides tools for accelerating the evaluation process. In particular, it can use *design of experiments* methods to generate simulation configurations in a way so that maximum information about the behaviour of the control mechanism is obtained using a minimum number of simulation runs.

– The *analysis and visualization* tools provide a way to interactively browse and review simulation execution and results at different spatial and temporal resolutions. This assists researchers during the development and debugging process and allows them to find out how the tested mechanisms perform under different conditions. The aggregated results, as well as the visualizations, are generated based on the detailed low-level event log recorded during the simulation, containing all the important events related to passengers (`passGotInVehicle`, `passGotOffVehicle`) and drivers with their vehicles (`vehicleMove`) and all the communication between the agents (e.g. `passSentRequest` or `requestConfirmed`).

3.3 Control Mechanisms

Unless there are too many different kinds of interactions between the agents, the incorporation of studied control mechanism into the testbed only requires implementing several classes and methods. For example, in the most simple case, the user only needs to extend the `DispatchingLogic` class and implement its `processNewRequest(Request r)` method.

From the perspective of the testbed's user, the classification of control mechanism into *centralized, distributed* or *hybrid* class depends only on whether the driver agent's actions are controlled centrally by (single or multiple) dispatcher agents, locally by the drivers themselves or the combination of both. The reasoning logic for individual agents and central authorities is implemented by extending specific methods of abstract classes `PassengerLogic`, `DriverLogic` and `DispatchingLogic` (see Tables 1, 2 and 3). Decentralized mechanisms are suitable in situations when communication capabilities are restricted, or when the

Table 1 Abstract methods of `PassengerLogic` class, implementing the behaviour of passenger agents

`sendRequest(Request r)`: Called by the testbed whenever this passenger is supposed to announce a new travel request `r`, according to input data. The passenger should contact other agents (dispatcher or drivers) within this method.
`processProposal(Proposal p)`, `processRejection(Rejection r)`: Two methods that are called when the passenger receives a trip proposal `p` specifying details about the trip (e.g. price or arrival time) or rejection `r` of his older request from a driver or dispatcher.
`vehicleArrived(String driverId, String vehicleId)`: Called when a driver arrives to pick the passenger up. Typically, the passenger just gets on board this driver's vehicle.

Table 2 Abstract methods of `DriverLogic` class, implementing the behaviour of driver agents

`processNewRequest(Request r)`: A method called whenever the driver receives a new travel request `r` from a passenger or dispatcher. Here, the driver should react by sending his trip proposal or request rejection.
`processNewAcceptance(Proposal p)`: Called when the driver's trip proposal `p` is accepted by the passenger. Here, the driver usually plans his route and starts driving.
`processNewRejection(Proposal p)`: If driver's proposal `p` is rejected, the testbed calls this method.
`processPassengerGotIn(String passengerId)`: Called when the passenger gets on board this driver's vehicle.

Table 3 Abstract methods of `DispatchingLogic` class, implementing the behaviour of dispatcher agents

`processNewRequest(Request r)`, `processNewAcceptance(Proposal p)`, `processNewRejection(Proposal p)`: The methods with similar meaning as in `DriverLogic` class with the exception that the dispatcher usually negotiates with passengers and only sends instructions and routes to drivers.

agents are independent and self-interested but can still benefit from collaboration (e.g. ridesharing).

Dynamic control mechanisms (sometimes called "online", especially in DARP context) process the travel demand requests when they are announced. On the other hand, *static* (or "offline") mechanisms need to know all the requests in advance. The testbed grants the driver or dispatcher agents the access to requests only after they are announced by the passengers. Nevertheless, to also address the requirements of static mechanisms, several benchmarks in which the travel demand is announced long time in advance are available.

4 Experiment Process

After the tested mechanism is incorporated into the framework, the actual experimentation using the testbed follows a three-step process[6] (see Fig. 2).

[6]This section provides a high-level overview of testbed's usage. More detailed tutorial can be found at http://github.com/agents4its/mobilitytestbed/wiki.

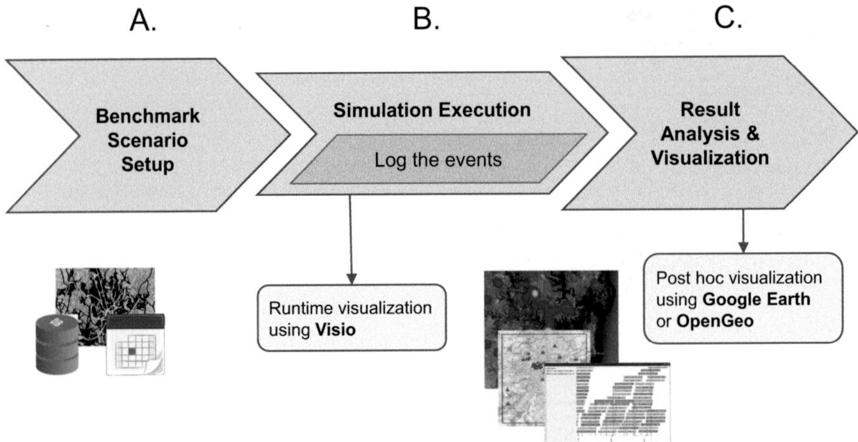

Fig. 2 Three-step process of the experiment (setup, simulation, evaluation)

4.1 Scenario Definition and Setup

First of all, the user needs to set up and *configure the scenario* under which he wants the control mechanism to be evaluated. The scenario is described in terms of a benchmark package, which consists of the following files:

1. *Road network*—the road network in the experiment area represented in the *OpenStreetMap (OSM)*[7] format
2. *Driver agents*—description (in JSON[8]) of all the relevant drivers with their initial positions and the properties of their vehicles including the capacity, fuel consumption, CO_2 emissions or non-standard equipment (e.g. wheelchair accessibility)
3. *Travel demand*—the exact representation (in JSON) of travel demand containing all the passenger agents with their associated trip details: origin and destination coordinates, time windows, announcement time and special requirements

4.2 Simulation Execution

Once the model is set up, the user invokes the simulation engine to execute the simulation. The AgentPolis engine employs the discrete event simulation approach [4] in which the operation of the target system is modelled as a discrete sequence

[7]http://openstreetmap.org/.

[8]JavaScript Object Notation (JSON): http://json.org/.

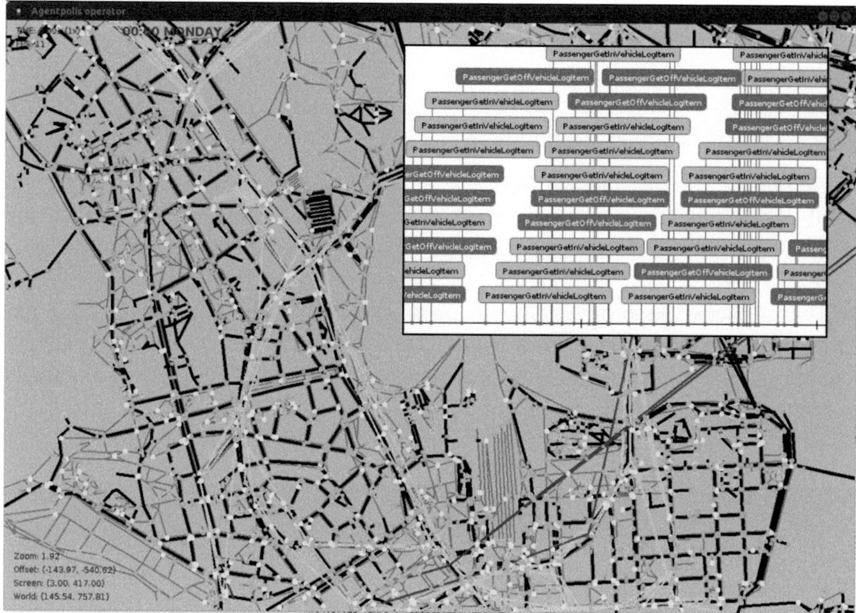

Fig. 3 Runtime view of a running simulation. Road network, `Passenger` and `Driver` agents are shown. Simulation events are depicted in the overlay window

of (possibly concurrent) events in time. Each event occurs at a particular time, with precision to milliseconds of the simulation time, and marks a change of state of the modelled system. Since there are no changes occurring between consecutive events, the simulation can directly jump in time from one event to the next, which, in most cases, makes it more computationally efficient than time-stepped approaches.

The simulation progress can be presented visually during runtime, using the internal visualization component of AgentPolis. It is capable of displaying the transport network and agents within the model, along with a convenient visualization of all the ongoing events (see Fig. 3).

4.3 Result Analysis and Visualization

From the low-level event log recorded during the simulation run, the testbed calculates a range of higher-level, aggregate performance metrics. By default, these include:

- Total vehicle distance driven
- Total fuel consumption
- Total values of CO_2 emissions

– Average vehicle productivity (passengers per hour)
– Passenger's total travel time statistics (average, median and maximum)
– Passenger's on-board ride time statistics
– Passenger's waiting time statistics
– Total runtime of control algorithms

Additional metrics can be defined. In addition to low-level event logs and highly aggregated metrics, the testbed also provides the means to visualize the simulation runs and results in the geospatial and temporal context, using external tools.

The interactive geobrowser *Google Earth*[9] can display the log of a simulation run exported in *Keyhole Markup Language* (KML).[10] It is capable of displaying a large number of agents, along with simple geometry and screen overlays, over a realistic satellite imagery and 3D model of the environment (see Fig. 4). Google Earth

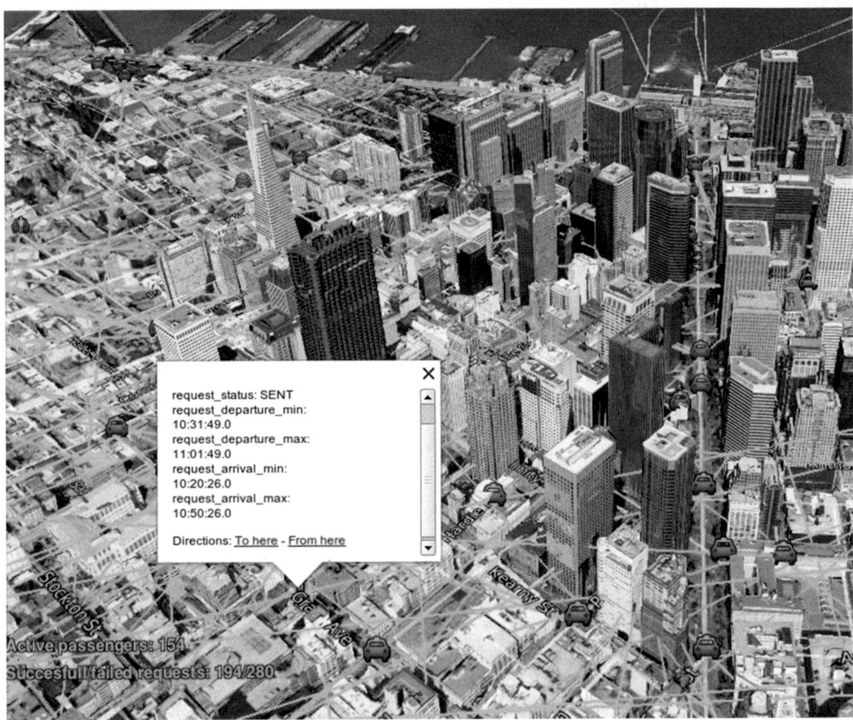

Fig. 4 Simulation run of a taxi-sharing scenario exported in KML format and displayed by Google Earth. The input benchmark was based on historical traffic and demand data from San Francisco, 2008

[9]http://earth.google.com/.

[10]http://developers.google.com/kml/.

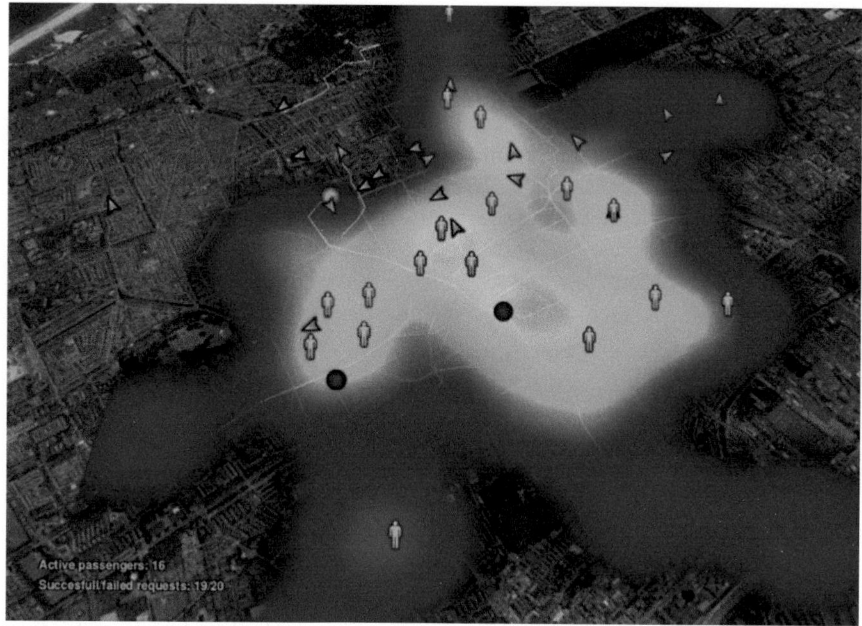

Fig. 5 Heat map representing the spatial distribution of successfully served trip requests in Hague, Netherlands

can be further used to display the values of metrics as they vary across different areas. For example, Fig. 5 shows a heat map representing the spatial distribution of successfully served passenger trip requests.

5 Example Study

To demonstrate how the testbed can be used, we implemented and evaluated a control mechanism based on *parallel tabu search heuristic* by Attanasio et al. [2], which is considered a state-of-the-art algorithm for dynamic multi-vehicle dial-a-ride problem (DARP). Mobility systems like taxi-sharing schemes governed by centralized dynamic DARP algorithms can be considered autonomic—they are *automatic* (serve incoming requests without external intervention), *adaptive* (modify current plans of driver agents based on new requests) and *aware* (monitor the state of the system continually and act accordingly).

5.1 Scenario Setup

Using our *benchmark generator*, we prepared two collections of scenarios[11]: one was situated in the urban core of Hague, Netherlands, covering the area of 80.09 km^2, while the other collection was set in Prague metropolitan area in Czech Republic, spread over 5938.64 km^2. The transport requests of passenger agents were generated with temporal distribution taking into account peak/off-peak hours based on our empiric knowledge and uniform origin-destination distribution over all the nodes of our transport graph.[12] Each collection contained 24 scenarios—one for every combination of the number of driver agents (10–35 drivers, increasing by 5) and request frequency (from 100 up to 175 requests per day, increasing by 25).

5.2 Implementation of the Control Mechanism

Since this particular control mechanism is centralized in the sense that the dispatcher agent has complete power over the behaviour of all the drivers, we only needed to extend the abstract class `DispatchingLogic` and implement its method `processNewRequest(Request r)`, which is called every time the passenger agent announces a transport request.

5.3 Simulation Results

First, we analysed the relation between *request frequency* and *success rate*, computed as a ratio of successfully served requests and all the announced requests, with different *numbers of driver agents*.

We learned that in Prague we would need roughly 30 drivers to satisfy at least 90 % of 150 daily requests, whereas in the smaller city of Hague, we could maintain the same success rate with only 15 drivers (see Fig. 6).

Once we had the estimation of optimal driver count, we were interested in the approximate distance driven by them on a daily basis. According to the experiments, to satisfy 150 requests per day, 30 drivers in Prague would drive 1722.29 km, while 15 drivers in Hague only 753.01 km (see Fig. 7).

---

[11] Another use case for the testbed can be found in [6], where we compared standard taxi and taxi-sharing service in Sydney, Australia.

[12] Users are free to define their own location-specific temporal distributions of requests based on historical data or empiric knowledge. Also, since version 2.0., the testbed's benchmark generator can use the density of certain points of interest within OSM map to distribute requests in space.

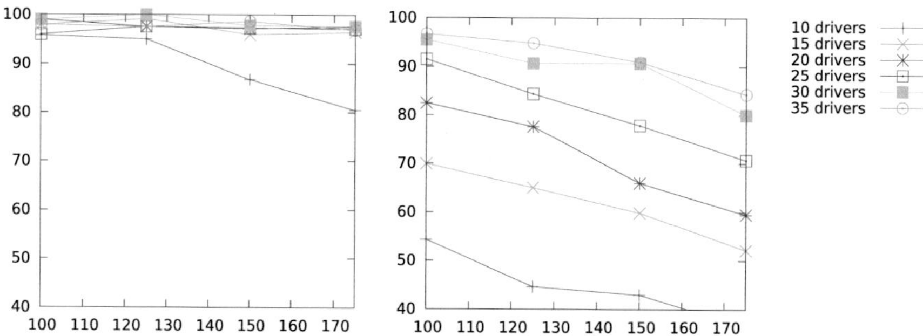

Fig. 6 Success rates in % (axis y) in relation to request frequency (axis x), with different numbers of drivers in Hague, Netherlands (*left*), and Prague, Czech Republic (*right*)

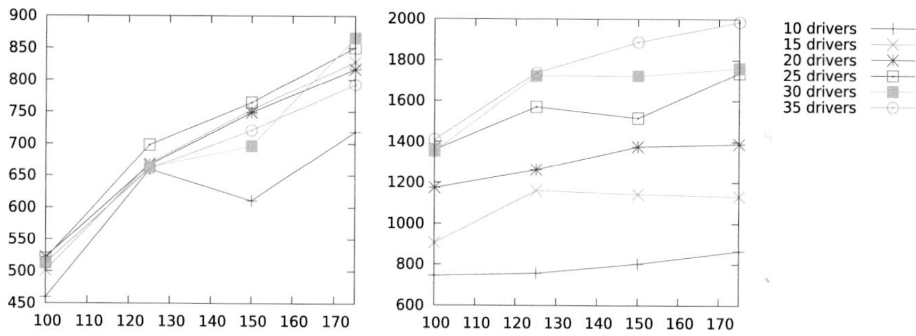

Fig. 7 Total distance in km driven per day (axis y) to serve increasing numbers of requests (axis x) by different numbers of agents in Hague, Netherlands (*left*), and Prague, Czech Republic (*right*)

This way, we were able to estimate operational costs and initial investments needed to serve a specific demand in two different cities. We were also able to study a number of other metrics (see the enumeration in Sect. 4.3) and relations between them.

In addition to performance metrics, we were able to study the visualization of the system's behaviour. During the experiments in Prague, we noticed that while in the morning the drivers were mainly situated in the city centre, after a few hours, the majority served a long-distance request and ended up isolated at the edge of the service area, unable to serve new requests originating in the centre quickly enough, because they were too far away (see Fig. 8). This leads to significant decrease in service's success rate in the afternoon and evening hours. Discovering this problem via visualization allows us to take steps towards improving the control mechanism (e.g. by sending secluded drivers back to more busy areas even before the requests are announced).

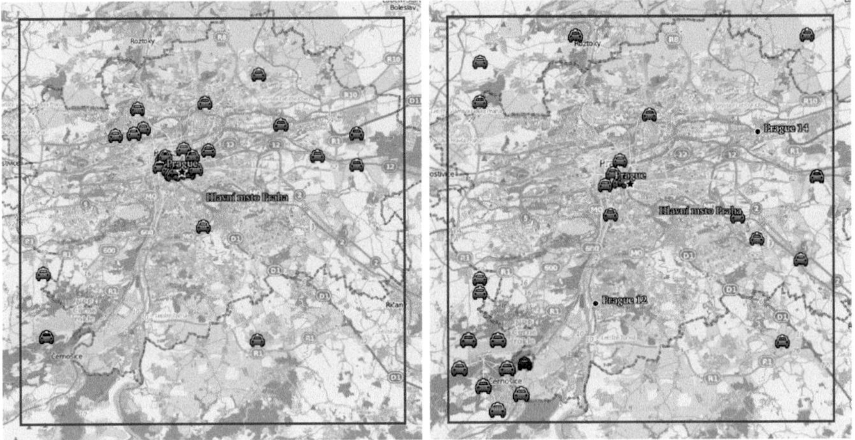

Fig. 8 Spatial distribution of drivers during the experiment in Prague metropolitan area at 5:00 (*left*) and 23:59 (*right*). In the later hours, many drivers were left isolated at the edges of the service area, unable to serve the requests originating in the city centre quickly enough

6 Conclusion

The presented testbed for simulation-based evaluation of autonomic mobility systems allows its users to incorporate their own control mechanisms, to evaluate them with respect to a variety of performance metrics and to compare their performance to alternative mechanisms under identical conditions using benchmark scenarios, based on realistic real-world or synthetic data. As such, *Flexible Mobility Services Testbed* can assist researchers in developing new control mechanisms, and it can help policy makers and transport operators assess the mobility services and schemes prior to their deployment. The testbed is freely available at http://github.com/agents4its/mobilitytestbed/.

Acknowledgements This work was funded by, Ministry of Education, Youth and Sports of Czech Republic (grants no. 7E12065 and LD12044) the Technology Agency of the Czech Republic (grant no. TE01020155) and by the European Union Seventh Framework Programme FP7/2007–2013 (grant agreement no. 289067).

References

1. Agatz, N., Erera, A.L., Savelsbergh, M.W., Wang, X.: Dynamic ride-sharing: a simulation study in metro Atlanta. Proc. Soc. Behav. Sci. **17**, 532–550 (2011). Papers selected for the 19th International Symposium on Transportation and Traffic Theory
2. Attanasio, A., Cordeau, J.-F., Ghiani, G., Laporte, G.: Parallel tabu search heuristics for the dynamic multi-vehicle dial-a-ride problem. Parallel Comput. **30**(3), 377–387 (2004)

3. Bailey Jr., W.A., Clark Jr., T.D.: A simulation analysis of demand and fleet size effects on taxicab service rates. In: Proceedings of the 19th Conference on Winter Simulation, pp. 838–844. ACM, New York (1987)
4. Banks, J., Carson, J.S., Nelson, B.L., Nicol, D.M., et al.: Discrete-Event System Simulation. Pearson Prentice Hall, Upper Saddle River (2005)
5. Bodin, L., Golden, B.: Classification in vehicle routing and scheduling. Networks **11**(2), 97–108 (1981)
6. Čertický, M., Jakob, M., Píbil, R.: Analyzing on-demand mobility services by agent-based simulation. J. Ubiquitous Syst. Pervasive Netw. **6**(1), 17–26 (2015)
7. Cheng, S.-F., Nguyen, T.D.: Taxisim: a multiagent simulation platform for evaluating taxi fleet operations. In: Proceedings of the 2011 IEEE/WIC/ACM International Conferences on Web Intelligence and Intelligent Agent Technology-Volume 02, pp. 14–21 (2011)
8. de Dios Ortuzar, J., Willumsen, L.G.: Modelling Transport. Wiley, New Jersey (1994)
9. Deflorio, F.P., Dalla Chiara, B., Murro, A., SpA, M.A.: Simulation and performance of DRTS in a realistic environment. In: Proceedings of 9th Meeting EWGT on Intermodality, Sustainability and ITS/13th Mini EURO Conference on Handling Uncertainty in the Analysis of Traffic and Transportation Systems (2002)
10. Diana, M.: The importance of information flows temporal attributes for the efficient scheduling of dynamic demand responsive transport services. J. Adv. Transp. **40**(1), 23–46 (2006)
11. d'Orey, P.M., Fernandes, R., Ferreira, M.: Empirical evaluation of a dynamic and distributed taxi-sharing system. In: Proceedings of ITSC 2012, pp. 140–146. IEEE, Anchorage (2012)
12. Drewe, P.: What about time in urban planning & design in the ICT age. In: Proceedings of the CORP Conference (2005)
13. Edwards, D., Elangovan, A., Watkins, K.: Reaching low-density urban areas with the network-inspired transportation system. In: 15th International IEEE Conference on Intelligent Transportation Systems (ITSC), 2012, pp. 826–831. IEEE, Anchorage (2012)
14. Fu, L.: A simulation model for evaluating advanced dial-a-ride paratransit systems. Transp. Res. A Policy Pract. **36**(4), 291–307 (2002)
15. Geoffrion, A.M.: The purpose of mathematical programming is insight, not numbers. Interfaces **7**(1), 81–92 (1976)
16. Haghani, A., Banihashemi, M.: Heuristic approaches for solving large-scale bus transit vehicle scheduling problem with route time constraints. Transp. Res. A Policy Pract. **36**(4), 309–333 (2002)
17. Hall, R.W.: Discrete models/continuous models. Omega **14**(3), 213–220 (1986)
18. Hauptmeier, D., Krumke, S.O., Rambau, J.: The online dial-a-ride problem under reasonable load. In: Proceedings of the 4th Italian Conference on Algorithms and Complexity, CIAC '00, pp. 125–136. Springer, London (2000)
19. Horn, M.: Multi-modal and demand-responsive passenger transport systems: a modelling framework with embedded control systems. Transp. Res. A **36**(2), 167–188 (2002)
20. Jakob, M., Moler, Z.: Modular framework for simulation modelling of interaction-rich transport systems. In: Proceedings of ITSC 2013. IEEE, The Hague (2013)
21. Jlassi, J., Euchi, J., Chabchoub, H.: Dial-a-ride and emergency transportation problems in ambulance services. Comput. Sci. Eng. **2**(3), 17–23 (2012)
22. Kamar, E., Horvitz, E.: Collaboration and shared plans in the open world: studies of ridesharing. In: Proceedings of IJCAI 2009, vol. 9, p. 187 (2009)
23. Kephart, J.O., Chess, D.M.: The vision of autonomic computing. Computer **36**(1), 41–50 (2003)
24. Klügl, F.: Agent-based simulation engineering. PhD thesis, Habilitation Thesis, University of Würzburg (2009)
25. Langevin, A., Mbaraga, P., Campbell, J.F.: Continuous approximation models in freight distribution: an overview. Transp. Res. B Methodol. **30**(3), 163–188 (1996)
26. Lioris, E., Cohen, G., de La Fortelle, A.: Overview of a dynamic evaluation of collective taxi systems providing an optimal performance. In: 2010 IEEE Intelligent Vehicles Symposium (IV), pp. 1110–1115. IEEE, San Diego (2010)

27. Lipmann, M., Lu, X., Paepe, W.E., Sitters, R.A., Stougie, L.: On-line dial-a-ride problems under a restricted information model. Algorithmica **40**(4), 319–329 (2004)
28. Pěchouček, M., Jakob, M., Novák, P.: Towards simulation-aided design of multi-agent systems. In: Programming Multi-Agent Systems, pp. 3–21. Springer, Heidelberg (2012)
29. Quadrifoglio, L., Dessouky, M.: Insertion heuristic for scheduling mobility allowance shuttle transit (MAST) services: sensitivity to service area. In: Computer-Aided Systems in Public Transport. Lecture Notes in Economics and Mathematical Systems, vol. 600. Springer, Heidelberg (2007)
30. Quadrifoglio, L., Dessouky, M.M., Ordóñez, F.: A simulation study of demand responsive transit system design. Transp. Res. A Policy Pract. **42**(4), 718–737 (2008)
31. Regan, A.C., Mahmassani, H.S., Jaillet, P.: Dynamic decision making for commercial fleet operations using real-time information. Transp. Res. Rec. J. Transp. Res. Board **1537**(1), 91–97 (1996)
32. Schuetz, S., Zimmermann, K., Nunzi, G., Schmid, S., Brunner, M.: Autonomic and decentralized management of wireless access networks. IEEE Trans. Netw. Serv. Manag. **4**(2), 96–106 (2007)
33. Shinoda, K., Noda, I., Ohta, M., Kumada, Y., Nakashima, H.: Is dial-a-ride bus reasonable in large scale towns? Evaluation of usability of dial-a-ride systems by simulation. In: Multi-agent for Mass User Support, pp. 105–119. Springer, Heidelberg (2004)
34. Stein, D.M.: Scheduling dial-a-ride transportation systems. Transp. Sci. **12**(3), 232–249 (1978)
35. Uhrmacher, A.M., Weyns, D.: Multi-Agent Systems: Simulation and Applications. CRC Press, Boca Raton (2010)
36. Wilson, N.H.M., Sussman, J., Goodman, L., Hignnet, B.: Simulation of a computer aided routing system (CARS). In: Proceedings of the Third Conference on Applications of Simulation, pp. 171–183. Winter Simulation Conference (1969)

Multi-Agent Traffic Simulation for Development and Validation of Autonomic Car-to-Car Systems

Martin Schaefer, Jiří Vokřínek, Daniele Pinotti, and Fabio Tango

Abstract In this chapter, we present the concept of an integrated multi-agent simulation platform to support the development and validation of autonomic cooperative car-to-car systems. The simulation allows to validate the car-to-car coordination strategies in various traffic scenarios in variable technology penetration levels (i.e. mixing different strategies) and user acceptance of such system as an external observer and/or as a part of the traffic (human in the loop with intelligent cooperative guidance system). The platform combines features of realistic driving simulation, traffic simulation with flexible level of detail and AI controlled vehicles. The principal idea of the platform is to allow the development and study of complex autonomic distributed car-to-car systems for vehicles coordination. The platform provides a development environment and a tool chain that is necessary for the validation of such complex systems. Autonomic car-to-car systems are based on coordination mechanisms between agents, where an agent represents a reasoning unit of a single vehicle. The road traffic is modelled as a multi-agent system of cooperative agents. The interaction between the agents brings autonomic properties into the emerged system (e.g. the traffic adapts to a blockage of a lane and vehicles merge into a second lane). The system also exhibits autonomic properties from a single user perspective. The driver approaches the system in a form of a driver assistance system—we can refer it as an autonomic driver assistance system. The driver is interacting only with the assistance system via a human-machine interface (HMI). The autonomic driver assistance system is hiding the complexity of multi-agent interactions from the user. The related agent of the single vehicle is

M. Schaefer (✉) • J. Vokřínek (✉)
Department of Computer Science, Faculty of Electrical Engineering, Czech Technical University in Prague, Prague, Czech Republic
e-mail: martin.schaefer@fel.cvut.cz; jiri.vokrinek@fel.cvut.cz

D. Pinotti
RE:Lab s.r.l., Reggio Emilia, Italy
e-mail: daniele.pinotti@re-lab.it

F. Tango
Centro Ricerche Fiat – E/E Systems, Orbasano, Italy
e-mail: fabio.tango@crf.it

T.L. McCluskey et al. (eds.), *Autonomic Road Transport Support Systems*, Autonomic Systems, DOI 10.1007/978-3-319-25808-9_10

responsible for an interaction with other agents in the system without any user's intervention.

Keywords Autonomic car-to-car systems • Development and validation • Multi-agent simulation

1 Introduction

In general, our work is motivated by the two main aspects that are common in the automotive and transportation domain—safety and efficiency.

Safety is the key motivation for technological innovation in the automotive industry. The human factor is often the cause of traffic accidents. Most car manufacturers are developing intelligent systems to reduce the influence of inattention or imperfect reasoning of humans. Such systems are mostly deployed as so-called advanced driver assistance systems (ADAS). The driver is still in control of the vehicle and receives suggestions or warnings from these systems. Nowadays, some systems that even actively control the vehicles (e.g. Lane Keeping Assist) have become common. Ultimately, no driver is needed at all in a fully autonomous car. So far, we considered vehicle whose autonomy is based on the vehicle's perception of the environment via sensors. A vehicle like this is designed as a single autonomous robot. Major enhancement of this approach can be achieved by introducing a cooperation between multiple such vehicles. The concept of connected vehicles (C2X communication-equipped vehicles) can broaden the single vehicle's perception by the information received from others via a dedicated communication channel.

In addition to safety, traffic efficiency is the second aspect being addressed by researchers in the automotive and transportation domain. The key assumption is that the capacities of highways are currently used inefficiently because of the reactive control performed by humans. Human drivers usually do not cooperate with the others, and they have very limited or late knowledge about states and intentions of other vehicles. Hence, this fact provides a ground to develop cooperative car-to-car techniques to enhance these features towards a more safety driving yet more efficient usage of the current infrastructures. Such techniques widely exploit the autonomic properties of the system—the self-awareness of the individual vehicles, communication-based shared awareness on the traffic level and a wide range of possible learning and adaptive methods increasing both safety and efficiency of the cooperative traffic.

The ADAS or autonomous vehicles are examples of already existing applications aiming to improve the road safety. Accident-free traffic or at least reduction of the number of accidents is an actual ongoing challenge in the related research areas. The recent achievements in autonomous car development and advanced drive support systems raise research questions about user acceptance of such systems and their effectiveness from the traffic perspective in case of high penetration. The development of next-generation car technologies relies on usage of driving and traffic simulations for testing and validation. The simulations allow to study both the user acceptance and the effectiveness from the traffic perspective. Nowadays, a traffic simulation can be used to evaluate the effects of new technologies on the traffic, while the driving simulators are used to perform human-in-the-loop tests of various in-car equipment.

The characteristics that make car-to-car systems autonomic are discussed in detail in Sect. 2. We discuss the autonomic car-to-car systems as a multi-agent environment where the emergence via interaction of individual agents brings autonomic properties to the global system. From the driver's point of view, the autonomic car-to-car system is considered as an autonomic driver assistance system. A sample implementation of car-to-car systems is introduced in Sect. 3, and the introduced platform is described in detail in Sect. 4. We demonstrate that the platform can be integrated with a proprietary driving simulator and that can be used to perform a human-in-the-loop validation of the driver assistance system. This feature is demonstrated on the pilot experimental validation of the Cooperative Lane Change Assistant in Sect. 5.

2 Role of Autonomic Car-to-Car System

An autonomic car-to-car system relies on the ability of cooperating vehicles to detect and resolve potential dangerous situations. Such situations are normally handled by drivers, but with fast development of autonomous vehicles, the autonomic properties of the cars themselves and car-to-car systems became extremely important. From the perspective of this chapter, the involved vehicles do not necessarily need to be autonomous self-driving cars, but every vehicle is equipped with an agent capable of providing an autonomic behaviour. Such a behaviour consists of a detection of the potentially dangerous situation and suggestion of a corrective maneuver, cooperation abilities by means of information exchange or conflict resolution negotiation. Various examples of such information exchange are in the scope of car-to-car (C2C) or car-to-infrastructure (C2I) communication systems that are under development by the major players of the automotive industry.

Although it is possible that cars will be fully autonomous in future, drivers are still responsible for controlling cars nowadays. There is a necessity of cooperation even within a car between a driver and the agent providing cooperation with other cars. The diversity of drivers makes it challenging to design the human-machine interface (HMI) or the related software agent itself; so, suggestions of systems are beneficial. The suggestions must be acceptable and executable by drivers and thus the car-to-car system is designed to fulfil this requirement. Here, we see the need for autonomicity of the system. The car-to-car system—in a form of the autonomic driver assistance system—must be adaptable to a particular driver. The adaptation or configuration of the system is a complex task in general, and thus we expect that a self-configuration and self-adaptation of the agent can lead to better acceptance of such systems by its users.

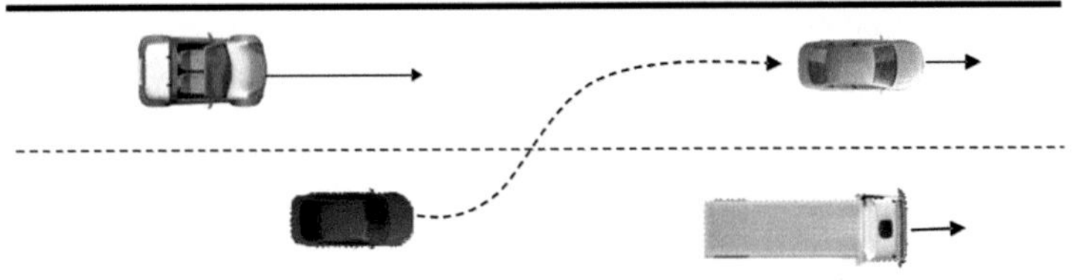

Fig. 1 Example of the dangerous situation of the lane change maneuver

The principles of autonomic car-to-car system features can be demonstrated on a practical example. An example of the situation that exhibits potential hazards is a lane change maneuver. Imagine a situation depicted in Fig. 1. The red car approaches a slowly moving truck and has to safely overtake. The maneuver is straightforward, but the situation is also influenced by a behaviour of other cars in the left lane.

The lane change maneuver is considered to be one of the most difficult driving tasks and special attention is needed: It is estimated that crashes resulting from an improper lane change constitute almost 8 % of all car accidents [6]. A common kind of dangerous situation may occur if the driver underestimates the speed of an approaching vehicle or overlooks it at all. It has been shown that drivers' perception of inter-vehicle distances is often insecure, especially at high velocities [19]. Autonomic lane change assistant (LCA) systems may help human drivers in avoiding severe accidents. An LCA monitors adjacent lanes and keeps the driver informed of the presence of other nearby vehicles. Furthermore, in a case of conflicting resources (i.e. a section of a lane is aimed by two vehicles), a cooperative LCA can considerably improve the handling of resources, boosting a beneficial collaboration between drivers [11]. Moreover, a cooperation among road users should also be associated with an efficient cooperation between the LCA system and a human driver [8], meaning that a proper HMI needs to be built. The example scenario consists of a vehicle, which brakes on a highway, forcing the ego vehicle (i.e. the one driven by the human) to overtake/lane-change while paying attention not to enter in a collision with other vehicles in the adjacent lane that are already overtaking.

The autonomic cooperative car-to-car system detects the situation in advance and performs a twofold action: first, it informs a driver suggesting the right maneuvers, and second, it interacts directly with the other agents, for an automatic resolution of the conflicts. The system suggests the driver via a proper HMI and at the same time the vehicles in the area (within a certain range related to the influence of C2I and C2C running communication exchanges) cooperate in order to avoid any unexpected unsafe behaviour. This cooperation is carried out by using negotiation algorithms for a collision avoidance [24]. This is done in accordance with the traffic perspective, where a set of vehicles is in competition for space and time, and they cooperatively solve their spatiotemporal conflicts.

3 Autonomicity of Car-to-Car System

The source of autonomicity in the car-to-car system is the interaction of the agents implemented to fulfil their local requirements. The interaction is an important aspect of the autonomic car-to-car system. The agents can be designed with various levels of interaction capabilities. We describe in the following sections, the features that can be introduced with increasing interaction capabilities.

3.1 Local Interaction Agents

An agent that senses its operational environment and does not communicate with other agents is the basic unit to form a car-to-car system. The coexistence in the same environment and common objectives (e.g., collision-free drive) are the aspects that imply that there is an implicit coordination among the agents, so that we claim that they form a car-to-car system. The car-to-car system composed of such agents can already begin to exhibit some of the autonomic properties. The system as a unit is self-configured and self-optimized as the effect of local autonomy of agents and their interactions.

Well-defined behaviour of the single agents can lead to desired features of the complex system. The design of the complex heterogeneous traffic system as one unit is difficult to be done, but the system can be composed by many simpler agents.

There are several approaches to design such an agent. The methods can be reactive (e.g., method described in [1] using velocity obstacles) or based on dynamic planning (e.g., a method particularly based on the constraint-based planning [2]). The traffic environment is very dynamic and the behaviour of agents can be hardly predicted; thus, the planning horizon of the agents is in seconds at the operational level or tens of seconds to few minutes at the tactical level. A longer planning horizon is not possible without a reliable communication and information exchange between agents.

3.2 Communicating Agents

Introducing a car-to-car communication brings possibility to enhance the cooperation of the agents. The basic communication may utilize standardized car-to-car broadcast protocols, but there is a need for algorithm-specific information exchange for more advanced cooperation. Desires or plans of each agent can be shared with agents in its neighbourhood, and a negotiation or well-specified coordination protocol is necessary in certain traffic situations.

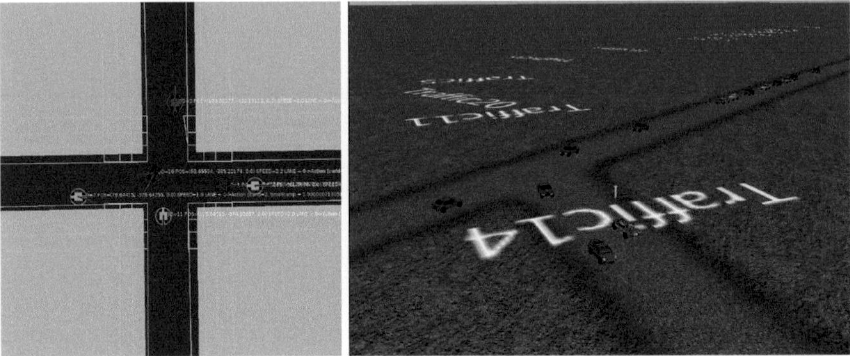

Fig. 2 Traffic situations in which the cooperation is necessary. Visualization of collision avoidance method at x-junction (*left*) and all-way stop junction (*right*)

Let us consider a specific traffic situation in which the cooperation of vehicles is necessary. Figure 2 illustrates a junction without traffic signs nor lights. If vehicles approach the junction at the same time, the vehicle approaching from the right has the right-of-way. This rule can lead to a deadlock if there are vehicles on all incoming lanes. The cooperation is needed to solve the situation.

Now, let us again consider the car-to-car system as an autonomic driver assistance system. Assuming the agents are communicating with each other, the driver assistance system begins to exhibit more autonomicity than it did without communication. Let us explain the last claim. The driver does not know details of the communication, but she/he is provided with the result in a form of suggestions only. The car-to-car system continuously adapts itself to the ongoing execution of the driver and also considers other agents involved in the certain traffic situation. The motivation of the cooperative decision of the agents can be hidden from the driver. The internal interaction within the car-to-car system then introduces more autonomicity into the complex system.

3.3 Adoption of Cooperative Drive System

One of the most critical challenges today is a human driver acceptance of such a system. The incremental integration of the autonomic systems in the real environment will vary from a passive assistance system to an active car control. The key aspect of this process is the effect of the penetration of the system deployed and the heterogeneity of systems used.

Regarding a cooperative behaviour, let us remember a remark by Da Lio and colleagues [5] and Tango et al. [22]. The authors pointed out that mankind used animals, especially horses, as transportation systems for thousands of years. However, they have been replaced by motor vehicles in the last century, which has caused something to be lost: the intelligence of the animals and the interaction (cooperation) with humans (riders, in that case). In the recent book [17], Norman recalls the interaction between a rider and a horse as one example of how a future intelligent interaction should work: "Think of skilled horseback riders. The rider reads the horse, just as the horse can read its rider. (...). This interaction (...) is of special interest because it is an example of two sentient systems, horse and rider, both intelligent, both interpreting the world and communicating their interpretations to each other." (quotation from Da Lio's paper and Norman's book).

This means that the cooperation (we focus on this aspect, even if we know that interaction regards also "competition") occurs between two "sentient" systems; in our case, one is the human agent (the driver) and the other one is not anymore the animal, but the machine agent. Literature provides many works of such a smart collaboration. The H-metaphor (i.e., the rider-horse metaphor) is one of the most relevant and was proposed by Flemish, originally in the aerospace domain, as a guideline for interactions between a vehicle and its driver [7]. Other examples are present in activities of Heide [12] and Inagaki [13], or in works related to the human-robot interactions (see [9, 23]) and adaptive automation (see [18, 20]), where both the human agent and the machine agent can initiate changes in the level of automation, producing modes of automation more closely tied to the operator needs at any given moment.

In the scope of this chapter, the autonomic car-to-car system is equipped with an HMI manager, which provides, via a specific communication channel, the most appropriate HMI to convey warnings or recommendations to the driver: Inputs to the HMI also came from the cooperative driver model agent, so that the human-in-the-loop is made a part of the cooperative environment. Depending on the simulation environment and its inherent critical features, the warning/recommending strategies can either be visual, acoustic, or a combination of them. Examples of visual recommendations are shown in Fig. 3.

The self-configuration property of the HMI can be realized by self-adapting timing of the suggestion. The closed-loop between driver and HMI would allow to adjust the timing so that the driver is suggested on time and the maneuver is performed by the driver as suggested. For example, a driver who reacts slowly would get the suggestion earlier to be able to perform the maneuver at the desired moment.

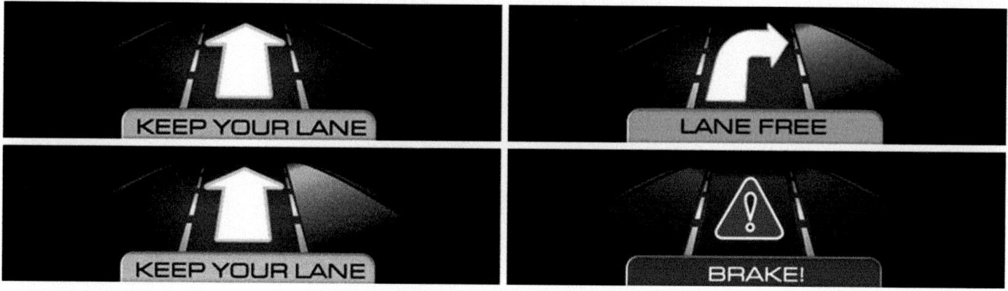

Fig. 3 Examples of visual recommendations of the cooperative driver assistance system

4 Simulation Platform

This section describes the platform for a development of autonomic car-to-car systems. The integrated multi-agent traffic simulation with human-in-the-loop testing abilities provides flexible support for a wide range of testing and validation possibilities for researchers and developers in the field of autonomic vehicles, cooperative drive, driver assistants, and HMI design and development. The system is able to integrate various driving simulators, car control techniques, autonomic cooperative car systems, and human-driven vehicles (an example of such an integration is demonstrated in [25]).

A schematic architecture of the multi-agent simulation system is depicted in Fig. 4. The left-hand side module is responsible for a realistic drive of all simulated vehicles controlled by both human and AI. AI-based vehicles execute instructions autonomously. The human-driven vehicle visualizes the instruction for a human driver using the HMI. Note that there is a reasoning agent for each vehicle. Not only for AI-driven vehicles but even for human-driven ones. The human driver interacts via his/her agent with the rest of the traffic. The multi-agent coordination then includes all the vehicles—both the human-driven and the AI-driven ones. The reasoning is distributed among agents or a centralized mechanism can be used. The model of the environment is a road network. Road networks are commonly

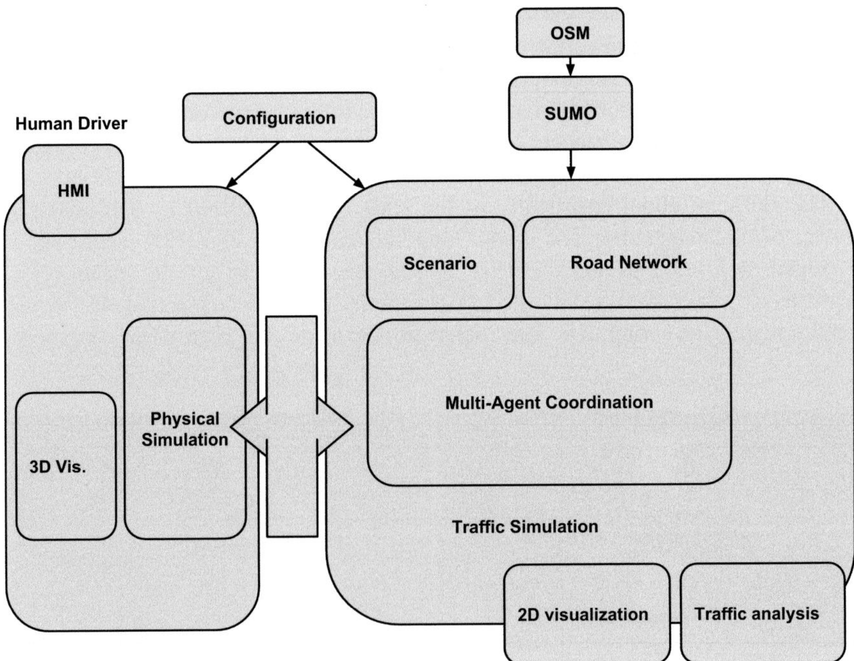

Fig. 4 Schematic architecture of the platform

used in traffic simulations, particularly, model of the SUMO Simulator [16] is adopted in our platform. It allows us to use SUMO tools to import map data (e.g., OpenStreetMaps) as it is shown in Fig. 4.

A physical state update is done in physical simulation module (see Fig. 4) according to agents' actions. Then, the updated physical state is sensed by the agents' sensors. The physics simulation can be performed in various external tools. The realism of the physics can vary with the tool that is used to model particular car. The usage of a driving simulator as a physics simulator brings additional features (e.g., possibility of human-driven vehicle in simulation and 3D visualization).

4.1 Cooperative Driver Model

The cooperative driver model is inspired by the cooperative trajectory planning algorithms widely used in computational robotics for conflict-free navigation of autonomous vehicles (e.g., aerial vehicles [4]). This model enables to plan the trajectory of the vehicle moving on a highway and to cooperatively check the trajectories of the vehicles for conflicts [14]. If a conflict occurs the trajectories of the vehicles are adjusted to be conflict free. This process is repeated to guarantee a cooperative safe drive on the highway. The model is composed of three main components: (1) a highway model, (2) trajectory planning algorithm, and (3) cooperative conflict resolution algorithm [24]. Altogether, these three components form the cooperative driver model that can be used in a multi-agent simulation for a validation of autonomic car-to-car systems.

In this chapter, we refer to the cooperative driver model presented in [24] that is based on a vehicle trajectory planning augmented by techniques from the domain of distributed artificial intelligence and already utilized in multi-agent systems. Altogether, it provides a multi-agent traffic simulation environment that can serve as a framework for evaluation of various cooperative strategies of autonomic car-to-car systems. Thus, it provides a base for further research towards defining representative quality metrics and comparing different approaches.

4.2 Human-Machine Interface

The human-machine interaction interface is designed to present the plan proposed by an autonomic driver assistance system. We prototype an "augmented reality"-based HMI in the OpenDS simulator to demonstrate the proposed concept of presenting proposed maneuvers by the autonomic car-to-car system.

Fig. 5 Example of HMI implementation. The basic setting of driving simulator with integrated driving assistance system (*centre*). The detail of augmented reality-based HMI that is implemented in the driving simulator (braking suggestion on left and lane change to left and acceleration suggestion on right)

The output of the HMI is designed to present the suggested maneuvers, i.e., plan. Figure 5 shows examples of HMI screenshots and a basic setting of the simulator to perform driving experiments. The desired lane is proposed by the blue colouring of the lane of the proposed lane. The speed instruction is projected into a rectangle in the heading direction. The transparency of the rectangle is being adjusted. The rectangle is red if braking is proposed and it is green if the accelerating is proposed. The colour intensity is proportional to the proposed speed change. This HMI implementation is a prototype integrated into the OpenDS simulator. Another external HMI device was used for the experimental validation in Sect. 5.

4.3 Traffic and Driving Simulation

The general concept of simulation platform presented in Fig. 4 was implemented by an integration of a multi-agent autonomous traffic simulation and a driving simulator. The implementation is described in this section and is also illustrated in Fig. 6. The traffic simulation implementation (on right) is based on the simulation toolkit Alite [15]. The component performs a multi-agent event-based simulation of all vehicles in the scenario. Each agent is responsible for controlling a corresponding vehicle. The multi-agent simulation allows to use various coordination and communication strategies of autonomic agents. An agent in this context is specified as an entity that can perceive and act in the environment. In Fig. 6, we present the implementation of the coordination mechanism by two particular methods. The SD agent is an implementation of a maneuver planning method based on keeping a safe distance after each maneuver execution [21]. An adapted optimized reciprocal collision avoidance (ORCA) mechanism of Berg et al. [3] is implemented in the ORCA agent. tHESE agent implementations are examples of approaches to coordination methods. The agents' sensors and actuators are used to provide interactions with the environment—a realistic driving simulator.

The integration of a realistic driving simulator enables the simulation to validate the system in the realistic-physics environment. Thanks to the openness and flexibility of the integrated simulator architecture, there is a possibility to incorporate

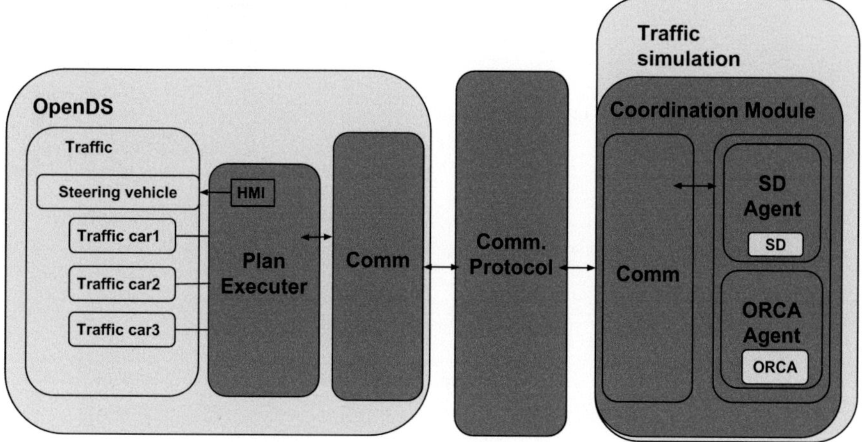

Fig. 6 Implementation scheme of integration of the OpenDS driving simulator with the developed multi-agent simulation platform

a wide range of driving simulators. An example of driving simulator integrated in the system is open-source Java-based simulator OpenDS.[1] Another example is the industrial stationary driving simulator CoopSim with the SCANeR™simulation engine[2] used for the following experimental validation.

5 Pilot Experimental Validation

The simulation system presented in this chapter has been used within the development of a cooperative lane change assistant (C-LCA) by the A.E.B. Technologies SpA. The simulator is owned by Reggio Emilia Innovazione and hosted at RE:Lab premises. The development of such a system consisted of many phases of simulations and testing within the traffic and user perspective. For the realistic user experience the SCANeR™driving simulation engine has been used.

The system is a fixed-base simulator that comprises a mock-up of a car with real driving controls, specifically a seat, steering wheel, pedals, gear, handbrake, and a digital simulated dashboard displaying a traditional instrumental panel, with RPM, speedometer and vehicle subsystem lamps (see Fig. 7). The scenario is projected on a frontal screen at the driver's field of view, together with the rear mirror displayed on the top of the field of view and the wing mirrors on the sides. Environmental sounds, such as the engine rumble, are provided through the loudspeakers. This

[1]www.opends.eu.

[2]www.scanersimulation.com.

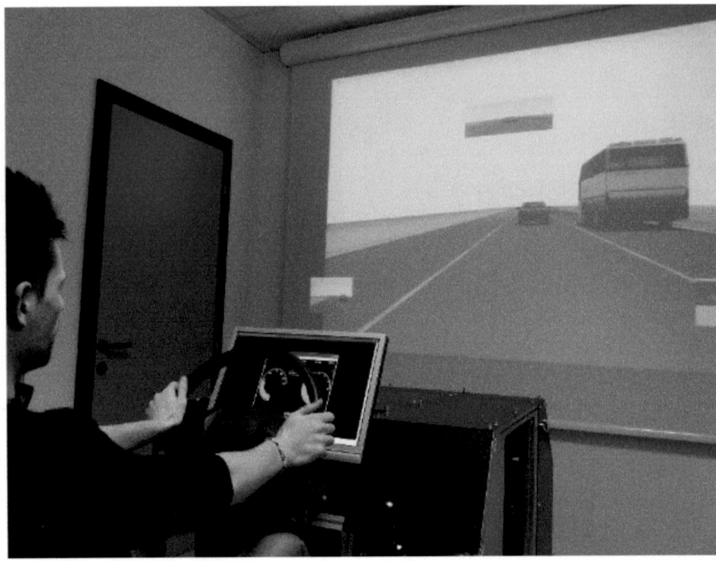

Fig. 7 Stationary driving simulator based on SCANeR™engine during the tests

driving simulator does not provide support for cooperative traffic scenarios out of the box. Its integration in the developed multi-agent simulation framework enables to simulate a wide range of cooperative scenarios.

Several driving experiments were carried out on the C-LCA with the following objectives:

- Testing the connection with the multi-agent coordination module and the cooperation among the agents.
- Validating the ongoing development of the Cooperative HMI by means of a test-and-develop loop approach.
- Estimating the efficiency of the cooperative driver model involved in the C-LCA in improving safety and driver's performance.
- Evaluating user's trust and acceptance of the autonomic driver assistance system and of the HMI.

The cooperative traffic scenario consists of agents with limited resources, and thus, potentially dangerous situations can occur. Hence, the focal point is not the ego-vehicle, but the environmental perspective becomes of paramount importance if we assume to change the ego-vehicle traditional perspective and switch it to an autonomic cooperative system point of view.

For this experimental study, 28 users were involved (14 males, 14 females – Mean age = 37.8, SD = 12.6). All participants had a valid driver's licence for at least 4 years and usually drive at least 5000 km per year. Participants were asked to perform a sequence of lane changes on a highway, in a traffic environment, which simulated a real driving situation. The lane change was induced by a brake of the

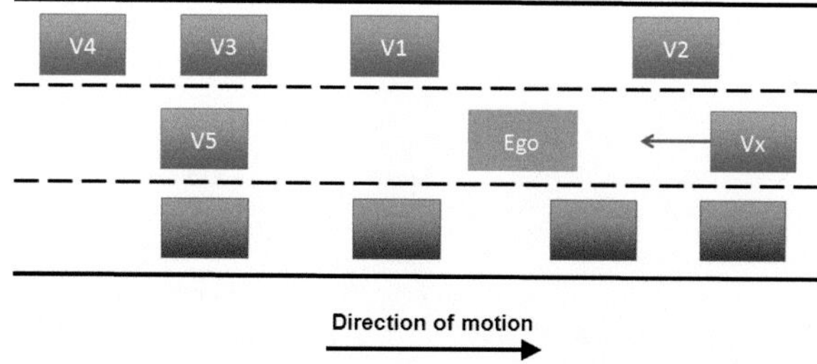

Fig. 8 Illustration of the driving scenario at the moment of VX braking

vehicle ahead the Ego car (VX, see Fig. 8) and the user was asked to overtake it, paying attention to the other vehicles around him/her. Every participant was asked to perform three runs:

1. Baseline situation (BA)
2. Non-cooperative warnings (NC)
3. Cooperative system (C-LCA) activated (CO)

The NC run was included in the study in order to compare the C-LCA system with a state-of-the-art ADAS implementation, to investigate the usability of this innovative cooperative system: Since this book is focused on cooperation, though, the experimental results from the NC run are not included in this chapter.

Before each driving session, the interviewer explained the driving task to the user; additionally, before the assisted runs, the interviewer described the operation and purpose of the C-LCA system under investigation, also by showing the screenshots of the visual interface. The main test session was then carried out, the driving scenario being the one illustrated in Fig. 8 while other vehicles are in transit around the Ego car, VX starts braking, so that the user must choose between changing lane or slowing down in turn.

Finally, participants were asked to fill out some questionnaires to address their interaction and confidence with the system, including the widespread NASA-TLX questionnaire to evaluate the workload [10]. The questions of the NASA-TLX are the following ones:

1. Mental demand: How mentally demanding was the task?
2. Physical demand: How physically demanding was the task?
3. Temporal demand: How hurried or rushed was the pace of the task?
4. Performance: How successful were you in accomplishing what you were asked to do?
5. Effort: How hard did you have to work to accomplish your level of performance?
6. Frustration: How insecure, discouraged, irritated, stresses, and annoyed were you?

Participant's answers to the workload questionnaire are shown in Fig. 9, on a scale from 0 to 20, for each of the six questions. The results indicate that the C-LCA system effectively reduced the perceived workload (total mean estimation: 44.4 vs.

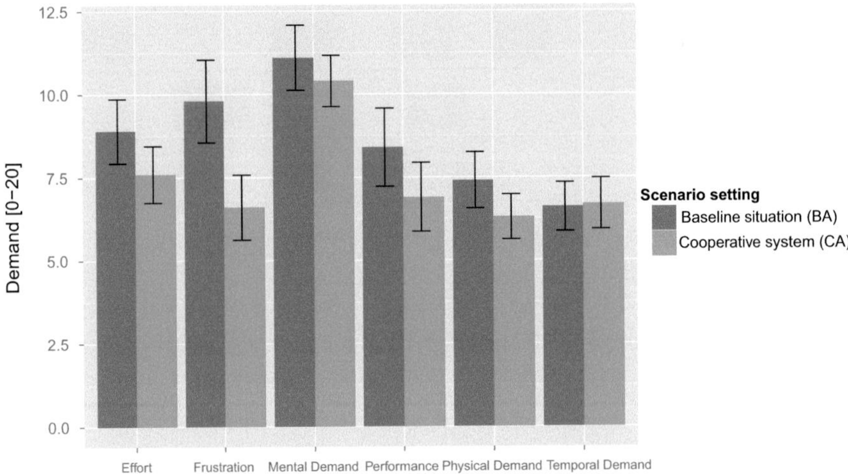

Fig. 9 Workload questionnaire outcomes comparing scenario setting with cooperative system and baseline situation. The average demand is presented with standard error bounds

52.1), thus supporting the users with the cognitive load induced by the driving task; in particular, the frustration indicator showed to be the most affected by the cooperative system, dropping from the original 9.8 (baseline run) to 6.6.

6 Conclusion

The multi-agent simulation of cooperative cars implemented by cooperative driver models is presented as a core of the autonomic car-to-car system. The integration of driving simulator enhances the system with a feature of the realistic drive. The interface between cooperative system and driver provided by the HMI manager allows human-in-the-loop simulation testing and validation.

Important autonomic properties are related to the multi-agent coordination mechanism. The parameters of the coordination mechanism can be continuously adapted according to the observed situation and execution in the environment. Since the road traffic environment is highly dynamic, it is expected that a dynamic parameter configuration can improve the performance of coordination mechanisms. This self-configuration property can be used for a variety of parameters, e.g., adaptation to the current weather condition or adaptation of perception radius to the actual vehicle speed.

The presented simulation system is designed to integrate various driving simulators and/or various car control and coordination strategies. There is a wide range of scenarios that can be covered by the developed simulation platform. The pilot experimental validation of the developed system on the lane change maneuver scenario is presented. A C-LCA HMI was developed and integrated in order to test the involvement of the human driver in a cooperative scenario (i.e., does he/she trust the cooperative system? Will he/she follow the recommendations coming from the HMI?). Feedback from the user experiments provide useful insight for the research in the field of the coordination strategies and ADAS, which may considerably increase driving safety and performance.

The presented results of the experiments indicate that both the stress and perceived workload are reduced with increasing functionality of the assistance system. Going back to the motivating horse-rider example, the cooperative system starts to play the role of the intelligent vehicle providing autonomic features and effectively reducing cognitive load of the driver. The next step of the development of driver assistance systems may address a group of autonomic features based on continuous feedback from driver, e.g., self-configuration and self-optimization of the HMI. The HMI provides instructions for a driver while it is continuously observing driver's execution and adjusting timing of instructions according to the driver's behaviour.

Acknowledgements This work was supported by the Ministry of Education, Youth and Sports of Czech Republic within grant no. LD12044.

References

1. Alonso-mora, J., Breitenmoser, A., Beardsley, P., Siegwart, R.: Reciprocal collision avoidance for multiple car-like robots. In: Proceedings of IEEE International Conference on Robotics Automation ICRA, pp. 360–366 (2012). http://www.disneyresearch.com/research/projects/DisplaySwarm/alonsomora12icra_paper.pdf
2. Anderson, S.J., Karumanchi, S.B., Iagnemma, K.: Constraint-based planning and control for safe, semi-autonomous operation of vehicles. In: 2012 IEEE Intelligent Vehicles Symposium, pp. 383–388 (2012). http://ieeexplore.ieee.org/lpdocs/epic03/wrapper.htm?arnumber=6232153
3. Berg, J.V.D., Guy, S., Lin, M., Manocha, D.: Reciprocal n-body collision avoidance. In: Robotics Research, pp. 1–16 (2010). http://link.springer.com/chapter/10.1007/978-3-642-19457-3_1
4. Cap, M., Novak, P., Selecky, M., Faigl, J., Vokrinek, J.: Asynchronous decentralized prioritized planning for coordination in multi-robot system. In: Intelligent Robots and Systems (IROS) (2013)
5. Da Lio, M., Biral, F., Galvani, M., Saroldi, A.: Will intelligent vehicles evolve into human-peer robots? In: Intelligent Vehicles Symposium (IV), 2012 IEEE, pp. 304–309. IEEE, New York (2012)
6. Fitch, G.M., Hankey, J.M.: Investigating improper lane changes: driver performance contributing to lane change near-crashes. In: Proceedings of the Human Factors and Ergonomics Society Annual Meeting, vol. 56, pp. 2231–2235. Sage Publications, Thousand Oaks (2012)
7. Flemisch, F.O., Adams, C.A., Conway, S.R., Goodrich, K.H., Palmer, M.T., Schutte, M.C.: The H-Metaphor as a Guideline for Vehicle Automation and Interaction Report No. NASA/TM-2003-212672. NASA Langley, Langley (2003)
8. Flemisch, F., Kelsch, J., Löper, C., Schieben, A., Schindler, J., Heesen, M.: Cooperative control and active interfaces for vehicle assistance and automation. Tech. rep., ATZ - Automobiltechnische Zeitschrift 9 (2008)

9. Goodrich, M.A., Schultz, A.C.: Human-robot interaction: a survey. Found. Trends Hum. Comput. Interact. **1**(3), 203–275 (2007)
10. Hart, S.G., Staveland, L.E.: Development of nasa-tlx (task load index): results of empirical and theoretical research. In: Hancock, P.A., Meshkati, N. (eds.) Human Mental Workload. Elsevier, Amsterdam (1988)
11. Heesen, M., Baumann, M., Kelsch, J., Nause, D., Friedrich, M.: Investigation of cooperative driving behaviour during lane change in a multi-driver simulation environment. In: Human Factors: A View from an Integrative Perspective. Human Factors and Ergonomics Society Europe Chapter, Toulouse (2012)
12. Heide, A., Henning, K.: The "cognitive car": a roadmap for research issues in the automotive sector. Annu. Rev. Control **30**(2), 197–203 (2006)
13. Inagaki, T.: Smart collaboration between humans and machines based on mutual understanding. Annu. Rev. Control **32**(2), 253–261 (2008)
14. Janovský, P.: Cooperative collision avoidance of road vehicles. Bachelor's thesis, Czech Technical University in Prague (2011)
15. Komenda, A., Vokrinek, J., Cap, M., Pechoucek, M.: Developing multiagent algorithms for tactical missions using simulation. IEEE Intell. Syst. **28**(1), 42–49 (2013). http://doi.ieeecomputersociety.org/10.1109/MIS.2012.90
16. Krajzewicz, D., Hertkorn, G., Rössel, C., Wagner, P.: Sumo (simulation of urban mobility). In: Proceedings of the 4th Middle East Symposium on Simulation and Modelling, pp. 183–187 (2002)
17. Norman, D.A.: The Design of Future Things: Author of the Design of Everyday Things. BasicBooks, New York (2007)
18. Parasuraman, R., Sheridan, T.B., Wickens, C.D.: A model for types and levels of human interaction with automation. IEEE Trans. Syst. Man Cybern. Syst. Hum. **30**(3), 286–297 (2000). doi:10.1109/3468.844354. http://ieeexplore.ieee.org/stamp/stamp.jsp?tp=&arnumber=844354&isnumber=18307
19. Roelofsen, M., Bie, J., Jin, L., Van Arem, B.: Assessment of safety levels and an innovative design for the lane change assistant. In: 2010 IEEE Intelligent Vehicles Symposium (IV), pp. 83–88 (2010)
20. Scerbo, M.W.: Theoretical perspectives on adaptive automation. Automation and Human Performance: Theory and Applications (A 98-12010 01-54), pp. 37–63. Lawrence Erlbaum Associates Publishers, Mahwah (1996)
21. Schaefer, M.: Noncooperative collision avoidance of road vehicles. Bachelor's thesis, Czech Technical University in Prague (2011)
22. Tango, F., Saroldi, A., Da Lio, M.: Implementation of a co-driver for continuous support. In: 19th World Congress on Intelligent Transportation Systems (ITS), Vienna (2012)
23. Thrun, S.: Toward a framework for human-robot interaction. Hum. Comput. Interact. **19**(1–2), 9–24 (2004)
24. Vokrinek, J., Janovsky, P., Faigl, J., Benda, P., Tango, F., Pinotti, D.: A cooperative driver model for traffic simulations. In: 11th IEEE International Conference on Industrial Informatics (INDIN), pp. 756–761 (2013)
25. Vokrinek, J., Schaefer, M., Pinotti, D.: Multi-agent traffic simulation for human-in-the-loop cooperative drive systems testing. In: Proceedings of the 2014 International Conference on Autonomous Agents and Multi-Agent Systems, AAMAS '14, pp. 1691–1692. International Foundation for Autonomous Agents and Multiagent Systems, Richland (2014). http://dl.acm.org/citation.cfm?id=2615731.2616128

Performance Maintenance of ARTS Systems

Finding and Managing Performance Deterioration by Undesired System Adaptation

René Schumann

Abstract Autonomic Road Transportation Support (ARTS) systems will operate with adaptive system behavior to make them self-managing. In this chapter, we discuss methods for analyzing the performance of these kinds of systems. The performance of these systems not only depends on the state of the environment but also on the adaptation the system has made so far. Analyzing the performance can hardly be done analytically; we have to rely on empirical studies. A structured way for implementing such analysis of adaptive systems, like ARTS, is presented. Furthermore, we discuss different approaches and provide examples how such problems could be encountered during the design of ARTS systems.

Keywords Adaptive behavior • Performance monitoring • Performance maintainance • Regulated autonomy • Self-stabilizing

1 Introduction

In the process of designing Autonomic Road Transportation Support (ARTS) systems, the goal is to enhance road transport support (RTS) systems with adaptive and self-managing capabilities. The self-managing capabilities for autonomic computing have been detailed, e.g., in [12]. According to [12], a system is considered to be self-managing if it has the following characteristics:

- Self-configuration: The system can automatically configure and reconfigure itself from the available system components.
- Self-optimization: The system can monitor its performance and can reconfigure or control resources to improve or maintain a specified functionality within specific quality boundaries.

R. Schumann (✉)
Institute of Information Systems, HES-SO Valais-Wallis, Sierre, Switzerland
e-mail: rene.schumann@hevs.ch

T.L. McCluskey et al. (eds.), *Autonomic Road Transport Support Systems*, Autonomic Systems, DOI 10.1007/978-3-319-25808-9_11

– Self-healing: The system will monitor their performance, diagnose problems, and recover from faults.
– Self-protection: The system will try to maintain its functionality when problems occur that cannot be handled by self-healing.

The goal is to allow ARTS to adapt to unpredicted situations and changes in their environment without human interaction. Thus, a key characteristic of an ARTS system in contrast to a conventional RTS system is that it can *adapt* its behavior. We classify these types of systems as *adaptive systems*.

Adaptive systems can be designed either with a central or decentralized design perspective. Assuming a centralized perspective, an adaptive system can be considered as a *model-based reflex agent* or as a more complex form of agent according to the classification of Russell and Norvig [18]. In such systems, the action selection mechanism uses the perceived state of the environment and an internal state. The internal state can store acquired knowledge about the environment, e.g., by machine learning techniques, or provide a knowledge base, e.g., needed for automated planning techniques (see, e.g., [6]). Both techniques can be used for implementing adaptive systems, like ARTS. Assuming a decentralized design focus, the overall adaptive system is not considered to be represented as one single agent but as a multi-agent system (MAS). Within a MAS, adaptation can also occur due to the interaction of agents, which is also known as emergent behavior [24] or emergence [23].

Of course, each agent in a MAS can also have the ability to learn and/or plan, which means that techniques can be combined. We are not going to address the design of adaptive systems in more detail within this chapter. Instead, in the following section, we just assume that a system is an adaptive one, e.g., an ARTS system. However, note that the techniques presented address issues of adaptive systems in general. Also the approach presented here can be used for sensitivity analysis of ARTS and RTS systems.

So if we are going to compare RTS and ARTS systems in a dynamic environment, i.e., the environment is changing during the runtime of the system, we would expect the ARTS system to show better performance than a conventional RTS in terms of a given common objective function. In the remainder of the chapter, we assume, without loss of generality, that the goal is to maximize an objective function. The adaptation of a system's behavior at runtime can either increase or decrease the resulting objective value, by which we measure the performance of the system. In case the objective is increased, we consider the adaption as *desired*; otherwise we consider it as *undesired*. Note that the adaptation of a system's behavior is per se not *desired* or *undesired*; both are possible.

During the design process of an ARTS system, it is the goal of the designer to implement a system which exposes desired adaptation in a dynamic environment, while avoiding the occurrence of undesired adaptation in any potential environment, in which the system might operate in.

Considering that ARTS systems are supposed to manage a critical infrastructure of our society, the maintenance of their performance becomes crucial. To realize this we must consider means to design and analyze ARTS to increase the level of confidence users and managers of the traffic infrastructure have in a particular ARTS system. Within this chapter, we focus on two aspects to increase the confidence in ARTS systems:

1. The identification of situations in which *undesired* adaptation of the system's behavior occurs,
2. means to avoid performance deterioration due to *undesired* adaptation.

Each of these aspects is discussed within a particular section, describing ideas, techniques, and limitations of the presented approaches. Of course, both aspects can be combined, e.g., to validate that a particular approach for avoiding unwanted adaptation provides the expected results.

2 Identifying *Undesired* Adaptation of System's Behaviors in ARTS

As we have outlined above, an undesired adaptation of a system's behavior is characterized by a deteriorating performance of the overall system over time, which are not caused by changes in the environment. We are not primarily interested in performance deterioration that is caused by changes in the environment. For example, a conventional RTS would show worse performance if the patterns in which the traffic arrives change over time. In such cases performance deterioration is caused by a changed environment. Given identical inputs, the system's performance would not change. We are interested in the effects of adaptation, i.e., the performance changes even for identical inputs.

Performance analysis can be performed either by analytical or empirical means. Considering the fact that we address here systems that can adapt and operate in an environment that changes in time, current analytical means are challenged. In fact, research providing formal proofs for the performance of systems operating in dynamic environments, or with adaptive behaviors, is a rather new field, and only a few publications exist that address the formal analysis of adaptive systems (e.g., [1, 4, 10, 25]).

The challenge with these approaches is that the potential state spaces of the environment and the adaptive system are hard to model, and if so, they are very large, even not countable infinite. But even if we are able to handle the huge search space, a more general problem arises. As we have outlined before, adaptive systems should be able to operate in environments not necessarily foreseen at design time. But to create an appropriate model for the analytical analysis, the environment of the system needs to be known. As outlined before, the potential state space is unknown at design time and therefore also at validation time. So even if we take the effort to identify all potential states, this would go against the design principle that the system should be able to operate in unknown environments.

As a consequence, researchers have investigated empirical methods to investigate the behavior of their adaptive systems (e.g. [11, 16, 21]). Empirical testing of ARTS systems is typically done by running a number of simulation runs of the adaptive systems in different simulated environments. So, e.g., consider a new traffic light management system is tested within a traffic flow simulator. This kind of simulation corresponds to testing. A problem that arises in the search for negative adaption occurs, as it is not expected to happen; it is unclear which situations, i.e., which setting of parameters of the model, should be tested for such a behavior. Thus to increase the probability, a large number of simulation runs under different environments need to be performed. This raises the need for more systematic approach to simulation studies.

In the design of a systematic approach for using simulations to investigate the system performance in various environments, we have to identify two situations that constrain our approach:

1. Simulation runs can be executed fast, e.g., due to a simplified model,
2. Simulations are considered to be slow[1]

In the first case, we can apply search techniques, similar to those presented by Hudson et al. [11]. In their methodology for testing self-adapting systems, they search for a parameter setting that causes the worst possible performance of the system. While this is promising in providing some approximation of lower bounds of the system performance, it has two potential drawbacks, as (a) it requires a large number of simulation runs and (b) in its current form it does not provide all parameter settings in which the performance is lower than an *acceptable threshold*.

As pointed out before, traffic simulations can be computationally expensive by themselves, i.e., it can take several minutes computing time to run the simulation, and therefore the application of this approach is limited. This observation is supported by the research addressing the calibration of a traffic simulation model (see, e.g., [7–9, 15]). In this line of research, various methods are discussed to minimize the number of required simulation runs to calibrate the model. Thus, for the empirical investigation of ARTS, which will be based on traffic simulations, these techniques mentioned above seem to be less suitable. Therefore we need a methodology to find the effects of undesired adaptation of the system's behavior that requires less computational efforts.

In the following, we describe the principles of systematic simulation that can be used to search for the occurrence of undesired adaptation. First, it is required to find situations that could occur, in case the ARTS system does not perform well. Second, it needs to be investigated if the bad performance is caused by a degenerated scenario (which very likely will never occur in reality) or if we have found a *performance hole* in the system. In the following, we outline this methodology and concepts in more detail.

[1]A traffic simulation for 1 h of real traffic can take several minutes in computational time.

2.1 *Strategies for Identifying Performance Decrease of Adaptive Systems*

Within a simulation study, we have to explore the behavior of the ARTS system in different scenarios, e.g., different traffic conditions. Therefore it is necessary to have a simulation model that has been calibrated with a *base* scenario. Also it is required that we can modify the scenario by modifying the parameters of the simulation model. And finally, to enable an automated analysis, it is required that the control strategy for a given model can be exchanged in a similar fashion.

It has become clear so far that it is not sufficient to just simulate and evaluate the adaptive control system based on this single scenario. The scenario needs to be evolved. The *base* scenario is the starting point for a number of possible worlds that span from the initial scenario. Therefore the simulation model needs to be systematically modified, to evaluate how the ARTS system will perform in various possible worlds. The approach for implementing this type of analysis has been motivated by previous work, in particular [14]. The approach utilizes the concepts of *modifier* functions, or *modifiers* for short.

The *base* scenario is specified by a particular configuration of the parameters of the simulation model. A *modifier* function transforms a configuration of the simulation model parameters into another configuration. Thereby typically only one parameter is slightly changed. In this sense the *modifier* function implements a neighborhood relation between different configurations of the simulation model parameters. An example for a traffic simulation could be the increase of the traffic density by 1 %. By applying a *modifier* to a particular scenario, we evolve the environment in which the ARTS system is operating in. Attached to each *modifier* function is a probability value, which represents the expected probability of such a modification occurring in the world that we would like to simulate. *Modifier* functions are domain specific and need to be defined specifically for the simulation model and the ARTS system under investigation. Starting from a base scenario, we can, as outlined above, apply different sequences of a given set of *modifiers* to derive the space of possible worlds.

Note that in such a sequence each *modifier* can occur multiple times. An example for the search space starting from a *base* scenario (s) and a set of modifiers(m_1, m_2, m_3) is shown in Fig. 1.

It is clear that each simulation that tests the performance of an ARTS in one scenario can be time consuming. Also the number of possible worlds that can be generated from the *base* scenario is infinite, as the length of sequences of modifiers is not limited. To provide an analysis of an ARTS system in a reasonable amount of time, the different scenarios must be created and evaluated in a systematic way and not at random. Therefore, to evaluate the ARTS system, we need to provide an expansion strategy that defines in which sequence the different scenarios should be simulated. Therefore we use the associated probability values of each modifier.

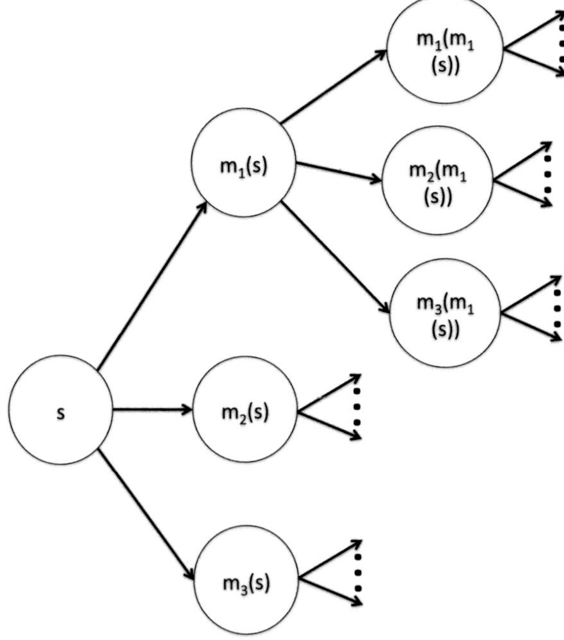

Fig. 1 Representation of the state space of possible worlds for a *base* scenario s and the three modifiers m_1, m_2, m_3

In fact we assume that each scenario has a probability of occurrence. Starting from the *base* scenario (which has the probability one), we can calculate the probabilities of all direct neighboring scenarios[2] created by applying the corresponding *modifier* function.

When expanding a particular scenario and computing its neighbors, we add the non-tested neighbors to a list of possible expansions within the space of possible scenarios. Scenarios to be investigated and expanded are taken from the head of this list, which is sorted by decreasing probability. By applying this strategy, we simulate the scenarios with a decreasing probability in which we believe they might occur. This strategy for investigating different scenarios in the simulation shows the *anytime* property, i.e., the simulation study can be stopped at any time, but can still guarantee that the most probable scenarios are tested within the limited amount of time. The *anytime* property makes this approach very suitable for situations, where we have to investigate any computationally expensive adaptive system, which is the case for traffic simulation and ARTS systems, as outlined above.

[2]The probability of a scenario can be computed by the probability of the modifier and the scenario from which it was derived.

2.2 Means for Identifying Decreasing Performance of Adaptive Systems

We have now described the principles and strategies for systematically exploring the space of possible worlds in which an ARTS could operate in. To execute simulation studies, as we have outlined, we need to put the simulation system, e.g., a traffic flow simulation, in the *loop*. As it has become clear so far, the execution of simulations needs to be automated.

A simulation controlling system has to start and stop the simulation and automatically modify simulation parameters to explore various environmental states. We rely here on existing work by others, e.g., [14] and our own experience [22]. The architecture of the simulation controlling system is shown in Fig. 2. To put the simulator in the loop, we need a `SimulationStudyController`. This component creates and maintains the experimentation plan, based on one of the strategies for searching in the space of different scenarios as outlined above. The scenario gets simulated in the conventional simulation system and is gathered during the simulation runs. Afterwards, it needs to be stored, which is done by the `ResultHandling` component. Also first evaluations can be implemented here. This can be used to start analysis as soon as the first data is available. Through this integration, initial results can be used to modify the experimentation plan automatically during runtime, e.g., new simulation runs can be scheduled. Thus, the experiment design, the data generation in the simulation, and the data analysis are not sequential phases. This provides further potential for accelerating simulation studies of ARTS systems. Here we do not discuss the details of the implementation nor potential improvements of the performance; instead we address the main principles and the usage of this simulation control system.

In the following we assume a simpler result handling component to provide a brief discussion. The amount of data generated by an automated simulation study can be quite large. Based on this data, we have to identify if a particular ARTS system has shown an *undesired* adaptation of its behavior. Undesired adaptation causes a deterioration of the performance of the ARTS system; thus, we can limit our further investigation to those scenarios in which we have measured a bad performance.

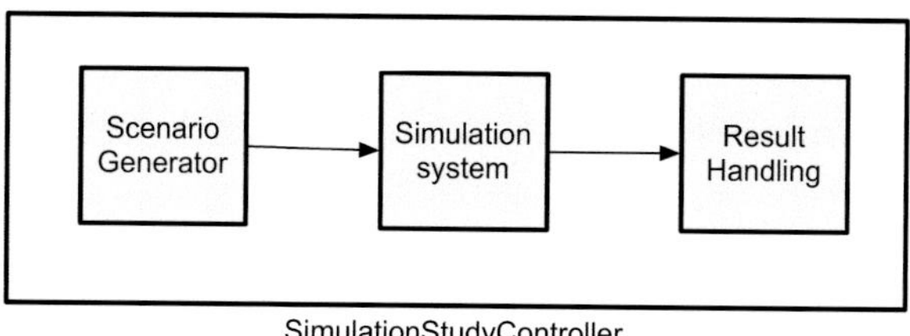

Fig. 2 Components of a simulation controlling system, figure adapted from [22]

Note that a bad performance of an ARTS system is not necessarily caused only by *undesired* adaptation, but it is a necessary observation. Also RTS that do not adapt their behavior can perform badly for particular scenarios, e.g., if the traffic density exceeds the available capacities. In such a scenario performance will decrease independently of the traffic control strategy.

Scenarios with a bad performance need to be investigated in more detail. A scenario causing the ARTS system to expose a bad performance can than be analyzed with different control strategies. If those control strategies have a significant better performance than the ARTS system, we have found a *performance hole* of the adaptive system. It is very likely that this was caused by an undesired adaptation or another flaw in the design of the system. In contrast, if the performance of the different control strategies is very similar, no control strategy can achieve a satisfactory performance. It is very likely that this is caused by a degenerated scenario. We have outlined above how such a degenerated scenario could be created for by the search strategy we apply.

If it is not possible to separate the control strategy from the model, we cannot provide a fully automated way of detecting performance hole in adaptive systems. Then data still needs to be interpreted by a domain expert. An expert, e.g., a traffic engineer, has to reconfirm if the particular bad performance was caused by the occurrence of a design problem (e.g., an undesired adaptation) of the control system, or if this performance is a consequence of the current ill-defined scenario. But by only presenting scenarios with a particular bad performance of the ARTS system to the expert, we already increase the probability of finding cases of undesired adaptation of the ARTS system.

To summarize, the presented approach provides a search heuristic for undesired adaptation of system's behavior. In particular when simulations are time intensive, we provide a strategy to investigate at least the most likely scenarios in a given time. Thus, we cannot provide any guarantees regarding the performance of the system in any arbitrary environment. Our goal is to increase the confidence level of ARTS systems. We have designed the approach in a way that it allows us to investigate the performance of ARTS in various possible scenarios. As the search for rather probable scenarios has the anytime property, we can increase the confidence level of the adaptive system by increasing the available computation time. The confidence level can be translated to the inverse probability of a particular sequence of modifications starting from a base scenario.

3 Avoiding Undesired Adaptation of System's Behaviors

As indicated before, an empirical approach cannot provide any formal guarantees that an adaptive system does not show undesired adaptation. Also we still intend to design ARTS systems in a way that they can expose desired adaptation of their behaviors to utilize the advantages of autonomic computing in traffic management. Therefore, performance maintenance of ARTS systems should already be addressed at design time. The focus of this section is to discuss the principles as to how ARTS systems can become more resilient against undesired adaptations. We consider here two principles: avoiding undesired adaptations (a) by design or (b) by self-regulation.[3]

3.1 Avoiding Undesired Adaptations by Design

During the design of an ARTS system, or any other adaptive systems, the focus is typically on exploiting the adaptation in favor of the performance of the system, e.g., by providing some autonomic computing features. This is, of course, necessary, but it is also necessary to consider the potential drawbacks of a particular control strategy that might cause undesired adaptations of the system's behavior, directly in the design phase. But this implies that potential undesired adaptations are known in advance. To give you a concrete example of such an approach to the domain of traffic routing, we present an example originally published in [5].

The task is to provide routing strategies for vehicles in an urban environment. In particular, in an urban environment, we have to consider the problem as a dynamic traffic routing problem because the problem structure changes while solving the problem, e.g., roads gets blocked while cars are navigating to their destinations. It is obvious that systems that can adapt its behavior could react to these changes at runtime to improve or at least maintain the overall system's performance. A widely used algorithm for solving dynamic routing problems is the well-known ant colony optimization (ACO) algorithm. The main idea of such a routing algorithm is that ants place information in the environment in the form of so-called pheromones. Pheromones evaporate over time. In case an ant needs to make a routing decision between two or more paths, it follows more likely the one with the strongest pheromone concentration. This stigmergy allows the system to adapt its behavior in order to find the shortest path between a start and an end point in a dynamic environment. For more information about ACO-like algorithms and their application in traffic, we refer to the literature, e.g., [2, 3, 13].

The underlying principle of ACO has a significant drawback for routing in urban environments with a high traffic density. If the traffic density is high, the ACO routing will cause traffic jams, as all vehicles follow the strongest pheromone concentration, as capacity on each road is limited. As ACO-based routing can handle dynamic environments, it can recover from these congestions, as cars will take a different route. But due to the principle of following other ants as a fundamental principle of the routing approach, these situations will emerge regularly in conditions such as heavy traffic, as it can be often found in urban areas today.

[3] It could be argued to subsume self-regulation, as an aspect of self-healing, according to the characterization used by Kephart and Chess [12], mentioned above.

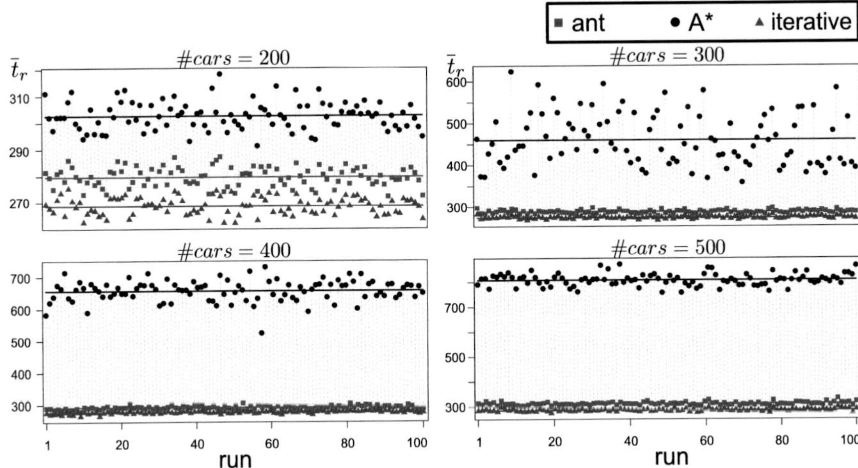

Fig. 3 Evaluation of the inverse ant-based routing, from [5]. *Horizontal lines* show average values

Based on the observation of these shortcomings of ACO-based routing, we have modified the principle of the routing algorithm in [5] to avoid the occurrence of the undesired behaviors of the system. We have presented an *inverted* ACO. It is inverse in the sense that a strong pheromone concentration will not attract more vehicles, but rather the contrary, making vehicles search for other paths. The idea is that ants try to avoid dense roads. Of course, this approach can only work if a number of alternative paths exist, and therefore it is better suited for urban scenarios rather than a highway system.

The pheromone concentration is considered to be a marker for the traffic density a vehicle can expect on that particular road. This information is used within an A* routing algorithm, determining the route for each vehicle. Experiments have shown that this routing algorithm provides a competitive performance, in terms of avoiding the occurrence of congested roads. The results presented in Fig. 3 have been created based on 100 start-goal settings with ten replications per run on the real road network of a small-sized city in Germany. Within these graphs the performance for the inverse ant-based routing, a simple A*, and an iterative algorithm is shown. Iterative routing refers here to a method that computes a dynamic user equilibrium (see, e.g., [17]). This is done by applying 50 iterations of a method, where all vehicles can plan their path, and 10 % can adjust their route based on currently computed travel times. Vehicles accumulate the knowledge about travel times over all iterations. So the iterative algorithms function here as a baseline; the inverse-ant routing is a one-shot routing mechanism like the original A* algorithm. All details of ant-inverse routing and about its evaluation can be found in [5].

In this example it has been demonstrated that by modifying an existing approach, the effects of potentially known undesired adaptations can be avoided or at least limited at the design phase. But this approach has particular drawbacks:

1. The problem needs to be known in advance; the systematic testing, we have presented in the previous section, can be used to analyze weaknesses. Then it is the task of the designer to provide hypothesis why the undesired adaptation of the system occurs and how it could be avoided.
2. Even if a weakness is identified and a method for fixing the strategy exists, it is still not sure that the modification of the control scheme does not introduce new instances of undesired adaptation. This is why the design process has to be done in an iterative way, where each iteration consists of a design and systematic testing phase.
3. Each modification is specific for the control strategy. It could become difficult to extract methods or patterns that can be used in the design of other adaptive systems.

3.2 Avoiding Undesired Adaptations by Self-regulation

Based on the previous discussion of the drawback of the avoidance by design, we discuss here a second approach to avoid these drawbacks.

The main idea is that one has to acknowledge the potential existence of undesired adaptation as a potential behavior of an adaptive system. Therefore it is necessary to change the architecture of an adaptive system to detect and counteract undesired adaptations (see, e.g., [20, 21]). Both approaches propose to add self-monitoring and self-regulating abilities to the system to maintain system's performance and avoid undesired behavior of the system.

The idea of self-regulation can be implemented differently. In the approach presented in [21], a set of rules indicate the presence of an error. These rules need to be defined at design time. A rule indicates a particular type of error. For each type of error, a policy needs to be defined that can recover the system at runtime. If an *error rule* fires, the corrective policy is applied. This approach can benefit from special knowledge about particular types of errors that could occur at runtime. But as not all possible instances of undesired adaptations can be anticipated, it requires an additional default rule, which catches all *unexplainable* performance deteriorations.

The approach of *regulated autonomy* [20] can be used as such a default rule, as it requires no special knowledge about the control scheme of the adaptive system. Its goal is to limit the degradation of performance below an acceptable level. For triggering the corresponding error rule, it is necessary to monitor the performance of the system, according to the given key performance indicators. The principle of the regulation is shown in Fig. 4. In this example we assume without loss of generality that the goal of the system is to minimize an objective function. It is necessary that a threshold indicates what can be considered as an *acceptable performance* for the

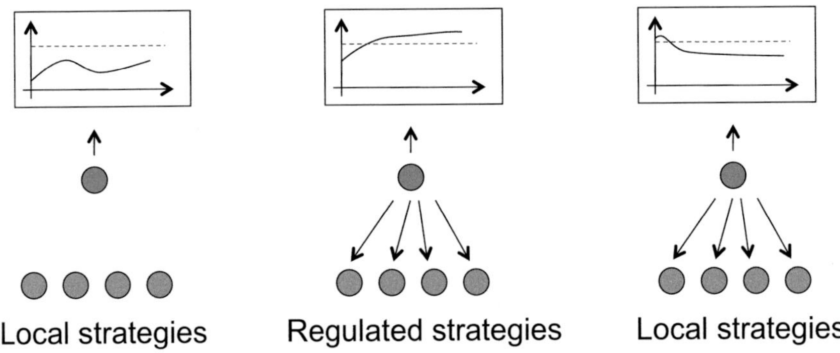

Fig. 4 The principle of regulated autonomy, presentation based on [20]

system. This threshold can be either statically defined or dynamically determined by simulating the behavior of a conventional RTS system based on the current state of the environment. As much as possible, the system's performance remains within an *acceptable* range. In the example in Fig. 4, below a given threshold (dashed line), we can exploit the advantages of the adaptive system. Note that in this example we used a static threshold value for value for simplicity.

In case the system measures a deteriorating performance, i.e. in this example the system's performance exceeds the defined threshold, the error rule fires and activates the self-regulation. This is when the control scheme of the system is exchanged at runtime. Like all correction activities, this strategy has to be predefined. It can be either a specific control that aims at quick improvements of the system's performance or the conventional RTS system. In particular, if we use an RTS strategy to dynamically compute the performance threshold, we could switch control from the ARTS to the RTS. In this phase we call the system regulated. What becomes necessary is that at this moment a new monitoring rule needs to be added, which later triggers the termination of the regulation of the adaptive system. Depending on the technique used for implementing the adaptive behavior, it can become necessary to modify the internal state of the adaptive system. This might be necessary to avoid a faulty adaptation applied by the system, which will reoccur if the internal state is not modified. We are not going into further details here, as we do not address here the technique-dependent aspects of implementing adaptive systems.

If the system's performance recovers, i.e., it drops below the performance threshold again, the regulation of the overall system needs to be released. This can be implemented via a monitoring rule and a corresponding action that reactivates the adaptive system again.

In [20], regulated autonomy has been implemented for a production planning problem (job shop planning). A current transfer to the domain of ARTS is currently missing. The principles of regulation put at risk not being able to exploit the gains of the adaptive system, if the overall system is constantly in the regulated state. But empirical results are promising. In an analysis about the fraction of time the system is regulated versus when it is controlled by an adaptive strategy, the results presented in [19] reported that the system was regulated about 25 % of the runtime, while the adaptive system was enabled for about 75 % of the runtime.

Even if a dynamic performance threshold with a conventional RTS is used and the RTS is used in the regulated state, it is currently not possible to prove any performance guarantee. But with this setup, it can only dip below the threshold performance for a short time, at the phase transition from deregulated to regulated. But an empirical validation for this is still missing.

4 Concluding Remarks

Within this chapter, we have argued that the ability of ARTS to adapt their behavior is a key feature to provide the additional value that autonomic computing can offer to traffic management. But we had to point out that adaptation can either be desired or undesired with respect to a given objective function of the system's performance. We have addressed techniques to deal with undesired adaptation in ARTS. In particular, we have pointed out on the aspects of:

- Identifying situations in which undesired adaptations of the system's behavior occur.
- Techniques for the design of ARTS to avoid or regulate the presence of undesired adaptations.

Both aspects are necessary for the future research in the field of ARTS but also adaptive systems in general. They are necessary to increase confidence in ARTS solutions and allow these systems to get out of the laboratories and into the operation of traffic infrastructure.

As discussed above, both aspects should also be integrated into the design process of adaptive systems early on. Additional work is necessary to integrate the techniques discussed in the design process of adaptive systems, like ARTS. Additional research is also needed to enhance techniques to handle faulty adaptation and system's recovery. Techniques like regulated autonomy can stop a performance degeneration but are not able to *repair* an adaptive system, which did not adapt in a proper way. This is necessary to avoid an adaptive system from oscillating between regulated and unregulated states.

References

1. Abdulla, P.A., Delzanno, G., Rezine, A.: Parameterized verification of infinite-state processes with global conditions. In: Damm, W., Hermanns, H. (eds.) Computer Aided Verification. Lecture Notes in Computer Science, vol. 4590, pp. 145–157. Springer, Berlin/Heidelberg (2007)
2. Alves, D., Ast, J.V., Cong, Z., Schutter, B.D., Babuska, R.: Ant colony optimization for traffic dispersion routing. In: Proceedings of the 13th International IEEE Conference on Intelligent Transportation Systems (ITSC 2010), pp. 683–688. IEEE, Funchal (2010)
3. Bedi, P., Mediratta, N., Dhand, S., Sharma, R., Singhal, A.: Avoiding traffic jam using ant colony optimization - a novel approach. In: International Conference on Computational Intelligence and Multimedia Applications, 2007, vol. 1, pp. 61–67 (2007)
4. Calinescu, R., Kikuchi, S., Kwiatkowska, M.: Formal Methods for the Development and Verification of Autonomic IT Systems. IGI Global, Hershey (2011)
5. Dallmeyer, J., Schumann, R., Lattner, A.D., Timm, I.J.: Don't go with the ant flow: ant-inspired traffic routing in urban environments. In: Vasirani, M., Klügl, F., Camponogara, E., Hattori, H. (eds.) 7th International Workshop on Agents in Traffic and Transportation (ATT 2012) Held at AAMAS 2012, pp. 59–68 (2012). Pre-proceedings
6. Falilat, J., Chrpa, L., McCluskey, T.L., Shah, S.: Towards application of automated planning in urban traffic control. In: Proceedings of the 16th International IEEE Annual Conference on Intelligent Transportation Systems (ITSC 2013), pp. 985–990. IEEE, The Hague (2013)
7. Flötteröd, G., Bierlaire, M., Nagel, K.: Bayesian demand calibration for dynamic traffic simulations. Transp. Sci. **45**(4), 541–561 (2011)
8. Flötteröd, G., Chen, Y., Nagel, K.: Behavioral calibration and analysis of a large-scale travel microsimulation. Netw. Spat. Econ. **12**(4), 481–502 (2012)
9. Ge, Q., Menendez, M.: Final report of calibration study for vissim (csv). Project report, Institute for Transport Planning and Systems (IVT) ETH Zürich (2012)
10. Güdemann, M., Ortmeier, F., Reif, W.: Formal modeling and verification of systems with self-x properties. In: Yang, L., Jin, H., Ma, J., Ungerer, T. (eds.) Autonomic and Trusted Computing. Lecture Notes in Computer Science, vol. 4158, pp. 38–47. Springer, Berlin/Heidelberg (2006)
11. Hudson, J., Denzinger, J., Kasinger, H., Bauer, B.: Efficiency testing of self-adapting systems by learning of event sequences. In: Proceedings of the 2nd International Conference on Adaptive and Self-adaptive Systems and Applications (ADAPTIVE 2010), pp. 200–205 (2010)
12. Kephart, J.O., Chess, D.M.: The vision of autonomic computing. Computer **36**(1), 41–50 (2003)
13. Krömer, P., Martinovic, J., Radecký, M., Tomis, R., Snásel, V.: Ant colony inspired algorithm for adaptive traffic routing. In: Proceedings of the Third World Congress on Nature and Biologically Inspired Computing (NaBIC 2011), pp. 329–334. IEEE, Salamanca (2011)
14. Lattner, A.D., Bogon, T., Lorion, Y., Timm, I.J.: A knowledge-based approach to automated simulation model adaptation. In: Biaz, S. (ed.) Proceedings of the 43rd Annual Simulation Symposium (ANSS'10), Spring Simulation Multi-Conference (SpringSim'10), pp. 200–207 (2010)
15. Liu, H., Yu, Q., Ding, W., Ni, D., Wang, H., Shannon, S.: Feasibility study for automatic calibration of transportation simulation models. In: Proceedings of the 44th Annual Simulation Symposium, pp. 87–94. Society for Computer Simulation International, San Diego (2011)
16. Miller, J.H.: Active nonlinear tests (ANTs) of complex simulation models. Manag. Sci. **44**(6), 820–830 (1998)
17. Raney, B., Nagel, K.: Iterative route planning for modular transportation simulation. In: Proceedings of the Swiss Transport Research Conference, Monte Verita (2002)
18. Russell, S.J., Norvig, P.: Artificial Intelligence: A Modern Approach. Prentice Hall Series in Artificial Intelligence, 2nd edn. Pearson Education, Upper Sadle River (2003)
19. Schumann, R., Lattner, A.D., Timm, I.J.: Management-by-exception - a modern approach to managing self-organizing systems. Commun. SIWN **4**, 168–172 (2008)

20. Schumann, R., Lattner, A.D., Timm, I.J.: Regulated autonomy: a case study. In: Mönch, L., Pankratz, G. (eds.) Intelligente Systeme zur Entscheidungsunterstützung,Teilkonferenz der Multikonferenz Wirtschaftsinformatik, pp. 83–98. SCS, München (2008)
21. Serugendo, G.D.M., Fitzgerald, J., Romanovsky, A.: Metaself – an architecture and a development method for dependable self-* systems. In: Shin, S.Y., Ossowski, S., Schumacher, M., Palakal, M.J., Hung, C.C. (eds.) Proceedings of the 2010 ACM Symposium on Applied Computing (SAC), pp. 457–461. ACM, New York (2010)
22. Timm, I.J., Schumann, R.: Performance measurement of multiagent systems: towards dependable MAS. In: Proceedings of the 2009 Spring Simulation Multiconference ADS, BIS, MSE, MSEng. Simulation Series, vol. 41, pp. 177–184. SCS, San Diego (2009)
23. Wolf, T.D., Holvoet, T.: Emergence and self-organisation: a statement of similarities and differences. In: Brueckner, S.A., Serugendo, G.D.M., Karageorgos, A., Nagpal, R. (eds.) Proceedings of the International Workshop on Engineering Self-Organising Applications, pp. 96–110. Springer, New York (2004)
24. Wooldridge, M.: An Introduction to Multi Agent Systems, 2nd edn. Wiley, Chichester (2009)
25. Wooldridge, M., Fisher, M., Huget, M.P., Parsons, S.: Model checking multi-agent systems with mable. In: Proceedings of the First International Joint Conference on Autonomous Agents and Multiagent Systems: Part 2. AAMAS '02, pp. 952–959. ACM, New York (2002)

Learning-Based Control Algorithm for Ramp Metering

Martin Gregurić, Edouard Ivanjko, and Sadko Mandžuka

Abstract Significant slowdowns in road traffic induced by increased traffic demand cause breakdowns and, consequently, congestion on roads. On urban highways, these congestion problems are most noticeable near on-ramps. To resolve traffic congestion on urban highways, it is necessary to apply new traffic control approaches like ramp metering, variable speed limit control (VSLC), etc. Today's cooperative ramp metering algorithms adjust the metering rate for every on-ramp according to the overall traffic state on the highway and can establish additional cooperation with other traffic control subsystems. To avoid some problems of usability and effectiveness of today's complex highway control systems, an approach based on autonomic properties (self-learning, self-adaptation, etc.) is proposed in this chapter. A new cooperative control method based on an adaptive neuro-fuzzy inference system is described. It can establish cooperation between VSLC and ramp metering. The new solution is tested using the CTMSIM macroscopic highway traffic simulator and Zagreb bypass as test model.

Keywords Adaptive neuro-fuzzy inference system • Autonomic systems • Cooperative systems • Intelligent transportation systems • Ramp metering • Variable speed limit control

1 Introduction

Despite the fact that urban highways are originally planned to provide high level of service (LoS), congestions and slowdowns occur daily. In spatial aspect on- and off-ramps on urban highways are common places for congestions since they are the merging points of mainstream and on-ramp traffic flow. In temporal aspects, congestions are common during peak hours [1].

The latest solution for mitigation of traffic congestion is to apply new traffic control approaches from the domain of intelligent transportation systems (ITS).

M. Gregurić (✉) • E. Ivanjko • S. Mandžuka
Department of Intelligent Transportation Systems, Faculty of Transport and Traffic Sciences, University of Zagreb, Vukelićeva 4, HR-10000 Zagreb, Croatia
e-mail: martin.greguric@fpz.hr; edouard.ivanjko@fpz.hr; sadko.mandzuka@fpz.hr

T.L. McCluskey et al. (eds.), *Autonomic Road Transport Support Systems*, Autonomic Systems, DOI 10.1007/978-3-319-25808-9_12

One of the most used ITS approaches for mitigation of congestions on highways is ramp metering. The main objective of ramp metering is to increase the throughput of urban highways by restricting access of on-ramp traffic [2]. Nowadays ramp metering is used in cooperation with additional traffic control approaches (subsystems) like variable speed limit control (VSLC), prohibiting lane changes, driver information systems, etc.

The usability and effectiveness of ramp metering and other highway control systems significantly depend on its ability to react upon unforeseen situations such as incidents, vehicle breakdown and rapid changes in traffic demand within a short time interval. To cope with this problem, a new learning-based local ramp metering control algorithm based on the adaptive neuro-fuzzy inference system (ANFIS) has been proposed by the authors in [3]. To cover the wide range of traffic scenarios on the bypass of the city of Zagreb, a case model is simulated using three distinctively different ramp metering algorithms (ALINEA, SWARM and HELPER). All three algorithms are chosen as teaching algorithms for the proposed ANFIS-based ramp metering algorithm [3]. To enable simulation of cooperative ramp metering, authors augmented the cell transmission model simulator (CTMSIM) macroscopic highway traffic simulator in [4] and presented first proof of concept results of the extension of the original proposed ANFIS-based ramp metering with cooperative properties in [5]. In this chapter, the authors present continuation of the research on this topic with the emphasis on an improved learning criteria function, on-ramp queue length analysis and extension of the simulation run on a full day (24 h).

This chapter is organised as follows: Section 2 briefly describes concepts and problems which can be mitigated by the application of ramp metering. The description of possibilities for the application of autonomic properties in ramp metering is given in the third section. In Sect. 4, a brief description of the used CTMSIM simulator is given. Then, Sect. 5 describes the proposed ANFIS-based ramp metering learning framework. Section 6 contains simulation results of the comparative analysis of implemented ramp metering algorithms, VSLC and cooperative approaches. The chapter ends with a conclusion and a description of future work.

2 Ramp Metering

The main goal of ramp metering is to reduce the impact of a downstream bottleneck on the mainstream highway traffic by restricting the access of on-ramp traffic to the mainstream traffic [6]. However, while reducing the downstream bottleneck, ramp metering may cause the traffic to spill over onto feeder arterial roads as the on-ramp queue length increases. Such situation is known as the spillback effect [2]. The location of the downstream bottleneck and the spillback effect are shown in Fig. 1. Additionally, Fig. 1 shows an elementary ramp metering installation for one metered on-ramp.

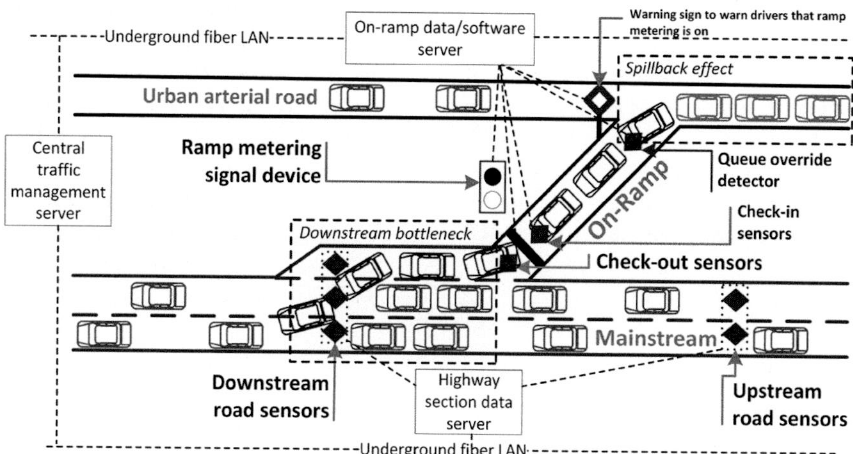

Fig. 1 Illustration of downstream bottleneck and spillback effect location with ramp metering infrastructure [4]

Generally it is possible to divide ramp metering algorithms into two major categories: local (or isolated) and coordinated [2]. Local strategies include ramp metering algorithms, which take into account only the traffic condition on a particular on-ramp and the nearby segment of the highway where they are applied. ALINEA is the most often used standard local ramp metering algorithm. The core concept of ALINEA is to keep the downstream occupancy of the on-ramp at a specified level by adjusting the metering rate [6].

Coordinated algorithms can be further divided into cooperative, competitive and integrated algorithms [7]. Cooperative algorithms involve additional computation of the metering rate after the local algorithm has provided its solution. The usual procedure is to detect the place of a bottleneck and enrol several upstream on-ramps to create virtual on-ramp queues. Virtual queues have the primary goal to stop forwarding additional traffic flow from an on-ramp into mainstream in order to mitigate any downstream congestion. The most representative algorithm of this concept is HELPER which is described in [8]. The competitive ramp metering algorithm contains local and global control logics. Independently of each other, these two control logics provide an appropriate solution for the current traffic situation. The more restrictive value is chosen as the final ramp metering value. The most representative algorithm of the mentioned ramp metering working concept is SWARM which is described in detail in [7]. Integrated algorithms are based on optimisation of a specific LoS value while considering constraints such as maximum allowable on-ramp queue, bottleneck capacity, etc. Most representative algorithms from this group are fuzzy logic-based algorithms. Two best examples of the algorithms based on fuzzy logic are the local traffic-responsive fuzzy logic algorithm developed at the University of Washington [8] and ACCEZZ fuzzy-based ramp metering algorithm optimised using evolutionary computing [9].

For measurement of the effectiveness of traffic control approaches, various LoS measures are used. LoS is defined as a group of qualitative measures which characterise operational conditions within a traffic flow and their perception by motorists and drivers [1]. The basic measures of service quality for ramp metering used in this work are travel time (TT) and Delay. TT is a simple measure which can answer the question of how much time one vehicle needs to travel through an observed highway segment. Using Eq. (1) the TT value can be obtained for each simulation step k with duration Δt [1]:

$$\mathrm{TT}_{k+1} = \sum_{i=1}^{I} \frac{\Delta L_i}{V_{i[k+1]}}. \tag{1}$$

where ΔL_i is the length of the cell i and $V_{i[k+1]}$ is the flow speed at cell i in time step $k+1$. Delay is defined as the difference between the actual time spent by all vehicles on a congested highway and the time spent in case they have travelled at free flow speed [10]. Delay also considers vehicles which are waiting in on-ramp queues or in mainstream queues caused by the bottlenecks. Equation (2) presents Delay in a small highway segment or cell i:

$$D_{i[k+1]} = \begin{cases} 0 & \text{if } n_{i[k+1]} \leq n^{C}_{i[k+1]} \\ \left(n_{i[k+1]}\Delta L_i + l_{i[k+1]}\Delta t - \frac{n_{i[k+1]}V_{i[k+1]}\Delta L_i \Delta t}{v_i}\right) & \text{if } n_{i[k+1]} > n^{C}_{i[k+1]} \end{cases} \tag{2}$$

where $n_{i[k+1]}$ is the number of vehicles (or mainstream density) in cell i at time step $k+1$, $l_{i[k+1]}$ is the number of vehicles at time step $k+1$ queuing in the on-ramp in cell i, v_i is the free flow speed in cell i and $n^{C}_{i[k+1]}$ is the critical density in the cell i at time step $k+1$. An additional measure for simulation result comparison is the queue length at on-ramps and the total time spend (TTS). TTS combines mainstream density and on-ramp queues into a single measure.

3 Autonomic Properties in Ramp Metering

Control theory and computer science have a significant role in the development and implementation of new ITS methods for highway management. Under the domain of computer and control sciences, autonomic computing provides self-properties (self-learning, self-healing, self-adaptation, etc.) which can be applied for the development of ramp metering algorithms. Autonomic computing aims to improve technical systems in a way to further reduce human involvement in them [11, 14]. Control methods based on autonomic computing provide an additional level of adaptive behaviour and other autonomic features such as self-calibration, self-adaptation and self-diagnostics to environments with high behaviour uncertainty such as highway traffic systems [12].

The most important property of autonomic computing for ramp metering and other highway control strategies is self-adaptation. It enables adaptation of the control system to the changing traffic conditions without human involvement [13]. This chapter presents a framework based on machine learning. Its main task is to select the best solution for a particular traffic situation, from the available learning datasets during the learning process.

4 Simulator CTMSIM

CTMSIM is an interactive simulator based on macroscopic traffic models specifically designed for highway traffic flow simulations. Macroscopic-based simulation tools are better and faster for evaluating coordinated ramp metering algorithms on larger highways' corridors. Reason for that is satisfying the ratio between simplicity (which enables faster simulation speed) and accuracy of their mathematical model. CTMSIM is based on the asymmetric cell transmission model (ACTM) and allows user-pluggable on-ramp flow and queue controllers [10]. Here only a brief description is given and more details about the original and augmented CTMSIM version can be found in our previous paper [4]. Details of the ACTM properties used in CTMSIM are explained in [10]. In order to apply ACTM, the highway is divided into I cells. For each cell a number of lanes, on- and off-ramps and corresponding fundamental diagrams can be defined. The duration of simulation is presented by K, which is divided into k simulation steps.

In order to simulate cooperative and autonomous highway control systems, the original CTMSIM version had to be appropriately augmented. In [4], a module which enables cooperative ramp metering and VSLC is described. Cooperative ramp metering module with VSLC can be seen in the upper part of Fig. 2. This module is important for the proposed ANFIS algorithm because its basic control logic is based on the cooperative ramp metering strategy. Furthermore, during the validation process, the ANFIS algorithm must be compared with other highway management strategies such as ALINEA, VSLC and cooperation between VSLC and ramp metering. All mentioned highway management strategies are implemented using the cooperative module and will be used to evaluate ANFIS's self-adaptive feature against other involved strategies.

4.1 *Cooperative Ramp Metering Module*

In [4], a module enabling cooperative ramp metering has been introduced. Furthermore, the HELPER ramp metering algorithm is implemented using that cooperative module. In this chapter, the HELPER algorithm is updated with an improved control logic, and it is used as one of the training ramp metering algorithms for the ANFIS algorithm as it is mentioned above. So, ANFIS has the task to learn cooperative

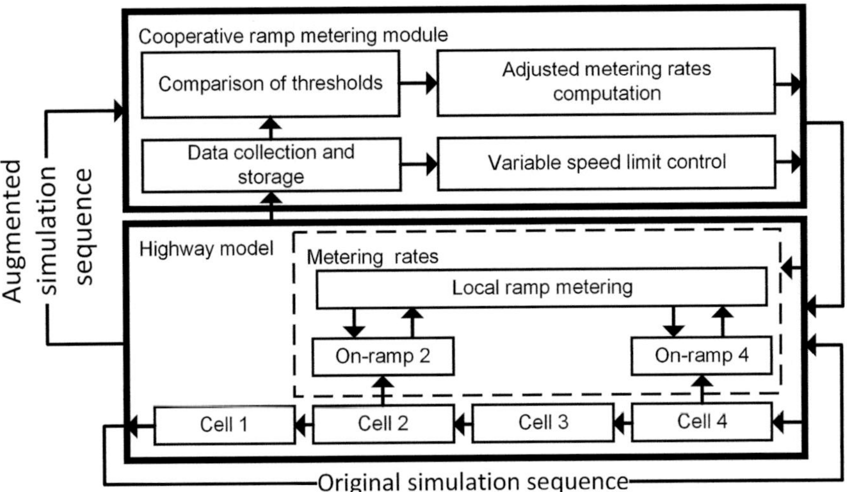

Fig. 2 Augmented CTMSIM simulation structure [4]

ramp metering behaviour based on the cooperative HELPER algorithm and apply that knowledge on a specific traffic situation.

The original CTMSIM simulation sequence goes only through defined cells in a particular time step. An additional simulation step is added. This step has access to data from all cells. At this step it is possible to compute optimal local ramp metering rates and VSLC values used in the next time interval [4]. The ANFIS algorithm conducts decisions about the current type of the control strategy based on data from all cells.

4.2 Variable Speed Limit Control Module

In [4], the stand-alone VSLC module is presented and compared against a no control situation. This newly developed control module and 24 h simulation run enable better insight into the operational work of the cooperative algorithms such as HELPER and ANFIS. Original equation for mean speed in the *i*th cell is changed into (3) in order to implement VSLC into the CTMSIM environment:

$$V_{i[k+1]} = \min\left(\frac{f_{i[k+1]} s_{i[k+1]}}{n_{i[k+1]}}, v_i, v_{i[\text{VSLC}]}\right), \tag{3}$$

where $v_{i[\text{VSLC}]}$ denotes the current VSLC value for the *i*th cell, $f_{i[k+1]}$ is the number of vehicles moving from cell i to cell $i+1$ during time step $k+1$ and $s_{i[k+1]}$ is the off-ramp flow in the *i*th cell.

5 ANFIS-Based Ramp Metering Learning Framework

Each of the aforementioned highway management strategies has its particular strengths, making it best suited for a specific traffic situation. For example, a ramp metering algorithm based on a local control strategy such as ALINEA is fast and efficient in resolving small congestions at on-ramps with low dependency on their neighboured on-ramps. The SWARM algorithm contains predictive logic that makes it efficient in mitigating congestions that are repeated in time and strength. The HELPER algorithm is effective in resolving back-propagation of heavy "shock waves" by using several upstream on-ramps with increased mutual dependency.

The main idea of the ANFIS algorithm is to cover the good properties of all mentioned strategies in the form of a formalised knowledge database. The algorithm consists of two parts: an inference control system and an artificial neural network (ANN) to tune the parameters of the control inference system [15]. In order to tune parameters of the control inference system, ANFIS conducts a learning process based on a learning dataset. The learning dataset contains a set of traffic solutions for one particular traffic scenario derived from different control strategies. The mentioned learning process will perform self-tuning in order to satisfy the defined criteria function [5]. New control knowledge will be formed and incorporated into the control inference system after the learning process is done. The control inference system at this point will have reactiveness on various traffic scenarios based on the newly formed knowledge learned from the teaching ramp metering control strategies [3]. It is possible to conclude that the offline learning process has indications of autonomy through the self-tuning and self-adaptation property by conducting the learning process without human involvement according to the criteria function results. The control inference system, which computes the metering rates, can be characterised as a control system extended with a learning feature which performs its self-tuning offline and self-adaptation online. In other words, the self-tuning feature of the ANN as part of the ANFIS algorithm provides a self-adaptation property to the inference control system for various traffic scenarios.

Self-adaptation of the inference control system to the various traffic situations is achieved by the mentioned knowledge database. Higher level of autonomy can be achieved by incorporating online learning into the ramp metering framework.

5.1 *Concept of an ANFIS-Based Ramp Metering Framework*

Recent work described in [15] and [16] includes the use of an ANFIS-based learning framework for the design of a ramp metering algorithm. This chapter extends the ANFIS framework by adding knowledge from an algorithm with cooperative ramp metering ability into the learning database. Primarily, the ANFIS algorithm uses an ANN to modify parameters of the Takagi–Sugeno Fuzzy Inference System (FIS) [17] according to the learning dataset. A FIS contains several types of parameters. The first set of parameters are related to the number, type and mathematical definitions of membership functions for each input and output. The second parameter is a knowledge database which contains IF-THEN rules. ANN optimises its interconnection structures through unsupervised learning and tunes both mentioned parameters of the FIS. This behaviour can be characterised as a self-tuning property of the ANFIS algorithm. The knowledge database which is learned from the other control logics is the core element that provides FIS self-adaptation to various traffic scenarios. Self-adaptation is the product of different control logics in the knowledge database.

In this approach, ANFIS is taught by using a hybrid learning algorithm (combination of feedback error propagation and least square error for learning) which is described in [16]. During the learning process, every element of the learning dataset (inputs only) is presented to the ANN. FIS is part of the ANFIS algorithm which actually provides control over the metering rates on every on-ramp. It contains a knowledge database which is essentially a set of fuzzy IF-THEN rules that can approximate non-linear functions. The reasoning mechanism provides an inference procedure upon the fuzzy rules and given inputs [17]. The result of the inference procedure is an appropriate control output. The used ANFIS ramp metering learning algorithm is shown in Fig. 3.

Different strategies are learned through tuning of the control inference system parameters. They are applied on several upstream on-ramps on the controlled highway segment regarding the congested one. For example, the congested on-ramp can be metered according to the knowledge acquired from the SWARM algorithm due to its control strategy which includes prediction. SWARM predictable logic can forecast the occurrence of congestion on a particular on-ramp and reduce TT of mainstream traffic but cannot efficiently reduce the impact of a “shock wave”. In order to override this problem, ANFIS can potentially use the knowledge obtained from the HELPER algorithm on exploitation of the on-ramp queue capacity and create a virtual queue on the previous upstream on-ramp. On the last on-ramp, ANFIS uses local control knowledge from the ALINEA ramp metering algorithm due to the lower dependency on the upstream on-ramp and lower traffic load. The described example illustrates the ANFIS property of self-adaptation to the specific traffic scenario by using its control knowledge.

Output (metering rate) is computed according to the input–output learning dataset, obtained by the teaching ramp metering algorithm which produces desired ration between overall TT and Delay for the currently measured traffic parameters (inputs for the ANFIS FIS). In the learning process, knowledge from the mentioned input–output dataset is extrapolated by the use of ANFIS ANN and implemented in the ANFIS FIS control structure through the calibration of its parameters. It is possible to conclude that the ANFIS algorithm achieves self-adaptation to the traffic situations under constraints such as the number of involved teaching ramp metering algorithms, diversity of the teaching ramp metering algorithm control logics, range of traffic situation presented to the teaching ramp metering algorithms and desired ration between involved LoS measures.

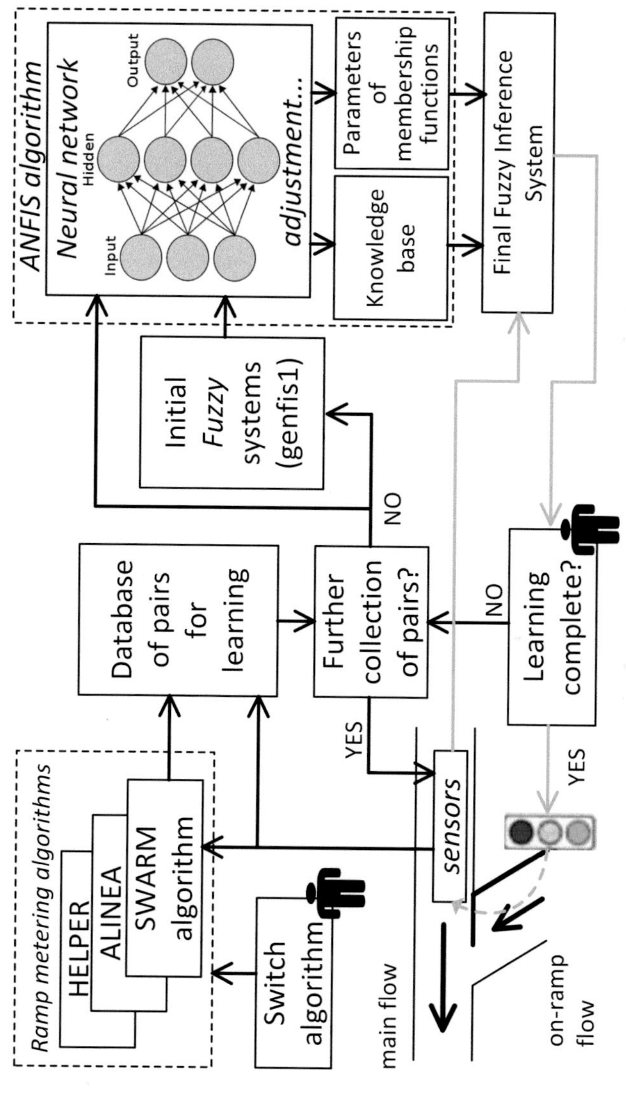

Fig. 3 ANFIS ramp metering learning algorithm [3]

5.2 ANFIS Learning Framework

The initial phase in the development of a ramp metering algorithm based on a learning framework is the creation of a learning dataset using an appropriate minimisation criteria [15]. Initial learning dataset is organised in the form of a matrix size $N \times B$. N denotes the number of 5 min intervals in a day multiplied by the number of used teaching ramp metering algorithms (three in this chapter) and the number of cells used in the model. B denotes the number of traffic parameters which are extrapolated from the available simulation results (speed, density, demand, flow, on-ramp queue, metering rate, Delay and TT).

Three simulation runs are performed under the same traffic model parameters and traffic demand dataset, while the ramp metering computation for every simulation run is conducted using a different algorithm, called teaching ramp metering algorithm. In the created matrix, every 5 min interval for every simulation model cell is saved for the three 24 h simulations, and it is represented by one of the three rows of traffic parameters. Matrix rows with parameters contain values such as density, flow, speed, metering rate, etc. These parameters can be divided into two categories: inputs for the ramp metering algorithm and their output (metering rate for every on-ramp of the simulation model). Inputs are computed according to the simulation model settings, traffic demand dataset and influence realised by the ramp metering algorithm control actions. Furthermore, for each of the three mentioned simulation runs, there are three different outputs (metering rates) for a particular 5 min simulation interval derived by the three teaching ramp metering algorithms.

So, the matrix N contains three sets of traffic parameters for each cell. These traffic parameters describe the solution quality derived by the particular ramp metering teaching algorithm for the same 5 min interval and particular cell. For every three rows in the matrix N, which are representing the same 5 min interval, the best traffic solution from all teaching ramp metering algorithms has to be selected. This is done by using the following criteria function:

$$f(r) = 0.6 \cdot \mathrm{TT} + 0.4 \cdot D, \tag{4}$$

where $f(r)$ is the metering rate function and D is the Delay as mentioned above. In our previous paper [5], the ratio between TT and Delay is balanced. In this chapter, TT is multiplied by a higher value regarding Delay. This means that the ANFIS algorithm should learn solutions which have an emphasis on lower TT values. The mentioned changes in the criteria function provide the possibility to verify potential autonomous behaviour of the ANFIS ramp metering algorithm.

The self-adaptation properties should provide ANFIS possibility to extract and learn solutions from the learning dataset which provide higher TT values compared to the Delay. At this point, the matrix contains only one row for every 5 min interval. Mentioned row represents the optimal control solution for a particular 5 min interval. Optimal solution for a particular 5 min interval contains the corresponding output or metering rate, derived by the teaching ramp metering algorithm, which is selected according to the criteria function.

The second step in the creation of an ANFIS-based ramp metering algorithm is to select suitable inputs which have the most significant impact on the metering rate [3]. The exhaustive search method is selected for this task. It uses brute force optimisation by conducting the learning process for several ANFIS models for only one iteration. Each of these ANFIS models has a unique combination of inputs. The combination of the inputs used into the ANFIS model, which produce the lowest learning error during only one learning iteration, is selected to be used for further learning.

The presented ANFIS model has two input variables (e.g. x density of main traffic flow, y on-ramp queue length). Each input variable has five membership functions and one output in the form of a ramp metering rate value. Upon completion of the learning process, results derived by the ANFIS algorithm and the input validation dataset are compared with output training data. Based on the difference between these two values, a degree of matching is derived in the form of root mean square error (RMSE). Higher RMSE values are reported during the learning process due to lack of real Zagreb bypass traffic data. Furthermore, an additional reason for generally higher values of the RMSE is the relatively small traffic dataset which is applied for the simulation of use case model.

6 Simulation Results

The urban highway section between the nodes Jankomir and Lučko on the Zagreb bypass is selected to be the use case simulation model. Traffic demand data for each on-ramp for the use case model is reconstructed by the use of interpolated traffic data from the Ljubljana bypass. Furthermore, this section provides a comparative analysis which involves the following highway control strategies: commonly used ramp metering algorithms (local ALINEA and SWARM and cooperative HELPER), stand-alone VSLC, cooperation between VSLC and HELPER and the proposed ANFIS learning-based approach.

6.1 Zagreb Bypass and Traffic Flow Data

The section between nodes Jankomir and Lučko on the Zagreb bypass has been used as the use case model due to the combination of increased traffic load during the whole day and significant effect of daily migrations [18]. Additionally, this section contains many close on- and off-ramps making it suitable for the implementation of cooperative ramp metering strategies [19].

The use case model is implemented under the augmented CTMSIM simulation environment in order to verify the functionality of the newly developed highway management strategy. It is developed based on the constructional parameters of the Zagreb bypass. The traffic dataset used for the use case model is reconstructed according to a traffic data obtained at the Ljubljana bypass due to the lack of detailed traffic data from the Zagreb bypass. The Ljubljana bypass has the same bypass role as the Zagreb bypass with similar intensity of the daily peak hours. Additionally, in the summer season, many tourists are using both bypasses when travelling to the Croatian seaside. All mentioned characteristic traffic behaviours make its traffic behaviour patterns similar to Zagreb's. The Ljubljana traffic behaviour patterns can be used to create the input traffic data for the simulation model of the Zagreb bypass.

The traffic data derived from the Ljubljana bypass were originally arranged in 1 h time intervals, while CTMSIM uses 5 min time intervals. To solve this problem, a cubic spline interpolation over the traffic data from the Ljubljana bypass has been made. In order to adjust the daily traffic demand characteristic, average daily traffic flow values from [19] are used to ensure that daily vehicle number realistically describes the traffic demand of the Zagreb bypass. The characteristics of the ACTM model in-flow curve and curve of the traffic demand of cell 14 are shown in Fig. 4.

In Fig. 5, it is possible to see the model of the Zagreb bypass between nodes Lučko and Jankomir created using the ACTM methodology. Every segment of the

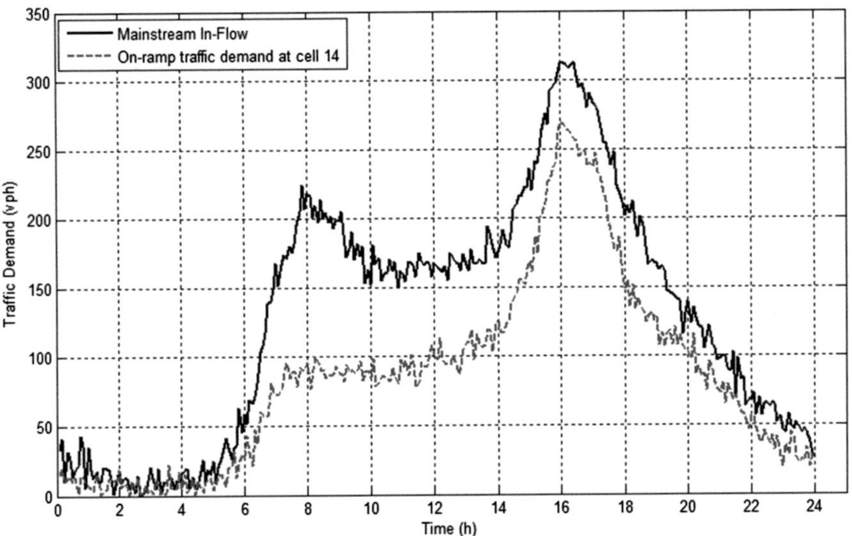

Fig. 4 In-flow curve of the mainstream traffic and the traffic demand of cell 14

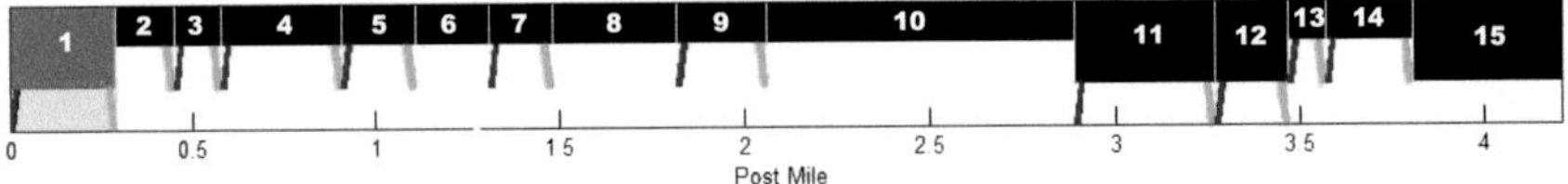

Fig. 5 ACTM model of the Zagreb bypass section between nodes Jankomir and Lučko

urban highway is presented by a cell which can contain on-ramps (blue lines) and/or off-ramps (green lines). The first cell is denoted in yellow. The section of Zagreb bypass between Jankomir and Lučko is modelled with 15 cells as denoted with corresponding numbers in Fig. 5. In order to verify operational work of the cooperative highway management strategies, the 14th cell is set to generate high traffic demand. Such a step creates a downstream congestion resulting in a "shock wave" propagating upstream. So, the creation of upstream virtual queues can be observed during simulation. This enables also the evaluation of the learned cooperative properties of the ANFIS algorithm.

6.2 Cooperation Between On-Ramps

The results of the comparative analysis, which involve results from all previously mentioned algorithms, are shown in Table 1. The trained ANFIS algorithm has been deployed and simulated using the same highway model as for the other involved highway management strategies, including the teaching ramp metering algorithms. As presented in Table 1, among the stand-alone ramp metering algorithms, the competitive algorithm SWARM has achieved the best average TT value due to its restrictive nature. The lowest Delay was achieved in the simulation scenario without ramp metering. In this basic scenario, all vehicles from the on-ramps are immediately merged with the mainstream if the mainstream maximal capacity of a cell, which contains mentioned on-ramp, is not exceeded. The relation between TT and Delay can be observed in Fig. 6.

The proposed ANFIS-based approach has produced the second lowest average TT value compared to the other ramp metering algorithms involved in the analysis. On the other side, ANFIS has produced highest Delay values compared to the other ramp metering algorithms, which is the consequence of the generally low TT values. The mentioned ANFIS results are induced due to the higher value of the coefficient assigned with TT in contrast to the coefficient assigned with Delay in the criteria function presented in Eq. (4). The ANFIS algorithm shows promising results regarding its ability to select solutions, which can produce lower TT values but higher Delay values during the learning process.

Table 1 Results of comparative analysis between different ramp metering algorithms

	No control	ALINEA	SWARM	HELPER	VSLC	HELPER + VSLC	ANFIS
Average TT (min)	14.46	7.39	5.58	6.82	10.5	6.80	6.48
Average Delay (vh)	6.06	6.8	8.03	7.29	8.05	7.59	10.18
TTS (h*vh)	19.4	22.07	28.36	20.97	19.48	23.92	24.82
Average queue (veh)	0	16	18	17	13	18	19
Maximum queue (veh)	0	40	49	40	15	42	42

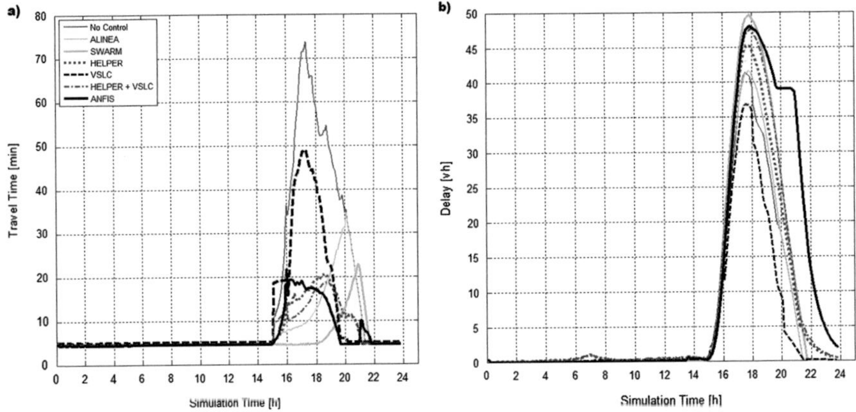

Fig. 6 Comparative analysis according to (**a**) TT and (**b**) Delay

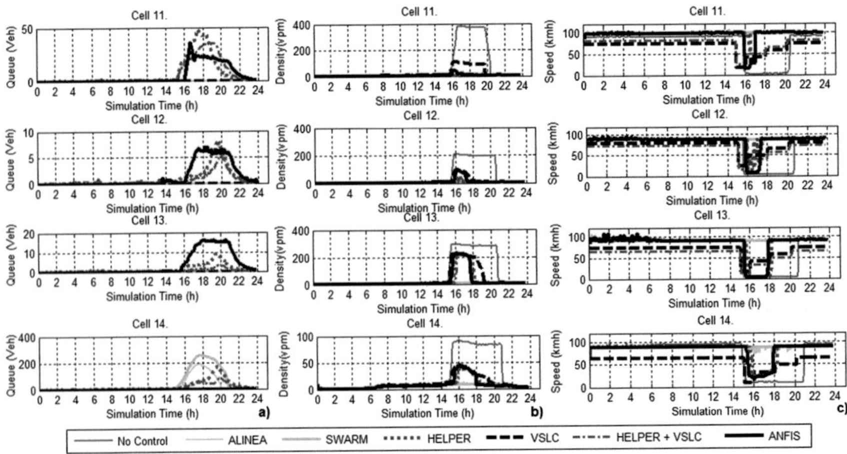

Fig. 7 Analysis of on-ramp queue (**a**) mainstream density (**b**) and speed (**c**)

HELPER as the teaching ramp metering algorithm provides knowledge of cooperative control between on-ramps. The cooperative strategy of the HELPER algorithm maintains increased mainstream throughput by distributing vehicles and consequently the waiting time to the "slave" on-ramps queues. This behaviour causes longer queues at "slave" on-ramps and consequently extends average Delay at the controlled segment of highway. As shown in Fig. 7a, it is possible to conclude that stand-alone HELPER and HELPER in cooperation with VSLC create virtual queues at three upstream "slave" on-ramps at cells 11, 12 and 13. This reduces the impact of congestion back-propagation on the mainstream throughput which consequently decreases TT. Furthermore, based on Fig. 7a, it is possible to conclude that ANFIS algorithm has learned a ramp metering strategy based on cooperation between on-ramps. ANFIS algorithm starts to create virtual queues at "slave" on-ramps at the time when the HELPER algorithm also begins to create virtual queues. This is evidence that the ANFIS algorithm is capable of learning cooperative behaviour between on-ramps.

Furthermore, ANFIS has achieved a TTS value which is in the range of the all involved ramp metering strategies. The TTS takes into account on-ramp queue length, which generally has more vehicles in the case of ANFIS algorithm due to its specific knowledge base. Its knowledge base is based on the understanding of the situation of which and where virtual queues should be applied in order to provide predefined balance between TT and Delay.

Results of the ANFIS algorithm regarding queue length at "slave" on-ramps are the consequence of the combination of two factors. The first factor is related to the lower overall TT values compared to Delay. Mentioned values are achieved by the ANFIS algorithm due to adequate setup of the criteria function, which is used in the learning dataset development. The second factor is related to the collected knowledge, which is characterised mainly by a restrictive nature induced by the SWARM and ALINEA teaching algorithms. The mentioned factors result in longer queues at the "slave" on-ramps compared to queue lengths at the "slave" on-ramps achieved by the stand-alone HELPER algorithm. This effect can be seen in Fig. 7a at cell 13. The ANFIS ramp metering algorithm produces the longest queues at the "slave" on-ramps compared to the other ramp metering algorithm used in the analysis. The absence of a queue at the congested on-ramp is the reason for the longer queues at the "slave" on-ramps.

6.3 Variable Speed Limit Control

VSLC is applied in the cells 11, 12 and 13. The main goal of VSLC is to gradually decrease the speed of the upstream flow before congestion starts in cell 14. Such approach firstly decreases mainstream speed but enables higher mainstream speed during the congestion period unlike the scenario without any control [4]. The graph group (b) in Fig. 7 shows that VSLC can prevent traffic standstill during most of the congested periods. Additionally, the application of stand-alone VSLC achieved best average Delay compared to other traffic control methods.

6.4 Cooperation Between On-Ramps and VSLC

In cooperation with the core ramp metering system, VSLC can provide better control over the involved traffic flows [20, 21]. The main function of the cooperation between the HELPER ramp metering algorithm and VSLC is to reduce the mainstream speed in all segments of the highway between the last "slave" on-ramp and congested on-ramp [5].

As shown in Fig. 6b, it can be concluded that VSLC has lower influence on Delay if the mainstream density is decreased by HELPER's exploitation of on-ramp queues. Furthermore, Fig. 7a shows that cooperation between HELPER and VSLC produces shorter on-ramp queues in sections affected by virtual queues (cells 11, 12 and 13) compared to the situation with the application of HELPER as a stand-alone ramp metering algorithm.

7 Conclusion and Future Work

In this chapter, autonomic properties of ramp metering algorithms and other highway management strategies are considered. Furthermore, possibilities to apply cooperative control in urban highway management are described. Simulation requirements necessary to simulate cooperative highway management systems and verify its autonomic properties are explained. An augmented version of the macroscopic highway simulator CTMSIM is used to perform a comparison of the described approaches.

In order to include self-tuning and self-adaptation properties into ramp metering, ANFIS is used as a foundation of a learning-based cooperative ramp metering framework. In this framework several standard ramp metering strategies (local ALINEA, competitive SWARM and cooperative HELPER) are utilised to create a learning dataset. Additionally, the learned ANFIS algorithm is compared with standard ramp metering algorithms used for the creation of its learning dataset. All simulations are made using the same use case model of the urban highway. The use case simulation model is created based on the constructional parameters of the Zagreb bypass (segment between nodes Lučko and Jankomir). Traffic data used for simulation correspond to real-world traffic situations.

At this point, it is possible to conclude that the ANFIS-based ramp metering algorithm has learned a restrictive behaviour with higher values of TT compared to the SWARM and ALINEA teaching ramp metering algorithms. Similarities between the behaviour of the HELPER and the ANFIS ramp metering algorithm regarding cooperative work between on-ramps can also be noticed. The ANFIS-based learning framework has created a unique ramp metering algorithm based on different ramp metering control knowledge in order to satisfy the desired ratio between TT and Delay in the used criteria function. According to obtained simulation results, the developed ANFIS ramp metering framework has the potential to be a suitable learning platform for complex cooperation between different highway management subsystems.

Acknowledgements The research reported in this chapter is supported by the FP7, Collaborative Project Intelligent Cooperative Sensing for Improved Traffic Efficiency, ICSI (FP7-317671), and by the EU COST action TU1102, Towards Autonomic Road Transport Support Systems. The authors wish to thank Nikola Bakarić for his valuable comments during the writing of this chapter.

References

1. Barcelo, J.: Fundamentals of Traffic Simulations. Springer, New York (2010)
2. Papageorgiou, M., Diakaki, C., Dinopoulou, V., Kotsialos, A., Wang, Y.: Review of road traffic control strategies. Proc. IEEE **91**(12), 2043–2067 (2003)
3. Gregurić, M., Buntić, M., Ivanjko, E., Mandžuka, S.: Improvement of highway level of service using ramp metering. In: Proceedings of ISEP 2013 (2013)
4. Gregurić, M., Ivanjko, E., Mandžuka, S.: Cooperative ramp metering simulation. In: Proceedings of MIPRO 2014, pp. 1204–1209, 26–30 May 2014
5. Gregurić, M., Ivanjko, E., Mandžuka, S.: New concepts for urban highways control. In: Proceedings of REAL CORP 2014, pp. 423–432, 21–23 May 2014
6. Papageorgiou, M., Kotsialos, A.: Freeway ramp metering: an overview. In: Proceedings of IEEE 5th ITS Conference, pp. 271–281 (2002)
7. Zhang, M., Kim, T., Nie, X., Jin, W.: Evaluation of on-ramp control algorithms, California PATH Program - Research Report UCB-ITS-PRR-2001-36, Berkeley (2001)
8. Bogenberger, K., May, A.D.: Advanced coordinated traffic responsive ramp metering strategies. Working Papers, California Partners for Advanced Transit and Highways (PATH) - UCB (1999)
9. Bogenberger, K., Vukanovic, S., Keller, H.: ACCEZZ - adaptive fuzzy algorithms for traffic responsive and coordinated ramp metering. In: Proceedings of 7th AATT, pp. 744–753 (2002)
10. Kurzhanskiy, A., Varaiya, P.: CTMSIM - an interactive macroscopic freeway traffic simulator, Berkeley (2008)
11. Huebscher, M.C., McCann, J.A.: Survey of autonomic computing - degrees, models and applications. J. ACM Comput. Surv. **40**(3), 1–31 (2008)
12. White, S.R., Thomas, J., Hanson, J.E., Whalley, I., Chess, D.M.: An architectural approach to autonomic computing. In: Proceedings of ICAC'04, pp. 2–9 (2004)
13. Jimoh, F., McCluskey, T., Chrpa, L., Gregory, P.: Enabling autonomic properties in road transport system. In: 30th Workshop of the UK PLANSIG 2012 (2012)
14. Xu, J., Zhao, M., Fortes, J.A.B.: Cooperative autonomic management in dynamic distributed systems. In: Proceedings of SSS 2009, pp. 756–770 (2009)
15. Yu-Sheng, C., Li-na, W., Yu-long, P., Xian-Zhang, L.: On-ramp neuro-fuzzy metering for urban freeway. J. Transp. Syst. Eng. **10**(3), 136–141 (2010)
16. Feng, C., Yuanhua, J., Jian, L., Huixin, Y., Zhonghai, N.: Design of fuzzy neural network control method for ramp metering. In: Proceedings of 3rd ICMTMA 2011, vol. 1, pp. 966–969 (2011)
17. Angelov, P.: An approach for fuzzy rule-base adaptation using on-line clustering. Int. J. Approx. Reason. **35**(3), 275–289 (2004)
18. Štefančić, G., Marijan, D., Kljajić, S.: Capacity and level of service on the zagreb bypass. Promet Traffic Transp. **24**(3), 261–267 (2012)
19. Ministry of infrastructure and spatial planning of the Republic of Slovenia, Traffic counting - The analysis of automatic traffic counting, DVD ISSN 1580–3864 (2011)
20. Ghods, A., Hosein, K., Ashkan, R., Tabibi, M.: A genetic-fuzzy control application to ramp metering and variable speed limit control. In: Proceedings of IEEE ISIC 2007, pp. 1723–1728 (2007)
21. Hegyi, A., De Schutter, B., Hellendoorn, H.: Model predictive control for optimal coordination of ramp metering and variable speed limits. Transp. Res. C **13**(3), 185–209 (2005)

An Autonomic Methodology for Embedding Self-tuning Competence in Online Traffic Control Systems

Anastasios Kouvelas, Diamantis Manolis, Elias Kosmatopoulos, Ioannis Papamichail, and Markos Papageorgiou

Abstract Recent advances in technology, control and computer science play a key role towards the design and deployment of the next generation of intelligent transportation systems (ITS). The architecture of such complex systems is crucial to include supporting algorithms that can embody autonomic properties within the existing ITS strategies. This chapter presents a recently developed adaptive optimization algorithm that combines methodologies from the fields of traffic engineering, automatic control, optimization and machine learning in order to embed self-tuning properties in traffic control systems. The derived adaptive fine-tuning (AFT) algorithm comprises an autonomic tool that can be used in online ITS applications of various types, in order to optimize their performance by automatically fine-tuning the system's design parameters. The algorithm has been evaluated in simulation experiments, examining its ability and efficiency to fine-tune in real time the design parameters of a number of traffic control systems, including signal control for urban road networks. Field results are in progress for the urban network of Chania, Greece, as well as for energy-efficient building control. Some promising preliminary field results for the traffic control problem of Chania are presented here.

Keywords Intelligent transportation systems • Self-tuning • Adaptive fine-tuning

---

A. Kouvelas
EPFL ENAC IIC LUTS, CH-1015 Lausanne, Switzerland
e-mail: tasos.kouvelas@epfl.ch

D. Manolis • I. Papamichail (✉) • M. Papageorgiou
Dynamic Systems and Simulation Laboratory, Technical University of Crete, 73100 Chania, Greece
e-mail: dmanolis@dssl.tuc.gr; ipapa@dssl.tuc.gr; markos@dssl.tuc.gr

E. Kosmatopoulos
Democritus University of Thrace, 67100 Xanthi, Greece
e-mail: kosmatop@ee.duth.gr

T.L. McCluskey et al. (eds.), *Autonomic Road Transport Support Systems*, Autonomic Systems, DOI 10.1007/978-3-319-25808-9_13

1 Introduction

Despite the continuous advances in the fields of control and computing, the design and deployment of efficient large-scale traffic control systems remains a significant objective. This is mainly due to the complexity and the strong nonlinearities involved in the modelling of traffic flow processes. Practical control design approaches are often based on simplified models for the system dynamics, as the use of more complex models is virtually infeasible in most real-life applications. As a result, although the derived regulators are theoretically optimal, they usually exhibit suboptimal performance.

As the complexity of systems grows, the need to build into them the means to manage and maintain themselves becomes necessary, particularly in the case of large-scale, heterogeneous control systems. Systems need to be self-directing, self-configuring, self-maintaining, self-protecting and self-optimizing. One consequence of self-managing systems is that their interaction with people is set more at a "service" level than a "command" level. As a result, a traffic control centre manager will interface with future autonomic systems by communicating goals, priorities and tasks which the systems will solve.

The ultimate performance of a designed or operational traffic control system (e.g. urban signal control or ramp metering or variable speed limits) depends on two main factors: (a) the exogenous influences, e.g. demand, weather conditions and incidents, and (b) the values of some design parameters included in the control strategy. Every time a new control algorithm is implemented in the real world, there is a period of (sometimes tedious) fine-tuning activity that is needed in order to elevate the control algorithm to its best achievable performance. Fine-tuning concerns the selection of appropriate (or even optimal) values for a number of design parameters included in the control strategy. Typically, this procedure is conducted manually, via trial-and-error, relying on expertise and human judgement, without the use of a systematic approach. Currently, a considerable amount of human effort and time is spent by experienced engineers, practitioners and traffic operators on tuning operational systems. In many cases, the result of this manual procedure does not lead to a desirable outcome in terms of a measurable performance metric.

Some isolated examples of autonomic properties such as self-adaptation have found their way into Intelligent Transportation Systems (ITS) and have already proved beneficial. A recently developed methodology that combines the principles of traffic engineering, automatic control, optimization and machine learning and enables online self-tuning autonomicity for operational traffic systems is presented in this chapter. This problem has been discussed in depth in [1] where the algorithm AFT (adaptive fine-tuning), which was originally introduced in [2], is analysed and tested in different simulation environments. This autonomic online procedure is aiming at replacing the conventional manual optimization practice by embedding self-tuning capabilities in control strategies. AFT can self-adjust the tunable parameters of control systems, so that they reach the maximum (measurable) performance that is achievable with the utilized control strategy. The method can also be used for automatic readjustment of "aged" systems.

Given the positive feedback from the simulation investigations for different control problems, the algorithm is currently implemented in the field for energy-efficient building control, as well as the urban traffic control of Chania, Greece. Some preliminary results from the latter field implementation are also presented here. The results demonstrate the applicability of the algorithm and its efficiency in solving the tuning problem of real-life operational control systems.

2 Background

2.1 Problem Formulation

Consider a general discrete-time control system which is dictated by different feedback-type regulators, and its underlying dynamics are described by the following nonlinear first-order difference equation:

$$z(t+1) = F\left(z(t), u_i(t), d(t), t\right), \quad z(0) = z_0 \tag{1}$$

where $z(t), u_i(t), d(t)$ are the vectors of system states, control inputs and exogenous (possibly measurable) signals, respectively, $t = 0, 1, 2, \ldots$ denotes the discrete time index, i denotes the regulator index and $F(\cdot)$ is a sufficiently smooth nonlinear vector function. Note that the proposed methodology can be applied to a control system even if the function F is unknown.

Consider also that one or more control laws are applied to the system (1), which are described as follows:

$$u_i(t) = \varpi_i\left(\theta_i, z(t)\right) \tag{2}$$

where $\varpi_i(\cdot)$ are known smooth vector functions and θ_i is the vector of tunable parameters for the ith regulator. Note that there is no restriction imposed neither on the form of (2) nor on the number of regulators applied. Furthermore, the discrete time index t may be different for each control law i.

The overall system performance is evaluated through the following objective function (performance index):

$$\begin{aligned} J\left(\theta; z(0), D_T\right) &= \pi_T(z(T)) + \sum_{i=1}^{I}\sum_{t=0}^{T-1} \pi_{i,t}\left(z(t), u_i(t)\right) \\ &= \pi_T(z(T)) + \sum_{i=1}^{I}\sum_{t=0}^{T-1} \pi_{i,t}\left(z(t), \varpi\left(\theta_i, z(t)\right)\right) \end{aligned} \tag{3}$$

where $\theta = \text{vec}(\theta_1, \theta_2, \ldots, \theta_I)$, π_T and $\pi_{i,t}$ are known non-negative functions, I is the number of regulators that needs to be tuned, T is the finite time horizon over which the control laws (2) are applied and

$$D_T \triangleq [d(0), d(1), \ldots, d(T-1)] \quad (4)$$

denotes the time history of the exogenous signals over the optimization horizon T. By defining $x = \text{vec}(z(0), D_T)$, Eq. (3) may be rewritten as

$$J(\theta; z(0), D_T) = J(\theta, x) \,. \quad (5)$$

AFT is an iterative algorithm which can be applied every T and will update the current system parameter vector θ so as to achieve better performance. Equation (5) indicates that the system performance depends on the vector of tunable parameters θ and the exogenous vector x. Assuming that the signal x is bounded (i.e. $|x(t)| \leq B, \ \forall\, t \in \mathbb{Z}$ for a finite value $B > 0$), it can be omitted from Eq. (5) as the objective is to optimize the expected value $E\,[J(\theta)]$ given the variations in x. In [3] it has been mathematically proven that the AFT algorithm asymptotically converges to the optimal solution of this problem.

The requirement for convergence itself is not sufficient in most practical implementations. Another crucial issue is the safe and efficient behaviour of the system. Algorithms similar to AFT, which enable systems with autonomic self-tuning properties, should also guarantee stable and sustainable system performance during the field deployment. The violation of this requirement in a practical application may cause serious problems (e.g. performance degradation, safety, etc.). For instance, in the case of operational traffic control systems, this could lead to serious problems (e.g. complaints, dangerous driving, etc.) that may force the traffic operators to cancel the self-tuning process. This requirement has been addressed successfully in [4] for the AFT algorithm.

2.2 *Theoretical Foundations*

The self-tuning problem discussed in the previous subsection is closely related to the problem of dynamic parameter estimation that has been studied for decades by many researchers. The problem of interest is to find the values of a vector $\theta^* \in \Theta$ that minimize the expected value of a scalar-valued performance function $E\,[J(\theta)]$ assuming that measurements of the function are available for different θ. The vector θ represents a collection of tunable (or adjustable) parameters that need to be tuned. The nonlinear function $J(\theta)$ is a scalar measure that summarizes the performance of the system and is assumed to be continuous in Θ. The vector θ^* represents the optimal solution, and the domain Θ reflects allowable values (constraints) on the components of θ and has to be a compact space.

Many stochastic approximation algorithms have been developed for the solution of this problem. Robbins and Monro [5] were the first to propose an adaptive technique for dynamic parameter estimation. Important extensions of this algorithm followed by Kiefer and Wolfowitz in [6], where the Finite Difference Stochastic Approximation (FDSA) algorithm was introduced. FDSA has provided the basis for many learning or parameter tuning algorithms in control engineering problems. An extension of FDSA is the Random Directions Stochastic Approximation (RDSA) algorithm, which was first introduced in [7] and makes use of many random perturbations of θ in order to come up with a good set of tunable parameters (based on the measurements of the performance criterion $J(\theta)$).

Finally, Spall in [8] introduced the Simultaneous Perturbation Stochastic Approximation (SPSA) algorithm for stochastic optimization of multivariate systems. This algorithm attempts to estimate the gradient $\partial J(\theta)/\partial\theta$ in one discrete time step by applying a random perturbation to the current vector θ, and it has been widely applied to parameter estimation problems. It is worth noting that SPSA does not guarantee the requirement of safe and efficient performance during the tuning process, mainly due to the use of random perturbations applied to the regulator parameters.

The theoretical intuition of AFT lies in the area of the algorithms mentioned above. However, its scope is to enable traffic control systems with autonomic self-tuning capabilities. In this chapter we explore the efficiency of AFT through simulation experiments. The problem of online self-tuning of the urban signal control strategy Traffic-responsive Urban Control (TUC) [9, 10] is investigated. A microsimulation environment of traffic flow is used for evaluating the performance of the algorithm.

3 The Self-tuning Algorithm

Figure 1 illustrates the working principle, while Table 1 denotes the variables used by the AFT algorithm. The basic functioning procedure of the self-tuning process may be summarized as follows:

- The traffic flow process (e.g. urban road network) is controlled in real time by a control strategy (of any kind) which includes a number of tunable parameters.
- At the end of appropriately defined periods (e.g. at the end of each day), the AFT algorithm receives the value of the real (measured) performance index (e.g. average speed over space and time for traffic networks). Note that the performance index $J(\theta, x)$ is a (generally unknown) function of the tunable parameters θ that need to be adjusted and the main external (measurable) disturbances x (i.e. demand).
- Using the measured performance (the samples of which increase iteration by iteration), AFT calculates new tunable parameter values to be applied at the next period (e.g. the next day) in an attempt to improve the system performance.

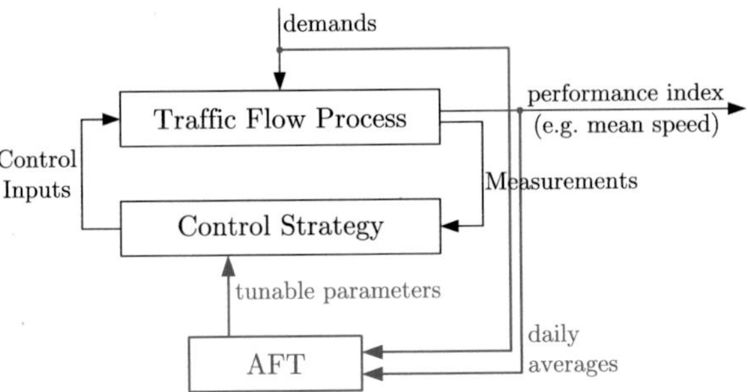

Fig. 1 Working principle of AFT for autonomic self-tuning of online traffic control systems

Table 1 Variables used within the AFT algorithm

k	Iteration index
ℓ	Past performance measurements index
J_ℓ	Performance value for the ℓth calibration experiment
$\hat{J}_\ell$	An estimate of J_ℓ obtained at the ℓth iteration
$\theta(k)$	The vector of tunable parameters at the kth calibration experiment
$\theta^*(k)$	The best set of tunable parameters until the kth experiment (according to the real measurements)
$\Delta\theta(k)^{(j)}$	Zero-mean random sequences (e.g. Gaussian), $j = 1, 2, \ldots, 2K$
$\Delta\theta(k)$	The perturbation picked by the algorithm in iteration k

- This (iterative) procedure is continued over many periods (e.g. days) until a maximum in performance is reached; then, AFT may remain active for continuous adaptation or can be switched off and reactivated at a later stage (e.g. after few months).

The main components used to develop the employed algorithm are summarized as follows:

- A universal approximator $\widehat{J}(\theta, x)$ is used (e.g. a polynomial-like approximator or a neural network) in order to obtain an approximation of the nonlinear mapping $J(\theta, x)$.
- An online adaptive/learning mechanism is employed for training the above approximator. Globally convergent learning algorithms (e.g. see [11]) are required for such a purpose.
- At each algorithm iteration k, many randomly chosen candidate perturbations $\Delta\theta(k)^{(j)}$ of vector $\theta^*(k)$ are generated (where $\theta^*(k)$ is the best set of parameters so far). The effect of each candidate set $\theta^*(k) + \Delta\theta(k)^{(j)}$ to the system performance is estimated by using the approximator mentioned above. The perturbation that corresponds to the best estimate (i.e. the one that leads to the best value for $\widehat{J}(\theta^*(k)+\Delta\theta(k)^{(j)}, \hat{x}(k+1))$, where $\hat{x}$ is an estimate of the external disturbances x) is selected to determine the new values for the tunable parameters $\theta(k+1)$ to be applied at the next period (e.g. the next day).

3.1 The Universal Approximator $\hat{J}(\theta)$

The universal approximator used in the simulation experiments in order to approximate the objective function $J(\theta)$ is a linear-in-the-weights polynomial-like approximator with L_g regressor terms, which takes the form

$$\widehat{J}(\theta) = \vartheta^T \phi(\theta) \tag{6}$$

where ϑ denotes the vector of the approximator parameter estimates and

$$\phi(\theta) = \left[\phi_1(\theta), \phi_2(\theta), \ldots, \phi_{L_g}(\theta)\right]^T. \tag{7}$$

The nonlinear functions $\phi_i(\theta)$ are given by

$$\phi_i(\theta) = S^{d_1}(\theta_{m_1}) \cdot S^{d_2}(x_{m_2}),\ d_i \in \{0, 1\} \tag{8}$$

where d_i, m_i are randomly chosen at each iteration of the AFT algorithm (with $m_1, m_2 \in \{1, 2, \ldots, n_\theta\}$, where n_θ is the number of components of vector θ) and $S(\cdot)$ is a smooth monotone nonlinear function. In the neural network literature [12], this function is usually chosen to be sigmoidal. In our simulations we choose

$$S(\theta) = \tanh(\lambda_1 \theta + \lambda_2) \tag{9}$$

where λ_i are non-negative real numbers initially defined by the user; after 4–5 iterations of the algorithm, the values of λ_i are optimized so as to minimize

$$\min \sum_{\ell=1}^{k-1} \left(J_\ell - \vartheta^T \phi_\ell^{(k)}\right)^2. \tag{10}$$

3.2 The AFT Algorithm Description

Below, we discuss in details the application steps of the algorithm. More precisely, the steps that are executed at every iteration are as follows:

- **Step 1:** *Calculate $2K$ random perturbations.* In this step K random perturbations are calculated (e.g. according to Gaussian distribution). The resulting $2K$ candidate vectors $\theta^*(k) \pm \Delta\theta(k)^{(j)}$ are then projected in Θ, in order to satisfy the problem constraints.
- **Step 2:** *Calculate the number of approximator regressor terms.* The number of the approximator's regressor terms $L_g(k)$ to be used in this iteration is calculated by $L_g(k) = \min\{2(k-1), \overline{L}_g\}$ with $\overline{L}_g$ a given upper bound.

- **Step 3:** *Calculate the number of past measurements.* The algorithm keeps a window of past measurements which moves along with the iterations. T_h is the upper bound of the number of past measurements AFT uses and it is defined by the user. In this step the starting point of the window in the past is calculated. The end point of the window is always $k - 1$.
- **Step 4:** *Produce the polynomial-like approximator.* After steps 2 and 3, the structure of the universal approximator may be formed and applied for nonlinear fitting to the data included in the window of the past measurements.
- **Step 5:** *Calculate the optimal approximator parameter estimates.* The optimal values of the approximator's parameters ϑ are calculated according to the solution of a least squares estimation method.
- **Step 6:** *Apply the* $2K$ *random perturbations* $\pm\Delta\theta(k)^{(j)}$ *to* $\widehat{J}(k)$. The $2K$ candidate vectors $\theta^*(k) \pm \Delta\theta(k)^{(j)}$ are applied to the approximator $\widehat{J}(k)$ for evaluation.
- **Step 7:** *Pick the best random perturbation (according to* $\widehat{J}(k)$*).* The vector $\theta(k)$ with the best estimated performance is selected for application in the next simulation experiment.

It is worth noting that similarly to RDSA, the proposed algorithm introduces random perturbations to the control design parameter vector θ. Besides, the use of random perturbations is crucial for the efficiency of the proposed algorithm as it provides the so-called persistence of excitation property, which is a sufficient and necessary condition for the neural approximator $\widehat{J}(\theta)$ to be able to efficiently learn the unknown function $J(\theta)$. However, due to the use of Step 6, the proposed methodology avoids poor performance or instability problems and guarantees safe and efficient performance. As shown in [2, 3] using strict mathematical arguments, the performance of the system can be, in the worst case, similar to the system performance without the self-tuning property plus some random term. The magnitude of this term is proportional to the magnitude and variance of the exogenous inputs x.

3.3 Efficient Stochastic Stepsizes α_k

The first step of the AFT algorithm makes use of an arithmetic sequence $\alpha(k)$ which plays a critical role, often determining whether the algorithm converges or diverges. These factors are sometimes referred to as stepsizes but also gains or learning coefficients, depending on the field of application. The choice of the gain sequence $\alpha(k)$ is critical for the performance of stochastic approximation methods. In many applications, a constant stepsize is used (instead of a decaying one) as a way of avoiding gains that are too small for large k. On the other hand, there is considerable appeal to the idea that the stepsize should depend on the actual trajectory of the algorithm. When the stepsizes depend on the observations they are called stochastic stepsizes. For large-scale problems, it is possible that we have to estimate hundreds of parameters. It seems unlikely that all the parameters will approach their optimal value at the same time (wide variation in learning rates can occur). Stochastic stepsizes try to adjust to the data in a way that keeps the stepsize larger while the parameter being estimated is still changing quickly.

Conditions guaranteeing that the stochastic approximation iterate converges to θ^* as $k \rightarrow \infty$ are presented in many places (e.g. [13]). All the existing proofs require three basic conditions about the applied stepsizes:

$$\alpha(k) \geq 0, \quad k = 0, 1, \ldots, \tag{11}$$

$$\sum_{k=0}^{\infty} \alpha(k) = \infty, \tag{12}$$

$$\sum_{k=0}^{\infty} \alpha(k)^2 < \infty. \tag{13}$$

Equation (11) requires that the stepsizes must be non-negative. The most important requirement is (12), which states that the infinite summation of stepsizes must be infinite. If this condition is violated, the algorithm might stall very early without reaching the optimal solution. Finally, condition (13) requires that the infinite sum of the squares of the stepsizes is finite. A good intuitive justification for this condition is that it guarantees that the variance of the estimate of the optimal solution goes to zero in the limit. The three conditions mentioned above provide a careful balance in having the gain $\alpha(k)$ decay neither too fast nor too slow.

For our experiments, we introduce an adaptive technique for the calculation of stepsize $\alpha_i(k)$ (where i refers to the ith component of vector θ), at each iteration of the AFT algorithm k. This technique is based on the signs ($\pm$) of the product of the differences $\Delta\theta_i(k)$, $\Delta\theta_i(k-1)$ picked for the last two iterations. If there are frequent sign changes, this is an indication that the iterate is near θ_i^*; if the signs are not changing, this is an indication that the iterate is far from θ_i^*. This forms the basis for an adaptive choice of the gain $\alpha_i(k)$, where a larger gain is used if there are no sign changes and a smaller gain is used if the signs change frequently.

Given the desirability for a gain sequence that balances algorithm stability in the early iterations and non-negligible gains in the later iterations, the form used in AFT is

$$\alpha_i(k) = \frac{\alpha(0)}{\alpha(0) + K_i}, \tag{14}$$

which satisfies the three conditions mentioned above.

Initially $K_i = 1, \forall i$ and then for every iteration $k = 2, 3, \ldots$, we have

$$K_i = \begin{cases} K_i & \text{if } \Delta\theta_i(k)\Delta\theta_i(k-1) > 0 \\ K_i + 1 & \text{if } \Delta\theta_i(k)\Delta\theta_i(k-1) < 0. \end{cases} \tag{15}$$

This form is inspired by the famous learning method RPROP [14]. This formula takes into account only the sign of $\Delta\theta_i$ and acts independently on each θ_i. This way, every component i of vector θ converges with a different rate according to the frequency of sign changes.

4 Simulation Experiments

In order to evaluate the efficiency of the self-tuning algorithm, extensive simulation experiments have been carried out. The microscopic simulation environment Aimsun was used in order to replicate a real-world implementation of the algorithm. In our experiments the TUC strategy [9, 10] is used to regulate the signals of the city of Chania, Greece, in real time. The system autonomously self-tunes its design parameters using the AFT algorithm. All the data utilized in Aimsun and TUC (turning rates, lost times, staging, saturation flows) are provided by the operators of the Traffic Control Centre of the city and correspond to the data of the real network. This section presents the simulation results, comparing the performance of the TUC strategy, when AFT is used for autonomic self-tuning of a predefined set of design parameters, with the base case (no AFT case). In the base case, the aforementioned parameters of the original TUC system have been manually fine-tuned to virtual perfection by the system operators [15].

4.1 Network and Simulation Setup

Chania, located at the north-western part of Crete, is the capital of the prefecture of Chania and covers 12.5 km^2. Figure 2 exhibits a satellite view of the trial urban road network (red bullets correspond to the controlled junctions), which has a total length of approximately 8 km and consists of 16 controlled junctions.

Figure 3 represents the model of the network developed for the simulation investigations. It consists of 16 signalized junctions (nodes) and 60 links (arrows). Each network link corresponds to a particular junction phase. Typical loop-detector locations within the Chania urban network links are either around the middle of the link or some 40 m upstream of the stop line. Split, cycle and offset control modules of the TUC strategy are applied to the network for all simulation investigations. For the implementation of the AFT algorithm, the following design values were used: $T_{\mathrm{h}} = 90$, $\bar{L}_{\mathrm{g}} = 150$, $K = 100$ and initial values to λ_i according to $\lambda_1 = 100$, $\lambda_2 = 0$. Finally, a simulation step of 0.25 s is considered for the microscopic simulation model.

Fig. 2 Satellite view of the Chania urban road network

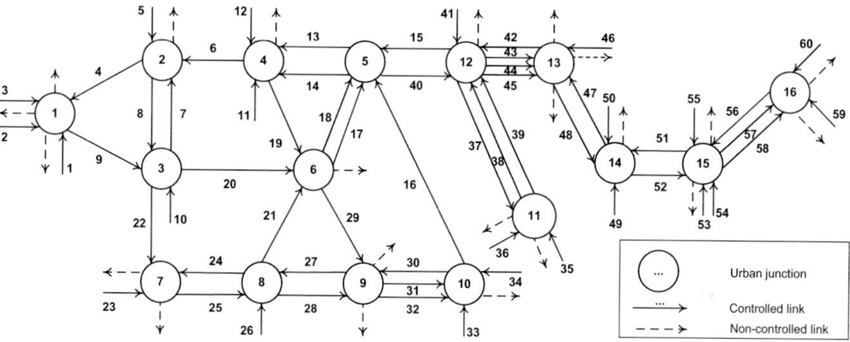

Fig. 3 Simulation model of the urban road network of Chania

4.2 Demand Scenarios and Integration with Aimsun

In order to investigate the performance of AFT under different traffic conditions, two basic traffic demand scenarios (time history of vehicles entering the network in the network origins during the day) were designed based on actual measurements, each with a simulation horizon of 4 h. Scenario 1 comprises medium demand in all network origins, while scenario 2 comprises high demand and the network faces serious congestion for some 2 h, with some link queues spilling back into upstream links. For simplicity, we assume that a demand scenario with a time horizon of 4 h corresponds to a day. Each day (iteration of the AFT algorithm) a randomly perturbed 5 % width version of the basic demand scenarios is produced and the assessment criterion is gathered from the Aimsun simulator. Then, the design parameters of the TUC strategy are updated by AFT according to the calculated assessment criterion.

The overall closed-loop scheme consists of two main control loops as inner and outer loops. The inner loop is used by the TUC strategy to produce the traffic signal settings. More specifically at each control cycle, Aimsun delivers the (emulated) occupancy measurements at the locations where detectors are placed (as in real conditions). These measurements are used by the control modules of the TUC strategy to produce the traffic signal settings (splits, cycle and offsets). The signal settings are then forwarded to the microsimulator for application. The outer loop is used by AFT to update the design parameters of TUC. More specifically, at each day, Aimsun delivers the mean speed for the whole urban road network (this is the measurement of the performance index $J(\theta)$). The mean speed is used by the AFT algorithm in order to produce the new values for the design parameters of split, cycle and offset control modules of TUC (the vector θ). The new set of the design parameters is then forwarded to TUC for application and so forth.

4.3 Results from the Simulation Experiments

Table 2 presents the average results for a series of replications for the simulation of the two demand scenarios. The self-tunable system exhibits an improvement of around 17 % and 36 %, respectively. The diagrams in Fig. 4 compare the network-wide mean speed of the original TUC system (blue line) versus TUC system combined with the self-tuning algorithm (red line) for the network described above and two different demand scenarios. Scenario 1 (Fig. 4a) reflects medium demand in all network origins, while scenario 2 (Fig. 4b) reflects high demand whereby the network faces serious congestion with some link queues spilling back into upstream links. In both diagrams, it can be seen that the application of the AFT algorithm leads to better performance compared to the original TUC system. More precisely, the AFT algorithm aims to optimize the overall system performance within a few days (iteration number in x-axis), by efficiently self-tuning the design parameters for all TUC's control modules (89 parameters in total). The combined system first increases and then maintains the daily mean speed of the network at higher levels

Table 2 Comparison of the 50 days' average space-time speed (ASTS) for many simulation experiments

Demand scenario	No AFT ASTS (km/h)	No AFT St. deviation (km/h)	AFT ASTS (km/h)	AFT St. deviation (km/h)	ASTS improvement (%)
1	16.29	0.71	19.13	0.86	17.46
2	9.67	1.63	13.19	0.82	36.33

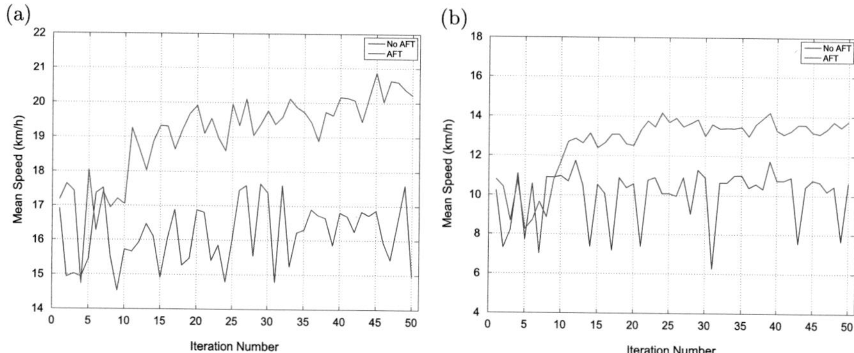

Fig. 4 Daily mean speed trajectories with and without the use of the AFT algorithm: (**a**) scenario 1, (**b**) scenario 2

than the initial day (which corresponds to the initial values of the parameters), eventually leading to a local maximum value of performance.

5 Preliminary Field Results

During the write-up period of this chapter, a field implementation and testing of the AFT algorithm took place in the city of Chania under the research project AGILE (funded by the European Commission, FP7-ICT-5-3.5). The overall system outlined in this chapter was implemented in the Traffic Control Centre of the city. More specifically, TUC was controlling the traffic signals in real time, while AFT was running in parallel, embedding self-tuning capabilities in the overall system.

Due to the fact that this is the first field experiment of the AFT algorithm to the traffic domain, some choices had to be made so as to enable a careful and gradual evaluation. The urban road network of Fig. 2 is considered for the field experiment, albeit it is separated in two regions; Region 2 consists of junctions 15 and 16 in Fig. 3, while Region 1 comprises all other junctions. Each region is controlled by its own TUC algorithm, with independent cycle times. Also, two independent versions of the AFT algorithm are running in parallel with TUC, embedding self-tuning capabilities for each region. Thus, there are two distinct experiments running at the same time. The main reason for clustering the junctions into two regions is that Region 2 is remote from the rest of the network (no offsets apply among the regions), and moreover its congestion patterns, and hence suitable cycle times, are different than for the rest of the network. It should be mentioned that traffic in Region 1, which comprises the city's CBD, is more stochastic in its behaviour, mainly due to uncertain but frequent illegal or double parking that may change the network characteristics and junction capacities in an unpredictable way.

In this first running experiment, we have chosen only four parameters for each region to be automatically tuned by the respective AFT algorithms. The four parameters determine the real-time specification of the cycle time and were found in earlier simulation-based work to influence the performance of TUC. The criterion that AFT tries to maximize is the overall mean speed. More specifically, the space-time averaged network mean speed is calculated daily based on detector data in each network link, for the period 8:00 a.m. to 2:00 p.m., which includes most of the morning and early-afternoon traffic peaks. The algorithm receives also the daily total demand (as the most important external factor for performance), which is the sum of the time-averaged (8:00 a.m. to 2:00 p.m.) flows measured by detectors at the network origins. Every day is an AFT iteration, while a total of 29 days of results (no weekends) are presented.

Figure 5 shows trajectories of parameters under AFT tuning over iterations (blue lines). The starting values of the parameters are those used in the operational system and have been manually fine-tuned in the recent past. At the beginning, some conservative bounds have been used for the parameters (red lines). The parameter of Fig. 5a is seen to hit the upper bound several times; hence we decided to change it (on the fly) as seen at iteration 15. This was also done with other parameters' upper or lower bounds.

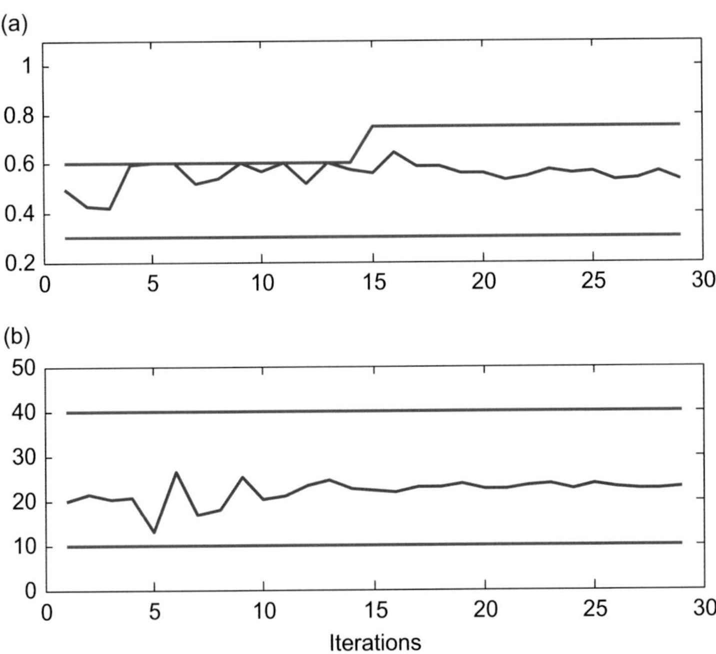

Fig. 5 Examples of trajectories of parameters (*blue*) over iterations (days) and their bounds (*red*)

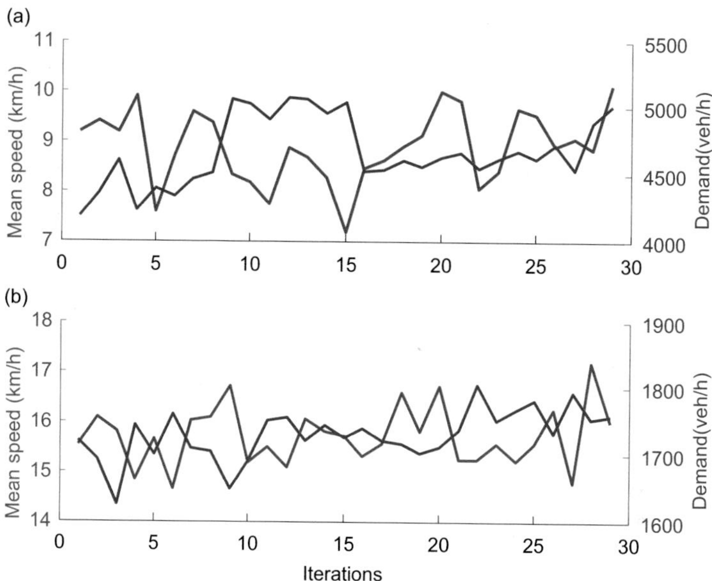

Fig. 6 Overall mean speed (*red*) and total demand (*blue*) vs. iterations: (**a**) Region 1; (**b**) Region 2

Figure 6 displays the overall mean speed and the total demand of the two networks (Region 1 and Region 2) over the available iterations. A difficulty in assessing these preliminary results is due to the fact that, in contrast to the simulation investigations, the demand is changing daily without evidence for stationary average or standard deviation. If everything else is constant, the mean speed is a decreasing function of the demand; as a result it is not possible to judge on any possible improvements by observing only the mean speed (as with the simulation results of Fig. 6). In the following, we present two ways of addressing this difficulty.

The first way is to split the available days into two groups according to their respective total demands. For Region 1, groups 1 and 2 comprise all days with demand above and below 4650 veh/h, respectively, while for Region 2, groups 1 and 2 comprise all days with demand above and below 1725 veh/h, respectively. Figure 7a, b presents the Region 1 results for the two groups, along with corresponding regression lines. It can be seen that for lower demands, there is a very slight average deterioration over iterations, while for higher demands, there is a strong improvement of about 20 % over the iterations. AFT operates for all demands and strives a total improvement. This does not exclude partial deteriorations for subdomains of demand. Figure 7c, d presents the corresponding results for Region 2, where a clear average improvement is visible for both demand groups.

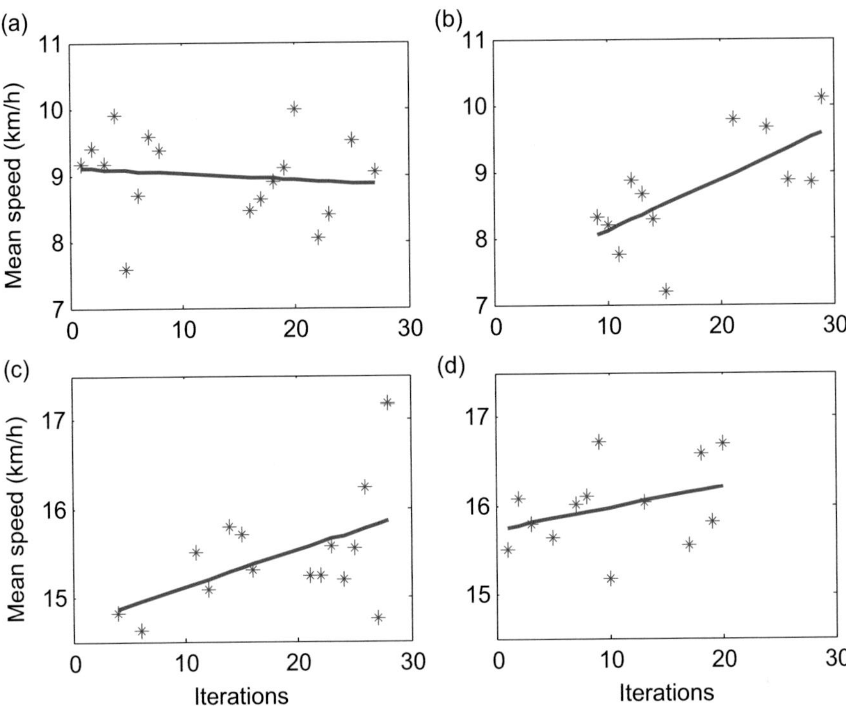

Fig. 7 (**a**) Mean speeds of Region 1 for iterations with demand lower than 4650 veh/h; (**b**) mean speeds of Region 1 for iterations with demand higher than 4650 veh/h; (**c**) mean speeds of Region 2 for iterations with demand lower than 1725 veh/h; (**d**) mean speeds of Region 2 for iterations with demand higher than 1725 veh/h

A second way to evaluate the results is by introducing a criterion which integrates the demand and mean speed. Such an evaluation criterion, which is used regularly in various studies (e.g. it is one of the three national performance criteria for Australia), is the product of the daily overall mean speed and the corresponding total demand. This is sometimes called "production" and expresses essentially the amount of veh$*$km/h^2 served by the traffic network. Figure 8 displays the evolution of this criterion over iterations for the two regions, along with the corresponding regression lines. This criterion clearly indicates that AFT achieves significant improvement to the mean speed of the network over iterations.

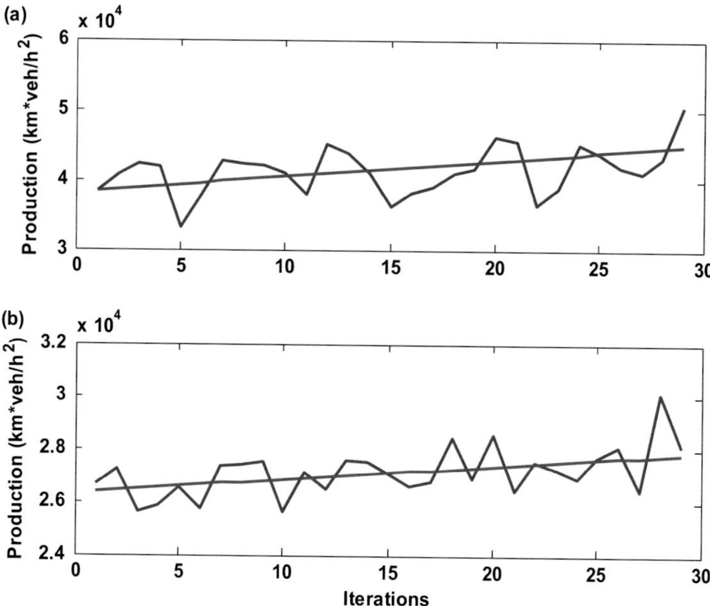

Fig. 8 Production over iterations: (**a**) Region 1 and (**b**) Region 2

6 Conclusions

This chapter investigated the efficiency of the AFT algorithm for the problem of optimizing the design parameters of traffic control systems. This adaptive optimization methodology aims at replacing the conventional manually based optimization practice with an autonomic procedure. Simulation results have been presented demonstrating that the self-tuning algorithm (AFT) leads to better network performance (in terms of daily mean speed) compared to the original TUC system. This underlines the superiority of the autonomic optimization procedure over the case where the design parameters are manually fine-tuned by field experts.

Given the conclusion of the simulation investigation, it was decided to proceed with a field implementation in the traffic network of Chania, Greece. In conclusion, the available preliminary field results of AFT are very promising and encouraging. The results confirm that despite the inhomogeneous demands, AFT evolves the control parameters so as to lead to better network average performance over time.

More field investigations have been planned in order to study in more details the impact of the strongly varying demand. One of the questions that need to be answered is the following. How many and which parameters should be selected for fine-tuning? A big set of parameters could give more degrees of freedom in the problem, but it could also lead to over-parameterization. In conclusion, the set of parameters that will be used should be the one with the highest impact on the problem to be solved and should take into account the control strategy characteristics and of course some successful simulation results.

Acknowledgements The research leading to these results has been partially funded by the European Commission FP7-ICT-5-3.5, Engineering of Networked Monitoring and Control Systems, under the contract #257806 AGILE.

References

1. Kouvelas, A.: Adaptive fine-tuning for large-scale nonlinear traffic control systems. Ph.D. dissertation, Technical University of Crete, Chania (2011)
2. Kosmatopoulos, E.B., Papageorgiou, M., Vakouli, A., Kouvelas, A.: Adaptive fine-tuning of non-linear control systems with application to the urban traffic control strategy TUC. IEEE Trans. Control Syst. Technol. **15**(6), 991–1002 (2007)
3. Kosmatopoulos, E.B., Kouvelas, A.: Large-scale nonlinear control system fine-tuning through learning. IEEE Trans. Neural Netw. **20**(6), 1009–1023 (2009)
4. Kouvelas, A., Aboudolas, K., Kosmatopoulos, E.B., Papageorgiou, M.: Adaptive performance optimization for large-scale traffic control systems. IEEE Trans. Intell. Transp. Syst. **12**(4), 1434–1445 (2011)
5. Robbins, H., Monro, S.: A stochastic approximation method. Ann. Math. Stat. **22**, 400–407 (1951)
6. Kiefer, J., Wolfowitz, J.: Stochastic estimation of a regression function. Ann. Math. Stat. **23**, 462–466 (1952)
7. Ermoliev, Y.: On the method of generalized stochastic gradients and quasi-fejer sequences. Cybernetics **5**, 208–220 (1969)
8. Spall, J.: Multivariate stochastic approximation using a simultaneous perturbation gradient approximation. IEEE Trans. Autom. Control **37**(3), 332–341 (1992)
9. Diakaki, C., Papageorgiou, M., Aboudolas, K.: A multivariable regulator approach to traffic-responsive network-wide signal control. Control Eng. Pract. **10**, 183–195 (2002)
10. Diakaki, C., Dinopoulou, V., Aboudolas, K., Papageorgiou, M., Ben-Shabat, E., Seider, E., Leibov, A.: Extensions and new applications of the traffic-responsive urban control strategy: coordinated signal control for urban networks. Transp. Res. Rec. **1856**, 202–211 (2003)
11. Kosmatopoulos, E., Polycarpou, M., Christodoulou, M., Ioannou, P.: High-order neural network structures for identification of dynamical systems. IEEE Trans. Neural Netw. **6**(2), 422–431 (1995)
12. Huang, G.-B., Chen, L., Siew, C.-K.: Universal approximation using incremental constructive feedforward networks with random hidden nodes. IEEE Trans. Neural Netw. **17**(4), 879–892 (2006)
13. Bazaraa, M.S., Sherali, H.D., Shetty, C.M.: Nonlinear Programming: Theory and Algorithms, 2nd edn. Wiley, New York (1993)
14. Riedmiller, M., Braun, H.: RPROP – a fast adaptive learning algorithm. In: Proceedings of ISCIS VII, Universitat (1992)
15. Kosmatopoulos, E., Papageorgiou, M., Bielefeldt, C., Dinopoulou, V., Morris, R., Mueck, J., Richards, A., Weichenmeier, F.: International comparative field evaluation of a traffic-responsive signal control strategy in three cities. Transp. Res. **40A**(5), 399–413 (2006)

Electric Vehicles in Road Transport and Electric Power Networks

Charalampos Marmaras, Erotokritos Xydas, Liana M. Cipcigan, Omer Rana, and Franziska Klügl

Abstract Electric vehicle (EV) market penetration is expected to increase in the next few years. Transport electrification will affect both the road transport and the electric power network, as EV charging will be influenced by events that take place on the road network (such as congestion, weather, etc.) which subsequently have an impact on the potential load imposed on an electricity grid (based on where EV charging takes place). An EV is therefore seen as a link between transport and energy systems, and their interdependencies are important. In this chapter an EV is modeled as an autonomous agent with a set of predefined high-level goals (such as traveling from origin to destination). Algorithms for the routing and charging procedures of EVs are presented. A multi-agent simulation is carried out, based on a number of scenarios, which demonstrates interactions between transport and energy systems, showing how an EV agent is able to adapt its behavior based on changes within each of these systems.

Keywords Multiagent simulation • Electric vehicle • Charging station • Autonomous behaviour

1 Introduction

Environmental and energy security reasons have identified electric vehicles (EVs) as a major part of future road transport networks. This integration of EVs will affect transport networks due to their particular characteristics, such as the frequency and the time needed for recharging an EV battery. Apart from playing a major part in

C. Marmaras (✉) • E. Xydas • L.M. Cipcigan
School of Engineering, Cardiff University, Cardiff, UK
e-mail: MarmarasC@cardiff.ac.uk; XydasE@cardiff.ac.uk; CipciganLM@cardiff.ac.uk

O. Rana
School of Computer Science and Informatics, Cardiff University, Cardiff, UK
e-mail: RanaOF@cardiff.ac.uk

F. Klügl
School of Science and Technology, Örebro University, Örebro, Sweden
e-mail: franziska.klugl@oru.se

T.L. McCluskey et al. (eds.), *Autonomic Road Transport Support Systems*, Autonomic Systems, DOI 10.1007/978-3-319-25808-9_14

road transport networks, EVs are expected to influence significantly the electric power networks. Considering a typical battery capacity of 30 kW, the energy needs for recharging this vehicle are almost double the average daily needs of a house. EV charging will affect significantly the load profiles unless smart grid control techniques are applied to either limit when (in time and location) charging is carried out or for how long. Several studies indicate that uncontrolled charging of EVs will increase the peak demand of a power system, resulting in feeder voltage excursions and equipment overloads, especially in already stressed networks [1, 2]. It is obvious that the integration of EVs will affect both systems, and it has therefore become necessary to identify possible ways of making this integration more efficient.

Autonomic computing approaches play an essential role in EVs: the driver should be supported by adaptive route guidance that takes account of traffic state, battery state, available charging stations, etc., ensuring that the overall objective to reach a destination in the preferred way can be realized. At the same time the electricity network also needs to self-adapt to the changes in demand. One way to facilitate EV integration is by using analysis tools built specifically to determine the effects of adding large numbers of mobile loads to the grid using information from transport models. Such analysis tools would attempt to predict where an EV is likely to charge, thereby providing an estimate of potential load likely to be exerted on the electricity network at that point. In [3, 4] agent-based models (ABMs) are developed to control the charging of EVs. These ABMs consider constraints coming from the electric power network; however, a road transport system perspective is not studied. Approaches to model EVs in both the electric power and road transport system are presented in [5, 6]; however, in both cases each system is modeled independently.

This chapter proposes an integrated simulation-based approach, introducing the EV as an intelligent and autonomous component living in both road transport and electric power systems. Using a multi-agent simulation platform, we model both systems and demonstrate how (under various scenarios) EV behavior can be adapted to changes in the underlying road transport and/or energy network. Autonomic computing aspects like adaptability and self-management are demonstrated in this context. An adaptive routing algorithm is used to ensure EVs reach their destination in the minimum time. The route planner adapts to battery consumption constraints and adjusts the EV's route to include the necessary recharging stops. In addition, a charging management mechanism exists to coordinate the EV charging requests. This mechanism adapts the EV charging demand to the overall demand limitations of the energy network, so that normal operation is maintained.

2 Multi-Agent Simulation

In multi-agent simulation, autonomous decision makers are conceived of as (simulated) agents who interact with each other and with a simulated environment resembling the real context of the original actors [7–9]. With origins both in social science simulation and complex system analysis, multi-agent simulation is now used in many application domains with traffic and transportation being a major one (for a recent review, see [10]). Multi-agent simulation models have been published at all levels of transportation ranging from mobility simulations to tactical and strategic levels (e.g., route and mode choice, or travel demand), or combining all levels. Besides addressing objectives that cannot be solved with traditional simulations such as the effect of behavioral response to traffic information or testing different forms of communication between vehicles and infrastructure, the vision behind all of them is to achieve more realistic travel decision and traffic participation models. Multi-agent systems therefore form the paradigm of choice when modeling behavior of EVs that are able to carry out autonomic decision making, while factoring in the current state of the energy and road transport network. Each EV has one or more goals (e.g., reach destination by a certain time) that it attempts to achieve in an autonomic manner (based, generally, on an approximate understanding of its environment).

Various tools and platforms for multi-agent simulation have been developed. There are several surveys comparing various simulation platforms, such as NetLogo (http://ccl.northwestern.edu/netlogo/) or Repast (http://repast.sourceforge.net/). The choice of the simulator often involves trading off the complexity of an agent with the complexity of potential interactions. Some simulators enable complex agent behavior to be modeled (with limited support for interaction), whereas in other contexts, agent behaviors are expected to be simple but with more complex, often emergent, interactions. In this study, we apply SeSAm [11], which is a domain-independent modeling and simulation platform enabling domain experts to design, implement, and run multi-agent simulations on their own. Models and their context are represented in a high-level language mainly based on variable sets for entity bodies and activity diagrams for specifying agent behaviors. Implementation is carried out using visual programming language primitives, which can be extended with a plug-in concept for integrating advanced functionality written in the Java programming language. Plug-ins providing basic functionality for traffic simulations are available and have been used in this work.

3 Modeling Framework

In this work, a generic model was created that aims at capturing the interplay between traffic participation and charging interaction for showing the overall effect of an autonomic control. For that aim, EVs were simulated in a complex environment, dealing with intrinsic limitations (energy requirements, battery capacity), as well as external constraints (road network topology, traffic, charging station availability).

A routing algorithm was developed for the EV to choose the optimal route to the destination defined by the EV owner. The routing algorithm considered dynamic road congestion data and geographical information of a transport network (such as the nodes and links of the route, and the route length), as well as consumption data of the EV. For the evaluation of the algorithm, a test network was developed, consisting of nodes and links. Nodes represent an area that can contain charging stations, and links represent the roads that connect these nodes. Each link has time-dependent congestion values for different times of the day, based on which the preferred route is selected.

The model also includes an algorithm for charging station aggregators to manage the charging requests from EVs. It is assumed that dispersed public and private (home) charging stations exist, installed at the nodes of a transport network. Public charging stations are used by all EV agents in order to recharge their batteries. Home charging stations are assumed to exist at all nodes of the transport system. In this model, two charging station aggregators are modeled, one for public stations (public station manager) and one for private stations (private station manager).

As stated before, the model was simulated using SeSAm [11], in which each type of entity constitutes an agent class with the same characteristics and behavior. Independent variables are used for the static characteristics of each agent class, indicating a parameter that cannot be affected by other entities, e.g., an EV's battery capacity. Additionally, dependent variables exist in every entity's behavior, influenced by the interactions of the various entities within the same environment. Each agent has a reasoning engine, which enables the agent to follow a particular predefined behavior, modeled as activity (behavioral states) and transitions. Each activity defines a sequence of actions that are executed and can trigger different procedures in the same entity and/or in other agents. Time-dependent variables are used to capture the dynamic state of the agent and make sure that transitions between the various activities of each agent take place in the correct sequence. All interactions between agents follow request-response logic; thus each request must precede the corresponding response. Following this rule, all agents are modeled with an "idle" state in which they just wait to receive an answer from another agent. This is critical for coordinating the agents, as during this state, other agents perform various actions that need to be executed prior to this agent's next action, e.g., one agent uses the result of another agent's calculation.

In this model both a simple road transport network and a small part of an electric power distribution network are modeled, along with their main components. Although the size of the network being considered is intentionally small to facilitate clear analysis, this does not limit the generality of the model, as it is expandable and applicable to larger networks. Our intention is to demonstrate the linkage and dependencies between these in the context of EV charging.

3.1 Modeling the Road Transport Network

The modeled example road transport network consists of eight nodes (N1–N8) and nine links (A–I). The topology is presented in Fig. 1. Each node represents a small geographical area that contains a number of charging stations and is connected with other nodes through links. The links represent the roads connecting one area to

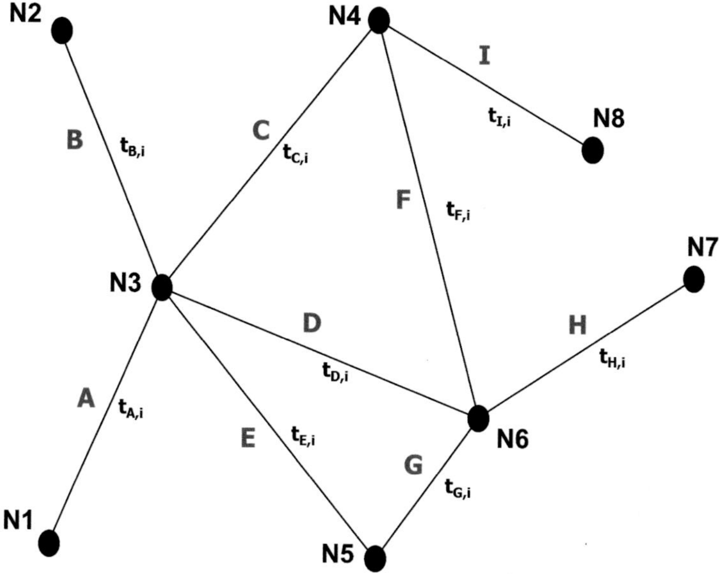

Fig. 1 Network topology

another. In this case study the congestion on the roads is expressed based on the time an EV has to spend on each link. These values are affected by both temporal parameters (e.g., the time of day and the day in the week) and spatial parameters (e.g., the length of each link). The hourly and daily change of the average congestion in the roads was obtained from the hourly traffic distributions for 1 week from the UK Department for Transport [12].

According to [12], on weekdays the roads are congested mostly at early morning hours (7:00–8:00) and early evening hours (17:00–18:00), something that is directly related to the hours of driving to and returning from work. However, this is not the case for weekends, where the peak is found at noon (11:00–12:00). Obviously, when a road is congested, the average vehicle velocity on that road is low. This hourly change of the average velocity on a link, in combination with the length of each link, resulted in the congestion values (*t*-indices on links in Fig. 1). Those indices represent the time that an EV has to spend on each link/road and consequently the average velocity on this road. Velocity also affects the energy consumption of the EV and consequently its battery state of charge (SoC). Every modeled EV agent's energy consumption and speed follow the relationship presented in Fig. 2.

Each geographical area represented by a node contains a number of charging stations. In this model, two different types of charging stations were considered, the private (home) charging stations and the public charging stations. Each station type is modeled with an agent class; therefore each charging station is an agent able to take an autonomous decision about which vehicles it should provide access to for charging purposes.

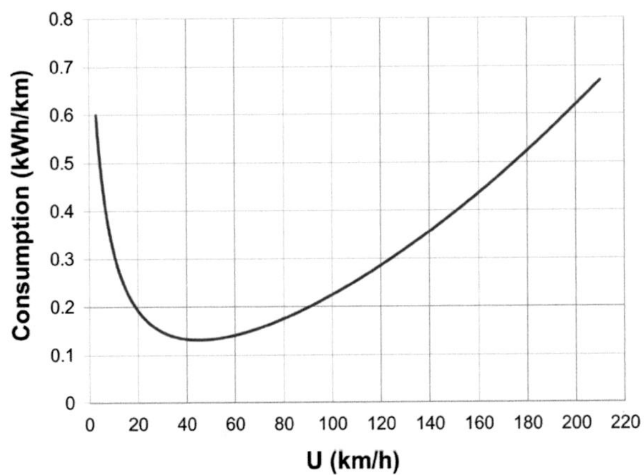

Fig. 2 Energy consumption versus speed for an EV agent

The private station agent represents a residential charging point that is unique for every home in the model. Each agent of this type is located at a node; it has a unique ID, a charging rate of 3 kW, and a common manager, the "private station manager." Each station has a reservation array, which is modified by the private station manager according to the EV requests and the power system's technical characteristics.

The public station agent represents a public charging point located at the central nodes, available to every EV in the model. Usually the charging rate of this type of stations is high (in our case we have specified a charging rate of 11 kW), and this means shorter charging periods than the private stations. Each station of this type has a unique ID and a common manager, the "public station manager." The reservation idea is the same, and the reservation array is now modified by the public station manager. As these stations are public and can only serve one EV per time slot, the possibility for an EV to charge at a public station is subject to the station's availability.

3.2 Modeling the Electric Power System

Figure 3 shows the topology of the modeled example electric power distribution network. This network is layered on top of the modeled road transport network, supplying energy to all nodes. As seen from Fig. 3, the electric power distribution network follows the structure of the UK Generic Distribution Network [13] and consists of eight low-voltage (LV) feeders, two medium-/low-voltage transformers, and one medium-voltage (MV) feeder. The operation of each entity is described by an agent class; therefore every component of the power system constitutes an agent.

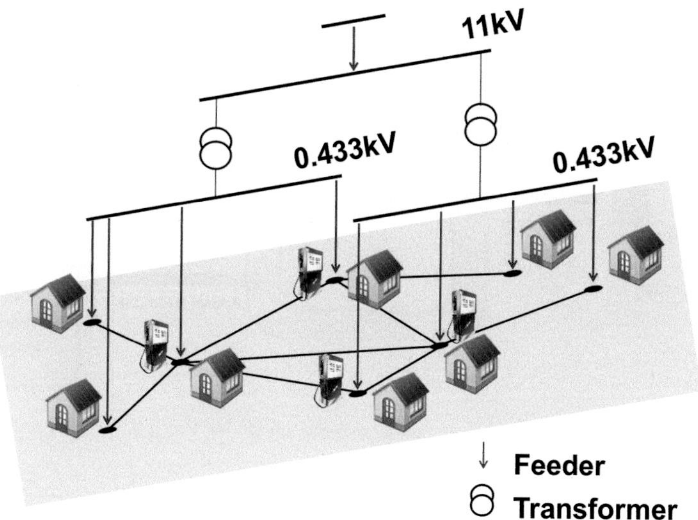

Fig. 3 Topology of the electric power network

Each node of the transport network is provided with energy by one LV feeder. Every LV feeder is connected to a number of charging stations (public and/or private charging stations), as well as to a number of houses. Such houses are not represented by any kind of agent in our current simulation; however, the aggregated electricity demand for all houses at one node is defined as the "No-EV Demand" variable. The LV feeder agent's task is to monitor the demand of all charging stations on the corresponding node and inform the corresponding transformer agent for the total demand. Following the UK Generic Distribution Network specifications [13], a MV/LV transformer has four LV feeders. Therefore, in our case, each transformer agent supplies energy to four LV feeder agents and consequently to four nodes of the transport model. The transformer agent's task is to monitor the demand of the corresponding LV feeders and inform the MV feeder agent when a demand variation occurs. The MV feeder is the highest point in our power system network and its demand curve shows the total electricity demand in our model.

All these agents are part of the simulated power system model, and each of them is working under specific operating limits, according to [13]. These limits must not be exceeded; otherwise the stability of the power system is at risk.

3.3 Modeling the Charging Station Aggregator Agents

Two essential entities exist in this model; the private station manager agent and the public station manager agent. The architecture of the charging station aggregator agent is presented in Fig. 4.

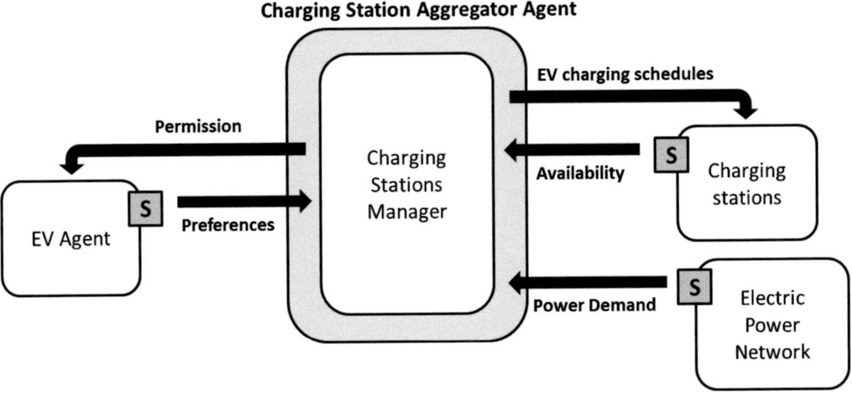

Fig. 4 Architecture of the charging station aggregator agent

Both charging station aggregators communicate and interact with the electric power network, EV agents, and the corresponding type of charging stations (e.g., the private station manager is responsible for the private charging stations). They try to achieve different goals; thus their behavior is not the same. However, both agents work to ensure that the overall electricity network remains in a stable state by managing the charging requests accordingly.

The Private Station Manager

The private station manager communicates with EVs in order to satisfy their requests for charging at a particular private station. This agent is also responsible for maintaining stability in the electric power system—communication links exist between this agent and the power system network entities.

Different charging strategies have been proposed in the literature regarding private (domestic) charging stations. In the early stages of EV integration, the number of the EVs is expected to be relatively small, and the EV owners will charge their vehicles without any controlled scheme (uncontrolled charging scenario) [3, 14]. With the EV number gradually rising, the EV owners could be incentivized to charge their vehicles following a dual-tariff scheme, to reduce their energy cost and at the same time decongest the peak hours (dual-tariff scenario) [3]. In more mature stages of EV integration, the charging station managers will have contractual agreements with the power system operator, and they will be paid based on ancillary services they provide. Advanced control algorithms for EV charging will be applied to optimize the network operation and charge only in the off-peak hours of the demand curve (Smart scenario—valley fill) [3, 14–16]. The impact of the different charging scenarios on the demand curve is presented in Fig. 5.

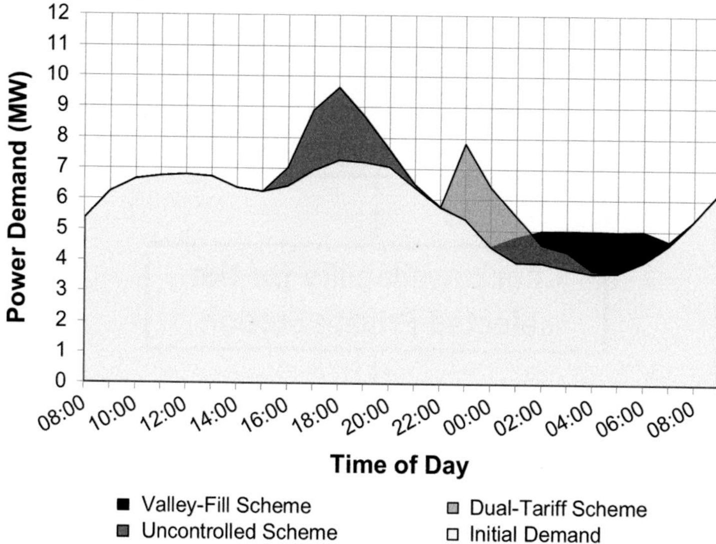

Fig. 5 Architecture of the charging station aggregator agent

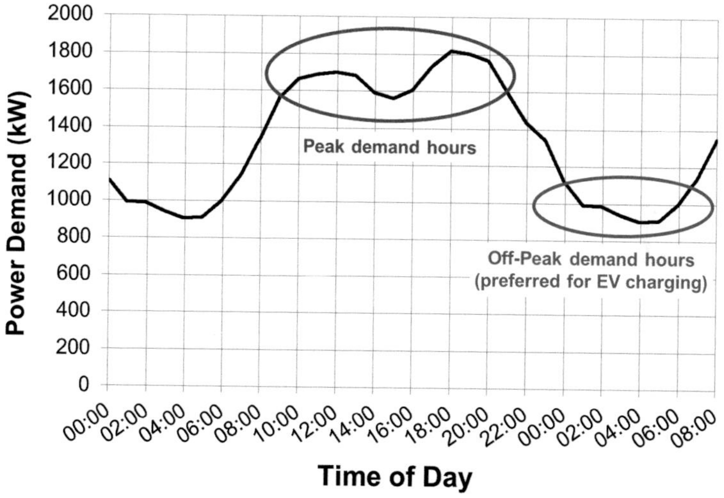

Fig. 6 Valley-filling strategy

For this model, it is assumed that the private station manager provides valley filling services in order to flatten (as much as possible) the total electricity demand (see Fig. 6).

The lowest parts of the demand curve (off-peak hours) are preferred for charging EVs. During night and early morning hours, the electricity demand is low. At those

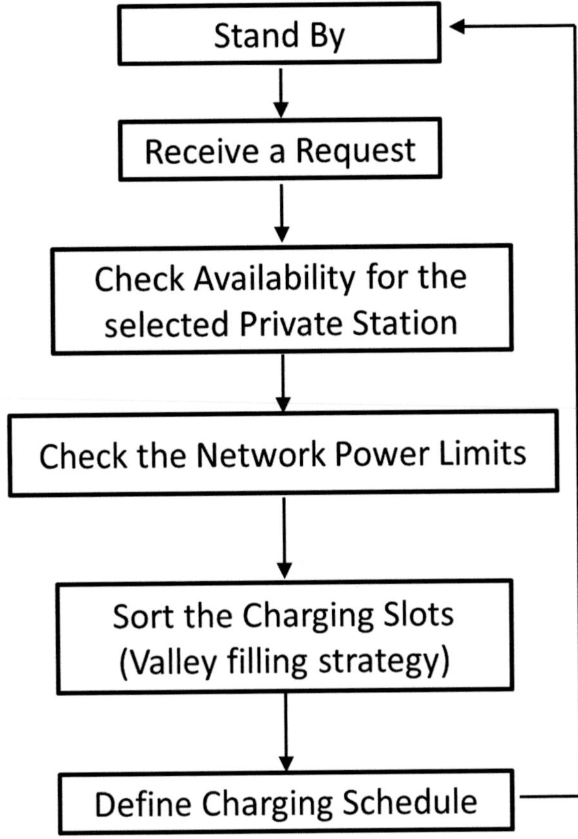

Fig. 7 Flowchart of the private station manager behavior

times, it is preferable to charge EVs because the charging impact on the power system is at minimum.

As outlined previously, the private station manager is responsible for all requests regarding charging at residential/domestic charging points. These requests contain information about the time that the EV will arrive to and depart from the "home" node, as well as their energy requirements. When a request from an EV is received, the private station manager reserves the necessary charging slots according to the network's technical constraints and the charging strategy in place.

Figure 7 shows the main operations of the private station manager agent. This agent is responsible for coordinating EV requests in a way that the technical limits of the power network are not violated (not exceeding the nominal values of the components of the power system). As soon as the private station manager defines and communicates the EV charging schedule, it returns to "standby" mode, waiting for a new request. Thus, in situations which offer some charging flexibility (e.g., the EV could stay connected for more than needed to fully charge), the charging station manager will autonomously define the charging schedule that supports overall stability of the network.

The Public Station Manager

In addition, the public station manager agent attempts to satisfy all requests regarding charging in a public charging station. These requests are divided into two types, one for charging at a final destination (final booking request) and one for a recharging stop (mid-stop booking request) in case the EV agent is not able to reach the final destination with the initial state of charge (SoC) of the battery.

Figure 8 illustrates the basic steps of the public station manager agent operation. Initially, this agent is in the "standby" mode. This means that the agent remains idle until a new request is received. When the request is received, the public station manager checks the status of every public station at the specified node and reserves the necessary charging slots.

In the case of a mid-stop request, the public station manager agent receives a request for charging accompanied by a list of all public charging stations within the EV's driving range. In addition, it receives the specific period of time when the EV will want to charge at each public charging station. The public station manager checks for any possible violations in the power network and selects the

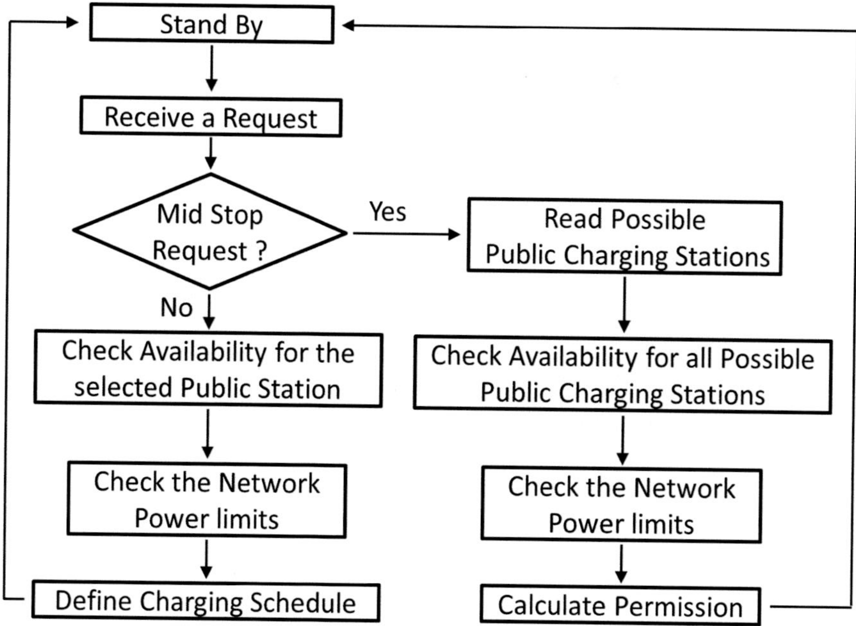

Fig. 8 Flowchart of the public station manager behavior

nearest station that meets the requirements. Permission is granted to the EV, and the requested charging slots are reserved. With a final booking request, the EV requests charging slots only at a specific node of the network (the EV's destination node). The public station manager takes into consideration the station's availability and charging rate, as well as the technical constraints of the power network, and reserves the appropriate number of charging slots. After completing this task, the public station manager agent waits until a new request is received.

3.4 Modeling the EV Agent

The EV agent is the most important agent in the model. It represents an EV living in two systems, the transport and the power system. The EV agent interacts with the other agents, makes calculations, and takes decisions regarding potential future actions that can be carried out. It moves along the links toward a node and stops for charging (or not) at a particular charging station. Its autonomic decision making and behavior adapt to the behavior of the other EV agents it can observe, based on the status of the other simulated objects in the system. The EV agent's architecture is presented in Fig. 9.

Each EV agent has a "home node" representing the EV owner's domestic location and a private charging station at that node, called a "home station." At this station, only that particular EV can charge. Each EV's behavior is illustrated in Fig. 10.

At the beginning, the EV agent selects a destination node—in our test scenario, it randomly defines it—and the time the EV will spend there. Subsequently, the EV uses an exhaustive breadth-first search algorithm to calculate all possible routes (unique sequence of links) to reach the defined destination. For each possible route, it calculates the time needed and the energy consumption for the whole trip. Both parameters are time dependent, so the EV agent calculates the estimated time of arrival to each link of the route in order to compute the total time/energy needed for

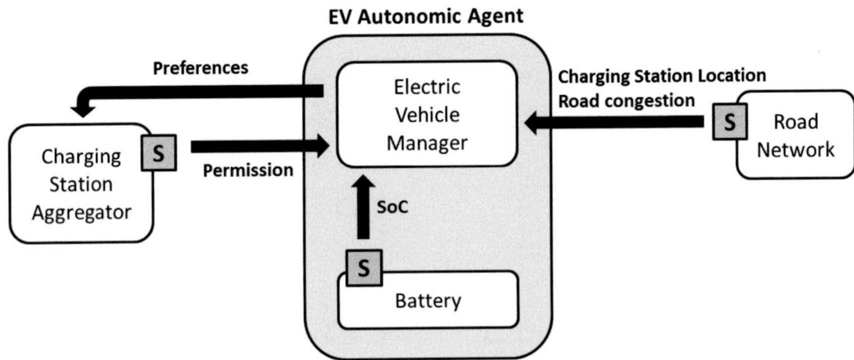

Fig. 9 Architecture of EV agent

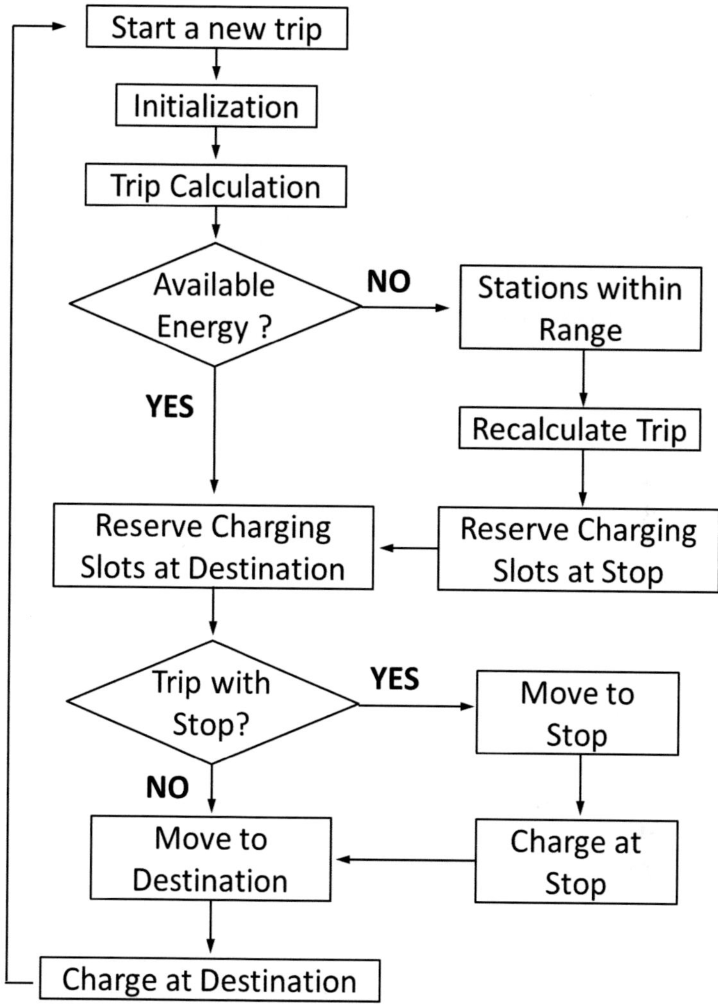

Fig. 10 Flowchart of the EV agent behavior

each trip. The EV agents select the route with the minimum trip duration according to (1):

$$\min T^{S\rightarrow D}_{\mathrm{Route}_i} \tag{1}$$

where:

$i = 1 \ldots N$
S is the starting node of the trip
D is the destination node of the trip

N is the number of possible unique routes from S to D
$\text{Route}_i = \{l_1 \dots l_k \mid k \text{ links connecting } S \text{ with } D\}$

$$T^{S\to D}_{\text{Route}_i} = \sum_{j=1}^{k} t_{l_j}$$

$t_l =$ is the time spent on link l of Route_i

The total traveling time is calculated based on the congestion values of every link along the route (t-indices in Fig. 1), while the energy consumption is calculated based on speed as depicted in Fig. 2. According to these calculations, the route which has the smallest time duration is selected. In case the EV does not have enough charge in the battery for the selected route, the EV agent considers a stop for recharging. Based on the available energy (state of charge of the battery), an EV agent finds all the public stations within its driving range, and for each one plans a new route that includes the necessary recharging stop. After this, the EV agent communicates with the public station manager to reserve the necessary charging slots. The optimal route is now selected based on the minimization of the total traveling time (2), including the recharging time at the selected station. The necessary recharging time T^M_{ch} is calculated based on the EV's energy requirements to complete its trip and the nominal power of the charging station:

$$\min(T^{S\to M}_{\text{Route}_i} + T^M_{\text{ch}} + T^{M\to D}_{\text{Route}_m}) \tag{2}$$

where:

M is the recharging node of the trip

$$T^M_{\text{ch}} = \frac{\text{Energy}_{\text{wanted}}}{\text{Power}_{\text{station}}}$$

In case the available energy is sufficient for the initial route or the calculations for a recharging stop have finished, the EV agent considers charging at the destination (if there is such an option). To do this, the EV agent calculates the estimated time of arrival at the destination and the energy needed at that time to maximize the SoC of the battery. Based on the type of station at the destination (private or public station), it communicates with the private or public station manager agent, respectively, to reserve charging slots for recharging.

When the trip is defined and the charging slots are reserved, the EV agent starts moving. In case the selected route includes a recharging stop, the EV will travel to the node of the recharging station and charge according to the schedule. When the specified recharging time is over, or the selected route does not include a recharging stop, the EV will move to the destination node. Arriving there, the EV will start charging (if there is such an option at that node) for the reserved period. After this, the procedure is repeated. Thus, the EV exhibits autonomic behavior by selecting/suggesting route and charging stops, while the user sets destination (location) and time. Routing is adapted based on the current traffic situation.

4 Simulation Results

The simulation we used to validate our approach consisted of 80 EV agents, all living in the described example networks. The EV agents consume energy from their batteries when moving, and as a result their battery's SoC is decreased. On the contrary, when the EV agent is charging, its battery's SoC is increased. In the following we will illustrate the properties and dynamics of the modeled system using a particular example.

Figure 11 follows the SoC variation of a randomly selected EV agent in a simulation run. There are periods that the SoC is increasing, indicating a charging event, and periods where the SoC is decreasing indicating consumption (movement). A constant SoC indicates that the EV remains static at a node (not moving) but with no charging activity for that time. This figure also shows a recharging stop at a public charging station (between 16:00 and 17:00) before reaching the next destination (in this case the "home" node). Once it arrives home, the EV will not charge immediately, but it will follow the specified charging schedule defined by the private charging station manager agent. The scheduling strategy of this agent is "valley fill"; thus the off-peak hours are preferred. As shown in this figure, the EV agents don't recharge in every node, but they make a recharging stop (at a public charging station) only if their SoC is low, decongesting the charging infrastructure network and consequently the electric power system. Supported by the route planner, they start charging as soon as they arrive at the public charging station avoiding waiting periods and queues. This behavior proves the awareness of the EV agents, as they make decisions according to their environment.

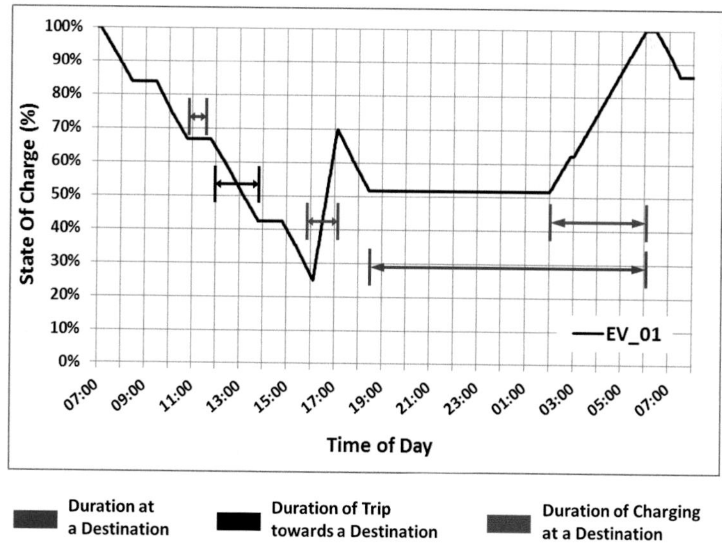

Fig. 11 EV-01 agent's SoC variation for 1 day

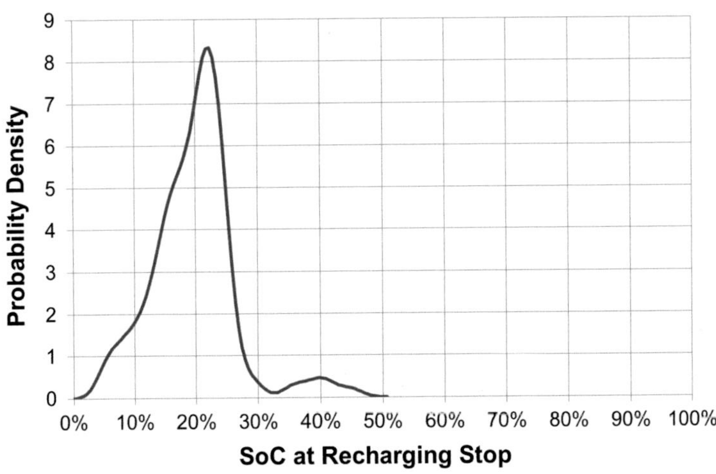

Fig. 12 Probability density of SoC at a recharging stop

The probability density of the EVs' SoC when they choose to make a recharging stop is presented in Fig. 12. Studying this figure, we realize that EV agents show a weak "survival instinct," as the majority of the recharging events in public charging stations occur at low SoC levels trying to avoid running out of energy. Recharging events at relatively high SoC levels would indicate strong "survival instincts," a phenomenon also known as "range anxiety" of the EV drivers. However in this model, the autonomic behavior of the EV agents reduces the risk of not reaching their destination.

Figure 13 presents the demand from all public charging stations in 1 day. The majority of public charging events occur during the afternoon, when the average level of SoC for most EVs is low. The events are random in terms of start (connection) time and duration (energy requirements); thus the fluctuation in the demand curve is high.

The total electricity demand in the modeled network is illustrated in Fig. 14. In this figure, we can distinguish the two charging periods, one between 14:00 and 20:00 and one between 22:00 and 07:00. The first period is related to charging events from public charging stations, while the second is associated to charging events from private charging stations. Comparing the energy in both periods (area between the red and black lines), we can see that the demand from public charging stations is less than the demand from private charging stations. The first is very fluctuating due to the randomness of the recharging events; however, its magnitude is restricted to the necessary energy requirements for reaching the next destination. The latter is supplied in an adaptive and smart fashion trying to minimize the impact on the electric power network, indicating the self-healing properties of the model.

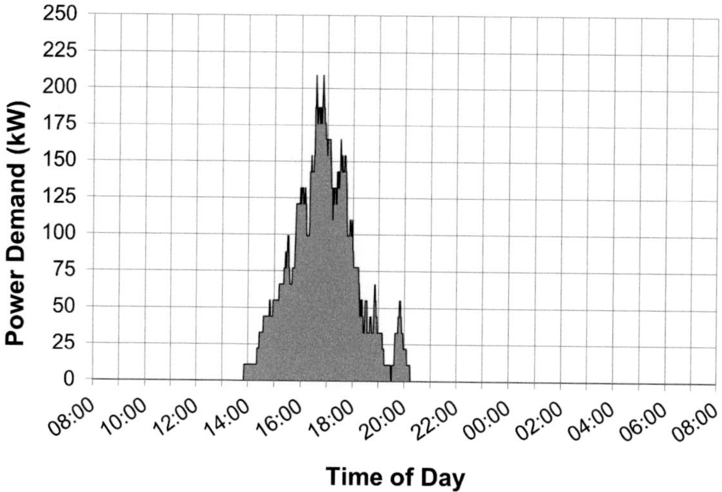

Fig. 13 Demand from public charging stations

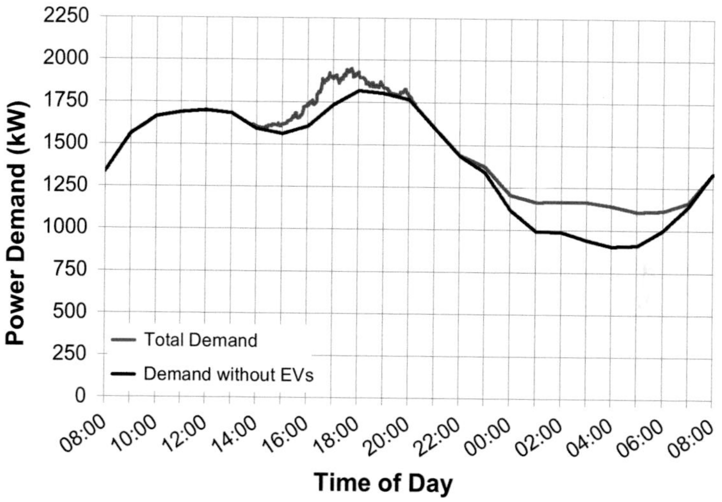

Fig. 14 Total demand in the MV feeder level

5 Future Development

With our existing model and simulation, more scenarios can be considered to analyze the overall system in depth. By changing the number of the EVs within the model, the limitations of the existing electric power network in terms of charging capability will be investigated. However, further improvement is needed to reduce the simulation time. As seen from Fig. 15, the simulation time on an average

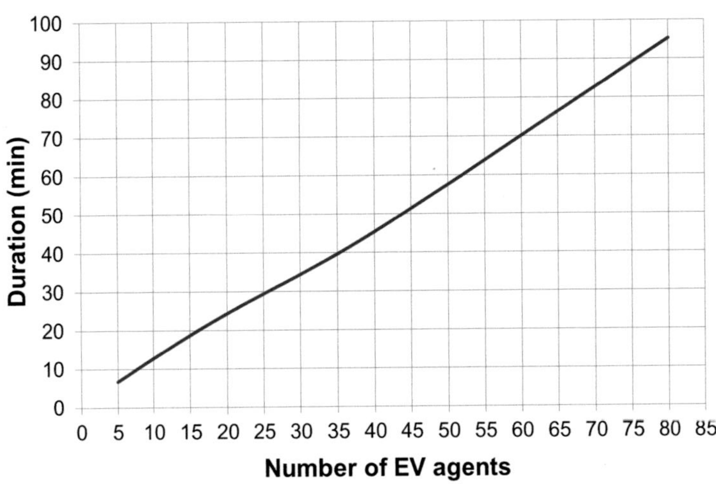

Fig. 15 Simulation time for different numbers of EV agents

PC (Intel i3 processor at 3.2 GHz with 8 GB of RAM) increases linearly with the number of EV agents, making the simulation of a large-scale scenario time consuming.

By changing the location and the number of charging stations at the transport network, the EV travel behavior will show the utility value of each location, indicating the most and least visited stations. By applying the model on larger networks, the results become more interesting, as the EVs could travel longer distances needing perhaps more than one recharging stop. Activity-based trip patterns, representing activity patterns of a single or multiple days, can be integrated in the EV agent's behavior, simulating a more realistic scenario for EV owners. The simulation can also be improved by considering more detailed congestion models for the links based on finer-grained traffic models. Additional stochastic parameters can be introduced in the transport network (e.g., a link becomes unavailable due to an unexpected event), to observe the agents' reactions and understand the impact on both the transport and electric power network.

Simulating the EV's behavior in future road transport and electric power networks offers an opportunity to understand how the number and location of public charging stations affect the route of an EV and the power demand of low-voltage distribution networks. Making the system more stochastic, the operation of both systems under a non-normal situation can be analyzed. Observing EV behavior under different situations with multi-agent simulations will help understand the impact of future EV integration on both systems and to better understand how a variety of differing roles within both networks could coexist. Therefore, authorities will have knowledge of possible irregularities or needs for adjustments/reconfiguration in order to allow and support the EV adoption in the future.

6 Summary

This research developed a multi-agent system-based simulator for the integration of transport and electricity networks capable of reproducing the behavior of an autonomous entity (electric vehicle) coexisting in both systems. One of the main aims of this simulation is to enable a variety of possible scenarios for the management of EV charging to be developed, bringing together two distinctly different but highly interrelated infrastructures. Multi-agent systems are good candidates to model and manage such applications considering geographically distributed entities (e.g., charging stations and electric vehicles) composed of autonomous and reactive entities which are proactive with social abilities.

The interactions between the different entities in both systems were studied, to understand their interdependencies. Future EVs could be supplied with an intelligent system able to communicate with other EVs and charging station managers. Such an intelligent system will inform EVs about road accident or traffic congestions on specific streets in order to avoid them and select alternative ways to reach their destination. Forecasting applications regarding road traffic conditions and/or electric power system status will be critical for a stable and optimal operation [17, 18]. Such systems could minimize the probability of an EV running out of energy—with range anxiety being one of the key considerations for EV users.

In future work, different real-world scenarios will be evaluated, with the developed simulation tool, using transport data from cities or regions combined with the topology of the electricity network in that region. If-then scenarios will be constructed to also find the optimum location of charging stations for planning application.

References

1. Papadopoulos, P., Skarvelis-Kazakos, S., Grau, I., Cipcigan, L.M., Jenkins, N.: Electric vehicles' impact on British distribution networks. IET Electr. Syst. Transp. **2**, 91–102 (2012)
2. Wang, Y., Guo, Q., Sun, H., Li, Z.: An investigation into the impacts of the crucial factors on EVs charging load. In: IEEE/PES Innovative Smart Grid Technologies Conference Asia (ISGT-Asia), Tianjin (2012)
3. Karfopoulos, E., Hatziargyriou, N.: A multi-agent system for controlled charging of a large population of electric vehicles. IEEE Trans. Power Syst. **28**(2), 1196–1204 (2013)
4. Papadopoulos, P., Jenkins, N., Cipcigan, L.M., Grau, I., Zabala, E.: Coordination of the charging of electric vehicles using a multi-agent system. IEEE Trans. Smart Grid **4**(4), 1802–1809 (2013)
5. Acha, S., van Dam, K.H., Shah, N.: Modeling spatial and temporal agent travel patterns for optimal charging of electric vehicles in low carbon networks. In: IEEE Power and Energy Society General Meeting, San Diego (2012)
6. Galus, M.D., Waraich, R.A., Noembrini, F., Steurs, K., Georges, G., Boulouchos, K., Axhausen, K.W., Andersson, G.: Integrating power systems, transport systems and vehicle technology for electric mobility impact assessment and efficient control. IEEE Trans. Smart Grid **3**(2), 934–949 (2013)

7. Gilbert, N.: Agent-Based Models. Quantitative Applications in the Social Sciences, vol. 153. Sage, London (2007)
8. North, M., Macal, C.: Managing Business Complexity: Discovering Strategic Solutions with Agent-Based Modeling and Simulation. Oxford University Press, New York (2007)
9. Klügl, F., Bazzan, A.L.C.: Agent-based modeling and simulation. AI Mag. **33**(3), 29–40 (2012)
10. Bazzan, A.L.C., Klügl, F.: A review on agent-based technology for traffic and transportation. Knowl. Eng. Rev. **29**, 375–403 (2013)
11. Klügl, F., Herrler, R., Fehler, M.: Sesam: implementation of agent based simulation using visual programming. In: AAMAS, pp. 1439–1440. ACM, New York (2006)
12. Department for Transport [Online]. http://www.dft.gov.uk/. Accessed 14 June 2014
13. Ingram, S., Probert, S., Jackson, K., The impact of small scale embedded generators in the operating parameters of distribution networks. In: DTI (2003)
14. Karfopoulos, E., Marmaras, C., Hatziargyriou, N.: Charging control model for EV supplier aggregator. In: IEEE/PES Innovative Smart Grid Technologies Conference Europe (ISGT Europe), Berlin (2012)
15. Momber, I., Gomez, T., Rivier, M., Mateo, C.: Benefits of EV supplier-aggregators and distribution system operators from applying smart charging of plug-in electric vehicles. In: CIGRÉ International Symposium on The Electric Power System of the Future: Integrating Supergrids and Microgrids Bologna, Italy (2011)
16. Rivier, M., Gomez, T., Cosset, R., Momber, I., Downing, N., Bower, E., Miller, P., Hartmann, N., Fengler, S., Joyce, C., Guerra, B.D., Lioliou, V.: New actors and business models for the integration of EV in Power Systems. In: MERGE Deliverable D5.1 (2011)
17. Xydas, E., Marmaras, C., Cipcigan, L.M., Hassan, A.S., Jenkins, N.: Electric vehicle load forecasting using data mining methods. In: 4th Hybrid and Electric Vehicle IET Conference, London (2013)
18. Xydas, E., Marmaras, C., Cipcigan, L.M., Hassan, A.S., Jenkins, N.: Forecasting electric vehicles charging demand using support vector machines. In: UPEC, Dublin (2013)

Traffic Signal Control with Autonomic Features

Iisakki Kosonen and Xiaoliang Ma

Abstract Inspired by diverse organic systems, autonomic computing is a rapidly growing field in computing science. To highlight this advancement, this chapter summarises the autonomic features utilised in a traffic signal control in the form of an operational control system, not simply a simulation study. In addition, the real-time simulation is used to refine the raw sensor data into a comprehensive picture of the traffic situation. We apply the multi-agent approach both for controlling the signals and for modelling the prevailing traffic situation. In contrast to most traffic signal control studies, the basic agent is one signal (head) also referred to as a signal group. The multi-agent process occurs between individual signal agents, which have autonomy to negotiate their timing, phasing, and priorities, limited only by the traffic safety requirements. The key contribution of this chapter lies not in a single method but rather in a combination of methods with autonomic properties. This unique combination involves a real-time microsimulation together with a signal group control and fuzzy logic supported by self-calibration and self-optimisation. The findings here are based on multiple research projects conducted at the Helsinki University of Technology (now Aalto University). Furthermore, we outline the basic concepts, methods, and some of the results. For detailed results and setup of experiments, we refer to the previous publications of the authors.

Keywords Autonomic computing • Fuzzy control • Multi-agent systems • Optimisation • Real-time traffic simulation • Signal group • Traffic signal control

1 Introduction

Autonomic computing mimics self-sustaining organic systems, which are capable of self-protection, self-healing, self-adaptation, and so on. These features enable independent self-management in complex and uncertain environments. The goal

I. Kosonen (✉)
Transportation Engineering, Aalto University, Espoo, Finland
e-mail: iisakki.kosonen@aalto.fi,

X. Ma
Traffic and Logistics, KTH Royal Institute of Technology, Stockholm, Sweden

T.L. McCluskey et al. (eds.), *Autonomic Road Transport Support Systems*,
Autonomic Systems, DOI 10.1007/978-3-319-25808-9_15

here then is to demonstrate how various autonomic methods can be utilised in traffic signal control. Arguably, the first traffic signal control was carried out by traffic officers given that the human mind represents the ultimate capability in organic autonomic systems. Thus, the presented traffic signal control method attempts to capture some of those features of the human mind by mimicking these traffic officers.

There are several urban traffic control systems (UTCS) on the market. The most widely used systems are SCOOT [1], SCATS [2], MOVA [3], and UTOPIA/-SPOT [4]. These systems are based on a control loop, which minimises a cost function. The cost function can involve several aspects, e.g. delays, emissions, and public transport priorities. Therefore, these UTC systems have at least some autonomic features, such as being policy driven and adaptive. The aforementioned control systems are phase oriented, i.e. they have predefined phases.

Most of the research in traffic signal control focuses on the optimisation of phase-oriented systems. In these optimised systems, the parameters include the split, cycle, and offset, as well as the order of the phases. For example, in [5], a multi-agent approach with fuzzy control was studied by employing the type-2 fuzzy sets. Likewise, distributed W-learning was used to optimise a phase-oriented signal control [6]. In optimising the split, Shirai et al. [7] utilised the spring model, while Oliveira and Camponogara [8] used a model with predictive control.

To our knowledge, very little research exists on so-called signal group control, in which the phases are not predefined. Kronborg, Davidsson, and Edholm developed the SOS controller, in which Webster's delay calculation was used to determine the green extension of the individual traffic signals [9]. Wong et al. [10] studied group-based signal control; however, their definition for "group" denoted not the signal group but a group of traffic flows. In addition, Niittymäki [11, 12] and Kosonen [13] introduced the use of fuzzy logic with a signal group control. In a review of agent-based systems [14], no other examples of a signal group-based control were referred to, except the system proposed here.

In this chapter, we focus on the signal group control that has been adopted, especially in the Scandinavian countries. Unfortunately, the prevailing concept of a signal group remains somewhat confusing. In fact, the term "signal group" refers to one logical signal. The term "group" refers to the fact that often one logical signal can be represented by multiple physical signal heads in the field (i.e. primary and secondary signal heads). To avoid this confusion, we adopt the term "signal agent" instead of "signal group agent".

These signal agents behave in an autonomic way, pursuing to start green, but limited by other agents due to the safety factors. Here, the multi-agent approach is applied within a junction, not only between the junctions. The main benefit of the signal group control is that phases are composed on demand. As a consequence, unusual phases are possible, such as an all-red rest state and all-green state for pedestrian signals. The Swedish version of the signal group control is called LHOVRA [15].

The drawback of the prevailing commercial signal group controllers is the lack of real-time modelling and autonomic features like self-optimisation and self-calibration. The present systems rely on detectors for traffic actuation, but they do not have a cost function that can be optimised. Thus, this chapter aims to demonstrate how to improve the signal group control with various autonomic features.

The results of this effort are detailed across several sections. In Sect. 2.1., we apply a multi-agent real-time simulation to the processing of the sensor data, refining the detector occupancies into a microscopic traffic situation model. The self-calibration features related to this real-time simulation are presented in Sect. 2.2. Subsequently, Sect. 3 deals with the actual control algorithm; the signal agent and a multi-agent control with fuzzy logic are presented in Sects. 3.1–3.3. In Sect. 3.4, the self-optimisation with neural networks is explained, and an ongoing research project related to coordinated signal group control is introduced in Sect. 3.5. Finally, conclusions and future research are discussed in Sect. 4.

Due to the large number of simulations and field studies undertaken over the years, it is not feasible to present the detailed setup and results of each study within the constraints of this chapter. However, more detailed descriptions and results can be found from the references.

The basic architecture of the proposed control method is demonstrated in Fig. 1. The actual traffic as shown generates sensor data (samples), which is generalised by

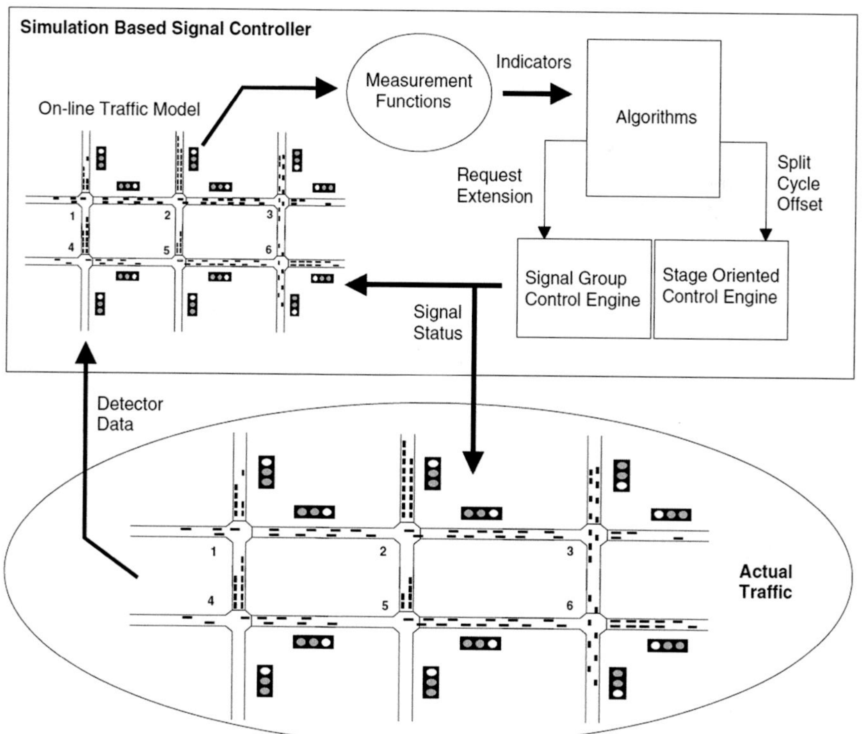

Fig. 1 The basic architecture of a signal control system based on a real-time simulation

using an online simulation. By using the microsimulation model, various indicators or measures of effectiveness (MoE) can be derived and applied as control input.

The artificial intelligence (AI) used for decision making here is fuzzy logic, but the architecture is not limited to any specific form of AI. The control decisions are delivered through a control engine, which can be phase oriented or signal group oriented. Subsequently, this chapter focuses only on the latter option, demonstrating the autonomic features related to this approach.

2 Sensory Processing

2.1 Multi-Agent Real-Time Modelling

Human operators are actually fairly adept at managing traffic flows through a junction. A human operator, such as a traffic officer, has a built-in modelling system, which converts the data from the senses into a comprehensive situational awareness. The human sensory processing system does not passively analyse data but rather acts more similarly to an active modelling and predicting system. During the control operation, previously acquired knowledge (cognitive model) is complemented with real-time information from the senses. The basic concept of applying a real-time simulation remains the same, i.e. to combine previous knowledge (the simulation model) with real-time detector input (the senses). This postulated real-time simulation approach provides an effective means for continuous and comprehensive situational observation.

Microscopic simulation is a form of multi-agent modelling, whereby the vehicle/driver functions as the agent with some degree of intelligence and autonomy. Only microscopic modelling embodies the capability of identifying individual objects (agents) and modelling their interactions. The simulation model is utilised to generalise the samples (detector data) over space and time. Through this dimension of time, the simulation model can also predict how situations will evolve in the short term. In the microscopic model, the previous knowledge involves all of the static features such as the detailed geometry, the lane topology, the detector positions, and so forth. This model may also include many statistical features like average driver behaviour and traffic composition.

The minimum requirement for this is that all vehicles have to be detected at least once (on arrival to the junction area). On arrival, each vehicle is detected and immediately inputted into the simulation model [16]. With additional sensor information, the accuracy of the model can be further improved with the self-calibration features described in Sect. 2.2. In principle, any type of additional sensor technology can be utilised to improve the accuracy [e.g. loop detectors, infrared (IR), radio-frequency identification (RFID), Bluetooth, video, radar, and the Global Positioning System (GPS)].

From the perspective of a seamless comprehensive picture, the simulation model can produce higher-order measures indicating traffic fluency, safety, economy, and environmental aspects. These refined indicators (e.g. delays, queues, stops, fuel consumption, and emissions) can be inputted for the reasoning process in the traffic signal control.

2.2 Self-calibration

Self-calibration is one of the key autonomic features. In a real-time simulation, calibration of the model is not simply a one-time event. The model itself needs to identify the discrepancies between its own state and the sensor data. Based on these differences, proper adjustments are undertaken to ensure the continued accuracy of the model.

The sensor system for traffic lights is usually based on stationary vehicle detectors, like the inductive loops. The sensory processing system relies on the detection of vehicles as they enter the junction area and then predicts the vehicle movements. This prediction tends to drift away from reality over time. Therefore, self-calibration features are necessary in order to correct the prediction using information from the other detectors.

One primary source of error is the vehicle speed, since a typical detector provides the occupancy information only. When detected and generated, the simulated vehicle is afforded its normal cruising speed. When both the actual and simulated vehicles have reached the next detector, the speed difference can then be calculated and the speed of the simulated vehicle adjusted accordingly. It is also important to recognise the vehicle types correctly. The length of the detection pulse indicates the length of the vehicle, given that the speed level is known.

The turning movements are another potential source of error. One approach for this is to maintain a table of turning probabilities. Unfortunately, this table needs to be updated periodically based on average detector counts. With this method, individual vehicles can be incorrectly predicted despite the accuracy of average turning flows. However, a more accurate approach utilises a detector at the beginning of the pocket lane. When a vehicle is detected, then the closest simulated vehicle in the main direction will be forced to change to the pocket lane.

The queue length is an important indicator of the traffic situation, but it is quite sensitive to cumulative errors. Even small errors in vehicle counts can accumulate to create large discrepancies in queue lengths over time. Therefore, the self-calibration features should focus on the detectors, which are occupied over a longer time than the normal vehicle passing time. These detections indicate that the end of the queue reaches the detector. If the simulated situation fails to reflect this, it may become necessary to add or remove vehicles in order to calibrate the queue length.

Moreover, other types of sensors can be employed to improve the calibration performance. For example, a vehicle with a positioning system can indicate the queue length as the moment of stopping. The measured travel times (via RFID or Bluetooth) can be compared to simulated ones in order to calibrate vehicle speeds and other parameters. Additional video or radar systems can provide detailed data about driving behaviour, which can be applied to calibrate the parameters of the vehicle dynamics.

It is worth bearing in mind that driving behaviour is not constant over time. For example, the density of the traffic can affect car-following gaps as well as the lighting, weather, and road friction. Ideally, a "perfect" self-calibration feature should learn these changes on a continuous basis.

2.3 *Self-healing*

The problems with the sensor systems are often hardware failures, and the physical self-healing capability may not be a realistic option. However, at the software level, it may be possible to replace actual data with the statistical equivalent. In this regard, the most common problem is often a broken detector. This can be diagnosed if there is no activity over a certain period. In the event of a malfunctioning input detector, one possible self-healing feature would be starting to generate vehicles randomly according to the average daily/weekly patterns.

Another type of error can occur with overly sensitive sensors. In this case, the sensor reacts to vehicles in adjacent lanes. By analysing the correlations between vehicle positions and sensor occupancies, it is possible to identify if a detector is not working properly. A self-healing action here would enable incorrect detections to be filtered out automatically.

3 Decision Making

3.1 *The Signal Agent*

In order to highlight the autonomic behaviour in a signal control, it is again worth considering the role of a human operator (e.g. the traffic officer in the junction). There are two levels of autonomy in the behaviour of the officer. On the conscious level, the officer is autonomous, i.e. no external agent is in direct control, and can thus freely perform tasks within the limits of the traffic rules.

The other autonomic level is subconscious. On this level, previously learned skills produce fast and detailed responses to various traffic situations without much effort on the conscious level. Over time, the traffic officer is also learning to perform better, so there is arguably self-optimisation in the control operation. These subconscious operations are in essence mappings between the inputs and outputs, so they can be implemented in multiple ways. Here, fuzzy inference is applied to produce the mappings and neural networks for the self-optimisation.

In the same fashion, we used fuzzy logic to provide the signal agent with the necessary intelligence. Fuzzy logic can be characterised as calculations with words. In fuzzy logic, all rules and inputs can affect the final output to some degree [17].

This differs significantly from binary logic (true/false), whereby only one branch of the decision tree is followed. As such, fuzzy logic is a deterministic algorithm without any autonomic features. While there exists plenty of literature about fuzzy sets in general, this chapter focuses on the application of fuzzy logic to signal controls.

We do not claim that fuzzy logic is the best of all options, only that it is suitable for signal controls. Generally speaking, fuzzy logic is suitable when the desired mapping can be described as explicit rules provided by a human expert. This is the case in traffic signal controls. The traffic officer or signal control planner's knowledge can be transformed into a form of rule sets, which are then implemented into the control algorithm.

Fuzzy logic as such involves no self-adaptation or learning. The self-adaptation can be included by adjusting the parameters of the algorithm, i.e. the fuzzy rule sets and fuzzy membership functions. This will be explained in Sect. 3.3.

The signal agent is basically making decisions about its own green time (Fig. 2). To enable this, the signal agent requests data from the real-time simulation model regarding the number of approaching vehicles. This input (APP) involves only those vehicles, which are controlled by this particular signal agent. Obviously, a high number of arriving vehicles shift the decision towards extending the green time.

The other input requested by the signal agent describes the number of queuing vehicles (QUE). These vehicles waiting behind the red signal(s) can belong to any number of conflicting signal agents (i.e. they cannot go green at the same time). A high value of QUE puts "pressure" on the signal agent to terminate its green signal early.

Once the signal has entered a green state and the minimum green time has elapsed, the signal agent starts using a fuzzy inference object to determine whether to extend or terminate the green. This decision is repeated after each extension

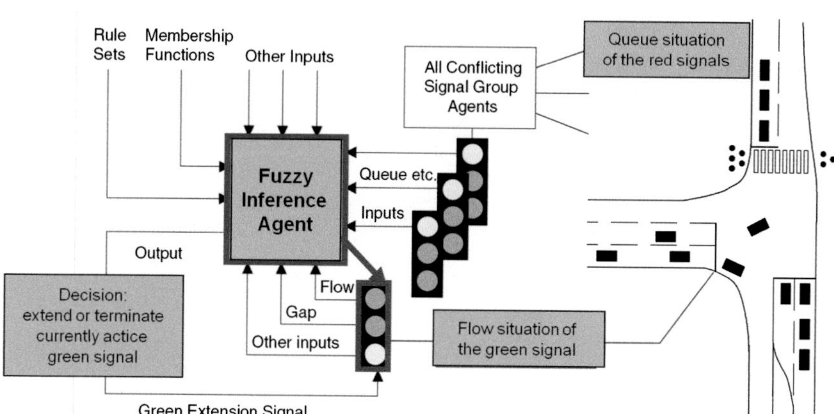

Fig. 2 The signal agent with the fuzzy inference object

(0–10 s), and zero seconds means termination of the green time. The fuzzy inference object is a general-purpose object that performs the fuzzy inference according to the fuzzy rules and the fuzzy membership functions (initialised from an input file). The fuzzy output has to be defuzzified into a strict value, before returning the result to the signal agent.

3.2 Multi-Agent Process

Human decisions are most often the result of a group process. This process can be simulated with a multi-agent control approach. In our case, rather than one traffic officer in the middle of a junction, we assume a group of officers each representing one traffic signal. While controlling their own signal, the agents also negotiate with each other to work out the optimal solution within the junction.

The general goal is to maintain the flexibility of phase sequences, while at the same time improve the decisions related to signal timing, phasing, priorities, and coordination. In a multi-agent approach, each signal agent has its own objectives. The basic objective of a signal agent is to obtain and maintain the green state, whenever there are vehicles requesting the green. Similar to those human groups, it is not always possible to act immediately but rather to adapt the behaviour or delay the action according to the states and objectives of the other agents.

In Fig. 3, the concept of a generic multi-agent control is demonstrated with a simple junction. In more complex junctions with plenty of dedicated lane signals, pedestrian crossings, and public transport priorities, the advantages of a flexible multi-agent control become more evident.

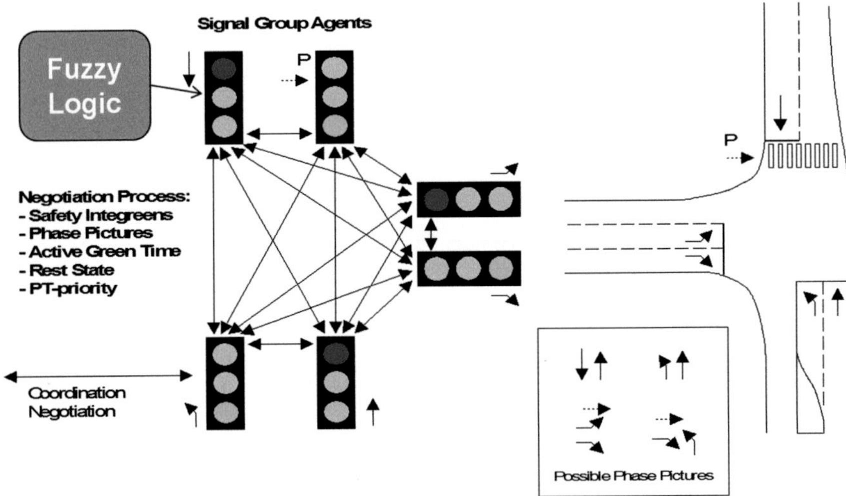

Fig. 3 Multi-agent signal group control in a simple junction [18]

A signal agent starts the transition to the green state through the intergreen and amber states. During the green signal, the other (conflicting) signal agents can create pressure (QUE) to terminate the active green. During the green extension, the APP value is decreasing because of the queue discharge, and the QUE value is increasing because of the queue build-up behind the conflicting signal agents. Depending on the traffic situation, the green extensions become increasingly shorter and finally reach zero, meaning the active green is terminated. After the active green extension, the signal agent can return to red or remain as passive green. If a signal is on passive green, any conflicting signal agent can terminate it immediately. During the green time, any other nonconflicting signal agent can start its own green state and green extension.

After termination of the green signal(s), the other conflicting signal agents have to decide which is next to start green. Obviously, if there is only one candidate with traffic demand, the choice is clear. However, there is often more than one pending signal agent. If they are not in conflict, they can start at the same time; conversely, if they are in conflict, they have to work out who is first in the queue. The agents have autonomy, but only within the limits of traffic safety, i.e. the safe intergreen time must be maintained at all times between conflicting signal agents.

To ensure some equality of opportunity to start green, we use a revolving priority order. The signal agent that had the last green receives the lowest priority (it can still get the green if there is no higher priority signal pending). The signal agent with currently the lowest priority gets the highest priority, and the others move down one step. If there is pending (traffic demand) for the highest priority signal agent, it can start green first. Otherwise, the signal agent(s) at the next priority level is offered the opportunity to start green. In this way, there are no fixed phases; instead, every agent receives an equal chance to start green, if it is pending to do so.

Within this framework, the signal agents have to negotiate and compose a mutual control strategy, which addresses at least the following objectives, listed in order of priority:

- Safety (intergreen management)
- Equality (assuring each direction has a possibility to get green and handling public transport priorities)
- Timing objectives (several objectives: delays, queues, stops, emissions, energy, etc.)
- Minimising transitions (find an optimal rest state when there is no demand)

3.3 *Fuzzy Logic Green Extension*

The presented methods and system were developed during the FUSICO project (FUzzy SIgnal COntrol) at the Helsinki University of Technology (HUT). The FUSICO software has some similarities to the object-oriented HUTSIM microsimulation software [13]. From signal timing point of view, the most crucial object type is the fuzzy logic green extender, which is connected to the signal agent as described in Sects. 3.1 and 3.2.

In the simulation studies and field testings, our main interest was to find out the performance of the detector logic (gap seeking) versus the fuzzy logic (Fig. 6). With the FUSICO software, we were able to replicate the operation of ordinary signal group controller, by applying the detector logic for green extension. The detector logic provides a simple gap-seeking method for the green extension of the signal agent. In the fuzzy control, we replace the simple detector logic with the fuzzy green extension. While the gap seeking uses the detector pulses only, the fuzzy green extension can utilise the situational awareness provided by the real-time simulation and the other signal agents in the same junction.

Our first step was to implement the fuzzy green extension method introduced by Pappis and Mamdani [19]. In this method the green extension can be 1–10 s. If the fuzzy logic results were equal to the maximum, then a new extension is started after 10 s. Otherwise the green signal will be terminated after the extension time has elapsed. This procedure will be repeated to the maximum of six times.

The Pappi and Mamdani version of the fuzzy logic green extension was found to be a bit inflexible and to cut the green short too easily. Therefore a new version (FUSICO) of the fuzzy green extension was introduced. In this mode, the green extension can get a value of 0, 3, 6, or 9 s. The green signal is terminated only if the result is 0 s; otherwise new extension will be started after the present one expires. The FUSICO version turned out to be more consistent with regard to the traffic situation and provides more sufficient amount of green time.

The basic approach is similar in both versions of green extension. For each consecutive green extension, a different set of fuzzy rules is applied. The membership functions remain the same all the time. In the beginning, the rules allow easy extension of the green time regardless of the queue(s) behind the conflicting red signal(s). After each completed green extension, the rules make it more and more difficult to extend the green; thus the pressure by the queuing vehicles starts to have an effect. Eventually the green will be terminated regardless of the traffic situation since there is a given maximum green time that cannot be exceeded.

The presented signal control method has been evaluated in simulations and tested with field installations. In Fig. 6, the results of a simulation study are shown. The average delay per vehicle is shown as the function of the overall traffic demand in the junction. Our base line here is the ordinary signal group control (gap seeking) since this is the prevailing controller type in Scandinavian countries. Despite the simple logic, the performance of a gap-seeking signal group control is fairly effective. Both types of fuzzy signal control perform better than the base line, but the FUSICO performs slightly better than the Pappis–Mamdani. The fuzzy logic can improve the performance by 10–20 % (see Fig. 4) when compared to gap seeking [20]. However, the gap-seeking algorithm can react more quickly to the arriving single vehicles, which explains the better performance in low-demand situations. These results presented here can be further improved with the self-adaptation feature described in the next section.

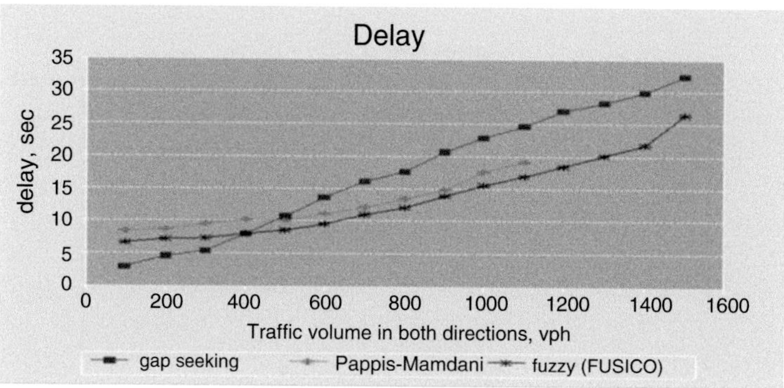

Fig. 4 Demonstration of performance of the fuzzy signal group control against the detector logic-based signal group control (gap seeking).

3.4 Self-adaptation

The fuzzy logic used for the signal control is based on transferring expert knowledge into the rule sets. A traffic signal control expert states the rules and membership functions for use in the control operation. The expert knowledge is generic and may not be optimal for all junctions with various traffic demands.

In this regard, self-adaptation can be implemented in different ways. The one presented here is based on neural networks [21]. Here, the performance is evaluated by delays only, but in more advanced versions, multiple objectives can be handled. At the moment, we are working on evolutionary algorithms for multi-objective optimisation [22].

The self-adaptation is used to fine-tune the membership functions. In this case, reinforced learning tunes the parameters of the fuzzy inference. After each round of a completed green extension, the simulation model provides feedback on the efficiency of the decision made by returning the delay caused by the signal control.

In neural network-based reinforced learning, the information regarding the inputs (APP, QUE) and the consequences (delay) are used to evaluate the performance of the control. Based on the evaluation, the membership functions of the APP and QUE will be modified gradually until no further improvement is achieved (Fig. 5).

With self-adaptation of the membership functions, the performance of the fuzzy signal control can be improved and adapted to various types of junctions or to long-term changes in traffic volumes. In Fig. 6, an example of the results is shown. About a 1-s decrease on the average delay was achieved with traffic flows of more than 400 vehicles per hour.

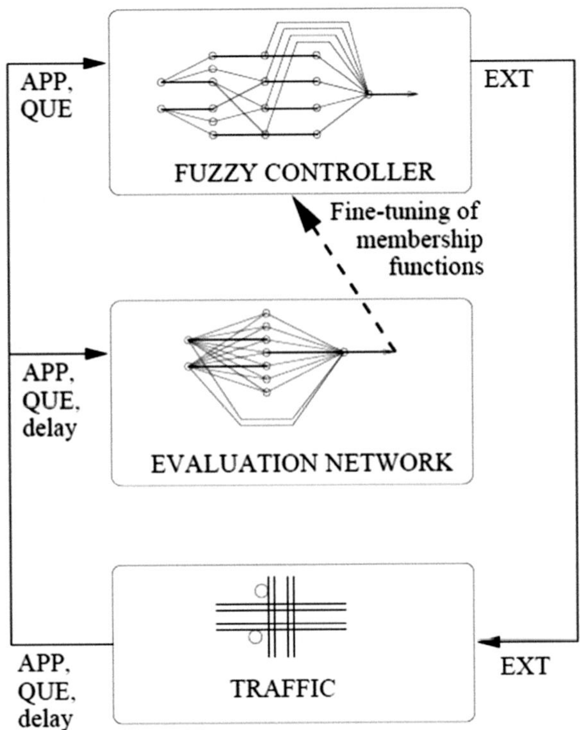

Fig. 5 Self-adaptation by reinforced learning

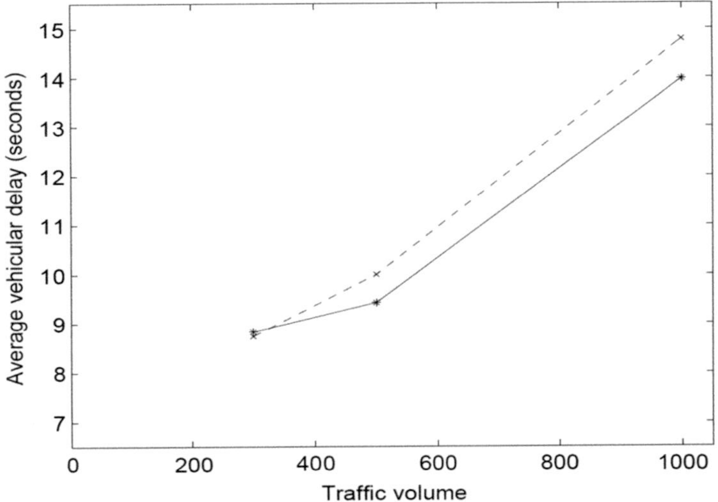

Fig. 6 The average delay before (*dashed line*) and after the self-adaptation

3.5 Autonomic Signal Coordination

In multi-agent area control, one agent is most commonly controlling one junction. However, we aim here to outline a multi-agent area control based on signal agents. The basic principle is the same as in a single junction case, but the negotiation process is extended to the neighbouring junctions. In the multi-agent signal group control, the agents aim to compose green waves for different directions in as flexible of a manner as needed. In addition to green extensions, the negotiation can be applied to phase sequencing and to public transport priorities. This research activity is currently ongoing; therefore within this chapter we can only demonstrate the basic concepts, but not the performance.

There are many possibilities for composing an area control strategy. One possible approach is proposed in Fig. 7. In this example, the signal agents in each junction negotiate regarding the green extensions, as in Fig. 3. In this coordinated operation, this negotiation process is affected by external signals from the neighbouring junctions.

Each signal agent generates two additional outputs for requesting or extending the green signal in the downstream junction. The basic concept is to increase the priority of a moving platoon especially on a main road where a green wave is desired. The increased priority has an effect through the fuzzy inference system. A moving platoon of a certain size and density can be compared to public transport vehicles. In this way, a moving platoon receives priority over other vehicles.

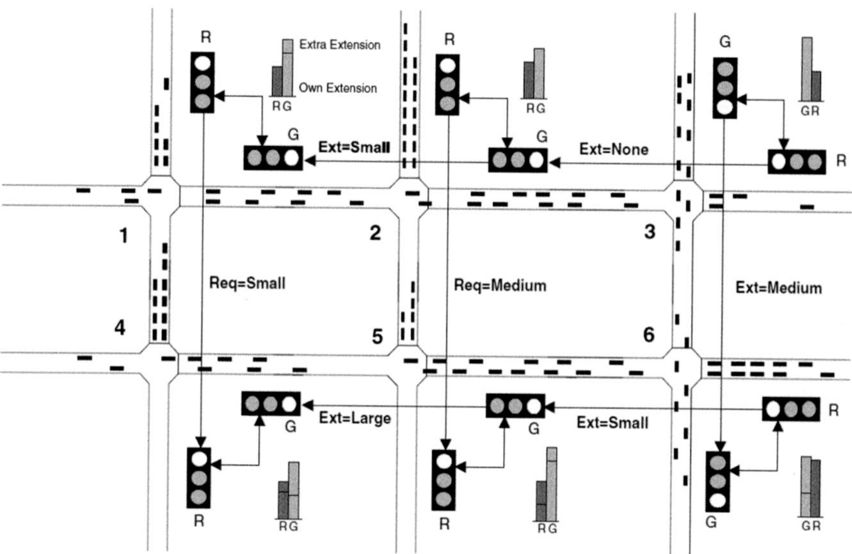

Fig. 7 Outlining a coordinated multi-agent signal group control [18]

This priority can lead to a green extension, early green, or extra phase. A green signal can be given an extra extension due to an approaching platoon. An early green (or red truncation) can be achieved by letting the approaching platoon put extra pressure on the conflicting signal groups to terminate their green signals. An extra phase can be arranged by affecting the priority order of pending signal agents. In this way, green waves can be created in an autonomic way on demand.

The benefit of this approach is that the actual bus priorities can be implemented in the same manner. In the case of buses, there can be additional inputs that affect the weight of the bus request. Factors such as the length of delay, the number of passengers, and the importance of the line could affect the bus priority decisions.

4 Conclusions

This chapter presents an intelligent traffic signal control method based on autonomic signal agents. Each signal agent is attached through a fuzzy logic controller, which handles the interactions with the other agents. The decision process in these interactions is improved with an autonomic self-optimisation feature. Moreover, a multi-agent approach is also used in the sensory processing in the form of a real-time simulation. Autonomic features also involve self-calibration of the simulation during the real-time operation.

The contribution of this chapter rests in the combination of three methods: multi-agent signal group control, real-time simulation, and fuzzy logic. To the best of our knowledge, the presented system or combination of autonomic methods is unique. In this chapter, we do not claim that fuzzy logic or neural networks as such are the best possible choices. The intelligence of the system is encapsulated into objects, which can be replaced with other types of artificial intelligence, while the basic architecture remains unchanged. This approach provides a basis for further research based on the presented system.

Plenty of studies have been carried out both in simulation and field studies. Several versions of fuzzy inference, defuzzification, etc., have been tested. The isolated signal control has already been tested in the field in many cities, especially in the city of Tampere in Finland. Moreover, public transport priorities have been implemented and tested with the presented method. Special features for high speed junctions have also been tested.

This research work has been carried out in several projects by the Helsinki University of Technology (now Aalto University). We aim to continue the research cooperation between Aalto University and the Royal Institute of Technology (KTH). As such, we will continue developing and evaluating the coordinated signal control presented here. In addition, the self-optimisation will be further improved with multi-objective optimisation and evolutionary algorithms.

References

1. Robertson, D.I., Bretherton, R.D.: Optimizing networks of traffic signals in real time: the scoot method. IEEE Trans. Veh. Technol. **40**(1), 11–15 (1991)
2. Sims, A.G., Dobinson, K.W.: The Sydney coordinated adaptive traffic (scat) system philosophy and benefits. IEEE Trans. Veh. Technol. **29**(2), 130–137 (1980)
3. Vincent, R.A., Peirce, J.R., Webb, P.J.: Mova traffic control manual (1990)
4. Maoro, V., Taranto, C.D.: Utopia. In: Proceedings of 6th IFAC/IFIP/IFORS Symposium on Control, Computers and Communications in Transportation. IFAC, Paris (1989)
5. Gokulan, B.P., Srinivasan, D.: Distributed geometric fuzzy multiagent urban traffic signal control. IEEE Intell. Transp. Syst. **11**(3), 714–727 (2010)
6. Dusparic, I., Cahill, V.: Using distributed w-learning for multi-policy optimization in decentralized autonomic systems. In: Proceedings of the 6th International Conference on Autonomic Computing, pp. 63–64. ACM, New York (2009)
7. Shirai, T., Konaka, Y., Yano, J., Nishimura, S., Kagawa, K., Morita, T., Numao, M., Kurihara, S.: Multi-agent traffic light control framework based on direct and indirect coordination. In: Proceedings of 7th International Workshop on Agents in Traffic and Transportation, pp. 9–17 (2012)
8. de Oliveira, L.B., Camponogara, E.: Multi-agent model predictive control of signaling split in urban traffic networks. Transp. Res. C Emerg. Technol. **18**(1), 120–139 (2010)
9. Kronborg, P., Davidsson, F., Edholm, J.: Sos - self optimising signal control, development and field trials of the sos algorithm for self optimising signal control at isolated intersections. Technical report, TFK, Sweden (1997)
10. Wong, S.C., Wong, W.T., Leung, C.M., Tong, C.O.: Group-based optimization of a time-dependent transyt traffic model for area traffic control. Transp. Res. B Methodol. **36**(4), 291–312 (2002)
11. Niittymäki, J., et al.: Fuzzy traffic signal control: principles and applications. Ph.D. thesis, Helsinki University of Technology (2002)
12. Niittymäki, J.: Using fuzzy logic to control traffic signals at multi-phase intersections. In: Computational Intelligence, pp. 354–362. Springer, Heidelberg (1999)
13. Kosonen, I.: HUTSIM-Urban traffic simulation and control model: principles and applications. Ph.D. thesis, Helsinki University of Technology (1999)
14. Chen, B., Cheng, H.H.: A review of the applications of agent technology in traffic and transportation systems. IEEE Trans. ITS **11**(2), 485–497 (2010)
15. Al-Mudhaffar, A., Archer, J., Cunningham, A.: Resolving the driver's dilemma: improving vehicle actuated signal control for safety and performance. In: World Conference on Transport Research (2004)
16. Čapek, K., Kosonen, I., Luttinen, R.T.: Sink&source – an approach for real-time corrections of an online microscopic traffic simulation. In: 13th World Congress and Exhibition on Intelligent Transport Systems (ITS) and Services, p. 8, London (2006)
17. Zadeh, L.A.: Fuzzy sets. Inf. Control **8**(3), 338–353 (1965)
18. Kosonen, I.: Multi-agent fuzzy signal control based on real-time simulation. Transp. Res. C Emerg. Technol. **11**(5), 389–403 (2003)
19. Pappis, C.P., Mamdani, E.H.: A fuzzy logic controller for a traffic junction. IEEE Trans. Syst. Man Cybern. **7**(10), 707–717 (1977)
20. Pursula, M., Niittymaki, J.: Evaluation of traffic signal control with simulation – a comparison of the pappis-mamdani fuzzy control vs. vehicle-actuation with the extension principle. In: EURO-Conference, Newcastle (1996)
21. Bingham, E.: Reinforcement learning in neurofuzzy traffic signal control. Eur. J. Oper. Res. **131**(2), 232–241 (2001)
22. Ma, X., Jin, J., Lei, W.: Multi-criteria analysis of optimal signal plans using microscopic traffic models. Transp. Res. D Transp. Environ. **32**, 1–14 (2014)

TIMIPLAN: A Tool for Transportation Tasks

Javier García, Álvaro Torralba, José E. Florez, Daniel Borrajo, Carlos Linares López, and Ángel García-Olaya

Abstract Multi-modal transportation is a logistics problem in which a set of goods has to be transported to different places, with the combination of at least two modes of transport, without a change of container for the goods. In such tasks, in many cases, the decisions are inefficiently made by human operators. Human operators receive plenty of information from several and varied sources, and thus they suffer from information overload. To solve efficiently the multi-modal transportation problem, the management cannot rely only on the experience of the human operators. A prospective way to tackle the complexity of the problem for multi-modal transportation is to apply the concept of autonomic behavior. The goal of this chapter is to describe TIMIPLAN, a software tool that solves multi-modal transportation problems developed in cooperation with the Spanish company Acciona Transmediterránea. The tool includes a solver that combines linear programming (LP) with automated planning (AP) techniques. To facilitate its integration in the company, the application follows a mixed-initiative approach allowing the users to modify the plans provided by the planning module. The system also integrates an execution component that monitors the execution, keeping track of failures and replanning if necessary. Thus, TIMIPLAN showcases some of the needed autonomic objectives for self-management in future software applied to road transport software system.

Keywords Multi-modal transportation • Mixed initiative • Automated planning • Operations research

1 Introduction

Multi-modal transport is an emerging field [1] that presents many different kinds of challenges for software development. Following the classification of problems in [2], this work focuses on the operational aspects of multi-modal operators, users

J. García (✉) • Á. Torralba • J.E. Florez • D. Borrajo • C.L. López • Á. García-Olaya
Departamento de Informática, Universidad Carlos III de Madrid, 28911 Leganés, Madrid, Spain
e-mail: fjgpolo@inf.uc3m.es; atorralb@inf.uc3m.es; agolaya@inf.uc3m.es; dborrajo@ia.uc3m.es; carlos.linares@uc3m.es

T.L. McCluskey et al. (eds.), *Autonomic Road Transport Support Systems*, Autonomic Systems, DOI 10.1007/978-3-319-25808-9_16

of the multi-modal infrastructure, and services who take care of the route selection for a shipment through the whole multi-modal network. In this work, we deal with multi-modal transportation that is characterized by the combination of at least two modes of movement of goods, such as road, rail, or sea. The development of multi-modal transportation has been followed by an increase in multi-modal transportation research [2] and tools development. However, there are relatively few applications to solve the multi-modal transportation problem. The logistics research usually focuses on only one mode of movement of goods, whether by road, rail, or sea. Multi-modal transportation is more complex than the unimodal one. There are two observations that make multi-modal transportation problems quite challenging. On one hand, the optimal path is not the shortest path anymore; instead, additional costs have to be taken into account at the nodes where a new transportation mean is applicable—e.g., money and/or time. On the other hand, a new class of constraints has to be observed which (to make things harder) is dependant on each node—e.g., operating an exchange of transportation mean can actually involve other subproblems as it happens when moving freights from a truck to a ship. Additionally, the transport processes are subjected to a number of noisy inputs, like weather conditions, subjective driver decisions, or incidents which can neither be predicted nor controlled.

In most cases, a human operator is in charge of the route selection for each shipment and manually replanning when failures occur such as traffic jams or damaged trucks. Thus, the transport management is strongly influenced by the human operator manager, who decides how to manage the services according to his competence about the transport needs. The human operators receive plenty of information from various sets of resources and thus they suffer from information overload. In order to efficiently solve the multi-modal transportation problem, the management cannot rely only on the valuable experience of the human operators. A way to tackle the complexity of the problem for multi-modal transport management is to apply the concept of autonomic behavior. In this chapter, we propose a new decision support system (DSS), TIMIPLAN, implementing some autonomic properties for self-management, to solve a real problem assisting the operators in the task of planning the transportation routes for each service in multi-modal transport [3]. Firstly, TIMIPLAN presents the requested services and proposes a solution that the users may accept or change using a mixed-initiative approach. Thus, we advocate that a truly autonomic system should also reflect on when it needs the help from humans and interact with them if deemed appropriate. Secondly, TIMIPLAN also allows execution control, as autonomic systems do [4]. Therefore, TIMIPLAN performs a cycle of monitoring the plan execution, analyzing deviation from the original plan (as in the case of traffic jams or damaged trucks), replanning when unexpected situations are found, and executing the new plans. This cycle requires the system to sense, interpret, and deliberate about: goals to be achieved; available actions; changes in the state; and resource or environmental constraints. TIMIPLAN can plan and act effectively after such deliberation in unexpected situations such as traffic jams, damaged trucks, or new transport requests. In these situations the self-healing objective of TIMIPLAN arises, being the heart on which the tool is built upon.

In achieving that objective, TIMIPLAN has the following attributes: self-monitoring of its current state (e.g., truck positions) and self-adjusting and control of itself in unexpected situations (e.g., damaged trucks).

The remainder of this chapter is organized as follows. Section 2 gives a brief summary of the multi-modal transportation problem introducing some of the main approaches used to solve it. Section 3 describes the multi-modal transport problem. Section 4 presents the TIMIPLAN decision support tool with a detailed explanation of the application workflow and its modules. Lastly, Sect. 5 presents the conclusions.

2 Related Work

There are already some published works in the multi-modal transport task. However, none of these works solves the complete logistic problem, focusing on other problems associated with multi-modal transportation or on subproblems that do not represent all the constraints [2, 5]. In [2], the authors discuss the opportunities for operations research (OR) in multi-modal freight transport. The chapter reviews OR models that are currently used in this emerging transportation research field and defines the modeling problems which need to be addressed. In [6], the authors present a case study applying an interactive vehicle routing and scheduling software to a brewing company in the UK. They explain how a commercial tool was applied to schedule the day-by-day (operational) vehicle routing and scheduling to distribute the goods. This tool was specific for the brewing problem, and the operator that manages the tool needs a previous training process to manage all variables involved. In our case, the solution is quite domain independent, with less user-knowledge requirements and human intervention, which enables self-management.

There is little research in solving the whole problem of planning the multi-modal transportation route for all services. Some works model the problem as a multi-commodity flow network and use heuristics to obtain suboptimal solutions [7, 8]. For example, in [7] the problem is modeled as a multi-objective multi-modal multi-commodity flow problem. That work uses relaxation and decomposition techniques to break the original problem into a set of subproblems. A re-optimization approach helps to produce valid solutions when this relaxation of constraints leads to infeasible ones. In [8], the problem is solved using a linear programming compilation. The constraints considered in those works are similar to the ones considered here, but they are not exactly the same due to differences related to the company organization. For example, in our case the requested services are given with fixed pickup and delivery times instead of time windows. Additionally, the above works do not offer the ability of monitoring the proposed solutions and replanning to unforeseen situations, which is an essential requirement for self-management.

Regarding decision support systems, there are many works dealing with the monitoring of goods. In [9] the authors recall the relevance of monitoring and review the different technologies and applications that have been used in this aspect. While other systems consider several kinds of sensors, like radio-frequency identification

(RFID) tags on the containers or goods, TIMIPLAN only assumes that the trucks are provided with a GPS sensor so their location is known. Although there are many works dealing with the monitoring of goods, trucks, or means of transport, very few works use this monitoring information for self-management. The applications are used only to provide information, and they delegate all responsibility for decision making in unexpected situations to human operators. Instead, TIMIPLAN self-adjusts in unexpected situations such as damaged trucks or new services, and it requires very little human intervention.

There have been some architectures in the literature which use state-of-the-art plan generation techniques, plan execution, monitoring, and recovery in order to address complex tasks in real-world environments [10]. However, they are designed mainly as robotic control architectures. Lastly, there has also been some work using automated planning for enabling autonomic properties in road traffic support systems [11]. In this case, they are only focused on diverting the flow of regular traffic during unplanned circumstances, and hence, they do not solve a real logistic problem.

3 Problem Description

We define a multi-modal logistics problem as the tuple $\langle G, F, C, R, B, S \rangle$ where G is the network graph; F, C, R, and B are the sets of trucks, containers, trains, and ships, respectively; and S is the service that should be fulfilled. The nodes in G represent the locations where the goods should be picked up or delivered as well as the intermodal choice locations: ports and train stations. We work in a real problem, where goods can be picked up and delivered in any location all over peninsular Spain, its islands, and some cities in Europe and Morocco. In order to reduce the number of locations involved in the whole problem, we make an approximation based on the first three numbers of the postal code. The error in the number of kilometers induced by this approximation is small in comparison with the total kilometers of most services. This allows us to bound the number of locations to 600 and cache the number of kilometers and transportation time between each pair of locations in our database, speeding up the problem loading process.

A service $s \in S$ specifies pickup and delivery operations, each one with a location and service time that indicates the time at which the corresponding location is available for the pickup or the time at which a delivery service should be performed. To complete a service only a container $c \in C$ is required, but it can be moved by using a combination of vehicles: trucks, trains, and/or ships. Each truck $t \in F$ has information relative to the location and time at which it will be available and its corresponding driver's accumulated driving time. If a truck is selected, it should travel to pick the container up and either visit all locations of the transportation request (pickup and delivery locations) or transport it to the next transportation means (train station or port), where the rest of the plan might involve one or several other transportation vehicles. Trains and ships have a timetable specifying their

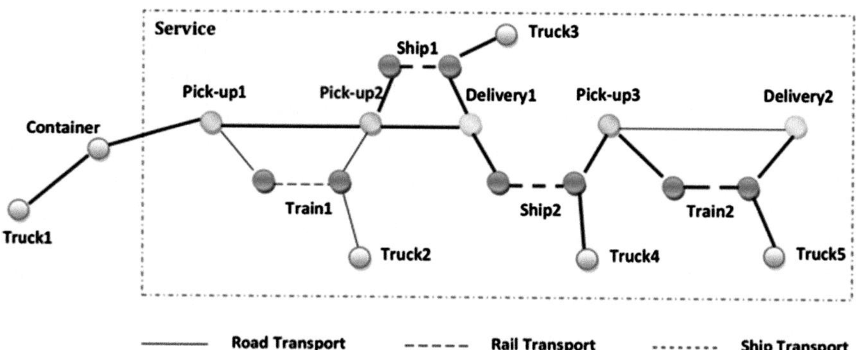

Fig. 1 Example of multi-modal transportation graph. A possible transportation route is *highlighted*

movements and the load and unload actions can only be executed when they are at a station/port. The resulting plan should satisfy the given service times of the locations involved. For instance, if the truck and container arrive early, they have to wait at the location until the next transportation mean is available. If the truck and container arrive late, there will be a cost penalty (e.g., when transporting perishable goods, as bananas). In multi-modal transportation, several trucks are usually needed (Fig. 1).

Each service may be completed by different routes: either single mode routes, as all road, or multi-modal routes, as combining trucks with ship and/or rail. In the case of the Spanish company, they are mostly based on ship transportation, so most services involve at least one ship segment. The trucks are defined by their average speed, the cost per hour when they are stopped, and the cost per kilometer when they are loaded and when they are not (moving an empty truck has different cost than moving it loaded). Moreover, the trucks have temporal and resource constraints imposed by legal regulations about the number of continuous driving hours. When the drivers have driven during some time, they have to rest. The concrete maximum continuous driven time and the minimum rest time vary for each truck.

Several constraints have not been included in the previous description of the problem, due to the difficulty of formalizing them or because they depend on information that is not available in the system. For example, there are soft goals related to the places where the drivers prefer to stop or to the client's preferences about vehicles and/or containers used to transport their goods. Also, human planners have expert knowledge about the probabilities of new services arising at each zone. They use that knowledge to reserve trucks or containers in these zones or to make movements that prepare all resources for future unknown services. Given that it is impossible to predict all potential soft goals to be taken into account when planning, we use a mixed-initiative approach to help the user take into account those constraints that cannot be easily handled by TIMIPLAN.

The planner is executed every day in the evening for the next day. A daily problem has approximately 600 locations (summing up all pickup and delivery locations, as well as initial positions of trucks, containers, ships, and trains), 175,000 edges among those locations, 300 trucks, 300 containers, 300 services, 50 train segments, and 150 ship segments. The company imposes a time limit of 2 h for computing the daily plan. More services are requested through the day and must be planned as they come.

Currently, the problem is solved by human experts who assign the resources of each service and the multi-modal route to deliver the goods. The company divides the planning problem between several headquarters, each one responsible of planning the services in one part of Spain. Each of them has its own resources, including trucks and containers. Resources can be shared among several headquarters if one of them requests it through phone calls. Thus, the current approach necessarily leads to suboptimal solutions, due to the local view of all the available resources. The main areas of improvement highlighted by the company are planning all the services at once and reducing the number of kilometers done by trucks without any goods.

4 TIMIPlan

The tool, TIMIPLAN, solves multi-modal transportation problems. It receives as input the positions of the set of all available resources (initial state) and a number of services to be performed (goals), and it has to generate a plan with actions including the load of goods in containers in different places, the unload on others, and the assignment and movement of the available resources (trucks, containers, ships, trains, etc.) to achieve all goals. Also, it must take into account several constraints, such as pickup and delivery times or driving hours, as well as all related costs. The objective is to minimize the cost of servicing all the daily requests. TIMIPLAN is composed of a set of modules as shown in Fig. 2.

The input for the multi-modal task is the list of services to accomplish and the list of available resources (initial locations of each resource, costs, constraints, etc.), both in XML format, that are extracted from the company database. The output is a plan for each service. This plan can be graphically inspected on a map which includes points where the actions are performed and the routes followed by the vehicles. The Web access component performs different queries to Web portals like Google Maps,[1] postal codes services, or traffic information. The main module fuses all the gathered data to generate the problem description and delegates the work to the planning and monitoring modules. Once TIMIPLAN creates the problem description, it is given to the planner, which combines operations research (OR) and automated planning (AP) techniques, as described in more detail in [3]. The mixed-initiative module allows the human experts to interact with TIMIPLAN to

[1] Webpage: http://maps.google.com.

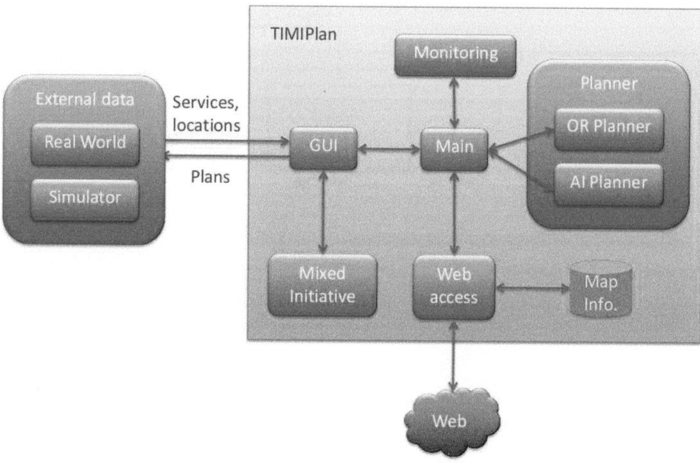

Fig. 2 TIMIPLAN architecture

include additional information in the problem (constraints and goals that cannot be formalized explicitly), or to validate the plans for solving unexpected failures. The monitoring component allows TIMIPLAN to detect deviations from the original plan, or new services to be planned for that arise everyday, and triggers replanning when necessary. The system also incorporates a simulator that allows the analysis of potential plan alternatives generated by the user.

TIMIPLAN has to support two modes of operation: offline and online. The offline mode runs everyday to generate the next day's planning. The user interacts with the generated plan modifying it and chooses the definitive plan. In the online mode, the system monitors the position of each resource and the execution of actions and replans when necessary. During this phase, the user is notified of every incidence that affects the predicted execution for the plan (Fig. 3).

4.1 Planning Module

This module can be understood as a core of deliberative reasoning and decision making in the proposed architecture. Most current autonomic computing systems tend to rely on reactive rather than deliberative reasoning. However, techniques as automated planning are proliferating into the realization of the properties of autonomic computing [11]. The potential role of automated planning in autonomic computing was originally highlighted in [12]. The use of such type of deliberative reasoning is particularly suitable for self-adjustment, because, in the context of multi-modal transportation, it can reason about unforeseen or unexpected situations in the road network and come up with plans achieving desired transport goals with

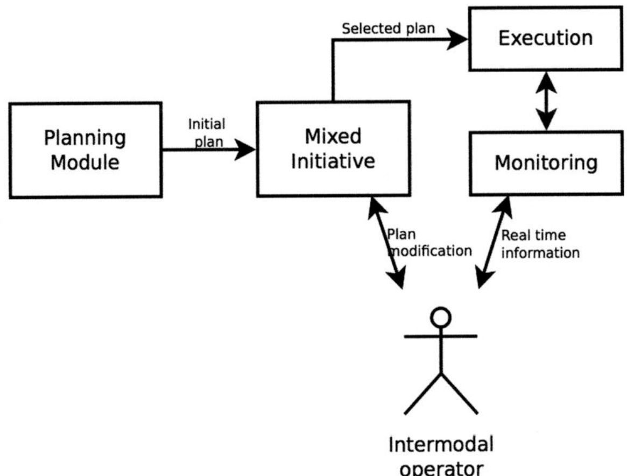

Fig. 3 TIMIPLAN user interaction workflow

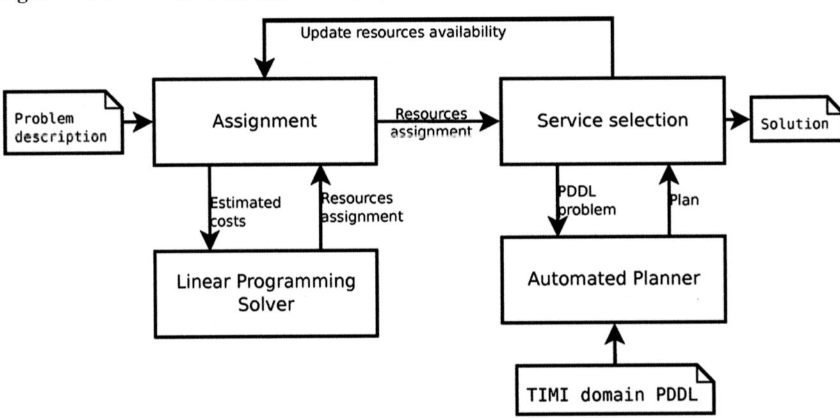

Fig. 4 Workflow of the TIMIPLAN top-level algorithm

minimum cost. Building a reactive system can be a complex and time-consuming endeavor because of the need to precode all of the behaviors of the system for all foreseeable circumstances. So, our solution consists on making the system autonomic until it figures out that it needs the help from the user.

Our approach tries to exploit the benefits of techniques from automated planning and linear programming, decomposing the problem into two parts: the assignment problem and the planning problem. The assignment problem decides which resources will be used in each service. We use a linear model that estimates the cost of each assignment. The planning problem decides the transportation route, taking into account all the nonlinear constraints, but limiting the number of resources to those selected by the assignment problem.

Figure 4 shows the TIMIPLAN top-level algorithm workflow. First, we compute the assignment of trucks and containers to services using an LP approach that selects the resource assignment for each service that minimizes the estimated total cost. Then, our approach sequentially solves the problem. For each service, the algorithm follows three steps. The first step consists of selecting the truck and containers that had been selected in the solution of the assignment problem as the ones that minimize the total plan cost. Then, the planning module is used to select a path from a first pickup point to the last delivery point over the transportation route of each one of the selected services. This path includes all the actions that fulfill the given set of constraints, including the sequence of the transportation modes used (where several trains and/or ships can be used) with the minimum cost. Finally, to allow the use of the selected trucks and containers in other services, their position and availability time after attending the planned services are updated in the assignment problem. The problem of the assignment of trucks and containers to services is refined using the LP algorithm, and the new resource assignment will be used in the next iteration. This approach balances the total cost obtained and the time required to compute the plan. More details can be found in [3].

4.2 Plan Visualization

When developing a real application, usability is a key issue. Figure 5 shows TIMIPLAN's graphical user interface (GUI). Users can access all the information

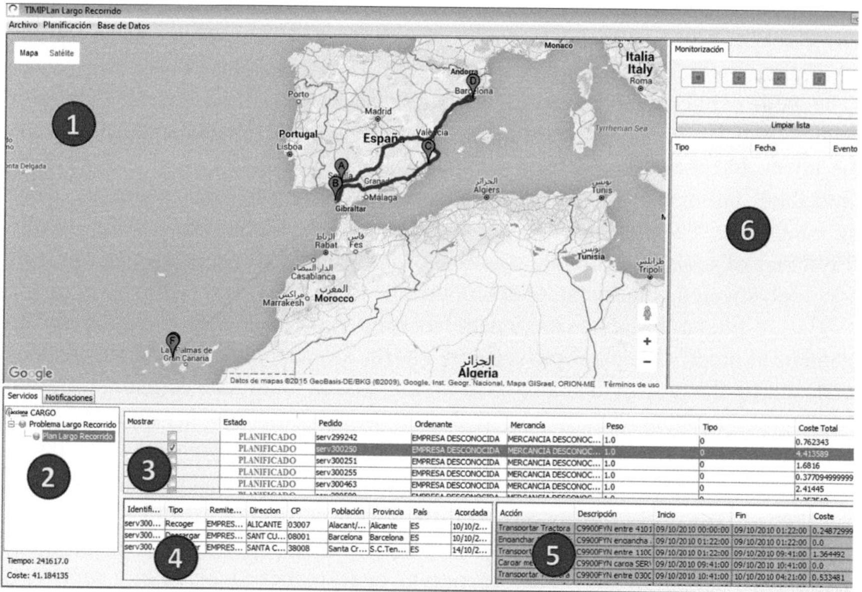

Fig. 5 Plan visualization interface

from this single view, avoiding the use of several windows and simplifying the problem comprehension. The window is divided into six frames:

1. Graphical map with the transportation routes of the selected services. It uses the Google Maps service.
2. Plan hierarchy for the mixed-initiative process.
3. List of services with their cost and information about the goods delivered and customer. The user can select a service to show more detailed information in frames 3 and 4 and has the option of showing its transportation route in frame 1.
4. Information about the pickup and delivery operations of the selected service.
5. Actions needed to complete the selected service with their time and resources involved. A color code identifies whether each action is being executed (purple), has been correctly executed (blue), has failed (red), or will be executed in the future (uncolored).
6. State of the trucks. Only available in the online mode in which the system monitors the position of each resource.

4.3 Mixed Initiative

TIMIPLAN implements a full planning process that allows the user to automatically obtain a complete plan from the services and the available resource description. That plan takes into account most of the constraints, but not all because some cannot be efficiently represented and handled by the system. For example, drivers prefer services near home or prefer to work only on week days or prefer to be located where their football team plays, or simply they do not want some of their preferences to be made explicit or to be recorded by any means. In addition, several failures or changes may occur once the services are planned (e.g., misunderstandings between the client and the transportation company about the conditions of the services, timetables, number of pickups and deliveries of a service, etc.), which are fixed by humans in real time through phone calls. Finally, human experts are usually suspicious of tools that provide solutions which cannot be changed, regardless of how sophisticated, intelligent, or autonomic the tool is.

Thus, a mixed-initiative component has been implemented to allow the human planners to modify the plans provided by TIMIPLAN, according to their suggestions made during the project, and also to fulfill the goal of letting the autonomic system decide when the help of users is needed.

We believe this is a key component of any self-management system that enables the solution of problems related to controllability or responsibility of computer decisions. TIMIPLAN collaborates with the users, updating the whole plan when the user proposes a change and allowing the comparison among different plans. In order to make changes on the operations or resources involved in a service, a new window is displayed, as shown in Fig. 6. It contains detailed information about

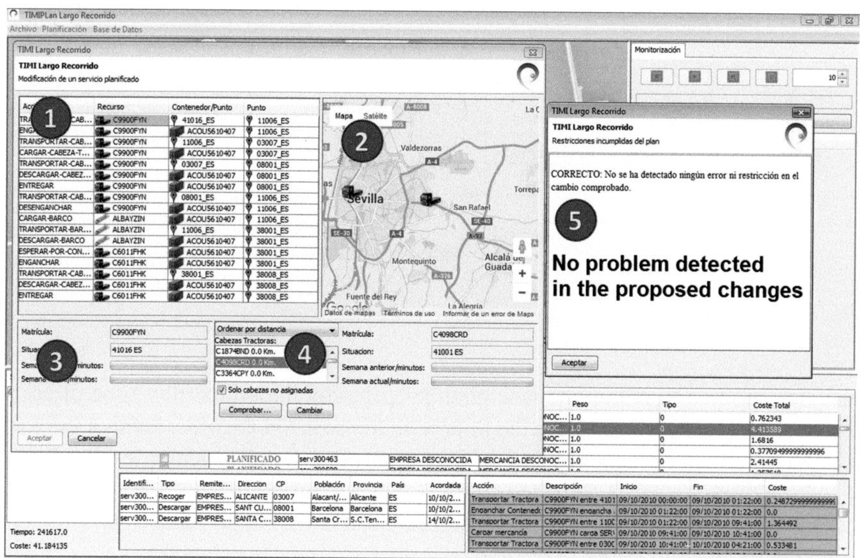

Fig. 6 Mixed-initiative interface

the resources and operations involved in the selected service as well as a list of alternative resources. The information is displayed over five frames:

1. Information about the actions planned for the service. For each action, the resources involved in it are shown, highlighting with an image the type of resource. The user may select an action to change the truck that currently performs it.
2. A map comparing the position of the previously selected truck with the new one for the action selected in frame 1. The proposed truck should be selected in frame 4 and appears in the map as a black truck. The truck in the current plan is shown in red.
3. Information about the truck that currently performs the action.
4. List of trucks that can be used in the action and information about the selected one. The user has the option to show all trucks or only the currently free ones.
5. A displayable window for checking if there are any problems with the changes proposed by the user. In the example, the proposed change does not incur in any constraint violation. When TIMIPLAN has to execute a plan where some constraints are violated, the user should be told, since it would go against the good "health" of the full system.

Currently, TIMIPLAN allows users to perform two kinds of modifications over the services. On one hand, it is possible to change means of transport, such as trucks, containers, or ships. The user selects the resource to change and a list of equivalent resources is displayed, with information about its location shown on the map. When a new resource is selected, TIMIPLAN replans the service, using the

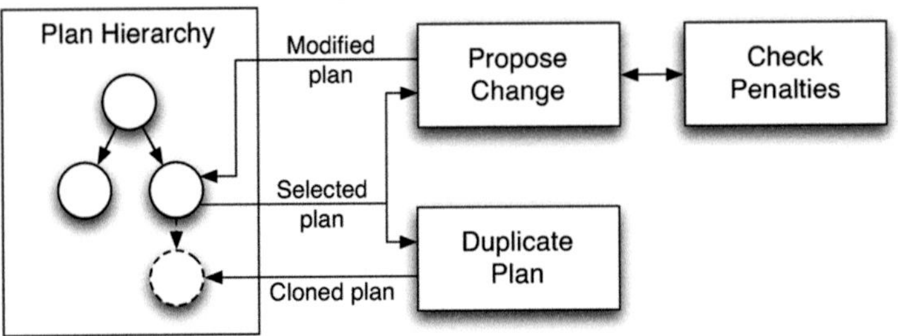

Fig. 7 Mixed-initiative workflow

planning module to obtain the new plan, propagating the availability time of each resource involved, and verifying the impact on the cost. On the other hand, users can change the order of the pickup and delivery operations for a particular service. Even if the operation order is included in the service description, the users may want to modify it due to changes in the customer preferences or to react to unforeseen problems in the availability of the goods. Before applying the changes, the user may check if they result in a penalty for violating a constraint, such as an operation delay. The system shows a comparison of the violated constraints in the plan with the new changes against those of the previous plan, including the cost difference between both options. The user may decide to apply the changes even if the cost is increased. TIMIPLAN propagates the effects of the changes: whether the plan is still valid (does not violate any constraint) as well as its new cost.

After trying some changes over the plan, the user may want to undo some of them or even compare two different plans. As the user changes the plan, she can store previous versions of the plan in a plan hierarchy. The root is the original plan proposed by TIMIPLAN and any plan on this hierarchy can be duplicated, adding a new node in the hierarchy to be modified. Thus, the user can compare different plans with their cost and keep track of the changes made (Fig. 7).

4.4 Monitoring and Replanning

After the interaction with TIMIPLAN, the user selects the final plan and starts its execution. The self-management in automatic control requires that the behavior of the system elements is monitored and analyzed, and the performance is used to plan and execute suitable actions to take or keep the system in desirable states [13]. In a similar way, TIMIPLAN monitors the plan execution retrieving information of the current state based on information from road sensors and trucks' positions, noticing the deviations from the expected plan execution and replanning if needed. Given that we are dealing with a real-time system, with a large number of resources involved, and that changing transportation routes already in execution may disturb the drivers, it is not possible to replan from scratch. In the monitoring mode, some of the resources assigned to one service cannot be changed: the trucks that have been already assigned to a service must be preserved. So, our replanning component consists on adapting the existing plan to the current state, aiming to perturb the original plan as little as possible (also known as *plan repair*), only modifying the services affected directly by the incidence. We consider three kinds of failures (incidences) that may occur during the monitoring process, and for each one TIMIPLAN is able to self-adapt with little or no human intervention: damaged trucks, new services, and traffic jams.

- **Damaged trucks:** Sometimes trucks may break down, being impossible for them to finish the services they are assigned to. In this case, only the services associated with the damaged truck are replanned (i.e., only a part of the original plan is modified). The replanning process is composed of two different steps: *assignment* of a new truck to replace the damaged truck and *planning* of the new transportation modes to complete the service. The assignment process selects the truck to replace the damaged truck following a greedy strategy: select the truck with the least estimated cost, taking into account whether it is associated with a previous service or not, its current location, and whether it is engaged with a container or not. The new selected truck drives to the damaged truck location, picks the container up, and continues the transportation route. If the damaged truck was associated with more services, a new truck is selected to replace it on each of them. The new times and action costs are propagated throughout the plan.
- **New services:** New services may arrive at any moment throughout the day. These services must be attended as they come, so TIMIPLAN proceeds in a similar way as previously; first, an *assignment* of truck(s) to complete the service and then *planning* the best transportation modes to complete it. The trucks are again selected following a greedy strategy, and only these trucks are considered for the planning problem. The actions planned to solve the new service are added to the original plan, with its corresponding action times and costs.
- **Traffic jams:** Traffic jams increase the duration of actions related to trucks' movements. These situations may occur at any moment during the monitoring process. TIMIPLAN monitors the positions of trucks and compares them to the expected positions in order to detect delays. If a truck is delayed due to a traffic jam, TIMIPLAN propagates the delay to all the actions that depend on that truck (in the same service or others using that truck), computing the new time and plan cost. If the delays create a constraint, violation TIMIPLAN alerts the user who decides if replanning is necessary.

Although it could be possible to use a different strategy of the greedy approach [14], Flórez et al. [15] demonstrate that the replanning process using this strategy is able to deal successfully with the daily damaged trucks and new services of the company (even in extreme situations). If some other unexpected situation arises during the monitoring process, this module delegates to the mixed-initiative component, allowing the human experts to solve it. The strength of the combined effort of system autonomic behavior and the user through the mixed-initiative component makes this tool an example on how to integrate man-machine

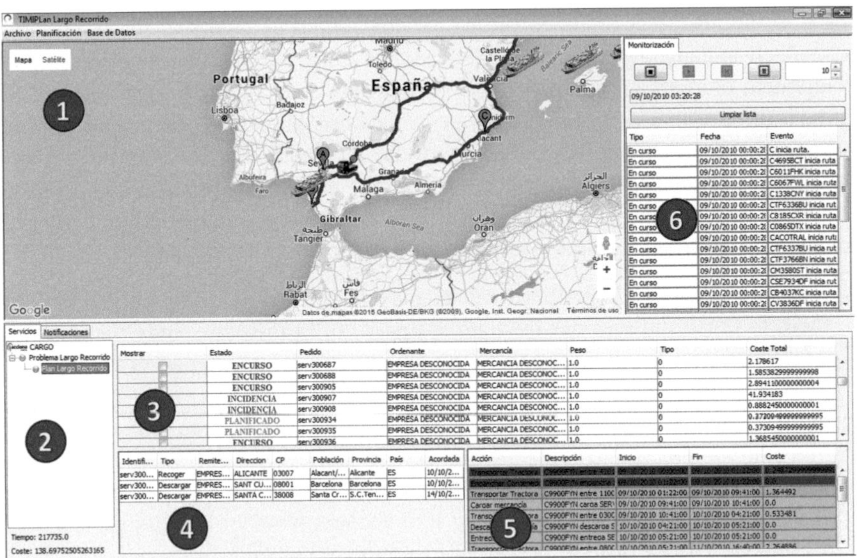

Fig. 8 Monitoring interface

in hard combinatorial control problems, as the ones arising in road transportation tasks. Figure 8 shows TIMIPLAN interface when the monitoring mode is enabled. As in the planning mode, the users can select the services they want to monitor and the transportation route is shown on the map. Also, the trucks associated with the service are shown too. Other resources such as ships are always shown. In the bottom part, the actions planned for each service are colored to highlight the current action and those which are finished. The cost of the plan is constantly being updated, allowing the users to monitor it.

Finally, an extensive experimentation has been conducted in order to test the planning, monitoring, and replanning capabilities of TIMIPLAN. Due to space limitations, we have not included it in this chapter, so we refer the reader to [3, 15, 16] for details.

5 Conclusions

In this chapter, we have introduced TIMIPLAN, a tool that successfully solves large multi-modal transportation tasks. We provide a formal model for the multi-modal transport problem and a good way to solve it that could be reused by researchers in the ARTS community for other tasks. Multi-modal transport usually involves the combination of a large number of resources, together with temporal constraints, resource consumption, cost functions, etc., which makes the decision-making process relying only on the experience of human operators not advisable. So, TIMIPLAN architecture incorporates some autonomic properties for self-management. One of the features which make TIMIPLAN self-managed is the use of a planning algorithm which combines linear programming and automated planning techniques. Automated planning enables control systems to automatically reason with knowledge of their environment and their actions, in order to generate plans and schedules to manage themselves. These properties make the automated planning particularly suitable for self-management and, in general, for automatic computing [12]. Additionally, automated planning uses a standard language, PDDL [17], for the definition of domain models and problems, making the modeling of any road transportation problem easier and, hence, making TIMIPlan easily generalizable to other ARTS scenarios.

In our case, the proposed planning algorithm is integrated within an application which offers a plan visualization interface with a mixed-initiative module. Hence, the users can access all the information and modify the plans accordingly. We believe that a pure full autonomic system in some domains, as the multi-modal transportation problem of the Spanish company Acciona Transmediterránea, is not adequate for three main reasons. Firstly, although the self-* components take into account most constraints, some others cannot be efficiently represented and handled by the system (e.g., drivers prefer services near home or prefer to work only on week days or prefer to be located where their football team plays, or simply they do not want some of their preferences to be made explicit or to be recorded by any means). Additionally, modeling all the knowledge (preferences, constraints, etc.) managed by experienced human operators for a multinational company like Acciona could be very time consuming and not always possible. We believe that our current solution is a viable solution that has also minimized the modeling time (programming effort) providing a good solution to the task. As a side effect, we have also separated the modeling difficulties, so that we deal with the best solution in terms of the multiple criteria problem of ⟨modeling time, quality of solution, and time to solve⟩. Secondly, some failures or changes may occur once the services are planned, which must be fixed by humans in real time through phone calls, according to company business rules. Lastly, and most importantly, human operators are reluctant to delegate their entire control of the planning processes to computer applications.

Regarding the latter, this does not mean that we cannot build real autonomic systems for those applications, but they then will most probably not be used by companies for some few more years (until the needed speed for decision making makes even for human operators the idea of being in the loop impossible). However, the application of real autonomic systems in such domains poses other challenges like the modeling of all the knowledge managed by very experienced human operators. So, TIMIPLAN collaborates with the users through a mixed-initiative component when needed in order to balance self-* properties with human control and responsibility.

Also, TIMIPLAN includes a monitoring mode to control the execution of all services, alerting the users when an incidence is detected. In other words, TIMIPLAN has the attributes of self-monitoring its existing current state (e.g., truck's positions, damaged trucks, traffic jams) and self-adjusting and control of itself (e.g., solving unexpected situations such as damaged trucks or new services). It is important to note that some of these attributes overlap; i.e., the existence of one requires the existence of the others. For instance, the self-adjusting property is not possible if the system is not self-monitoring. All the above properties confer on TIMIPLAN the ability of self-management with human intervention when deemed appropriate.

Acknowledgements This work has been partially supported by the CDTI (Spanish Ministry of Research) within the project CENIT2007-2002 (TIMI), the Spanish MICINN projects TIN2008-06701-C03-03 and TIN2011-27652-C03-02, and the UC3M-CAM project CCG08-UC3M/TIC-4141. We would like to thank the people from Acciona.

References

1. Bontekoning, Y.M., Macharis, C., Trip, J.J.: Is a new applied transportation research field emerging?–a review of intermodal rail-truck freight transport literature. Transp. Res. A Policy Pract. **38**(1), 1–34 (2004)
2. Macharis, C., Bontekoning, Y.M.: Opportunities for OR in intermodal freight transport research: a review. Eur. J. Oper. Res. **153**, 400–416 (2004)
3. García, J., Florez, J.E., Torralba, A., Borrajo, D., López, C.L., García-Olaya, A., Sáenz, J.: Combining linear programming and automated planning to solve intermodal transportation problems. Eur. J. Oper. Res. **227**, 216–226 (2013)
4. Lightstone, S.: Seven software engineering principles for autonomic computing development. Innov. Syst. Softw. Eng. **3**(1), 71–74 (2007)
5. Qu, L., Chen, Y.: A hybrid MCDM method for route selection of multimodal transportation network. In: ISNN '08: Proceedings of the 5th International Symposium on Neural Networks, pp. 374–383. Springer, Berlin/Heidelberg (2008)
6. Eibl, P., Mackenzie, R., Kidner, D.: Vehicle routing and scheduling in the brewing industry. Int. J. Phys. Distrib. Logist. Manag. **24**(6), 27–37 (1994)
7. Chang, T.-S.: Best routes selection in international intermodal networks. Comput. Oper. Res. **35**(9), 2877–2891 (2008). Part Special Issue: Bio-inspired Methods in Combinatorial Optimization
8. Moccia, L., Cordeau, J.-F., Laporte, G., Ropke, S., Valentini, M.P.: Modeling and solving a multimodal transportation problem with flexible-time and scheduled services. Networks **57**, 53–68 (2011)
9. Ruiz García, L., Barreiro, P., Bermejo, J.R., Robla, J.: Review. Monitoring the intermodal, refrigerated transport of fruit using sensor networks. Span. J. Agric. Res. **5**(2), 142–156 (2007)
10. Pinto, J., Sousa, J., Py, F., Rajan, K.: Experiments with deliberative planning on autonomous underwater vehicles. In: IROS Workshop on Robotics for Environmental Modeling, Algarve (2012)
11. Jimoh, F., McCluskey, T., Chrpa, L., Gregory, P.: Enabling autonomic properties in road transport system. In: 30th Workshop of the UK Planning and Scheduling Special Interest Group PLANSIG 2012 (2012)
12. Srivastava, B., Kambhampati, S.: The case for automated planning in autonomic computing. In: ICAC, pp. 331–332. IEEE Computer Society, Washington (2005)
13. Hariri, S., Khargharia, B., Chen, H., Yang, J., Zhang, Y., Parashar, M., Liu, H.: The autonomic computing paradigm. Clust. Comput. **9**(1), 5–17 (2006)
14. Fischer, K., Kuhn, N., Müller, J.P.: Distributed, knowledge-based, reactive scheduling in the transportation domain. In: Proceedings of the Tenth IEEE Conference on Artificial Intelligence for Applications, pp. 47–53, San Antonio (1994)

15. Flórez, J.E., de Reyna, A.T.A., García, J., López, C.L., Garcia-Olaya, A., Borrajo, D.: Planning multi-modal transportation problems. In: Proceedings of ICAPS'11. AAAI Press, Freiburg (2011)
16. Flórez, J.E., Torralba, A., García, J., López, C.L., García-Olaya, A., Borrajo, D.: Timiplan: an application to solve multimodal transportation problems. In: Proceedings of Scheduling and Planning Applications Workshop (ICAPS'10), Toronto (2010)
17. Ghallab, M., Howe, A., Knoblock, C., McDermott, D., Ram, A., Veloso, M., Weld, D., Wilkins, D.: PDDL-the Planning Domain Definition Language, Tech. Rep. (1998)

Applying the PAUSETA Protocol in Traffic Management Plans

Miguel Prades-Farrón, Luis A. García, and Vicente R. Tomás

Abstract The application of a traffic management plan (TMP) currently involves a manual negotiation between some agencies. Human operators from these agencies must negotiate with each other about who has to give each of the resources required by the TMP. This chapter proposes to use a new protocol, the Progressive Adaptive User Selection Environment by Type Agreements (PAUSETA) protocol, to support the autonomous deploying of a TMP. This protocol relies on a distributed combinatorial auction that preserves confidentiality and legal competences in the use of each resource in each agency. PAUSETA addresses the resources required by a TMP by type, that is, in the natural way that is given in a TMP, and it exhibits some self-* properties of an autonomic system. This protocol has been applied to a real traffic scenario to deal with a traffic incident. The analysis of the simulations performed show that PAUSETA provides results closely related to the ones obtained by a centralized system, thereby avoiding issues with regard to confidentiality about data or legal competences.

Keywords Combinatorial distributed auctions • Self-management • Traffic management plans

1 Traffic Management Plans

A traffic incident is an unexpected and serious situation in which response time matters a lot. As time goes by, traffic congestion produced by a traffic incident may extend to neighbour roads, and more importantly, injured people, if there are, will have less opportunities to survive. Therefore, it is fundamental for public administrations to apply the best tools available in order to reduce this response time. However, this is a difficult task because there are several independent agencies with different competences that must collaborate among them to deal with a traffic incident, for example, traffic police headquarters, hospitals, civil work agencies, fire

M. Prades-Farrón • L.A. García (✉) • V.R. Tomás
Engineering and Computer Science Department, University Jaume I, Castellón, Spain
e-mail: farron@uji.es; garcial@uji.es; vtomas@uji.es
http://www.aia.uji.es

T.L. McCluskey et al. (eds.), *Autonomic Road Transport Support Systems*,
Autonomic Systems, DOI 10.1007/978-3-319-25808-9_17

stations, etc. The usual way to coordinate these agencies is by means of a public administration which manually negotiates with them. This public administration uses previously offline developed traffic management plans (TMP) [1–3] when a traffic incident is detected.[1] Each TMP describes the scenarios, measures and actions to be deployed for dealing with a generic type of traffic incident. In the scenario part, it is described which is the current situation where the traffic incident has taken place. For each described scenario, there is a set of procedures to apply for solving it. This set of procedures is the measurement part of a TMP. Finally, the action part of a TMP describes the set of individual operations and tasks that each involved organization has to deploy to execute the selected procedures from the TMP (see Fig. 1).

However, the resources needed for the action and measurement parts may be provided for several of the involved agencies. For example, an ambulance can be provided by Hospital 1 or Hospital 2. Therefore, the public administration has to negotiate manually with the agencies which specific agency must provide each specific resource. This is a very time-consuming task, and, even more, it is possible

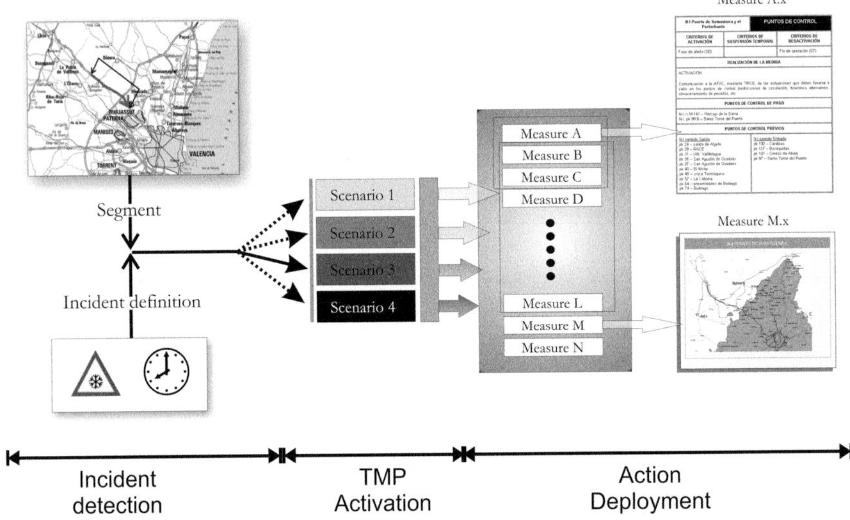

Fig. 1 In this figure the phases of a TMP activation are presented. First, once the agency responsible of the road management has detected and validated an incident, it activates the TMP for the current location, and by using this incident information, it determines the current scenario. Then, all agencies involved in the TMP start the coordination to develop the measures. To develop a measure, agencies must deploy individual actions. A measure can only be deployed when all agencies involved are ready to activate their individual actions

[1]The importance of making and using TMP in modern traffic management systems is reflected in the actions developed by the European Commission, both in the directive for the intelligent traffic systems (ITS) framework [9] and the action plan for the deployment of the ITS [10].

that, due to the fact that this task is performed manually, the agencies might finally allocate even more resources than the ones that are really needed.

There are several research proposals that could be used for supporting human operators of a public administration in this taken decision. These proposals [4–6] generally use a centralized system that calculates and imposes specific resources to be devoted from each agency. This decision is guided by fully updated information on the features and availabilities of each resource in each agency. For example, Fogue et al. [7] propose the allocation of resources by means of a search of a Pareto frontier driven by several utility functions measuring assistance quality, cost, reduced resource overuse and balanced resource deployment. Landa-Torres et al. [8] use another centralized searching solution based on harmonic algorithms and driven by minimizing distance and cost values to solve the concrete assignment of resources.

However, there are some real limitations that hinder the application in a real environment of a centralized system to decide what resources each agency should provide. This is due to several reasons. First, agencies may have different competences (nationwide, region-wide or local) to deploy the actions of a TMP and these competences cannot be transferred to each other. Second is the appearance of unexpected contingencies in each agency (e.g. a mechanical breakdown in a vehicle, or an illness of a worker). And, third, several agencies may compete with each other (e.g. a private and a public hospital), and therefore, they may be reluctant to provide their private data about the availability and features of their own resources to a central manager.

There is also another issue that must be taken into account when dealing with a centralized system. All involved agencies must trust that the resolutions of the centralized system have not been manipulated in a private and interested way. Therefore, each agency could manage its own resources more efficiently if decisions about required resources were taken in a distributed and coordinated way.

These identified problems in current approaches can be addressed by developing new distributed systems that exhibit autonomic properties in the deployment of a TMP. The general goal of an autonomic system is to support a self-management behaviour. In the system proposed in this chapter, this self-management behaviour is reached by using a new protocol for running combinatorial auctions. This feature allows to obtain a self-management behaviour from two different points of view:

1. A global one: once stated by the public administration how many resources of each type must be devoted for deploying a TMP, the set of agencies self-manage with each other for the overall required resources
2. A local one: each agency self-manages its own resources by means of their private valuations and by offering publicly some of them to the rest of agencies.

2 Auctions and Combinatorial Auctions

A known mechanism that is usually applied to resource allocation and that preserves some kind of privacy about data is an auction [11, 12]. The usual perspective of an auction is the one in which a bidder has the need to obtain a single item (or resource), and the auctioneer is the one who is in charge to assign it to the bidder who has a higher interest to get it. There is another point of view that can be applied when dealing with auctions: the auctioneer is the one that has the need to obtain an item (or resource), and the bidders are those who possess them. In this latter perspective, the private valuation of a resource by a bidder can be regarded as its private interest in giving it. For dealing with the action part of a TMP, the organization responsible of the incident management will play the role of the auctioneer. This auctioneer will ask for the resources to be allocated in a traffic incident to agencies that manage the resources, which play the role of bidders. Then, bidders will bid following their private preferences by using the auction rules. The auction will finish when a solution for the required resources will be obtained.

However, the requested resources may not be auctioned one by one but all at once. In this kind of auction, each agency can make bids for a different subset of these resources. For example, an agency may make a bid for giving two simple ambulances and another agency may make a bid for giving one simple ambulance and another fully equipped. This type of auction is called combinatorial. A great feature of combinatorial auctions is that a bidder can exploit the joint assessment of giving two, or more, resources simultaneously. By this way, a bidder exploits the synergy between its own resources: the sum of the separate utilities of two resources is different from the joint utility of them. [11]

One major drawback of combinatorial auctions is that the task for clearing the auction must be executed by the auctioneer. But, for doing this, the auctioneer must evaluate all possible combinations of bids, that is, the solution of this task involves to solve a well-known NP-hard problem [13].

One additional problem of combinatorial auctions is that because the calculation of the auction's winner is made by the auctioneer, the bidders have to trust that the process is clean, that is, there is not a deviation of the truthful response due to whatever private interest of the auctioneer.

A partial solution to the above-described problems is to use a distributed combinatorial auction. In this kind of auction, the calculation to determine the winner of the auction is distributed among the bidders. Therefore, the role of an auctioneer is mainly to verify that every bid done by a bidder meets the specifications of the protocol for a distributed combinatorial auction. Even more, the role of the auctioneer can be suppressed if there is a compromise among the bidders to comply with the norms of the auction. Note that since bids are public, they are known to all bidders. Therefore, the compliance of the rules can be observed by all bidders. One of the most well-known protocols for conducting a distributed combinatorial auction is the PAUSE (Progressive Adaptive User Selection Environment) protocol proposed by Kelly and Steinberg [14].

3 The PAUSE Protocol

The PAUSE protocol defines a set of rules to carry out a distributed combinatorial auction. The execution of this protocol is developed in several stages.

In the first stage, a classical English auction is performed for each one of the m resources that need to be allocated. The best bid for each specific resource is stored in a public set called *the set of best bids*.

Once this first stage is finished, a multi-round combinatorial auction is carried out for each one of the following stages. In every round, each bidder may make a *composite bid (CB)*. A CB is a set of bids covering all the m resources required, that is, a possible whole solution for the auction. The value of a CB is the sum of the values of each bid that composes it. Note also that each bid inside a CB may contain joint offers for more than 1 resource, that is, each bid is a combinatorial bid. For building up a CB, a bidder can use not only its own available bids but also those bids previously made by other bidders in previous rounds and stages. The auctioneer sets the minimum value in that a new CB must increase with respect to the previous CB within a given round. The auctioneer also updates the set of best bids with the bids of the current round. A stage ends up when there is a round with no new CBs. At the end of a stage, the best CB is recorded as the winner and the value of this CB is set as the initial value for starting the next stage.

The way the bids of a CB can be proposed by each bidder in each stage is subject to the following rule: at each stage k, for $k = 2, 3, \ldots m$, a bidder can only propose bids containing offers for no more than k resources. Therefore, in the stage $k = 2$, the bids in each CB can contain joint offers for 2 and/or 1 resource. In the stage $k = 3$, the bids in each CB can contain joint offers for 3, 2 and/or 1 resource and so on. At the last stage $k = m$, a bid in a CB may contain a joint offer for all the m required resources.

Note also that the calculation about which bidder is the winner of the auction falls into the bidders themselves. The overall process is public; therefore the bidders have no opportunity to manipulate the auction. However, by simply distributing the task of calculating the winner among a fixed set of bidders is not enough for solving this task efficiently. Bidders still have to deal with the calculation of the CB to propose in each round. Vidal and Mendoza [15] propose to use a set of approximate algorithms for helping bidders in this calculation. These algorithms apply greedy and hill climbing techniques to help bidders in the adoption of strategies for bidding a CB. The analysis of these strategies shows that these algorithms behave quite well in computation time, revenue obtained for each bidder and overall revenue of the auction when comparing with the optimal solutions computed by brute force.

Notwithstanding the use of these approximate algorithms for speeding up the calculation of the winner in an auction guided by the PAUSE protocol, there is also another intrinsic problem when trying to apply it in real settings. This protocol addresses each resource as an independent single entity. This makes the PAUSE protocol to be not capable of grouping resources with similar features in a same type. However, several application domains, for example, the management of traffic accidents, can be more naturally addressed if the required resources are identified by type and not individually. In other words, PAUSE can only negotiate for a heterogeneous set of resources, that is, each resource must be addressed in a unique way (e.g. the a_1 ambulance) without an option to address it in a generic or homogeneous way (e.g. an ambulance). Therefore, PAUSE shows serious practical difficulties for using it as a protocol to allocate resources for deploying a TMP, because the resources in a TMP are addressed in a generic way (e.g. three ambulances).

4 The PAUSETA Protocol

PAUSETA (Progressive Adaptive User Selection Environment by Type Agreements) is a protocol for distributed combinatorial auctions that deals with sets of homogeneous resources instead of heterogeneous (as PAUSE does). Therefore, an auction ruled by PAUSETA can address solutions from a higher level of abstraction than PAUSE. This new protocol is also developed in a finite number of stages, each of which may involve the execution of several rounds. Let t be the number of homogeneous sets in the auction and r_i, $1 \leq i \leq t$, be the type of resource i. Each r_i is associated with a finite set of specific resources. For example, r_1 represents the type of resource *ambulance* and there are three specific available ambulances associated with r_1: a_1, a_2, a_3. In PAUSETA, each bidder privately values its types of resources: the bigger the value, the more interested the bidder in giving one specific resource of this type. But not every resource of the same type must have the same value in a bidder. The valuation of a managed resource for a bidder may depend, for example, on the amount of its other managed resources available for the same type: when there are many, the valuation is higher, but this valuation is reduced as fewer dynamically managed resources remain available for this bidder as the auction progresses. Moreover, the valuation of a bid composed of more than one type of resource of a same bidder may include the synergy, that is, the potential benefit for a bidder of combining several resources of different type in a same bid. In a PAUSETA auction, each bidder tries to maximize the current best bid by making bids using the bigger values that are still available among the ones related to the resources managed by itself.

The number of stages in PAUSETA is t, as many as different types of resources are requested. In each stage k, $1 \leq k \leq t$, it is possible for a bidder to make bids for up to k types of resources, that is, in stage 1 a bidder can make bids for just one type of resource, in stage 2 a bidder can make bids for up to two types of resources, and so on. In PAUSETA no one plays the role of auctioneer, every bidder knows the resources requested by the auction, and the bids made by a bidder are broadcasted to the other bidders. A detailed explanation of the details of the PAUSETA stages is exposed below.

4.1 First Stage

The first stage behaves differently from the rest of stages. In this stage, an open-cry auction is performed, that is, an auction of a single step. Each bidder makes a set of bids containing as much available highest valuations for each type of resource r_i as specific resources of this type of resource r_i are requested in the auction. These bids are broadcasted to all bidders, so at the end of this stage, each bidder knows all these bids made by all the bidders. Each bidder stores these known bids in a local set called *the set of all bids (SAB)*.

4.2 Second Stage and Subsequent

From this second stage, the bidders must make *composite bids (CB)*, that is, a bid that contains as many valuations of types of resources as resources are requested in the auction. Therefore, each of these CBs is a complete solution for the auction. In each round within a stage k, $k \geq 2$, each bidder tries to outperform the current best CB making a new CB using bids from the SAB and its own private bids. Each one of the bids included in a CB within a stage k may be a *joint bid*, that is, a bid containing simultaneously as much as k values for resources of different type. Note also that for making a new CB, a bidder can use bids made for other bidders because these bids are already stored in the SAB. The new CB, if there exists, is broadcasted to the rest of bidders. When receiving a new CB, each bidder inserts the bids contained in the CB in its local copy of the SAB. A stage k ends up when no more rounds are possible. Then, it starts the next stage, the stage $k + 1$. The final solution of the auction will be the last CB made in stage $k = t$.

There is one constraint a bidder must follow when making up a new CB: the specific resource related to a value for a type of resource cannot be used more than once in a CB. In other words, a bidder complying this constraint avoids to make a new CB that includes repeated or not available values for any resource.

Two kinds of labels are proposed to be used by bidders in order to help them to manage this constraint. A label of the first kind of labels, *idUnique*, represents a specific value of a resource type. A label of the second kind of labels, *idsJoint*, is used to label each joint bid, and it comprises the labels *idUnique* and *idsJoint* of the values of the bids included in this joint bid.

4.3 The Bidding Strategy

One of the problems of a combinatorial distributed auction that follows a PAUSE style of auction is the calculus of the CB. This calculus is very expensive in computation time. Following the approach of Mendoza and Vidal [15], a new approximated algorithm for the PAUSETA protocol is proposed. This algorithm is based on a greedy paradigm for helping bidders to reduce significantly the computation time of a CB. The algorithm builds up a list with all the possible bids. These possible bids are the private ones and the ones stored in the SAB, subject to the limitation of size given by the current stage k. Then, it sorts this list by the square root of the relationship between the value of the bid and the amount of resources involved in it. Next, the new CB is calculated by choosing bids from this list that comply with the constraint described in the previous subsection. The code of this algorithm is the following:

```
1: Algorithm GreedyPausetaBid(i,k,M)
2: myBids ← theirBids ← idsUsed ← ∅
3: for b ∈ SAB do
4:     if b^bidder ≠ i then
5:         theirBids ← newBid(b^resource, b^bidder, b^value)
6: for b ∈ myOwnPrivateBids do
7:     if |b^resources| ≤ k then
8:         myBids ← myBids + b
9: g ← ∅
10: if myBids = ∅ then
11:     return g
12: bids ← theirBids + myBids
13: bids ← SortForGreedy(bids)
14: while bids ≠ ∅ do
15:     b ← first(bids)
16:     bids ← rest(bids)
17:     if ∃id ∈ b^IdJoint | id ∈ idsUsed then
18:         Next
19:     I_g ← resource in g
20:     if ∀ item ∈ b^resources |item ∩ I_g| ≤ |item ∩ M| then
21:         g ← g + b
22:         idsUsed ← b^idUnique
23:         for id ∈ b^IdJoint do
24:             idsUsed ← id
25: return g
```

There are three input parameters: i is the identifier of the bidder, k is the current stage, and M is the set of required resources.

The algorithm starts with two empty lists: *theirBids*, which will contain the bids made from other bidders, and *myBids*, which will contain the bids that bidder i can do. In lines 3–5, the list *theirBids* is calculated by iterating the SAB. In lines 6–8, the list *myBids* is calculated by using bids that involve an equal or less number of type of resources than k. The final CB to be returned will be stored in the list g. In lines 10–11, it is checked if this bidder has any bid to do. If there is not any bid, the algorithm returns an empty list. In line 12 *myBids* and *theirBids* are being jointed to form the new list *bids*. Line 13 sorts the list *bids*. In lines 14–24, the available resources which are not yet assigned from each available bid are added to the current solution, that is, the bids that hold the condition $\forall\ item \in b^{resources}\ |item \cap I_g| \leq |item \cap M|$ are added to the solution. When there are not any more bids to analyse, the algorithm returns g.

4.4 Properties of the PAUSETA Protocol

The PAUSETA protocol provides a feasible solution when at least one exists. The first solution is calculated by combining the individual bids provided by the bidders in the first stage. The execution of the auction in the following stages calculates new solutions that gradually improve the quality of previous solutions. However, for the final solution to be optimal, each bidder should calculate which CB is the best for each round and each stage. This involves to evaluate all possible combinations of bids, that is, an NP-hard problem [13]. The previously proposed bidding strategy based on a Greedy strategy runs in a polynomial computational cost, which increases the computational efficiency for the auction, but at the same time, it does guarantee to obtain a suboptimal solution that is better than other feasible solutions of lower quality. The autonomic property of self-optimization is captured by the fact that each bidder always tries to optimize its private interests via its own valuation of types of resources. This self-optimization is observed from a local point of view. The self-optimization for the overall solution can only be guaranteed by resolving the related NP-hard problem.

PAUSETA also provides more flexibility when comparing with PAUSE when expressing the autonomic property of self-configuration. This is due to the fact that PAUSETA is driven by types of resources instead of driven by specific resources. Therefore, the specification of the required resources can be expressed in a high level of abstraction. It is the work of the bidders to self-configure the specific resources to be included in each proposed solution according to the evolving valuation of the types of resources and the building of new CBs.

Also, PAUSETA shows a slight level of self protection by the way each bidder reduces the valuation for each managed type of resource as long as less specific resources within this type of resource are still available. By this way, a bidder tries to avoid running out of resources that may be needed for other unexpected events within the agency. This fact also allows the bidder to participate in future auctions for deploying other TMPs.

4.5 A Simple Test Case

In order to illustrate the behaviour of the PAUSETA protocol, a simple test case is shown. This test consists of a PAUSETA auction where two transport ambulances and one quick response ambulance are requested. Let n_{r_i} be the number of resources of the type of resource r_i managed by a bidder. There are two hospitals that can provide these resources. Hospital 1 (bidder p_1) has three transport ambulances and

Table 1 Resource values in hospital 1

p_1	Values					
r_1	130	120	110			
r_2	100	95				
r_1–r_2	240	235	230	225	220	215

Table 2 Resource values in hospital 2

p_2	Values
r_1	105
r_2	90
r_1–r_2	245

Table 3 Bids and CBs made during the auction

		Stage 2	
	Stage 1	Round 1	Round 2
p_1	$\{p_1, r_1, 130, id111\}$ $\{p_1, r_1, 120, id112\}$ $\{p_1, r_2, 100, id121\}$	$[\{p_1, r_1\text{–}r_2, 240, id111\text{–}id121\}$, $\{p_1, r_1, 120, id112\}]$	–
p_2	$\{p_2, r_1, 105, id211\}$ $\{p_2, r_2, 95, id121\}$	$[\{p_2, r_1\text{–}r_2, 245, id211\text{–}id221\}$, $\{p_1, r_1, 130, id111\}]$	–

two quick response ambulances available. The valuations for these resources are given by the expressions $v_{1r_1}(s_1) = 100 + 10 * s_1$ with $1 \le s_1 \le n_{r_1}$ and $v_{1r_2}(s_2) = 90 + 5 * s_2$ with $1 \le s_2 \le n_{r_2}$, respectively, transport ambulances (r_1) and quick response ambulances (r_2). The synergy relationship between both types of resources is stated as 10 units.

Table 1 shows the values of the resources of bidder p_1. For example, the type of resource r_1 is valued as 130, 120 or 100 following v_{1r_1} when p_1 has, respectively, three transport ambulances available to use in a bid, just two transport ambulances available because one transport ambulance is being used in another bid, or just one transport ambulance available because other two transport ambulances are being used in other bids. The values stated for the combinatorial bid r_1–r_2 are the six possible values of taking one value for r_1 plus one value for r_2 plus the synergy.

The other hospital, hospital 2 (bidder p_2), is closer to the location of the traffic incident than hospital 1. Hospital 2 has one transport ambulance and one quick response ambulance available. The valuations of these resources are given by the expressions $v_{2r_1}(s_1) = 85 + 20 * s_1$ with $1 \le s_1 \le n_{r_1}$ and $v_{2r_2}(s_2) = 80 + 10 * s_2$ with $1 \le s_2 \le n_{r_2}$, respectively, transport ambulances (r_1) and quick response ambulances (r_2). The synergy relationship between both types of resources is stated as 50 units. Table 2 shows the values of the resources in Hospital 2.

Once calculated the values for the resources in each bidder, the auction starts. In Table 3, the bids and CBs produced by p_1 and p_2 in each stage and round during the auction are showed.

A bid is represented as a tuple of four values: the bidder that makes the bid, a list of distinct type of resources, the overall value for the bid and the labels used. In the first stage, p_1 makes three bids: two values for r_1 and one value for r_2. Note that only two bids for values of r_1 and one bid for values of r_2 are made by p_1 because the solution just requires of two resources of type r_1 and one resource of type r_2. The bidder p_2 makes its bids given its available resources. Each bidder stores in its local copy of SAB these public bids and this first stage ends.

In the second stage, each bidder has to make a CB. Note also that in stage 2, a CB may contain bids for two types of resources. Bidder p_1 makes its CB $[\{p_1, r_1\text{–}r_2, 240, id111\text{–}id121\}, \{p_1, r_1, 120, id112\}]$ with value $240 + 120 = 360$ units in the first round. Note that the second bid in this CB is not $\{p_1, r_1, 130, id111\}$ because the label $id111$ is already used in the first bid of the CB. Bidder p_2 makes its CB $[\{p_2, r_1\text{–}r_2, 245, id211\text{–}id221\}, \{p_1, r_1, 130, id111\}]$ with value $245 + 130 = 375$ units. Note that as p_2 has only one resource of type r_1 and two are requested by the solution, p_2 has to take from its local copy of SAB a bid of p_1 for making up this CB. Each bidder updates its SAB with the new bids made by the other bidders and a new round starts. But, in this new round, any bidder cannot outperform the CB made by bidder p_2, so that this second stage ends. The auction also finishes because two types of resources in the solution requested are needed. The winner bid is the last one made by bidder p_2, so hospital 2 has to give one transport ambulance and one quick response ambulance, whilst hospital 1 has to give one transport ambulance.

5 Executing PAUSETA for Dealing with Traffic Incidents

PAUSETA could be used in the final step of a traffic incident resolution. Once the incident has been identified and a TMP has already been selected and it has been started to deploy it, the final decision on which agency must allocate which resources for each action could be reached using a distributed combinatorial auction.

In real settings, resources are not always in the headquarters of its agency, but they may be moving around the traffic scenario. For example, traffic police units may be patrolling on the roads. In addition, a resource type can be needed in one or more locations. For example, ambulances are only needed at the traffic incident location, but traffic police units are needed at several road points to enable and control alternative itineraries.

Each agency assigns a private value for each one of its managed resources and organizes them by type of resource. The valuation of each resource depends on (a) its current location and the distance to the place where they are needed, (b) the synergy to be applied when more than one resource type is combined in a bid and (c) the amount of available resources of the same type in the agency.

At the beginning of the execution of PAUSETA, all required resources (including type, amount and place to go) are determined by the agency that identified the incident. These data are communicated to the rest of involved agencies. All agencies act as bidders. Then, the execution of PAUSETA starts, and at the end of its execution, each organization will know which resources it must give and the location where they have to go.

The ring road of Castellón city (Spain) has been modelled with real traffic data for evaluating how well PAUSETA behaves. The model includes:

– The main road network involved. It includes roads CV-10, N-340, CV-1520 and CV-1551 with 35 km coverage. For the resources located initially in the city, only distances to the final allocations are being taken into account (urban streets have not been modelled).
– A traffic management plan (TMP) for emergencies with one scenario, three measures and nine actions.
– A set of bidders to model the different agencies involved in incident resolutions: three central traffic police stations (national, regional and local), two crane stations, two fire stations, three hospitals, two civil work stations and a varying number of traffic police units (from whatever central police station) patrolling on the road.

The test consists on the simulation of an incident in the CV-10 motorway. A truck with dangerous goods has an accident and the goods are spread on the road, closing the motorway to Barcelona city. Furthermore, two cars and one van are also involved. There are four injured people, and one of them is trapped inside the vehicle.

The measures set by the TMP to be deployed for this type of traffic incident are (a) to evacuate and care for injured people, (b) to clean the incident area and (c) to manage an alternative route to CV-10. Figure 2 presents the modelled area.

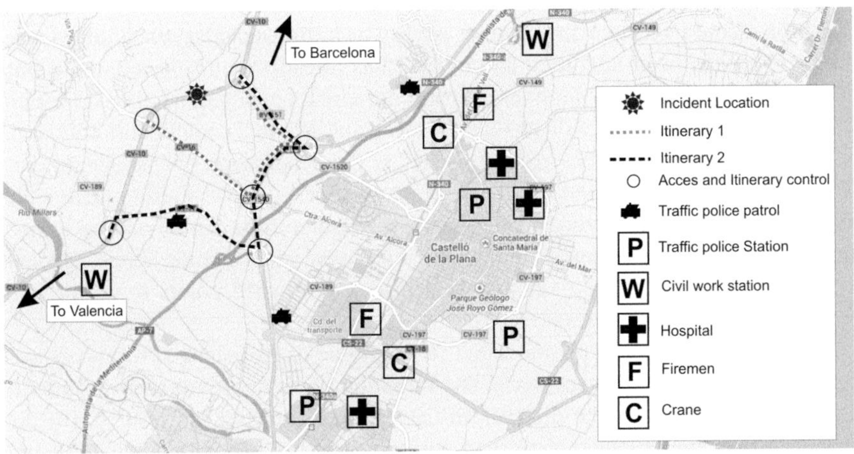

Fig. 2 Real environment modelled: the ring road of Castellón city

The resources to be deployed for dealing with the previous measures are three ambulances, one quick response ambulance, two urgency physicians, one heavy crane, two common cranes, two fire trucks, one maintenance road unit and eight traffic police units, two to go to the location of the incident and each one of the other six going to different places to direct the traffic of the alternative itineraries.

5.1 Evaluation Functions for the Resources of the Bidders

The interest of each resource in each agency is valued by using four parameters:

1. The base value for all resources is set to 100 units.
2. The synergy value between every pair of resources of distinct type is set to the 20 % of the base value, that is, 20 units for a base value of 100 units.
3. The amount of available resources of the same type increments the base value in 10 units by each one of them, that is, $v_{jr_i}(s) = 100 + 10 * s$. For example, if an agency has three resources of the same type, there are three different values $130, 120, 110$.
4. The influence of the distance to the location of the incident modifies the base value of this resource in 10 units by km, without going down the 0 value. For example, if a resource has a base value of 100 and it is located 3 km from the location of the incident, the base value of that resource is reduced to 70.

The PAUSETA model was implemented in a simulator. In order to evaluate the results provided by this PAUSETA simulator, they are going to be compared with the results provided by the optimal algorithm short common path (SCP). This centralized algorithm calculates the minimum accumulated distance among all resources, initial locations and final destinations. It uses a backtracking algorithm that returns that minimum distance. This centralized algorithm knows in advance of its execution all the update data about the availability of each resource in each agency. Its results provide a lower bound about total distance to be covered in each set of experiments, but it has three main drawbacks for applying it in a real traffic setting: (1) it has an exponential computational cost; (2) it calculates the solution regardless of the legal competences or preferences of each agency; and (3) it does not also take into account the communication time with the agencies for effectively deploying the solution provided.

In the first set of experiments, 100 distinct initial configurations were executed in both the PAUSETA simulator and the SCP system. Each configuration has a different position for traffic police units that are currently patrolling the road scenario. The results of this first experiment are shown in Fig. 3.

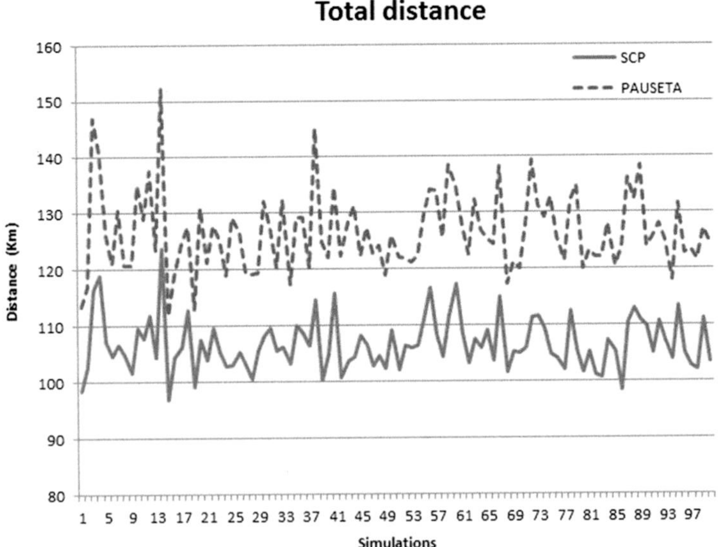

Fig. 3 Distance measured in km obtained in both simulators PAUSETA and SCP in each one of the 100 different configurations

The analysis of the results from this experiment shows that the PAUSETA simulator produces proportional results to the ones provided by the SCP system. The peaks and the valleys shown in the graph are simultaneously reached by both systems. Therefore, PAUSETA behaves as SCP. But PAUSETA also includes the interests and competences from each agency in providing the solution. This is the main reason because the total distance provided by each simulation is greater than its equivalent SCP simulation.

In the second set of experiments, the number of the traffic police units patrolling the road scenario was increased one by one, from 1 to 10. For each one of these values, 100 configurations were simulated by putting each available traffic police unit patrolling the scenario on different random initial locations in the road. Therefore, 1000 simulations in total were executed in the PAUSETA simulator and in the SCP system. The results provided by this experiment are shown in Fig. 4.

As the number of resources increases, the likelihood that any of them is closer to its final location also increases. Obviously, the total distance travelled decreases as more units of traffic police which are moving are available. Again, the analysis of the results from this experiment shows that the PAUSETA simulator produces results proportional to the ones provided by the SCP system.

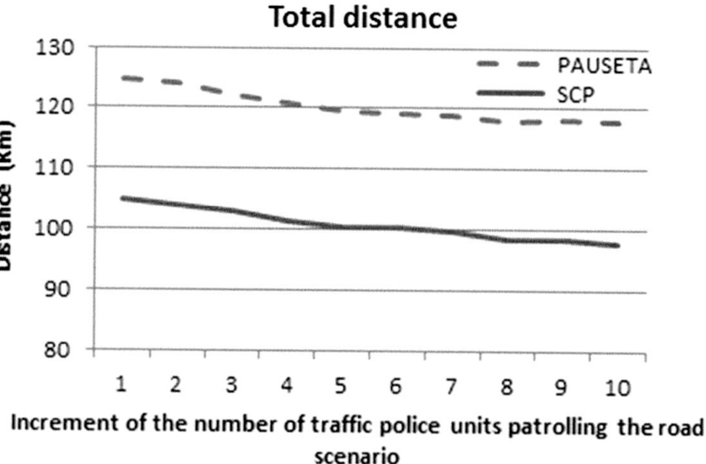

Fig. 4 Distance measured in km obtained in both systems PAUSETA and SCP in each one of the ten scenarios by varying the number of the available moving traffic police units. The value shown for each scenario is the average of the distance travelled by 100 different configurations

6 Conclusions

The different competences of the agencies involved in the actions to manage a traffic incident according to a TMP, and the difficulty of getting properly updated data on the necessary resources to treat it, hinder the real practical feasibility of research proposals based on centralized systems. Moreover, given that the reduction of the response time is critical, these centralized systems can compute the response very fast. But later, a human operator must manually negotiate with the involved agencies in the calculated solution to access effectively to its resources, which involves to devote a great amount of time.

The proposal presented in this chapter is to make the whole process of computation and negotiation by applying a combinatorial distributed auction ruled by the PAUSETA protocol. Experiments run in this model show that the results provided are consistent with those that would provide a centralized system in which there would be no impediments on competence grounds or by the use of real private updated data.

From an autonomic point of view, PAUSETA shows interesting behaviours that help to reach some self-* properties, mainly, self-management including self-configuration, self-optimization and self-protection.

Acknowledgements This work has been supported by Universitat Jaume I-Fundació Caixa-Castello research project number P11B2011-46.

References

1. EasyWay Project: DG-TMS-DG07. Traffic Management Plans for Corridors and Networks. Deployment guideline (November 2012)
2. Tomás, V.R., García, L.A.: A cooperative multiagent system for traffic management and control. In: International Joint Conference on Autonomous Agents and Multiagent Systems AAMAS05. ACM, New York (2005)
3. Belda, E., Tomás, V.R.: ITS for emergency resolution. In: Proceedings of 11th World Congress on Intelligent Transport Systems, Nagoya (2004)
4. Geem, Z.W., Lee, K.S., Park, Y.: Application of harmony search to vehicle routing. Am. J. Appl. Sci. **2**(12), 1552 (2005)
5. Figueiredo, L., Jesus, I., Machado, J., Ferreira, J., de Carvalho, J.: Towards the development of intelligent transportation systems. In: 2001 IEEE Intelligent Transportation Systems Proceedings, pp. 1206–1211 (2001)
6. Fogue, M., Garrido, P., Martinez, F., Cano, J.C., Calafate, C., Manzoni, P., Sanchez, M.: Prototyping an automatic notification scheme for traffic accidents in vehicular networks. In: IFIP Wireless Days (WD 2011), pp. 1–5 (2011)
7. Fogue, M., Garrido, P., Martinez, F.J., Cano, J.C., Calafate, C.T., Manzoni, P.: A novel approach for traffic accidents sanitary resource allocation based on multi-objective genetic algorithms. In: Expert Systems with Applications. Pergamon Press, Tarrytown (2012)
8. Landa-Torres, I., Manjarres, D., Salcedo-Sanz, S., Del Ser, J., Gil-Lopez, S.: A multi-objective grouping harmony search algorithm for the optimal distribution of 24-hour medical emergency units. In: Expert Systems with Applications. Pergamon Press, Tarrytown (2012)
9. European Commission: Directive 2010/40/EU of the European parliament and of the council of 7 July 2010 on the framework for the deployment of Intelligent Transport Systems in the field of road transport and for interfaces with other modes of transport (2010)
10. European Commission: Action Plan for the Deployment of Intelligent Transport Systems in Europe. Brussels,16.12.2008. COM(2008) 886 final version (2008)
11. Cramton, P., Shoham, Y., Steinberg, R.: Combinatorial Auctions. MIT Press, Cambridge (2006)
12. Caplice, C., Sheffi, Y.: Combinatorial auctions for truckload transportation. In: Combinatorial Auctions, Chap. 21, pp. 539–572. MIT Press, Cambridge (2006)
13. De Vries, S., Vohra, R.V.: Combinatorial auctions: a survey. INFORMS J. Comput. **15**(3), 284–309 (2003)
14. Kelly, F., Steinberg, R.: A combinatorial auction with multiple winners for universal service. Manag. Sci. **46**(4), 586–596 (2000)
15. Mendoza, B., Vidal, J.: On bidding algorithms for a distributed combinatorial auction. Multiagent Grid Syst. **7**, 73–94 (2011)

Index

T.L. McCluskey et al. (eds.), *Autonomic Road Transport Support Systems*, Autonomic Systems, DOI 10.1007/978-3-319-25808-9

Printed in the United States
By Bookmasters